SAVING OUR KIDS

SAVING OUR KIDS

from Delinquency, Drugs, and Despair

FALCON BAKER

Cornelia & Michael Bessie Books
An Imprint of HarperCollins*Publishers*

FIRST EDITION

Designed by Irving Perkins Associates, Inc.

Library of Congress Cataloging-in-Publication Data

Baker, Falcon.
    Saving our kids from delinquency, drugs, and despair / Falcon Baker.—1st ed.
      p. cm.
    "Cornelia & Michael Bessie Books"
    Includes index.
    ISBN 0-06-039115-4
    1. Juvenile delinquency—United States—Prevention. 2. Youth—Government policy—United States. I. Title.
HV9104.B335 1991   89-46516
364.3'6'0973—dc20

91 92 93 94 95 AC/HC 10 9 8 7 6 5 4 3 2 1

*For those teenagers
who so freely shared with me
the story of their lives,
their problems, and their dreams*

CONTENTS

INTRODUCTION by Kenneth B. Clark   ix

PROLOGUE: A Time to Begin   xi

PART I   THE BAD RESULTS OF GOOD INTENTIONS:
A NINETY-YEAR EXPERIMENT THAT FAILED

1. Juveniles and the Crime Problem   3
2. The Myth of the Juvenile Court   14
3. The Costly Myth of Rehabilitation   35
4. Even Prevention Has Failed   52
5. The Public School as Villain   61
6. Punishing the Victim: Status Offenders in the
Juvenile Court   81
7. Cultural Roots of Delinquency   95

PART II   THE ULTIMATE HOPE:
PREVENTION RECONSIDERED

8. Discarding False Assumptions   115
9. Delinquency and the Poverty Cycle   120
10. Escape from the Symbiotic Cycles of Delinquency,
Illiteracy, and Welfare Dependency   134
11. Intervention at an Early Age: The Child
Development Services System   156
12. Restructuring Schools to Meet Today's Challenges   173
13. Alternative Schools That Fight Illiteracy and
Delinquency   195

14. Shelter for Throwaways and Pushouts   211
15. Jobs Versus Delinquency   221
16. Juveniles and Drugs—a War That Was Lost   233
17. Toward a Winnable War on Drugs   253

PART III   SOCIETY'S LAST CHANCE:
           PUTTING JUSTICE INTO THE JUVENILE
           JUSTICE SYSTEM

18. The Family Court: Compulsory Prevention   273
19. Punishment as a Rehabilitative Tool   - 288 -
20. The Youthful Offender Court   - 299 -
21. Punishing the Juvenile Offender   311
22. State Offices of Children and Youth   324

     ACKNOWLEDGMENTS   331
     NOTES   333
     INDEX   339

INTRODUCTION

Falcon Baker has written about the turmoil of troubled youth. He has obviously identified with their struggle to attain and maintain a modicum of self-esteem. Although some have been successful in achieving this, he describes how a tragic self-destructive pattern leads to crime and delinquency, drugs and despair, in an increasing percentage of our youth. This is presented without professional jargon.

The system of juvenile justice is described in stark matter-of-factness, revealing how the process not only does not reduce or prevent further personal and social disintegration but all too frequently seems designed to increase the problems. As an advocate for the humanity of these young people, Baker describes a condition that strongly suggests that our society has not developed a workable system to prevent, remedy, or rehabilitate the personally and socially destructive behavior of these young people. His persistent empathy highlights the lack of empathy of the larger society. The cycle of social pathology involving sustained unemployment, poverty, inferior education, and social and racial stereotyping leads to a rejection of self and of social values. These are reinforced by a pervasive discriminatory education and a visibly negative social justice system which forms the foundation for a permanent underclass.

What is disturbingly plain is that the system of prevention, remedy, and rehabilitation which purports to redress the cycle of despair, delinquency, and crime ironically is not supported by the social services, the juvenile justice system, and the correctional institutions. A large proportion of young people who are trapped in the cycle of poverty, educational rejection, and self-destructiveness soon accept the negative social values of their peers and become defiant of social norms. As they are rejected by society, so they reject the society that rejects them.

Early symptoms of such defiance and social rejection can be observed in the rate of truancy and of social dropouts; later, violence, criminal activities, and such self-destructive behavior as drug abuse follow. The young pay a tragic price, as does society.

Those in control of the larger society view these behavior symptoms as socially destructive and seek to curb, punish, or rehabilitate the offender. What Falcon Baker makes clear is that these techniques are not now effective. The number of delinquents and young criminals is not decreasing. The first offender who is treated in the family court along with repeat offenders tends to become a more hardened criminal, insensitive to punishment. Baker makes a persuasive argument that young offenders who are treated in the juvenile courts should be separated from habitual delinquents and subjected to a more specific program of education in social values and self-esteem. Baker recommends that the juvenile justice system be restructured to allow early offenders to be brought before and supervised by a Youthful Offender Court.

It would seem that this approach, as part of a total pattern of realistic amelioration of poverty, effective education, and consistent manifestation of social values and racial justice, would reduce significantly juvenile delinquency as well as the number of older criminals. This clear, simple goal, implicit and embarrassingly explicit in Falcon Baker's book, would have to be accepted and implemented by pragmatic decision makers who are motivated by humanity, empathy, and enlightened self-interest.

—Kenneth B. Clark

PROLOGUE:
A TIME TO BEGIN

The woman in the apartment across the hall, knowing that I worked with delinquent youths, mentioned a story in the morning paper. A young black boy had been shot and killed while trying to hold up a neighborhood grocery. He had been brandishing a rusty old pistol which the police later said wouldn't even fire.

"A terrible tragedy," she said. "A young boy who could have stayed in school and gotten a job and made something of himself. But he was just too lazy, too trifling. Something for nothing, that's what these kids want. And look what it gets them."

I closed my eyes for a moment, searching for a reply.

"Yes," I finally agreed. "A real tragedy."

At the time I couldn't bring myself to tell her about the part I had played in that tragedy. Or, maybe, failed to play. Yes, the death was a tragedy . . . far greater than the neighbor envisioned.

I had just settled into a newly created position as Director of Delinquency Prevention Programs for the Louisville Public School System. Framed on the wall above my desk was a quotation from President Lyndon Johnson's Commission on Law Enforcement and

Administration of Justice, a challenge that I accepted as my personal crusade:

AMERICA'S BEST HOPE FOR REDUCING CRIME IS TO
REDUCE JUVENILE DELINQUENCY AND YOUTH CRIME.

Thus, delinquency prevention took on goals far more ambitious, far more significant than merely putting a stop to some of the peccadilloes of a few high-spirited students. It encompassed the nation's entire crime problem. It envisioned the rehabilitation of potential adult criminals *before* they became seriously involved in unlawful activities, rehabilitating them while they were still young and malleable.

So, there I was, ready to do battle with the dragons of crime, when a tough-looking teenager barged into my office. Cockily I motioned him to a seat. He slumped onto the chair, draped himself across my desk, and wasted no time in getting to the point. "I've gotta have a gig. And I mean quick. Damn quick!" His voice was menacing.

Here in the flesh was one of those statistics about whom I had so recently written in a book on delinquency for the Kentucky Crime Commission.

I had a fleeting flash of pride at being hip enough to know that a "gig" meant a job. Gradually I dug out the reason for the youth's urgency. Only two weeks earlier Dink had been released from Kentucky Village, the state's large reform school for hard-core delinquents.

It had been his second institutional commitment, the culmination of a long series of juvenile court appearances. Dink had just turned fourteen when the court sent him away the first time for an "attitudinal change." As a last resort the school system had filed multiple charges—habitual truancy, beating up a fellow student, destroying school property, and threatening a teacher. But the six months' stay had not cured him of delinquency. After release he had continued to be a frequent visitor in court on various charges.

The recent confinement had come when the patience of both the court and his probation officer had been exhausted—as punishment for trying to sell a TV set and a radio he had lifted from a neighbor. The sentence had been for an *indeterminate* length of time. After a ten-month stay he had been released, again having been "rehabilitated."

Upon returning home he discovered that his mother would not take him in again. As he was now seventeen and no longer listed as a student, she could not draw AFDC (Aid to Families with Dependent Children) payments for him. He was no longer of any value to her—just another mouth to feed.

His probation officer had warned, "Get off your ass and get a job . . . or else!" That had been the extent of the "help" offered by society's official advocate for an institutional returnee. So Dink had made the rounds of the service stations, fast-food joints, and grocery stores. He hadn't come close. It's hard enough for a young black to get a job under any circumstances; it's well nigh impossible for one who can't read or write well enough to fill out a job application and in addition has a record of two stays in a juvenile prison. I recall thinking during the interview that it was pretty cool of me to have refrained from asking how he'd gotten the fancy new duds he was wearing.

"Man, ain't none of them honkies gonna give me shit. I gotta get some bread. Man, I mean damn quick." His tone became a little more threatening. Even though the institutional authorities had declared him rehabilitated, they had failed to cure him of one unfortunate habit: at times he still got hungry.

Briefly I considered trying to persuade him to return to school, some vocational program perhaps. But as we talked he quickly torpedoed that idea. Apparently he had been a troublemaker from grade one. His academic career had consisted of more days being suspended than attending school. Year after year he had been "socially promoted" to get him out of the current teacher's hair, a common practice in many schools. It would have taken intervention from on high to persuade the school authorities to take back this over-school-age delinquent.

This was a pragmatic moment. It was no time to stop and theorize over who was to blame—his father who disappeared before he was born . . . his illiterate mother who existed on welfare . . . the schools that never taught him to read and write . . . the judge who thought sending him to a delinquency camp would solve his problems . . . the institutional therapists who worked on his "attitude" but ignored the basic causes of his delinquency . . . God, for having given him limited intellectual capabilities . . . our social system in general . . . or his own triflingness.

My ego began to ooze. Here was a real youth with a real problem asking me for real help. And I was flunking the test. No matter what he had done in the past, Dink still needed food and shelter. "Right now! Damn quick!" I was new in town and didn't know what help, if any, was available. Desperately I began reeling off names of places he might go to apply for a job. All the time I knew (as probably his probation officer had realistically known) that no one in his right mind was going to hire him.

The youth slammed his fist down on the desk. "Honkie, you ain't got no ears. You didn't hear me. I done said I spent my last fuckin' quarter for bus fare out here. I ain't got no damn bread to get to them places."

I grabbed at a straw. "That's where I can help you," I said, reaching for my billfold. "Here's ten dollars to pay for bus fares and something to eat while you hunt for a job."

For what seemed a long time he just stared at me. Then abruptly he got up and snatched the money. At the door he stopped, turned to stare at me again, and in contempt spat on the floor.

The end of the story merely involved playing out the scenario until the final curtain. Two weeks later I guess he really got hungry. In desperation he had tried holding up a neighborhood grocery. As I read the paper, I wondered if the rusty old pistol he was brandishing had been bought with my ten dollars.

"Yes," I had quietly agreed with the neighbor. "A real tragedy."

It is indeed a tragedy that our efforts to meet the needs of illiterate, untrained young Americans like Dink are so inadequate. A tragedy that our attempts to rehabilitate these wayward youths are such miserable failures. A tragedy that America has by far the highest rate of delinquency among all civilized nations.

For days Dink's death consumed my thoughts. There I was in a new job, all set to go out and slay dragons—slay them by doing more and more of the same things that had proved ineffective in the past.

Was I destined merely to tilt at windmills?

Dink's short life was a cameo statement of the problems with the juvenile justice system. The system is failing to rehabilitate delinquent youths . . . failing to protect society from the ravages of those young hoodlums. Undoubtedly the President's commission was correct: America's best hope for reducing crime is to reduce juvenile delinquency and youth crime.

But did anyone really know how this could be accomplished?

For twenty years I have searched for an answer to that troubling question. And in that time I have watched the severity and the violence of juvenile crime steadily increase year after year. As the public outcry for protection became louder and louder politicians grabbed for the quick, easy response: "Stop coddling these juveniles."

"Lock 'em up and throw away the key" became a popular refrain of the eighties. Legislators in three-fourths of the states passed more stringent laws, some making it possible for the court to consider life in prison and even the death sentence for mere children.

So juvenile institutions throughout the nation became jammed with up to 200 percent of rated capacity—causing a 300 percent increase in inmate violence. And millions upon millions of dollars have been allocated to build more and more juvenile prisons. Meanwhile taxpayers are paying an average of $25,200 a year to keep each of these troubled throwaway youths locked in what should be called "schools of crime" (New York State citizens pay $52,000, South Dakotans only $16,800).

And for what?

Most delinquents emerge from incarceration as hardened, embittered future adult criminals. After release 83 percent get into further difficulty with the law. The "quick, easy" solution has exacerbated the very problem it would solve. Critics, for example, make a good case arguing that Los Angeles's uncontrollable gang and drug problems were bred in the state's overcrowded, overused juvenile institutions.

There are no simple, easy answers to the problems of juvenile delinquency. It is bred and nurtured in a complex array of interrelated social, economic, and psychological factors. Because these haven't been taken into account, billions of dollars have been wasted on ineffective—even counterproductive—efforts to control criminal youths.

To counter this lamentable waste, Saving Our Kids *proposes a dual-accountability model for the juvenile justice system: making a youth accountable for his or her own actions, and at the same time making society accountable for those conditions which propel a youth into delinquency.*

To the delinquent the court would in effect be saying: "Perhaps you did get a rotten deal in life. If so, we'll do whatever we can to help you overcome those difficulties. But in the meantime, rotten deal or not, you are responsible for your behavior. Society cannot permit you or anyone else to break the law. Because you have done so, you must face the consequences. You are being punished for what you did. Although this first punishment is mild, it will become progressively more severe if you persist in crime."

And the court would be equally firm with those who abuse children, neglect them, discriminate against them, deprive them of a share in America's bounty, or cheat them of their right to loving care. Because the crime bomb in America is ticking away just waiting to explode, it is imperative that the courts really crack down—crack down on those guilty of *the making of a delinquent*, be it parents, schools, social agencies, the juvenile court, or society itself.

Because of the high costs, reactionaries looking for cheap solutions will dismiss the proposals in this book as being impractical and impossible. But again no cheap or easy solution exists. Expensive as they are these changes would be cost-effective in view of the tremendous price we pay for crime and the gigantic sums we spend for protection—estimated as high as $136 billion a year.

Barry Krisberg, president of the National Council on Crime and Delinquency, warns that the prison construction program that the United States has embarked on will eventually cost taxpayers some $250 billion. But despite the frenzied building of new prisons in America, it is impossible to keep up with demand. Thousands of prisoners are backed up in local jails awaiting an empty prison cot (over 1,200 in New York State alone). During the Reagan years the prison population steadily grew at a 10.9 percent annual rate—two and a half times the 4.2 percent average growth rate of the previous forty-five years.

California is usually found in the vanguard of efforts to fight crime. And there, in the first seven years of Governor George Deukmejian's administration, fourteen new prisons were built at a cost of nearly $2 billion. But this is only the start. Billions more must be poured into prison construction as the state struggles to cope with the projected increase in the inmate population—from 93,000 in 1990 to 153,000 by mid-1995.

As he dedicated the most recent state-of-the-art prison, Governor Deukmejian summed up his approach to crime prevention: "[This] symbolizes our philosophy that the best way to reduce crime is to put convicted criminals behind bars."

Saving Our Kids violently disagrees with the governor. Building more prisons is not the solution. Nor is hiring more police or passing tougher laws. Locking up more criminals merely exacerbates the vicious circle of crime, incarceration, and crime again. Instead, various proposals are offered in the following pages whereby the advice of the President's crime commission of twenty-five years ago can finally be implemented: reduce crime by reducing juvenile delinquency and youth crime.

It is time for America to cry *"Stop."* Stop using our resources to lock up the unfortunates of our society. Today one out of four black males in their twenties is either in jail, in prison, or on probation or parole. One out of four! Think about it. Among Hispanics it is one out of ten. Instead of spending billions to build new prisons, we need to use the money to develop ways to keep our citizens, both young and old, out of those prisons.

If we can plan a space station now projected to cost $120 billion and certain to go far higher before completed . . . if we can shrug off the prospects of having to find a half-*trillion* dollars to pay for the greed of savings and loan officials (a gloomier forecast of $1.4 trillion is made in a recent *Stanford Law and Policy Review*) . . . if we can shell out $300 billion annually just for armed defense against an unknown enemy, as we did for years . . . if America can afford to do these things, then surely we can afford programs that would save our children from delinquency, drugs, and despair (and, selfishly, save ourselves from the costs and the pain caused by their crime).

Congresswoman Patricia Schroeder, who has been on the Armed Services Committee for fifteen years, points out that whereas the average U.S. taxpayer in 1989 spent $1,200 to defend the free world, the average European spent $330 and the average Canadian only $200. When it comes to the Japanese the comparison is even more ludicrous. Despite their massive trade surplus, which is largely responsible for having made the United States the largest debtor nation in the world, we continue to spend billions on their defense while they spend only about $100 per taxpayer. The comparison worsens as we pay ever-increasing millions for the military to watch over our oil interests threatened by Iraq.

Congresswoman Schroeder asks rhetorically, "On what do these nations spend their tax money?" While we have been spending our tax money to defend them, they have spent theirs on free college tuition for their youths, comprehensive child care programs, extensive family health insurance. They are spending their tax money on those services that will be proposed here to break the symbiotic cycles of poverty and illiteracy and delinquency. And as a consequence their crime rate is a mere fraction of ours.

Even during the cold war the odds of America's being invaded by a foreign enemy were far less than the remote odds of a Communist takeover from within. Remote? Exceedingly so! But if the gap between the income of the affluent and that of the underclass continues to widen, the seeds of revolution could in time begin to sprout. We saw a preview of this in 1967 when the cry "Burn, baby, burn!" reverberated throughout America's ghettos. America was close to the point of revolution in the early 1930s until President Franklin Roosevelt defused the tension with programs for those suffering from hunger and homelessness. Those who would truly fight to protect the America we enjoy would best strive for the eradication of the root causes of poverty and crime.

With the end of the cold war, *now is the time* for America to initiate programs that meet the needs of its more unfortunate young citizens . . . children who otherwise may grow up to rob or do us in.

The proposals that follow are based not so much on humanitarian ideals as on enlightened self-interest. The widening gap between the haves and the have nots, the growing population of welfare-dependent teenage mothers, the increasing number of youths like Dink leaving our schools untrained and unqualified to hold a job— these make up the crime bomb that is ticking away . . . ticking away.

It is time for America to defuse that bomb.

America must turn a deaf ear to those reactionaries who will say the proposals in *Saving Our Kids* are too expensive . . . that in no way could we afford them *right now*. But it is because of our slowing economy and our rapidly escalating budget deficit, it is because of the drain on our economy from paying for the savings and loan fiasco and the costs of being policeman for the world's oil supply that make it imperative for us to start turning America around.

We must stop producing millions of uneducated, untrained dropouts who are candidates for welfare instead of industry, stop producing hundreds of thousands of drug-afflicted babies who threaten to bankrupt our health care system, stop producing thousands of babies born to unmarried teenagers whom welfare must pay for, stop producing that endless stream of young criminals who threaten not only our safety but the entire justice system, stop producing . . . The critical list goes on and on.

The proposals for *Saving Our Kids* are indeed founded in those humanitarian ideals that have made America great. But here they are presented as enlighted self-interest. The economic future of America demands it.

We must begin now.

PART I

The Bad Results of Good Intentions:

A NINETY-YEAR EXPERIMENT THAT FAILED

Chapter 1

JUVENILES AND THE CRIME PROBLEM

America the Beautiful . . . for Criminals

State and national officials annually announce that crime is up. Or down. But crime statistics are at best only educated guesses, and all too often are tainted by political expediency, sloppy recordkeeping, and outright deception. The softness of crime data was highlighted in 1986 when just a few weeks apart two divisions of the Department of Justice released their annual statistics. The Bureau of Justice Statistics (touting the administration's "success" in the war on crime) found that crime was down, having fallen to a thirteen-year low. The Federal Bureau of Investigation (seeking a congressional budget increase) reported that crime was up, having increased by 32 percent since 1976.

As statistics go, however, the body count of prison inmates is fairly hard to juggle. Shifts in the number of citizens behind bars reflect the intensity of the public's fear of crime and give some indication of the changing seriousness of criminal behavior. So, what has been the trend in America?

The decade of the nineties opened with more than a million Americans locked behind bars, a population that tripled just in the eighties. Increasing at a terrifying rate, it has reached a new record high each year for the past sixteen years. Prison administrators are now forced to add an average of sixty new beds every single day. Somewhere across the nation construction of a new prison is started every two weeks.

Even so, each year it is necessary to grant early release to tens of thousands of inmates because sardine warehousing has been deemed "cruel and unusual punishment." Forty-three states are under court order to correct overcrowding in all or part of their prison systems. During the summer of 1989 New York State administrators were forced to bed down three thousand inmates in prison gymnasiums, then double the capacity of some prisons by installing double-decker bunks. In California the system operates at 160 percent of capacity. And in Florida many felons serving two-year sentences are being released in four months in order to empty cots for newcomers knocking at the gates.

Jails are equally overcrowded. The problem, intensified by the drug crisis, threatens to bankrupt New York City. Bizarre and desperate measures have been necessary—mooring two old Staten Island ferryboats to be used as jails, and purchasing from England a floating barracks that had been used to house troops during the Falklands War. In Pine Bluff, Arkansas, a frustrated sheriff took fifty inmates from his bulging jail and chained them to trees outside the gates of the state prison.

Despite this surge in prison population, only some 3 percent of all felonies lead to imprisonment.

The Fear of Crime

Perhaps a more pragmatic measure of the problem is the fear that crime generates. Mass production of home burglar alarms is a growth industry, part of the annual expenditure of nearly $5 billion by frightened citizens to protect themselves.

The fear is not without justification. Each year one-fourth of all households are touched by crimes of violence or theft. America—the beautiful, the affluent, the powerful—this America in desperation locks up a larger percentage of its population than any country in the world except the Soviet Union and the Republic of South Africa, and even in those countries the prison population is decreasing as political dissidents are being released.

And violence! Consider murder, a crime for which statistics are fairly accurate. The United States has by far the highest homicide rate of all civilized nations—fifteen times that of England, twenty times that of Japan. The rate is so high, it compares with that of countries in the midst of war. In the past two years more Americans have been killed by criminal violence than died in the entire Vietnam War. Increased warfare among drug peddlers and rival juvenile gangs is daily pushing that figure off the top of the charts.

A child born in the United States today faces 1 chance out of 133 of eventually being murdered. For black males, 1 in 21 face that fate.[1] Five out of 6 of today's children will in their lifetime become victims of a violent crime—murder, rape, robbery, or aggravated assault.

When shadows from the setting sun encompass our city parks, out of fear we surrender them, letting young hoodlums and drug peddlers play their games of terror undisturbed. Recurring waves of muggings and holdups and vandalizing burglaries have left large areas of our major cities in shambles. Ravaged high-rise housing projects, built with multimillions of taxpayers' dollars, stand empty, ghostlike sentinels presiding over a war on crime that was lost.

Even in the quiet residential enclaves of the affluent one no longer walks the streets alone at night safely. We hide from the criminal, double-lock our doors, put bars across our windows, and install sophisticated electronic surveillance systems. As fear continues to increase law-abiding citizens may themselves, in time, become prisoners confined to their own fortified homes while criminals freely roam the streets. Already this fear holds residents of many drug-infested public housing complexes captive in their own apartments.

Twenty years ago Dr. Milton Eisenhower's National Commission on the Causes and Prevention of Violence foresaw the problem. It envisioned a "civilization" where the well-to-do would live in privately guarded compounds and move about in armored vehicles through "sanitized corridors" connecting one safe area with another.

With nostalgia old-timers look back forty or fifty years, when in small-town America most people left their doors unlocked, even when away from home for lengthy periods. And those homes that were locked could be opened with a skeleton key obtainable at the five-and-dime store. Even along the streets of Manhattan one could safely enjoy a leisurely evening stroll. It is not necessary to rely on statistics to know that in America the crime picture has been repainted with violent colors.

This book, however, is about juveniles—how they fit into this painful picture. Sadly, we will see, they are major contributors in two ways. As juveniles they are responsible for a large percentage of all serious crimes. And then many of these same delinquents grow up to become the chronic, experienced criminals of the adult world.

The Juvenile Role

These crimes of juveniles are not trifling affairs. The FBI classifies serious crimes under eight headings. Four are crimes of violence against persons: murder, forcible rape, aggravated assault, and robbery. Four are crimes against property: burglary, larceny-theft, motor vehicle theft, and arson. Youngsters under eighteen account for roughly one-third of all arrests for these eight Index crimes.

The peak age of arrests for FBI Index property crimes among both adults and juveniles is sixteen. A juvenile thirteen or older is nearly six times as likely to be arrested for one of these crimes as is the average adult. As for crimes of violence, the peak ages are seventeen and eighteen. Here the juvenile is twice as likely to be arrested as is an adult. After age eighteen the rate of criminal activity begins to drop sharply.

Two ominous trends have surfaced. One is the soaring degree of senseless, random violence exhibited in juvenile crimes. The other is the ever younger and younger age at which juveniles first become involved in serious crime.

Along with the increase in violent juvenile crimes such as murder, rape, and assault there has been an appalling surge in the viciousness of crimes committed merely for thrill and excitement. Aged and defenseless unfortunates, infants, street people, playmates—all have become targets. Anything goes. One popular juvenile game is following an elderly person home from shopping. When the apartment door is unlocked the victim is shoved inside and robbed, tied up, gagged, and at times raped and brutally beaten. Young hoodlums call it a "crib job" since it's like taking candy away from a baby. And even from affluent suburbs come increasingly frequent stories of children killing children—and parents. Between 1984 and 1989 the rate for arrests of juveniles ages ten through seventeen for murder doubled.

Violence fills the corridors of many inner-city schools. The National School Boards Association reports that *every month* over 5,000 teachers, 1,000 of whom require medical attention, and nearly 300,000 students are physically assaulted. Increasingly we hear reports similar to that from Los Angeles's Fairfax High School, where recently a student shot and killed a classmate during an argument over who could use the school's telephone booth. The president of the United Federation of Teachers last year urged the New York City Board of Education to increase its metal-detection program, in which security guards make surprise weekly visits to junior and senior high schools and search students with hand-held detectors like the ones used in airports.

And vandalism? California, for example, spends some $50 million a year on textbooks compared to nearly $100 million to clean up and repair buildings because of vandalism.

Even nondelinquents are becoming immune to the violence around them. In Milpitas, California, carloads of middle-class high school students repeatedly cruised by a secluded spot to view the body of a murdered fourteen-year-old classmate. Two days later a youth finally telephoned the police and a seventeen-year-old fellow student was arrested. Across the continent in Massachusetts a fifteen-year-old selected a fourteen-year-old classmate to lure into the woods, where he bludgeoned him with a baseball bat—just to find out how it would feel to kill someone. After showing off the corpse to two friends, he went with them to a pizza parlor to enjoy an evening snack. Only weeks later did one of them, unable to sleep nights, send an anonymous letter to the police.

Two boys aged twelve and fifteen tie a man to a tree in a park and set him on fire. For fun. To watch him squirm. In New York a fourteen-year-old kills two drug customers who owed him $150; a fifteen-year-old fatally beats an old man to death to improve his macho image. And in Rhode Island last year a 240-pound fifteen-year-old youth, known as "Iron Man," is given the maximum sentence of six years in the training school for four brutal murders, one of which—stabbing a neighbor woman fifty-eight times—had been done when he was thirteen. The other three had been committed while he was on juvenile court probation.

The Cute Little Offender

Some of these violent criminals are incredibly young. A few years back New York newspapers had great fun with the story of a cute nine-year-old who was arrested for holding up a bank with a toy pistol. The teller was sufficiently convinced to give him a hundred dollars. She had good cause to take the child seriously. That year in New York City alone some 2,000 youths eleven years old and younger were arrested on criminal charges, while across the nation over 200,000 subteen children were being arrested. These kiddie charges are not trivial. Half are for FBI Index crimes. In the latest two years for which figures are available, 43 children aged twelve and younger were arrested for murder or non-negligent homicide. A ten-year-old with a gun can be as dangerous as the most violent adult—maybe more so.

Increasingly one finds reports of these crimes by mere children: A twelve-year-old Little League star murders a visiting classmate in an argument over a baseball. He uses one of the several guns he kept in his bedroom. Another twelve-year-old stabs a friend for calling him a sissy. And yet another pulls out a pistol at school and kills the classmate making fun of his clothes. A nine-year-old Floridian terrorizes and extorts a dollar a day from each of several classmates. The stories go on and on . . . endlessly.

Crime no longer is just a young man's game; it's getting to be child's play.

The little ten-year-old brought into the station by the police after being caught breaking into a neighbor's house looks innocent enough. Certainly he seems harmless. Rarely will anything be done beyond calling his momma and telling her, when she comes to pick him up, that she should give him a sound spanking. The paper may even print a picture of the child sitting on the captain's desk and licking an ice cream cone.

But looks can be deceiving. This cute little fellow has a far greater potential for becoming a serious and/or violent juvenile *and* adult criminal than do older first offenders. Most fifteen- and sixteen-year-old *first offenders* are rebelling against adult authority or testing the limits of social permissiveness as a part of growing up. The vast majority will outgrow this antisocial behavior. But very young offenders are a different breed of cat. They likely reflect serious psychological or family maladjustment. Often their behavior mirrors physical or sexual abuse at home. Nearly always it is an indication of a severely distorted value system which is likely to get worse with time.

It may be considered an axiom of modern criminology: *The younger a juvenile is when first arrested, the more likely he is to become a habitual delinquent and, subsequently, a serious adult criminal.* For the juvenile justice system to excuse these offenders because of their young age may be doing them—and society—a grave injustice. Long before the juvenile court has begun to take their behavior seriously, criminal attitudes and behavior have already been firmly established, often irreversibly.

The Juvenile Delinquent Grows Up

David Bazelon while chief judge of the U.S. Court of Appeals for the District of Columbia declared: "Almost every one of the thousands of criminal defendants that have come before me has had a long record reaching back to age 10, 9, or even younger."[2] With the exception of those who commit certain crimes of passion and white-collar crimes, and also some adult drug addicts who turn to crime to support their habit, virtually all adult criminals had their vocational training during their juvenile years—they are youths for whom the juvenile justice system was a failure.

Most chronic delinquents continue their criminal careers into adulthood. An examination of the adult records of 210 serious California juvenile offenders, for example, found that in their first eight years of adulthood, 86 percent had been arrested for a total of 1,507 crimes, an average of nine times each.[3]

In 1988 the Bureau of Justice Statistics released a profile study of state prison inmates. Well over half admitted to having been previously convicted in a juvenile court, while among those being held for violent crimes nearly two-thirds admitted one or more juvenile convictions. These percentages do not include inmates who were uncooperative or were afraid to confess their juvenile crimes. Nor do they include those among the vast number whose juvenile arrests had been dismissed by the court or who had managed to escape arrest.[4]

The most extensive long-term study of juvenile crime ever undertaken was by Marvin E. Wolfgang and his associates at the University of Pennsylvania. They tracked into adulthood the 13,800 males born in Philadelphia in 1958. Among those youths who had as many as three arrests by age fourteen, 90 percent were later arrested as adults.

Not all delinquent juveniles pose a serious threat to society as adults. Far from it. Only a small fraction do. This was succinctly demonstrated in the Wolfgang study. During their juvenile years slightly over one-third of all Philadelphia youths had at least one arrest. *The vast majority of these, however, had only one or two brushes with the law.* After those original encounters they remained crime-free both as juveniles and as adults.

A much smaller group, however—roughly one-fourth of all those arrested—became chronic offenders. They were responsible for nearly three-fourths of all crimes committed by the entire group. Similar studies in Racine, Wisconsin, and elsewhere confirm that it is only a small core group of delinquents who contribute so extensively to the crime problem.

Obviously, if these few violent juveniles had been deterred while they were young, America would be a far safer nation. But the juvenile justice system has been an impotent dinosaur.

Part of the difficulty has been in identification. When first appearing in court most who later become habitual criminals seem little different from the many who outgrow their delinquent ways. Since we do not know which will eventually be dangerous, it would not only be exorbitantly expensive to lower the boom on all first offenders, it would be woefully counterproductive.

The Neat, Plain Solution

There are armchair criminologists who blame delinquency on irresponsible parents, or, conversely, on parents who maintain rules that are too rigid; and those who attribute it to courts that are too lax, or to law enforcement that is too zealous; to poverty and slums, or to too much affluency; to racial discrimination, or to racial inferiority; to a society that is too permissive, or is too materialistic; to association with bad companions; to lack of recreational facilities; poorly run schools; busing; unequal economic opportunities; declining religious faith; disintegration of family life; defective genes; television violence; child abuse . . .

You name it—someone will have insisted it is the cause of delinquent behavior. For many persons these divergent opinions are emotionally charged and blindly held. Actually, there is a measure of validity in each. Yet each is too limited, too pat, far too simplistic. Years ago H. L. Mencken, an acerbic political commentator, cynically observed that for every human problem, there is a neat, plain solution—and it is always wrong. Society has continually sought that "neat, plain solution" to the delinquency problem.

Unfortunately, it is not to be found.

Criminologists Voice Their Opinions

Academic explanations of delinquency flow along two broad pathways: the psychiatric and the sociological. Psychiatrists and developmental psychologists see the delinquent as an improperly socialized individual driven by inner turmoil and conflict. Frequently the cause is traced to defective family life, including physical or sexual abuse. The flawed personalities that result make them delinquent-prone. They are sick. They need treatment to be cured. In severe cases they should be sent to the hospital—the reform school—for intensive therapy. (Dink, my delinquent visitor in the prologue, had twice received the benefits of institutional therapy.)

Sociologists, on the other hand, see the delinquent as a youth unfortunately caught up in an imperfect social structure which needs to be improved. They see delinquency as being the price society pays for permitting the existence of poverty, inadequate housing, crime-infested slums, racial discrimination, or any of dozens of conditions that lead to family or community disorganization.

Most sociological theories sound convincing enough. Statistical research seems to back them up. Then invariably someone raises a barbed question: Why does one youth living in a certain sociological setting become delinquent while another in the same environment—even the same family—does not?

In the early fifties, during the Kefauver committee's investigations into the causes of crime, one witness made an impassioned plea in the Senate to reduce crime by eradicating city slums. He pointed to the severe deprivation and parental alcoholism in the slum background of a gangster who at the time was alleged to be the most dangerous criminal in America. But the impact of his testimony was blunted when it was pointed out that the gangster had a brother, raised in the same slum home, who had devoted his life to helping others as a foreign missionary.[5]

Of these two broad points of view, sociological theories have generally gained the most acceptance among academicians and criminologists. Yet the overwhelming preponderance of governmental and private efforts at reducing delinquency have been psychiatrically oriented—the treatment of "sick" youngsters in both institutional and community-based programs.

A puzzling reversal of priorities?

Not really. It is easier and far less expensive to attempt to treat a few delinquent individuals than it is to attempt to change the social structure. A more cynical explanation just might be that the rehabilitative therapy of delinquents is a major service industry. A large, vocal lobby of specialists depends upon delinquents for their living—a lobby that ranges all the way from probation officers and social workers to reform school guards and psychological therapists.

(Interlaced with both theories of delinquency causation is a biological component. Studies of twins raised separately in different environments, particularly identical twins, convincingly prove that many inherit a propensity to crime. Genetic inheritance unquestionably makes some more susceptible to those sociological and psychological factors which lead to criminal behavior. But this knowledge is not very helpful in reducing delinquency. Few children choose their parents. And barring Nazi-style genocide, there is small hope of significantly altering our society's genetic pool in the foreseeable future.)

In the final analysis neither of the two broad approaches has proved effective in curbing delinquency. *There is no documented proof that any large-scale program has ever made any discernible difference.*

Because of this failure—and the growing violence of juvenile crime—the public has become impatient and disillusioned with the juvenile court concept. In the 1980s there was a strong upsurge in what might be called the "man-in-the-street" point of view. Here the juvenile delinquent is seen as a little monster needing to be soundly punished and in extreme cases placed in a cage until the age of twenty-one.

"Getting tough" has become the prevailing mood.

According to this view, a juvenile is delinquent by choice. It's more fun, more profitable. He or she will shape up only if society cracks down hard enough. Make the punishment so tough that young hoodlums won't even dream of breaking the law again. Echoing a public television documentary, many loudly declare: "Old enough to do the crime, you're old enough to do the time."

A neat, plain solution!

In response to the ascendancy of this attitude state legislatures have toughened the delinquency statutes. More and more they are willing to treat violent and habitual delinquents as adults in adult courts. Last year a ten-year-old Cub Scout in rural Pennsylvania became the youngest child to be tried as an adult for murder. When the Supreme Court ruled by a 5–4 vote in 1989 that it was permissible to give the death penalty to youths for certain crimes committed when they were sixteen and seventeen, there were twenty-seven convicted of murder as juveniles sitting on death row. (Yet to be ruled upon is the question of those under sixteen.)

On May 18, 1990, Dalton Prejean became the first to die in the electric chair under this Supreme Court ruling. He had been found guilty of the murder of a state trooper when he was seventeen, and had served more than two years in a delinquency institution for killing a taxi driver when he was fourteen.

As courts have cracked down on delinquents, sending record numbers to institutions, child advocates are beginning to observe, "Doing time doesn't stop the crime." Those hardened, bitter young criminals are eventually released back into society. *There is convincing evidence that the rehabilitative experience may be doing more harm than good.*

The neat, plain solution is yet to be found.

Again the conclusion is reached that it is necessary to step back and take a critical look at the entire delinquency problem. But before attempting to establish guidelines for a more effective system, we must examine some of the myths that engulf the delinquency picture. These pervasive myths so cloud reality that both administrators and the public often fail to realize that good intentions are not enough.

Chapter 2

THE MYTH OF THE JUVENILE COURT

MYTH: *The juvenile court salvages wayward children and protects society by turning them away from lives of crime.*

REALITY: *The juvenile court is a sham. It neither rehabilitates delinquents nor deters other youths from criminal behavior. In fact, there is considerable evidence that it is itself a major contributor to the crime problem.*

THE RISE AND FALL OF GOOD INTENTIONS

Rising out of the feminine unrest that began to ferment in the second half of the nineteenth century was what Anthony Platt has aptly termed "the child-saving movement."[1] It produced child labor laws, universal and compulsory education, public playgrounds—*and* the juvenile court.

These "child savers" were primarily upper-middle-class women, firmly steeped in the Protestant ethic. To these women, being poor was equated with being immoral. Yet they looked with compassion upon children spawned in the crowded slums—products of mass immigration and rapid industrialization. Many of the children were being exploited in factories and sweatshops. Undoubtedly these undisciplined lower-class urchins would in time fall prey to the temptations of the street. But because of their tender age they could hardly be held responsible when they turned to crime. Instead of being punished by the criminal courts, they should be given compassionate supervision and rescued from lives of sin and corruption.

Thus was born the concept of a special court for juveniles. Under the doctrine of *parens patriae** the middle-class judge would become a surrogate father, providing the counsel and discipline the real fathers were incapable of delivering.

While it may be unfair to question in retrospect the motives of these Anglo-Saxon child savers, it should be noted that the ladies' motivation quite possibly was not so much benevolence as a desire to protect the existing social order by imposing their own puritanical definition of proper behavior upon the children of the slums. One matron sadly observed that children in the immigrant districts seldom tipped their hats to her, even though she was there solely to uplift them.

Be that as it may, in 1899 the Illinois legislature responded to pressure by establishing in Cook County the first court exclusively for juveniles. The movement spread with evangelical fervor throughout the nation. Rehabilitation, not punishment, became the philosophy of the day. Unlike other courts, here the concern was not the determination of guilt or innocence. Instead, a benevolent judge, sitting in as surrogate father, would chat in private with the child and interested adults. Together they would determine the course of action needed to salvage this bit of humanity. Since everyone in the informal proceedings would be concerned only with the child's well-being, neither attorneys nor legalistic restraints would be necessary.

Through this intervention the children, even though they had broken the law, would surely overcome the handicaps of an inferior heredity, irresponsible parents, and a crime-ridden environment. With rousing oratory it was proclaimed that the fatherly guidance of the judge and the court-ordered training in habits of honesty and

---

*From the medieval English doctrine permitting the Crown to intervene in the family relationship whenever a child's welfare was threatened.

industry would turn these young criminals into productive citizens.

It was, indeed, a noble vision.

But why sit around and wait for these street urchins to savor the false pleasures of illegal and immoral acts? Would it not be wiser to begin the redemptive process earlier in their lives? Why not intervene at the first indications of behavior that might forebode a criminal career?

So the state changed the definition of delinquency. The original Illinois Juvenile Court Act of 1899 had defined delinquency as "a violation of any law of the state or village ordinance." Over the next eight years the legislature progressively amended the act to include any *predelinquent* or *unsocialized* behavior.

Legislators throughout the country painted the definition of delinquency with a broad, moralistic brush. Stated in various terms in the different states, the court today has jurisdiction over three categories of juveniles (defined as under eighteen in most states):

1. Those who violate any state or local ordinance or criminal law
2. Youths who are beyond the control of parents or school, including runaways and truants
3. Others who fall within a catchall category variously described as being *in danger* of leading an idle, dissolute, lewd, or immoral life

The second and third categories are, of course, "crimes" for children only. They are referred to as "status offenses," meaning that these noncriminal acts are illegal only because of the special status of the individual—being a juvenile. Thus it is that thousands upon thousands of youths have been deprived of a great part of their freedom because of behavior that did not violate any criminal law.

Most state legislatures were satisfied with imprecise terms. Filling out the definition was left to middle-class judges. But a few states went into more detail. Arkansas, for example, added to the general categories a number of specifics. Among them:

> . . . visiting a public pool room or policy shop or place where any gaming device is operated; wandering about the street at night; attempting to jump on a moving train; writing or using any vile, obscene, vulgar, profane or indecent language; smoking cigarettes about any public place; and being guilty of indecent, immoral or lascivious conduct.[2]

About the only leeway the Arkansas legislators allowed their youngsters was in visiting houses of "ill repute." This was illegal only if the youth's visits became "frequent." Pragmatic legislators did not want to stifle practical education.

The juvenile court that evolved through the nation generally differs from the adult criminal court in five major ways:

1. *No finding of guilt.* Since juveniles are presumed to be too young to be legally responsible for their acts, technically the court does not find them "guilty" of an alleged crime, but rather they are "found to be delinquent" and in need of the services of the court.
2. *Punishment per se is a no-no.* Any disposition of the court is made in the name of "therapy" or "rehabilitation" rather than punishment.
3. *No legislatively fixed sentences.* Since rehabilitation is the goal, the sentence (called a "disposition") is determined by the individual's needs, not by the offense. Commitments to an institution are usually for an indeterminate time until the staff considers the youth to have been rehabilitated.
4. *Introduction of extraneous matters.* Since the hearing is not to determine guilt, the youth's social and family history, school record, and prior behavior are admissible and frequently carry far more weight than the severity of the alleged crime.
5. *Closed hearings.* In most jurisdictions the public and press are barred from juvenile hearings, supposedly to protect the reputation of the accused.

Only the most hardened Scrooge would argue against the humanitarian intent in the juvenile court concept. But alas! Good intentions don't make it so. The magnificent dream became a nightmare. The court not only failed society, it miserably failed the very children it was created to help. President Johnson's Task Force on Juvenile Delinquency, part of his massive mobilization in the war on crime, made this assessment;

> [The juvenile court] has not succeeded significantly in rehabilitating delinquent youth, in reducing or even stemming the tide of juvenile criminality, or in bringing justice and compassion to the child offender.[3]

The role of juveniles in the crime picture, as painted in the previous chapter, is compelling testimony to the failure of the juvenile justice system. Four major criticisms have been made: (1) the court has failed to protect society from the ravages of young criminals, (2) its compassion is a sham, (3) it is blatantly unjust, and (4) it does more harm than good.

1. FAILURE TO PROTECT SOCIETY

Out of a misguided compassion for young lawbreakers, the juvenile court does nothing to, *or for,* the vast majority until after they have become confirmed criminals. Up to half do not even have their day in court. At police headquarters or at the court's intake division they are given a warning and routinely released. Those sent to court fare little worse. Up to 90 percent are either dismissed, released into the custody of parents (many of whom couldn't care less), or placed on meaningless probation. Time and time and time again this "revolving door policy" operates—in and out, into the court and out on the street again.

This applies even to serious offenders. According to the most recent figures released by the Department of Justice, of those juveniles apprehended for violent offenses (homicide, rape, robbery, and aggravated assault) over two-thirds either were never brought to trial, or were placed on probation, or were released outright. Even among those arrested for homicide, only one-fourth ever served a day in an institution.[4]

In 1982 a *New York Times* investigative reporter dug into the records and discovered that despite the widespread instances of juvenile muggings, brutal beatings, rape, and murder that were terrorizing the city, only slightly over one out of every hundred of the youths who were arrested wound up in any sort of correctional institution.[5] Similar records of the court's failure to respond to serious juvenile crime are to be found in most major cities. A report from Chicago showed that before the court finally took any action more restrictive than mere probation, a delinquent boy had on the average been arrested 13.5 times, of which nearly two-thirds were for FBI Index crimes.

Because of a do-nothing court juveniles were literally getting away with murder. One twenty-year-old former drug hustler explained the increased use of juveniles: "The pushers get the young kids to hold the drugs 'cause if they get arrested they just go to children's court. The judge spanks their hands and tells them, 'Go home. Don't do that no more.' "

To knowledgeable and hardened delinquents the juvenile court is a joke. They sit bored with the hearings, yawning, laughing, scratching their genitals in an open show of contempt for the system. They know the chances of anything really happening are virtually nonexistent. At worst, they may be assigned to a probation officer with whom they can have fun playing a game of cat and mouse. Instead of being apprehensive, many look forward to their day in court. For a brief moment these habitual losers will be the center of attention.

The saga of one fifteen-year-old Harlem youth convicted in June 1978 for murder epitomizes the failure of the juvenile justice system. By the age of nine Willie Bosket, Jr., had accumulated a record of eight appearances in juvenile court, mostly for robbery. The court's idle threats had no deterrent effect. Finally, because he refused to go to school, his mother requested that he be sent to a delinquency institution.

Later he was transferred to the Brookwood Center for Boys, a maximum-security institution where he was among the youngest. Even so he intimidated and terrorized both the other inmates and the staff. In just one day he raped another boy, stole a truck, attempted to run over a social worker, and threatened the director with a crow-bar. When a psychologist attempted an interview the boy beat him up. After seven months of trying to "treat" this youth, the staff was more than happy to declare him "rehabilitated" and sign his release papers.

Back on the street Willie at age fifteen resumed his activities and purchased a pistol for sixty-five dollars. March 1978 was a busy month. When he and a cousin were surprised while trespassing in a train yard, Willie shot and seriously wounded a trainman. A week later, on a subway, he shot and killed a thirty-eight-year-old passenger. He was not caught for either offense, but two days later he appeared in court on a pickpocketing charge. The Transit Authority police advised the judge that the youth was "extremely dangerous," and a city attorney predicted from the past record that he would soon commit a more serious crime. But the judge released Willie to the custody of his mother. The next week the fifteen-year-old again held the loaded pistol three inches from a subway rider's left temple and squeezed the trigger. A cousin explained that Willie "gets a kick out of blowing people away."

This time Willie was caught and in family court admitted to having committed the two senseless murders plus the attempted murder. The judge handed down the maximum sentence—eighteen months in a "secure facility," after which, if he was not yet rehabilitated, he could be held in a "residential facility" for up to three and a half more years. At the discretion of the institutional authorities he could be released at any time.

The public outrage over this and similar demonstrations of the court's ineffectiveness was largely responsible for the New York legislature's passage, in 1978, of a law permitting district attorneys the option of trying as adults those juveniles over twelve who are charged with serious, violent crimes.

(Willie was released from the juvenile institution shortly after his twenty-first birthday, but three months later he was arrested for assault and sent to prison as an adult, this time for three and a half to seven years. The sentence was lengthened to twenty-five years to life after a conviction for assault and setting a fire in the prison, and in 1988 he was charged with attempted first-degree murder for stabbing a guard. At the trial he made a chilling pronouncement: "I laugh at this system because there ain't a damn thing it can do to me except to deal with the monster it created." For the next twenty years he is to live in silent isolation, confined to a cell stripped of everything including light fixtures. Even guards are not permitted to speak to him, leaving the flushing of his toilet the only sound he can hear.)

Following New York's lead three-fourths of the state legislatures have now responded to public concern by enacting get-tough laws. They either make possible or mandate the transfer of serious offenders to adult court. To date there have been conflicting reports on the effect of these harsher laws. Obviously they have not solved the juvenile crime problem. A recent study found that in the ten years following the enactment of New York's tougher law, only 14 percent of these "serious" offenders ever served a day in a correctional institution, and only 4 percent received sentences longer than those permitted prior to the 1978 law.[6]

The controversy over the effectiveness of trying hard-core offenders in adult courts misses the salient point. To suddenly treat these youths as adults after years of the do-nothing, slap-on-the-wrist policy is locking the barn door long after the horse has escaped. It is too late. Far too late. The juvenile court has already failed society—and failed these juveniles.

The tragedy of the court's failure to protect society is compounded by an ill-conceived policy. In virtually all states, when a delinquent officially becomes an adult his court record is "sealed," no matter how numerous or violent his past offenses may have been. Thus, he enters adult court as a criminal virgin and is given all the leniency afforded a first offender. He may prey on the public for many years before the accumulation of adult offenses causes the court to finally crack down.

2. COMPASSION IS A SHAM

The reality of the juvenile justice system is well curtained off by the myth that compassion is a hallmark of the court proceedings. My first glimpse behind that curtain came soon after I had begun a research project for the Kentucky Crime Commission.

On a Monday morning twenty-five years ago, Danny Diaz, a juvenile counselor of the state welfare department, came to my office with a handsome, sixteen-year-old black youth he had just found in the county jail. On the previous Friday afternoon, after getting off work at a garage, this juvenile *on his own volition* had gone to the police station and confessed that he and another boy had stolen a pistol from his employer, sold it for twenty dollars, and spent the money. Now his conscience bothered him. He wanted advice as to how he could make amends. The police at the station knew the juvenile court workers had already departed for the weekend. It was less trouble for everyone just to lock the boy in jail over the weekend. Society's reward for his courageous bit of honesty!

I began to feel a bit ill. But more was to come.

The juvenile counselor had the youth remove his shirt. His back was crisscrossed with long, ugly scars. Over the years his father, a religious fanatic, had whipped him with a cable. When the boy became old enough to obtain a job, he had run away from the small rural community. And the system's compassionate response to this troubled youth who asked for help? Well, after a brief investigation, the court decided it couldn't be bothered with a juvenile from another county. He was declared a runaway—and returned to his father, with the admonition that if he ran away again he would be sent to reform school.

Since that initial experience, from all across America, from the crowded ghettos out into the rural villages, I have heard variations on this story—the court's failure to show compassion and understanding to those who need help.

Except on occasions when some tragic incident occurs, the public remains largely unaware of—and unconcerned with—what goes on in the juvenile justice system. A youth hangs himself in jail. An institutionalized delinquent dies as a result of physical punishment. A juvenile boy is gang-raped in an unsupervised block of the jail. These incidents elicit an editorial in the local paper, at times even a speech at the PTA or Rotary Club. Concern quickly evaporates.

As rumors of the atrocities being done to children began to circulate one group did determine to get at the truth. Three thousand members of the National Council of Jewish Women in thirty states volunteered to take part in a year-long survey of the juvenile justice system. They sat in on court sessions and talked with judges, visited children in detention centers and training schools. Their reports were filed with hundreds of stories about good intentions that ended in human destruction.

Results of the study were published in 1975 in a volume entitled *Children Without Justice.*[7] It told the story of the council's discovery of the hurried hearings and harsh treatment of minor offenders in court, the deplorable juvenile penal conditions, and the inadequacy of rehabilitative programs. It concluded that the juvenile justice system is failing and that the human cost to children is too high to pay without a protest. This report is the flip side of a long-playing record about failure. One side tells how the court frequently does little to punish or deter hard-core juvenile offenders, and the other side how the same court system often brutalizes even minor offenders.

It is a paradox that boggles the mind.

At times the action is truly bizarre. In Ypsilanti, Michigan, a seven-year-old boy is ordered by the court to stand trial for rape. In Winter Springs, Florida, a six-year-old is arrested and booked in jail for slipping a thirty-five-cent package of bubble gum into his pocket at a convenience store.

In the past decade and a half the cruelty done to children in the name of juvenile justice has been documented by investigative reporters in more than a dozen books. A retelling of these exposés would not make pleasant reading. But it will be profitable to consider briefly one crusader who earned the right to be critical.

Patrick T. Murphy, as chief of the juvenile department of the Legal Aid Society of Chicago in the 1970s, tried to bring compassion to the system. Among the hundreds of victims he and his staff tried to rescue from the mangling care of the state's institutions were youngsters pumped full of tranquilizing drugs as punishment for swearing in the presence of women; teenage girls locked in "quiet rooms" (solitary confinement) weeks on end because they had been caught necking with boys; thirteen-year-old Matilda, tied to her bed for twenty-eight consecutive days for striking a matron; and Larry, placed in solitary confinement some fifty times, the longest for four months. Despite Larry's alleged unmanageable behavior he had been seen for a few minutes by a psychiatrist only once in thirty-two months.

After three years of trying to reform Illinois's juvenile justice system through legal pressure, Murphy could look back with some pride of accomplishment. Despite disappointments, there had been a few hard-fought victories. After several attempts in the state court and two trips to the federal court, a judge finally ruled that keeping two twelve-year-old boys tied to their beds in spread-eagle position for seventy-seven consecutive hours, clad only in skimpy hospital gowns and in full view of the other children, as punishment for "sexual acting-out" (an alleged homosexual embrace) was indeed "cruel and unusual punishment." Because of favorable court decisions some of the most abusive institutions were closed, the incarceration of runaways was considerably decreased, fewer children were being improperly placed in mental homes, and new regulations greatly limited the instances of "inhuman punishment."

Yet Murphy records in his book, *Our Kindly Parent—the State*,[8] that he found the entire juvenile justice system to be a wasteland of insanity. Reform was a hopeless task. It was like taking jabs at a great rubber balloon. Whenever legal pressure reduced the population in one of the state-financed dumping grounds for society's unwanted children, it automatically rose in others. He began to have the agonizing feeling that what he was doing was not only useless but also morally wrong. His legal battles were helping to make an unjust, outmoded, and never fully functioning system a trifle less abusive, and hence he was prolonging the life of a system that should be abandoned.

Letting the state play the role of a kindly parent had been a resounding failure. Originally Murphy had pleaded for more money to reform the system. But he saw millions poured into programs for rehabilitation that did little but subsidize middle-class bureaucrats and social workers. Instead of reform, he came to favor "doing away with the juvenile courts entirely, with the exception of the prosecution of older children who have committed serious felony offenses and adults who have physically abused children."

Public concern can close these abusive institutions. In Maryland after two suicides at Montrose, a large, overcrowded training school, a 1986 class-action suit brought by law professors at the University of Maryland finally led to the closing of the institution. The suit told in graphic detail of heartrending incidents, such as the eleven-year old, sent to Montrose for stealing a bike, who had been repeatedly raped by older boys. Because of his efforts to defend himself he had been accused of fighting, handcuffed, and placed naked in an isolation cell. Countless suicide attempts were listed.

The youths at Montrose were not hard-core delinquents. Less than 30 percent had been charged with acts of violence. Instead, they were largely status offenders and misdemeanants—primarily black "throwaways" from the streets of Baltimore. They were being held at an annual cost of $42,000 each. Even the Department of Health and Mental Hygiene admitted in court that at least half did not belong there.

3. THE JUVENILE INJUSTICE SYSTEM

Both ethical and practical reasons demand that justice be at the top of priorities for all courts, including the one for juveniles. Justice is a moral precept at the very roots of our Western civilization, and is essential if the democratic process is to work. Without it democracy would become a tyrannical dictatorship of the majority over the minority. Yet this essential ingredient is trampled upon daily in the juvenile justice system.

So rampant were the abuses of the court and so consistent the failure that finally in 1966 the U.S. Supreme Court in *Kent v. United States* spoke out:

> While there can be no doubt of the original laudable purpose of juvenile courts . . . there may be grounds for concern that the child receives the worse of both worlds: that he gets neither the protections accorded adults nor the solicitous care and regenerative treatment postulated for children.

This dual failure persists because serious flaws exist in the basic philosophy of the juvenile courts: First, the historical development of the juvenile court encouraged a discriminatory selection of disadvantaged youths to be brought before the court. Second, as rehabilitation, not punishment, is the avowed objective of the court, it is virtually impossible for the principle of fairness—"just deserts"—to prevail. And finally, because of the informality of the court, the system repeatedly violates the rights of juveniles.

A. Discriminatory Selection

There are two definitions of a juvenile delinquent: (a) a juvenile who has committed a delinquent act, and (b) a juvenile who has been *caught* for committing an illegal act and declared by the court to be a delinquent. The latter is an "official" delinquent. The former is a "hidden" delinquent. There is a vast difference.

Criminologists have long known that far more juveniles commit delinquent acts than are officially known to the courts. Periodically over the past forty years, dozens of self-reporting, anonymous studies of delinquent behavior have been conducted. All have come up with the same conclusion: virtually all juveniles—95 percent or more—admit to having committed one or more acts for which they could have been arrested and processed through the juvenile court. This finding is consistent across all social, economic, and racial groupings.

Even excluding trivial acts as well as underage drinking and uses of marijuana, the boys in one scientifically drawn sample confessed to an average of more than six offenses each. *Yet fewer than 3 percent of these offenses had come to the attention of the police.*

Milton Rector, while head of the National Council on Crime and Delinquency, raised a provocative question: Since delinquency is so widespread across class and racial lines, how is it that 98 percent of those youths being held in secure detention while awaiting trial are poor and disadvantaged?

The answer lies in the selection of youths to become involved in the juvenile justice process. The behavior of middle-class teenagers is frequently ignored while teenagers from low-income or racial-minority families, guilty of the same behavior, are tossed onto a treadmill of injustice. Shoplifting, for example, is only an "annoying phase" that middle-class teenagers are going through, but it is a prosecutable crime for those on the other side of the tracks. It doesn't even matter if the act was promoted by real need or hunger.

The disadvantaged encounter discrimination at each step along the way. First it comes from the police, the gatekeepers of the juvenile justice system. In some jurisdictions they arrest and take to the station as few as one-fifth of the youths they stop and question. The National Youth Survey at the University of Colorado's Institute of Behavioral Science is an ongoing longitudinal study of delinquent behavior among eleven- through seventeen-year-old youths. Studies there show that as a consequence of committing an FBI Index crime a black youth is twice as likely to be arrested as is a white youth *committing the same or an equivalent crime.* For minor offenses the probability is seven times as great.

The classic study of the criteria used in police decisions (and since confirmed by many other research projects) was made by sociologists Irving Piliavin and Scott Briar.[9] For nine months they observed the work of thirty officers in the juvenile bureau of a city of 450,000. (In return for the privilege of conducting the study they agreed not to name the city.)

In 90 percent of the encounters, the nature and seriousness of the youth's suspected offense had little to do with the action taken by the police. Instead, they relied on cues that they believed indicated the likelihood the juvenile was guilty. These cues were age, race, grooming, dress, and the youth's demeanor—cues that primarily indicate social class. Thus, in most instances well-dressed white youths, accomplished in such social amenities as saying "Yes, sir," were screened out of the justice system. They were released with a warning. The blacks and the poor were hauled to the station.

Herein is the first stage of a self-fulfilling prophecy. Prejudices, newspaper sensationalism, and past experiences have led police to believe that delinquency is primarily a product of the lower classes and racial minorities. On the basis of this belief, it is these youths who are selected to be taken to the police station, where they become "official" delinquents—and are counted in the statistics. Thus, through circular reasoning the policeman's original belief is confirmed. Consider what would happen should the police somehow be convinced that freckle-faced boys were the most delinquent-prone. Suddenly the courts would be flooded with freckle-faced delinquents. And the erroneous belief would be statistically "confirmed."

At the station and in the court's intake process the screening is further refined. Most of these juveniles pose no immediate threat to society. Yet they are frequently locked up in detention simply because the intake officer refuses to release them to lower-status parents who have been stereotyped as "irresponsible." Once they are in court, the punishment handed out to these second-class citizens—always in the guise of "treatment"—is inevitably more severe than that received by the few white, middle-class counterparts who were not screened out of the system.

Some years back a young white acquaintance of mine appeared in court for the *third* time. On this most recent spree he had been arrested for leaving the scene of an accident (a substantial fender bender), driving without a license, driving while intoxicated, threatening an officer while resisting arrest, possession of marijuana, and taking property worth more than fifty dollars (a group of road signs). He walked out of juvenile court with nary a strand of his well-coiffed hair out of place. Although this was his third bout with the law, the case was dismissed when the arresting officer "failed" to appear.

The only person to suffer even slightly from the escapade was the boy's divorced mother who had paid a five-hundred-dollar fee to a knowledgeable attorney. The point is not that my young friend should have been punished by the court. Most likely it was better that he was not. He is now settled down, leading a sedate life. But it is hardly justice that a lower-class black would have been punished for behavior considerably less reprehensible.

In most juvenile courts the judge is given a social history of the accused (a report on family background, school achievement, psychological makeup, and on and on) *before* he renders his decision. Professor Sanford J. Fox of the Boston Law School, in a speech reprinted in the magazine of the National Council of Juvenile Court Judges, pointed out the danger of these histories prepared by the court's social workers. Because so little is really known about the multiple causes of delinquency, the investigators feel compelled to delve into such useless details as the "record of a criminal grandfather, the alcoholism of cousin George, how long it took the child to walk, and whether he had to repeat the second grade." Professor Fox continues:

> The uncovering of such skeletons in the child's closet easily becomes an independent justification for intervening in his life. If his mother drinks, his father is unemployed, and his brother is in prison, the temptation to deprive the child of his liberty in big doses (the reform school), or little doses (probation) is overwhelming.[10]

Since such factors have no bearing on guilt or innocence, the practice is highly discriminatory.

But—the myth-loving diehard splutters—these children of the poor, the powerless, the uneducated, are precisely the ones for whom the juvenile court was created. The fact that the court concentrates on such children is proof the court is doing its job. Although nearly all youngsters at some time or another break the law, the vast majority of the really tough juveniles, the incorrigibles who make a career of crime, come from the lower echelons of society.

How true! Sadly true. Most middle- and upper-class youths committing hidden delinquencies, even at times very serious acts, do not turn out to be adult criminals (although they may in time falsify their income tax returns, cheat their clients, or sell confidential information to defense contractors). *But neither do most lower-class juveniles who are not caught and processed through the juvenile justice system turn out to be adult criminals.* Like their more well-to-do counterparts, as they get older they, too, grow out of their delinquent ways.

It just might be morally permissible to be unfair in the selection of youths if there were any evidence that those who are selected are actually being helped. There isn't. Most often the intervention only succeeds in locking the youth into a delinquent role. Had that high-rolling young acquaintance of mine been sent to a delinquency institution, he possibly would now be languishing in an adult prison.

"Different strokes for different folks" may have legitimate applications in social relationships. It is a policy that has no place in a court of justice.

B.   The Absence of "Just Deserts"

Because the juvenile court has traditionally embraced rehabilitation at the expense of justice, serious crimes are frequently treated lightly, trivial crimes seriously. In forty-five states the institutional commitment of a delinquent is an indeterminate sentence—that is, for an indefinite period until the authorities believe the youth has been rehabilitated.

The intent is noble. But the practice violates the delinquent's moral right to fair play, sometimes referred to as "just deserts"—punishment commensurate with the seriousness of the crime. A law that permits one youth to be held in an institution two, three, or four times longer than another guilty of the same or an even worse offense can hardly be expected to restore an erring youth's belief in the justice of society.

It is quite possible that institutional staff members feel frustrated in even attempting to rehabilitate the tough, hard-core delinquent but still have hope of helping the less serious delinquent. Thus, they hold on to the minor offenders. Or it simply may be that working with mild-mannered status offenders makes their job more bearable and so, perhaps unwittingly, they select the undesirables for early release. (Recall how Willie Bosket, Jr., the New York thrill murderer, was released as "rehabilitated" after terrorizing the staff for seven months.)

The indeterminate sentence is based on a false assumption: the belief that the institutional staff through tests, close observation, and gut feelings can determine whether or not a delinquent has been rehabilitated.

But they can't.

One of the many documentations of the gross inability of the staff to predict the future delinquency of their charges was made by Professor Harry Allen of Ohio State University's Center for the Study of Crime and Delinquency. The post-release behavior of 443 boys from a maximum-security institution was followed. The staff member each boy designated as "knew him best" was asked to predict whether or not he would get into further trouble with the law. In 371 of the 443 cases (84 percent of the time) the staff member was wrong. They erred in both directions. Tossing a coin would have produced a far more accurate prediction. Yet it is faulty judgments such as these that are the basis for release.

Many similar studies have made obvious the fallacy in the use of the indeterminate sentence. Since it is impossible to predict whether a youth has been rehabilitated or not, it is impossible to determine when the optimum time for release has been reached. The entire reason for the indeterminate sentence evaporates in a gust of good intentions.

C. Denial of Constitutional Rights

The rights of children have never had very high priority in America. It wasn't until 1976, for example, that a federal court finally ruled unconstitutional a Georgia law that permitted parents or guardians to commit unwanted children to mental institutions *without even a judicial hearing.* But the public has always assumed that the juvenile court's compassionate concern for a child's welfare would afford sufficient protection of the youth's rights.

This bit of wishful thinking has led to what often amounts to a kangaroo court. In the thirty-state survey conducted by members of the National Council of Jewish Women, it was found that over half of the court hearings lasted less than fifteen minutes. This assembly-line justice takes place because in most instances the decision has already been reached by a court social worker who put together the social history, often based on gossip and opinions of biased neighbors.

The year after the Supreme Court first voiced its concern about the juvenile court, it went further in the *Gault* decision and spelled out some of the constitutional guarantees needed for juveniles. This well-known 1967 case is an interesting example of what can occur—*and still does today*—under the juvenile court concept.

Fifteen-year-old Gerald Francis Gault and a friend were taken into custody by the Sheriff of Gila County, Arizona, on the complaint of a neighbor who had received a lewd telephone call. He was arrested and locked up in the children's detention home. At the hearing he denied making the offensive call. No attempt was made to prove or disprove this claim. The court's only contact with the complainant was a telephone call by a juvenile officer before the hearing. The request of Gerald's mother that the neighbor be brought to the hearing so her testimony could be challenged was denied. As neither the parents nor Gerald were allowed to see the referral report filed by the probation officer, they were unable to dispute any untrue or misleading statements.

On this basis he was sentenced to the state industrial school "for the period of his minority [until the age of 21], unless sooner discharged by due process of law."

When questioned later, the judge was uncertain as to what section of the law the boy had violated. He "thought" it had something to do with disturbing the peace, that is, using lewd language in the presence of another. Anyhow, he was convinced the boy was delinquent on the basis of his being "habitually involved in immoral matters." The reason for the habitual charge: two years earlier he had been questioned by the police about stealing a baseball glove (the police decided there was no foundation for the charge), and six months earlier he had been in the company of another youth who stole a wallet from a woman's purse.

The Supreme Court decision pointed out that if Gerald had been an adult and had been *legally proved guilty*, the maximum penalty would have been a fine of five to fifty dollars or a jail sentence of not more than two months. Yet he had received a sentence of up to six years and had been denied all the protections an adult would have had. The Court made it clear that juveniles, like adults, were entitled to:

1. The right to adequate representation by an attorney, either personally retained or appointed by the court
2. The right to be properly notified of the charges
3. The right to confront and cross-examine witnesses

Then in 1970 in the *Winship* case the Supreme Court went still further by ruling that, as with adults, the guilt of juveniles must be proved beyond a reasonable doubt.

Obviously this series of mandates by the U.S. Supreme Court has guaranteed the protection of juvenile rights. Obviously? Oh, no! Ten years after that first decision, David Gilman, counsel for the National Council on Crime and Delinquency, observed that "the practical effect of these cases has been hardly noticeable. Juvenile Court judges and staffs have resisted change in their practices, goals and procedures, simply by ignoring the decision entirely, or by subverting their spirit."[11]

Changes have been more of form than of substance. In many states, for example, as many as half of the youths appearing in court are still unrepresented by an attorney, even when facing long-term incarceration. When provided, the court-appointed attorney frequently does little more than interview the youth for a few minutes just before the hearing and then advise a guilty plea. He does it to "get help for the youngster," disregarding how damaging that "help" can be.

During the Christmas season ten years after the Supreme Court had demanded representation by an attorney, fourteen-year-old Robert May was arrested in a rural Mississippi town. He was charged with using a shotgun to rob a couple of fireworks stands and two nights later beating up a saleswoman while robbing a grocery. Indicted on four counts of armed robbery, Robert was sentenced a week later to forty-eight years in adult prison *with no chance of parole*. The slight (seventy-five pounds, four foot seven inches tall), bewildered youth was shipped off to join 1,800 adult felons in a Mississippi prison, where he was to remain until he was sixty-two years old. The youth's court-appointed attorney had plea-bargained the sentence. Robert's best interests had been protected by the "adequate counsel" demanded by the Supreme Court.

Despite the thousands of instances of violation of constitutional rights in the juvenile justice system, it is virtually unheard of for a court-appointed attorney to bother to file an appeal.

4. MORE HARM THAN GOOD

For a number of years many have realized that the juvenile court has been unsuccessful in protecting society. And there has been a growing suspicion that the court may even be causing irreparable damage to many youths.

Juveniles who have been subjected to the cruelty previously described have obviously been psychologically and physically harmed. But most apprehended delinquents are not so blatantly abused. And most institutions are not the hellholes publicized by investigative reporters. So what about the vast majority, the average, run-of-the-mill delinquents? How do they fare?

One observer who is eminently qualified to answer is Milton Lueger, former longtime director of the New York State Division of Youth and later head of the federal Office of Juvenile Justice and Delinquency Prevention. At the time he was president of the National Association of State Juvenile Delinquency Program Administrators, he was asked to appear at a Senate hearing on the problems of juvenile delinquency. In what has become an oft-quoted statement, he exclaimed:

> With the exception of a relatively few youths, it is probably better for all concerned if young delinquents were not detected, apprehended, or institutionalized. Too many of them get worse in our care.

Lueger's testimony is particularly revealing. He is no namby-pamby sentimentalist or dreamy-eyed armchair criminologist but has long been in the thick of the struggle. He knew that most juveniles quite normally outgrow their delinquent ways—that is, most of them will, provided their lives have not been messed up by the juvenile court. Rotary and Kiwanis clubs are filled with responsible citizens who successfully matured after a period of juvenile high jinks—matured without having had the services of the juvenile court. Conspicuously absent in those civic clubs, however, are the high-spirited youths who were unfortunate enough to have received "rehabilitative" services.

Since Lueger dropped his bombshell numerous studies have given further proof of what he had learned by experience. One of the most extensive of these was carried out by Martin Gold and his associates at the University of Michigan's Institute for Social Research. As part of a larger national study of adolescents, samples of teenagers from all forty-eight contiguous states were interviewed in depth. Youths who had been apprehended by the police in the previous six months were matched by age, sex, and race to youths who admitted having committed offenses similar in number and seriousness but had not been caught. The follow-up study found that those who had been caught were twice as likely to have committed additional criminal acts and been arrested as were their nonapprehended counterparts.

Commenting on the study, Gold said:

> Whatever it is that the authorities do once they have caught a youth, it seems to be worse than doing nothing at all, worse even than never apprehending the offender. Getting caught encourages rather than deters them from further delinquency.[12]

The reasons for this detrimental effect have been interwoven throughout this chapter. Young persons who believe that the punishment they received was unjust will bitterly seek revenge against society. The revolving-door policy whereby delinquents are brought into the court time after time, only to be released or placed on meaningless probation, encourages future lawlessness. The delinquent sees the court as a joke. It doesn't really give a damn whether they break the law or not. So why not do it?

It is difficult to summon any breath of sympathy for fifteen-year-old Willie Bosket, Jr., but it is uncomfortable to reflect on his claim that he is the "monster that society created." By the time he was nine the juvenile court had eight times turned an indifferent back on a kid desperately needing help and discipline. When he was eleven a psychological examination found him "precocious, warm and sympathetic," but in need of adult support if he was to "reach his above-average intellectual and creative potential." In response the court sent him to a maximum-security institution holding teenage murderers, rapists, and armed robbers.

Here he found the "support" he needed.

Andrew Cooper, publisher of the black-owned *City Sun Weekly* in New York, raised this issue: "Since he was black, did the system ever identify him as a person worth saving?" Because of the indifference, society is now paying hundreds of thousands of dollars to keep this monster caged.

It is indeed ironic that the juvenile court, which grew out of a concern for children, may at times be the very vehicle that propels a youth into a criminal career. But so convincing have been the many studies showing how detrimental the juvenile court actually is that in the 1970s the battle cry of child advocates throughout America became "diversion." Congress stated in the purpose clause of the Juvenile Justice and Delinquency Prevention Act of 1974 that the intent of the law is "to develop and conduct effective programs to prevent delinquency, *to divert juveniles from the traditional juvenile justice system* and to provide critically needed alternatives to institutionalization." (Emphasis added.)

What a testimony to failure this official statement represents! Diversion from an institution that had itself been created as a diversion of youths from the damaging effects of the adult court.

Sadly, the great hopes of the child savers, the vision they saw, have not come about. Apologists for the juvenile court are quick with explanations for its failure. They point to underfunded efforts, unqualified judges, overloaded courts, insufficient staffs, and a lack of dispositional alternatives. All of this is true. Destructively true. But the fact is that in the past two decades, after millions upon millions of dollars have been poured into projects designed to ease these deficiencies, the efforts have had no discernible effect on juvenile crime. Nor has the more recent effort to crack down on delinquents proved effective. The long line of recidivists being returned to the court continues to lengthen.

A major part of this sorry performance must be credited to the fact that the juvenile court has been blinded by another myth—the myth of rehabilitation. The next chapter will explore just how pervasive this myth has been.

Chapter 3

THE COSTLY MYTH OF REHABILITATION

MYTH: *Juvenile judges save delinquents from lives of crime by committing them to programs for rehabilitation.*

REALITY: *The belief that delinquents can be forcibly rehabilitated has been a costly bit of wishful thinking. The vast majority become far more delinquent because of their rehabilitative experience.*

Regardless of the euphemistic names given to delinquency institutions—reformatory, state training school, boys' industrial school, boys' camp, forestry camp—they brutalize children. It is claimed that these schools teach juveniles a trade. They do. The trade is crime. It is claimed that these schools change a delinquent's mental attitude. They do. He learns to hate. It is claimed that these schools can redirect a youth's motivation. They do. He becomes dedicated to getting even with a society that has excluded him.

How can it be that honorable men deliberately and knowingly

submit juveniles to the injustice and the cruelty cataloged in the previous chapter? The answer is simple. They do it with a clear conscience because America embraces a myth—the myth of rehabilitation. Americans have blind faith in the ability of science to accomplish miracles. It is easy to transfer this faith into a naive belief that some vague psychological activity, optimistically described as "therapy" or counseling, can change a delinquent youth into a law-abiding, responsible citizen.

The myth has been an expensive one—expensive in terms of the billions of dollars that have been wasted in the vain pursuit of therapeutic goals, even more expensive in terms of the thousands of young people whose lives have been mangled and futures destroyed. It is truly one of the great mysteries of the twentieth century how society has maintained the myth of rehabilitation despite the overwhelming evidence that coercive therapy simply does not work. But compassionate people are so fervent in their wish for it to work that they are blinded to disturbing facts.

For decades administrators and program directors managed to conceal the truth from the general public. But in the 1960s many people began to raise questions, among them the California legislators. They had become weary of being called upon, year after year, to build another and yet another juvenile institution. They demanded to know just what was going on. In response the California Youth Authority, which operates the world's largest juvenile correctional system, undertook a massive study of four thousand formerly institutionalized delinquents.

Their report, published in 1966, told the story of what had happened to those youths in just five years following discharge. Despite their rehabilitation, 44 percent of the males had already ended up in prison. Most of the remainder had been convicted of crimes for which they received jail sentences or fines. This study was particularly disheartening in that California is generally considered to have some of the most progressive juvenile programs in the nation.

Since then many studies have demonstrated the almost total failure of institutional programs in the rehabilitation of juveniles. Most surveys are even more discouraging, showing recidivism rates as high as 75 or 80 percent. Three out of four chronic juvenile offenders graduate into adult crime.

Massachusetts, under the leadership of Jerome Miller, then commissioner of the Department of Youth Services, was the first state officially to recognize and admit this failure of rehabilitation within an institution. In 1972, after discovering that the entrenched staffs of the scandal-ridden institutions were resistant to reform, Miller closed all of the state's large training schools. To the amazement of his critics, juvenile crime did not soar. *Instead, when the courts stopped sending delinquents to institutions, serious juvenile crimes declined.*

Why Not Try Psychiatry?

The most intensive psychiatrically oriented large institutional program has been that of the Boys Industrial School under the sponsorship of the famed Menninger Clinic of Topeka, Kansas. The delinquents, many of whom were only minor status offenders, were held an average of fourteen months so they could benefit from highly professional therapy. Staffing was a project director's dream. For 135 boys, there was a staff of 182, with 28 teachers (an average of 1 for every 5 boys). Included were psychiatrists, clinical psychologists, psychiatric social workers, and psychiatric residents from the Menninger School of Psychiatry.

With such an ideal setup, few people questioned the highly respected Dr. Karl Menninger when in 1968 he stated in his book *The Crime of Punishment*[1] that the school had a recidivism rate of between 4 and 9 percent—an unheard-of record in the annals of corrections. When, four years later, he repeated the claim in Senate hearings on delinquency, Senator Birch Bayh latched onto the statement as proof that delinquents can be rehabilitated if only enough money and energy are put into the effort.

Facts, however, belied the claim.

Even before Dr. Menninger appeared at the Senate hearing his clinic had published a little-circulated report showing that after release 65 percent of these mostly minor offenders had been rearrested. Furthermore, despite the clinic's great emphasis on education, only 15 percent had gone on to finish high school. In reality these delinquents were more likely to get into further difficulties than were those who did not receive the therapy—therapy of impeccable quality. The report ruefully admitted: "Statistical studies have shown that many boys who get into serious trouble with the law quickly become recidivists regardless of the kind of intervention."[2]

Despite the thousands of experimental projects, *there has been little scientifically verified evidence that psychotherapy—particularly group therapy—has been effective in reducing delinquent behavior.*

True, some youths have improved—but usually at about the same rate, at best, as has occurred simply with the passage of time.

This failure of rehabilitation is somewhat confusing to the reader whose knowledge of juvenile corrections comes solely from the Sunday feature section of the newspaper. The account of how a poor, wayward youth, habitually truant from school and repeatedly guilty of shoplifting, has been turned into an A student, a leader in the Boy Scout troop, and the principal support for his disabled mother, makes a tear-jerking story. Editors know it is the rare exception that is interesting, and there is no reader appeal in routine stories of program failure after failure.

In after-dinner speeches, proponents of institutional programs pound the podium and with trembling oratory proclaim that "even if just one youth is saved, it was worth the effort." A favorite example is Louis Armstrong, whose life was turned around after he learned to play the trumpet while in a reform school. (He was there not because of delinquency but because the state had no place for him after he had been abandoned by his prostitute mother.) A likely folklore successor to Armstrong is heavyweight boxing champion Mike Tyson, who may be the wealthiest man ever to have graduated from the "bad" cottage of a reform school. It was there that the pugilistic potential of this Brooklyn junior-high dropout was discovered. (Some may less admiringly suggest that the vicious brutality of his boxing style just might be a reflection of the brutality he experienced in the delinquency institution.)

Newspaper features and after-dinner polemics about saving one child, however, miss the point. The real questions are:

- Would some other approach have been more successful in saving a far greater number of juveniles?
- Could the money spent in an expensive institutional program have been used more effectively elsewhere?
- Would fewer of these youths have become hard-core delinquents if society had done nothing?

Maturational Reform

As has been previously noted, most delinquent youths grow out of their antisocial behavior—provided nothing disturbs that natural process. "Maturation reform" is the term devised by David Matza for this phenomenon whereby juveniles tend to become progressively less delinquent as they move toward adulthood. The maturing youth faced with paying the rent, buying diapers, and putting groceries on the table becomes weary of sowing wild oats and other juvenile peccadilloes.

Maturation reform seems to occur regardless of whether an individual juvenile is treated, punished, or ignored. But it seems to occur more readily among those youths who are not caught or given "treatment."

For this reason it is understandable that Allan Breed, for many years director of the California Youth Authority, declared that *"nothing in 25 years' experience has changed my early reaction that institutions do more harm than good."*[3] And the similar conclusion of Milton Lueger, longtime director of the other large state juvenile correctional system, the New York State Division of Youth, bears repeating here: "With the exception of a relatively few youths, it is probably better for all concerned if young delinquents were not detected, apprehended, or institutionalized. Too many of them get worse in our care."

GGI and the Highfields Fad

As the failure of large institutions became apparent small ones housing only twenty to forty youths came into favor. Attention focused on the Highfields (New Jersey) Treatment Program, a small residential institution which in the early fifties was set up in the former mansion of Charles Lindbergh, the site of the famous kidnapping. Staff reports claimed sharply more success than had been achieved in traditional large institutions. And despite the absence of independent evaluation, the program suddenly became the glamorous star of the correctional world. Program planners from across the nation beat a path to Highfields.

Here the treatment relied heavily on Guided Group Interaction (GGI), also known as Positive Peer Group Pressure and Positive Peer Culture. It was a technique so simple and so inexpensive that in the 1970s it became a widespread fad. Those who copied the program discovered that just any worker, trained or not, could run the groups. The fad grew into a national phenomenon, becoming the backbone of most juvenile correctional programs.

In 1969 the Select Committee on Crime of the U.S. House of Representatives conducting a two-year study of juvenile corrections visited institutions across the nation. Among them was the Red Wing

(Minnesota) School for Boys, where the staff stated that recidivism had dropped from 40 percent to 19 percent since they instituted the Positive Peer Culture method. The congressional committee was so impressed that in 1971 it published a report to the nation declaring that the program could rehabilitate virtually any type of delinquent. Furthermore, most any juvenile institution could be converted quickly and inexpensively to the new system.

Hosanna! Success at last!

As the name implies, the GGI system attempts to utilize the strong influence that adolescent peers have upon each other. Within the residential facility groups of eight to twelve youths live, work, play, study, and eat together. A two-hour formal group session is usually held daily; in the presence of the adult leader the teenagers probe the causes of their undesirable behavior.

When an individual is on the hot seat he or she is pressured to confess all past sins and to describe each transgression in gory detail. At times the pressure is painful physical force—being sat upon, slapped, screamed at directly into the ear, and subjected to other more severe "unapproved" actions. (A number of fatalities have occurred, as at a Kentucky youth camp where an asthmatic youth's arms were held tightly crisscrossed beneath his chin until, after twenty minutes, he stopped breathing.) From a list of character defects the group members decide which caused the delinquent to go wrong, tell him how he must change, and finally badger and harass him until he agrees to alter his attitude and behavior.

Outside the meetings the youths watch each other for violations of institutional rules or of group-imposed sanctions. Tattling is encouraged. This is "showing concern for others." In one group session I sat in on, a boy garnered points with the staff by squealing on four buddies. One was thinking about running away, a second had goofed off at the work detail, another had stolen a cigarette, and a fourth had been masturbating in the rest room. If one member breaks a major institutional rule—goes AWOL, hits a staff member, destroys public property—*all* members are punished by the staff along with the culprit: the others failed to show concern. Such a policy turns everyone into a vigilante.

Obviously, institutional staffs are loud in their praise. Their lives become much easier, since discipline is maintained by the inmates themselves. To obtain release from the institution, the youth must first obtain his group's agreement that he has satisfactorily "worked through his problems." This must then be confirmed by the staff.

Getting out becomes a con game—conning both the peer group and the staff.

On my first visit to a juvenile camp where GGI was utilized, I came away filled with enthusiasm. It was true. That elusive cure for delinquency had been found. I had talked at length with four boys who the staff informed me were nearly ready for release. The boys freely discussed with me their past mistakes and were profuse in their professions of determination to go straight. One boy wasn't even going to see his girl except on weekends—he'd need other evenings to study.

My enthusiasm collapsed three months later when I looked up those four boys. Two were already back in the detention center awaiting court hearings on new charges, one for breaking and entering, the other for purse snatching. The would-be student had been kicked out of school: he had been unable to adjust in a school that didn't want to bother with a former institutionalized delinquent. Only one had apparently managed to remain trouble-free for a whole three months.

These youths had not only conned the staff and their group, they had conned themselves. At the time, most genuinely believed that they could make it when they returned home—returned to the same home and the same community environment that had spawned their delinquency in the first place. The only real change had been that now they possessed an opportunity-limiting label—"reform school graduate." As such they were no longer welcomed in law-abiding company, in school, or by prospective employers. All they had really learned was how to be a con artist.

A Second Look at GGI

Long after programs modeled after Highfields had been established across the country, criminologists began to take a second look at the validity of the claims. Many flaws in the research method were discovered. Subjects had not been randomly assigned either to Highfields or to Annandale, the traditional large institute with which it was compared. Instead, Highfields's subjects had been hand-picked by the judge as promising candidates. Furthermore, the staff had been permitted to expel uncooperative, disruptive youngsters (and not include them in the statistics), a luxury the staffs of traditional institutions did not enjoy. When all significant variables were considered, the outcome at Highfields was little different from the conventional reform school's.

A year after the enthusiastic congressional report on Positive Peer

Culture at Red Wing, the Minnesota Department of Corrections published its research findings. The failure rate of boys approximately two years after release had already reached 55 percent, a far cry from the 19 percent reported to the congressional committee and considerably worse than Red Wing's record before adopting the new approach. In a slight understatement, the juvenile delinquency program planner for the Minnesota Crime Commission wrote me that "people are not as enthusiastic as they originally were about using the technique as a cure-all for all troubled kids."

Since that time dozens of research studies have consistently demonstrated that programs utilizing Guided Group Interaction have little positive effect. But amazingly, these carefully documented studies have failed to dampen the enthusiasm with which the "treatment" is embraced by administrators, even today. It is embraced because, as I have pointed out, it is an effective way to maintain discipline, it is inexpensive, and it brings joy to the soul of a counselor to hear a delinquent confess the error of his or her ways and promise to reform. The counselor is not around a few months later to witness the decay of those artificially induced promises.

Considerable space has been devoted here to Guided Group Interaction as a therapeutic tool, not because it is so much more unsuccessful than other strategies but because it points to the paucity of successful techniques and the inability to forcibly rehabilitate juveniles. Probably the principal reason for GGI's continued use is simply that the juvenile corrections industry has nothing more hopeful (or cheaper) to offer.

"Deinstitutionalization"

It became increasingly apparent that regardless of the therapy technique utilized, confinement in institutions was most often detrimental. (In addition to other failures, in 1986 seventy-four juveniles died while being rehabilitated, including twenty-one suicides and twenty-eight homicides.) So the battle cry of reformers changed to a fancy mouthful of a word, "deinstitutionalization." Professional journals were crammed with articles urging judges to commit delinquents to treatment programs in an open setting rather than to institutions. "Deinstitutionalization" became a code word that every program planner had to include in his application for grant money in order to show that he was hip to the latest fad. And fad it was.

The key to keeping youths out of institutions was to be community treatment. Basically this meant probation combined with some form of therapy. This could be as comprehensive as commitment to a nonsecure group home or as minimal as a once-a-week counseling session.

Hope springs eternal that the magic pill will be found. And again it seemed that the discovery had been made. Just as Highfields had become the guiding light in the movement for smaller institutions, now Achievement Place, a group home utilizing *behavior modification* techniques, became the star of the deinstitutionalization movement. Again administrators rushed to examine the new technique that was producing such exciting results: improvement in school performance, emotional behavior, conversational and social skills, attitudes, self-concepts, self-maintenance behaviors . . . and greatly reduced delinquent behavior.

Behavior Modification—the New Cure

Behavior modification is as old as the human family. Parents mold the behavior of children through rewards for good behavior, punishment for bad. Psychologists at the University of Kansas in 1967 adapted this concept to a group home for delinquents in Lawrence, Kansas. The idea was to give improperly socialized youths the home environment and character training they had missed. The most significant component of the program was the professional training given the foster parents before they were placed in charge of a home.

In the Achievement Place model, six to eight delinquents live in an open home with a married couple as teaching parents. Motivation for change is based on awarding points for good behavior and taking them away for improper behavior. A posted list specifies the points for over two hundred actions covering virtually everything conceivable. Among them: +50 for peeling a carrot, +100 for carrying in a grocery sack, +1,500 for doing a large homework assignment, −10,000 for fighting, −2,000 for forgetting school lunch money, −10,000 for lying. Points are given out on the spot and tabulated at the end of the day. Accumulated points may be exchanged for privileges such as snacks, watching TV, getting out of regular work, going to town.

The teaching parents are also instructed to provide social reinforcement with praise, affection, and support. As in the Guided Group Interaction technique, the youths are rewarded for reporting peer misbehavior, punished for not reporting. Residents quickly learn that if life is to be bearable they must do what the teaching parents "suggest." Again it is a technique successful in maintaining discipline and getting work done.

By 1981 when the government's Institute for Juvenile Justice and Delinquency Prevention released a book touting Achievement Place, it was already possible to list some eighty other books, journal articles, and Ph.D. dissertations that dealt with this newfound cure for delinquency. Across the nation new homes were being cloned almost daily. The National Teaching-Family Association was formed to coordinate these efforts. Six regional sites were established to train couples in behavior modification technique.

Only after the teaching-family model had begun its wildfire spread did the National Institute of Mental Health fund Mark R. Weinrott, Richard R. Jones, and James R. Howard to do a comprehensive evaluation of the approach. A longitudinal study was made of twenty-six teaching-family homes (including the original Achievement Place) that were alternative placements for delinquent youths. Follow-up data on these youths, three years after their release, were reported in 1982.

The evaluation report sounded like a rerun of the evaluation of the Guided Group Interaction fad of a decade earlier. Just as the early promise of Highfields did not stand up under careful scrutiny, now Achievement Place failed to live up to its promise. Delinquent activity was reduced only while the youths were living in the teaching-family homes. A year following treatment there was no significant difference between them and youths from comparison programs.

Again, in what sounds like a rerun, the negative findings of this definitive study failed to have a chilling effect on the enthusiasm. In the year the report was made there were 170 homes officially utilizing the program; two years later, in 1984, despite the report the number had increased to over 250.

Reasons for the failure are virtually the same as those that accounted for the failure of Guided Group Interaction. While he or she is in a behavior modification program a youth's actions are controlled by the promise of rewards and punishment. But not so afterward. In the real world the youth is no longer rewarded for being good; but crime provides rewards for being bad. And as with other rehabilitative programs, *in the end the delinquent is dumped back into the same family, the same community, and the same problems that existed before the "rehabilitation."*

Other nonsecure community residential programs have met with similar or even less successful results. One well-documented survey of eight such projects (including halfway houses, group homes, foster homes, and residential centers) showed that either they produced no significant differences over nonresidential control groups, or, as was the case in five of the eight programs, the residential groups did worse.[4]

Nonresidential community treatment programs have likewise been tried and found wanting. In some the youth has lived at home while spending the entire day in the program, others have operated during after-school hours, and still others only on the weekends. Some have required attendance at special or "alternative" schools. Programs utilizing intensive casework from social workers have been popular.

One highly publicized program of the sixties was the California Community Treatment Project. Success was claimed by keeping delinquents in the community under intensive supervision. Twenty years later researcher Jill Leslie Rosenbaum was able to obtain the post-release histories of 159 of 240 girls who had been in the program. Of the group, over half were white; two-thirds had been committed to the Youth Authority *only for status offenses*, mostly running away.

Rosenbaum published her report about this "successful" program in 1989. All but 6 of the 159 girls had been arrested as adults, most (70 percent) at least four times. Even excluding prostitution, drug offenses, and shoplifting, 82 percent had been convicted of at least one serious crime.[5]

Generally speaking, with very rare exceptions, community treatment projects have failed because most have been based on the very same techniques that over the years have proved to be no more effective, or less, than doing nothing.

Nothing Works?

The late criminologist Robert Martinson was commissioned by New York State officials to review the professional literature dealing with the rehabilitation of criminals. In his report made in 1975 he dropped a bombshell by declaring, in effect, that "nothing works." An uproar of protest arose among program administrators, particularly Ted Palmer and other California proponents of the state's community treatment programs for juveniles. So hot was the debate in the professional journals that the National Research Council was asked to settle the dispute. The Council set up the Panel of Research on Rehabilitative Techniques to examine not only the studies analyzed by Martinson but also research reports published after his cutoff date.

The panel's conclusion did not equivocate. Not only was Martinson correct, they declared, he did not go far enough. They were particularly critical of Ted Palmer's protest, concluding that he had taken at face value the overblown claims of project directors which in most instances proved to be wrong.[6]

A more recent survey of the professional literature concerning the impact of treatment on recidivism was published in a 1988 issue of *Crime and Delinquency*. The authors, Steven Lab and John Whitehead, reported that "the results indicated that juvenile correctional treatment fared no better than in earlier reviews." They noted that many of the "positive findings were based on dubious, subjective evaluations."[7]

In considering success or failure of a program, it is essential that the question be raised, *compared to what?* Take, for example, the widely known Provo, Utah, experiment, an intensive daytime community treatment project incorporating GGI and work incentive programs. The project proved to be more successful than institutionalization but less successful than mere probation. So—was it a success or a failure? Compared to what?

Youths assigned to an official probation officer to whom they regularly report usually have less recidivism than comparable youths committed to an institution. But generally they have more recidivism than those guilty of equivalent offenses who have only been given a firm admonition by the judge to stay out of trouble. When rehabilitation programs are compared, almost invariably the least restrictive, least intensive effort proves to be the most successful or—depending on the point of view—does the least damage.

Master of One's Fate

It has been naive to hope that the deep psychological scars from years of emotional stress or social and physical deprivation could be erased by forcing a kid into a few hours of something posing as therapy. Perhaps the failure is wrapped up in the human need to feel that one is master of his own fate. A youth sees society trying to force him to behave in a certain way. And while bowing his neck, the juvenile vows that nobody, but nobody, is going to tell him what to do.

This is "reactance," a psychological phenomenon that in varying degrees is common to us all, a phenomenon that makes it virtually impossible to control anyone's behavior by force except during the time the individual is under close surveillance and faced with punishment.

Reactance is not solely a juvenile phenomenon. It destroys the effectiveness of adult therapeutic programs that demand participation. Court-ordered rehabilitation programs for drug and alcohol abuse, for example, have been miserable, costly failures. Human behavior can be changed, but only if the individual *wants to change*. There were dire predictions about the hordes of junkies who would return from the Vietnam War: heroin use had been widespread. But the vast majority of addicted soldiers made the transition to a drug-free life with relative ease. Removal from the environment that nurtured the drug use, combined with a personal motivation to lead a normal civilian life, was all that was necessary.

The success of Alcoholics Anonymous and similar self-imposed programs can be attributed largely to their voluntary aspect. The alcoholic comes to AA wanting help, wanting to change, and frequently he does. When attendance is merely a court-ordered alternative to jail, the prognosis is far less hopeful. Similarly, many juvenile programs that would be helpful on a voluntary basis are destroyed by the demand to participate.

Delinquents will alter their antisocial behavior of their own volition if they can be shown that reform will bring a better life. Unfortunately, for many uneducated youths of the underclass legitimate opportunities are not readily available. For them crime holds the most hope for sharing in the material bounty of America.

No amount of "therapy" is going to overcome fourteen or fifteen years of the corrupting influence of family, friends, and environment. This influence began early in life, for some even dating back to inadequate prenatal nourishment or maternal drug or alcohol addiction. Showing concern for these troubled juveniles in their teenage years is at least a decade too late. Their criminality is rooted in deeper social problems which society must address if crime is to be reduced.

For a Few—Juvenile Prison

Up to now we have discussed court action only as an attempt at rehabilitation. But there is another reason, a critical one, for sometimes intervening in the life of a delinquent—the protection of society. It will always be necessary to lock up a small number of dangerous, psychotic youths for long periods of time. (The number is variously estimated to be between 3 and 10 percent of the delinquents now being institutionalized.) But no one should kid himself. This is not for rehabilitation. It is to protect the public from a violent criminal who just happens to be a juvenile.

With this select few, even to dream of rehabilitation is a joke. This was discovered in Massachusetts when Jerome Miller successfully closed the large secure institutions without increasing juvenile crime in the state. It became apparent, however, that a place was necessary for murderers, rapists, paranoid schizophrenics, child molesters, and the like, even though they were juveniles. In 1975, amid much fanfare about treatment for serious delinquents, the Worcester facility was opened with a projected maximum population of twenty-four and a staff of fifty. The thirty-two guards were labeled "child care workers."

A year later, after a machete-swinging youth held the guards at bay while others smashed down the door and escaped, the therapy program was revised. An ex-offender was hired as administrator, and another ex-offender with virtually no training or experience as a psychologist was given the title of "clinical supervisor of treatment." After a youth committed suicide under the new treatment program, the ex-offenders were fired and a clinical psychologist was again put in charge of the program. After a year he resigned in total frustration.

And what about the success of treatment in a maximum-security setting such as this? Of the boys held while the original therapeutic program was in full sway, every one had been rearrested for serious crimes within two years of release. Most were in adult prisons, serving long-term sentences. One had been killed attempting a prison escape. The results speak volumes about the dream of rehabilitating serious, violent delinquents.

Diversion—the Current Fad

In the previous chapter it was noted that the failure of the juvenile court has been so devastating that youth advocates and even Congress have pleaded for delinquents to be diverted from the destructive effects of the court. But like other reform movements in the juvenile justice system, "diversion" became a fad. In the late seventies and early eighties hundreds of books, monographs, and journal articles on the subject were published. Thousands of experimental projects were funded to keep minor offenders from becoming involved in the system.

There is nothing new about diversion per se. It has always occurred extensively (many would say too extensively). Most police merely give a stern lecture to some 50 to 80 percent of the youths they stop.[8] At the station upwards of 60 percent of those brought in are released after a warning or a call made to their parents. And of those remaining only half ever officially go before a judge. Even so, the National Advisory Commission on Criminal Justice Standards and Goals insists that the number of juveniles being brought to the court should be further reduced by at least 70 percent.

Unfortunately, diversion quickly lost its original meaning of totally diverting minor offenders from the justice system. Instead, it came to mean only diversion from *traditional* correctional programs (institutions, group homes, community treatment projects, and so on). Erring youths would be diverted into "new," less coercive treatment programs, supposedly on a voluntary basis.

Study after study has found, however, that "new" is only a new title to an old, unsuccessful treatment modality. And voluntary participation is an illusion. A youngster is given a Hobson's choice. Not very subtly he or she is threatened with court prosecution and possibly reform school for refusing to "volunteer" for the program.

As Donald R. Cressey and Robert A. McDermott explain in a book evaluating diversion projects, published by the National Institute of Law Enforcement and Criminal Justice:

> If "true" diversion occurs, the juvenile is safely out of the official realm of the juvenile justice system and he is immune from incurring the delinquency label or any of its variations— predelinquent, delinquent tendencies, bad guy, hard core, unreachable. Further, when he walks out of the door from the person diverting him, he is technically free to tell the diverter to go to hell. We found very little "true" diversion in the communities studied.[9]

Be that as it may, what has been the result of these thousands of so-called diversion programs?

Most evaluation reports have a familiar ring. Take, for instance, the Memphis-Metro Youth Diversion Project. As guideposts toward achieving the ultimate goal of reforming delinquents, the planners had written many subgoals into the proposal, e.g., organizing community resources, improving juvenile justice decision making, strengthening community-based service models, and so on. Early on there were glowing claims of program success. But listen to the face-saving gobbledygook in the final report: "All of the goals *except re-ducing the recidivism of diverted youths* were met either successfully or very successfully" (emphasis added).[10] Win the battle, lose the war.

A $10-million "National Evaluation of Diversion Projects" was sponsored by the U.S. Office of Juvenile Justice and Delinquency Prevention. The 1981 executive report succinctly summed up the findings: ". . . a diversion disposition was not more successful in avoiding stigma, improving social adjustment, or reducing delinquent behavior than normal justice processing or outright release."[11]

The greatest damage done by diversion has been that instead of removing youngsters from the system, it has actually drawn thou-sands upon thousands of additional status offenders and minor law-breakers *into* the system. The process is called "widening the nets." Police and court officials are under pressure to cooperate with the new program that has been established, often with great fanfare, in their community. But they are caught in a bind. They are being asked to endorse a program based on the stated belief that what they have in good faith been doing to young delinquents is actually harmful. Understandably their enthusiasm is lukewarm. Moreover, they rebel at releasing control over delinquents who they honestly believe can be straightened out by the system. As a result, they "cooperate" by diverting into the new program juveniles who oth-erwise would have simply been released. Many of these have com-mitted only exceedingly petty offenses. Others have committed no crime at all, having been referred by parents and schools for status offenses.

Diversion projects siphon off money to "treat" youths who should not have been there in the first place. As a result of widening the nets, more and more juveniles have suffered the debilitating effects of the juvenile justice system. They have been stigmatized. And they have been punished without even the safeguard of a court hearing. Again, what began as a noble reform movement ended up damaging the youths it was intended to help.

So much for the most recent of an ongoing series of misguided hopes that became fads.

The repeated failure of highly touted treatment modalities has left the juvenile justice system prey to the public's demand that something be done with these hoodlums. The resulting get-tough policy has come down most heavily on the minorities, the poor, and the uneducated, exacerbating the very problems society would solve.

The thousands of unfortunate youths caught in the crackdown are poured into overcrowded juvenile prisons at a cost of over a billion dollars a year. To punish each of these delinquents, taxpayers shell out as much in a single year as it would cost to provide them with a four-year college education. (In New York State the bill for each institutionalized delinquent is $53,000 a year.)

It is just possible that this billion dollars could be used in some other efforts which would provide greater protection to society . . . and greater hope to America's problem children.

Chapter 4

EVEN PREVENTION HAS FAILED

There is considerable agreement that prevention is preferable to rehabilitation. Unfortunately, no one seems to have discovered the magic formula for preventing delinquency. Many ideas have been touted, but when put to the test most have proved to be ineffective at best—often even counterproductive.

There are, we have noted, two approaches to delinquency prevention. One, the psychological, is the attempt to identify and zero in on potentially delinquent individuals. The other, the sociological, is the attempt to work with an entire population in areas known to produce a high percentage of delinquents, such as slum neighborhoods or low-achieving schools. The first approach, working with individuals, is the more popular. Not only is it far less expensive, it also is compatible with the commonly held myth that delinquents are "sick" individuals needing to be cured.

Predicting the Delinquent Individual

For over fifty years psychologists have dreamed of a project that would pinpoint for early treatment those children destined for lives of crime. This dream reached nightmarish proportions in 1970 when

President Richard Nixon asked the Department of Health, Education and Welfare to consider the possibility of administering psychological tests to every six-year-old in the nation. Those showing criminal inclinations (at age six!) would be required to undergo massive psychological and psychiatric treatment in after-school centers. If they persisted in antisocial behavior, they would be remanded to camps for more intensive therapy.

The proposal had been recommended to Nixon by Dr. Arnold Hutschnecker, a psychiatrist who, incidentally, had treated Nixon during his vice presidency. It was offered as an alternative to the recommendations made by the National Commission on the Causes and Prevention of Violence, headed by Dr. Milton Eisenhower, which had proposed massive urban reconstruction to eliminate some of the social conditions that breed crime.

In presenting his proposal, Hutschnecker stated: "No doubt there is a desperate need for urban reconstruction, but I would suggest another, direct, immediate, and—I believe—effective way of attacking the problem at its very origin by focusing on the criminal mind of the child. The aim is to prevent a child with a delinquent character structure from being allowed to grow into a full-fledged teenage delinquent or adult criminal."[1] It was a terrifying vision of a fascist state, complete with "treatment camps," swooping down to control the minds of children. Fortunately, the resounding uproar raised by child development specialists, educators, and civil libertarians caused the proposal to be quietly scuttled.

Most projects are less ambitious. But regardless of their scope, all programs that would zero in on the individual have one thing in common: they must first identify the potential delinquent.

And herein lies the problem.

Despite massive psychological research efforts to predict future delinquency—psychological tests, psychiatric evaluations, experience tables, sociological profiles—all have had extremely low predictive success. Overprediction is the biggest problem. All tests come up with a vast number of false positives, that is, predictions that a youth will become delinquent, when in actuality he does not. Thus, if any of these tests were applied randomly to large groups of youngsters, for example an entire classroom, many potentially erroneous and tragically self-fulfilling accusations would be made.

The most widely used predictive tests are adaptations of the true-false questions in the Minnesota Multiphasic Personality Inventory (MMPI). Here the two sides of the same coin are quickly apparent.

For example, future delinquents tend to answer "true" to the statement, "During one period when I was a youngster I engaged in petty thievery." But as such behavior is common among very young children, a "true" response may indicate an honest individual instead of a potential delinquent. Similarly, "I enjoy a race or game better when I bet on it" is approved by most future delinquents. But the future stock market guru may also be in agreement.

Predictions based on a sociological profile are equally unsatisfactory. Here the assumption is made that delinquency is the end product of adverse social conditions—the neighborhood, companions, economic status, and, most important of all, family relationships.

One of the best-controlled experiments to test the predictive power of a social profile was the New York City Youth Board Prediction Study. The Glueck Social Prediction Tables were given to a sample of 223 boys entering the first grade in a high delinquency area. (The Glueck Tables were also to have been the principal tool in Dr. Hutschnecker's national screening program.) Seven years later, 24 of the 37 predicted to become delinquents, or two-thirds, had *not* turned to crime (false positives), while 10 of the 186 predicted nondelinquents had become delinquent (false negatives). The project was declared to be "moderately successful" since the prediction was incorrect for only 15 percent of the boys. But sociologist Harwin Voss succinctly points out that there would have been one-third fewer errors if no test had been given and the staff had simply predicted there would be zero delinquents in the group.

The Self-Fulfilling Prophecy

While predictive techniques generally are failures, under certain conditions they can be accurate. This occurs when the prediction is made by or known to a person or persons having a significant influence on the child's development. It is particularly true for parents and teachers. The accuracy comes not from any special skill in crystal ball reading, however, but because these persons have the power to make their prediction come true—usually subconsciously.

It has been demonstrated that fourth- and fifth-grade teachers can very accurately predict which of their students will eventually wind up in juvenile court. But there is a catch. Having made the prediction, teachers unconsciously begin to treat the child as though what was predicted is already a fact. They become overly watchful, overly suspicious, overly ready to punish. Because of the psychological dynamics that come into play, particularly the influence of self-concept, the children tend to live up to the expectations of the teachers. They are expected to become delinquent—and many do!

Herein is the tragedy in many prevention programs. Because the screening tests are inaccurate, many youths are inappropriately labeled—predelinquent, potential delinquent, troublemaker, maladjusted. And because of these improper labels social, educational, and economic doors are slammed in their faces, thus setting in motion the same antisocial behaviors that are meant to be prevented.

Ineffective Social Services

The most popular ingredient of most major delinquency prevention programs has been the delivery of social services to those identified as predelinquent. Few projects have engendered as much hope as the Seattle Atlantic Street Center, a settlement house in a high-crime area. Three years went into designing the program and testing various methods for delivering services. School records and police files, along with extensive family interviews, were used to identify high-risk boys entering the seventh grade. These were divided into an experimental group and a carefully matched control group, each containing fifty-four boys.

Intensive social services lasting from one to two years were given the experimental boys *and their families* by specially trained male social workers. Caseloads were low. Workers obtained needed services for their clients, provided individual and group counseling, and served as recreation leaders. Eighteen months after the completion of the program an evaluation was made. The final report admitted:

> The study made by the Seattle Atlantic Street Center becomes the eighth known delinquency-prevention experiment of this type conducted in the United States. Like its predecessors, the experiment did not yield evidence that the rendering of a social service to carefully selected acting-out youths and their significant others was effective in moderating those youths' acting-out behavior.
>
> This unfortunate finding is particularly convincing in this instance, for, unlike previous delinquency-prevention exper-

iments, this study achieved a level of methodological rigor not usually found in prior experiments. . . .

To have this effort fail and to have this failure so well documented that few rationalizations can be made to mitigate the outcome inevitably raises the question of whether such interventive efforts should continue.[2]

Misplaced Faith in Organized Recreation

And what about delinquency prevention efforts aimed at an entire high-risk population?

Recreation was one of the first approaches to area-wide delinquency prevention. Many years ago social workers from the Chicago YMCA organized slum-area youngsters into athletic teams which competed at the Y gym after school and in the evenings. To everyone's dismay, delinquency increased. The reason? The Y closed its doors at 9:00 P.M. so the boys could go home and study. But the boys had other ideas. Out on the street they continued their camaraderie with various illegal pursuits and by wreaking vengeance on members of opposing teams. The Y had become a catalyst for the formation of youth gangs.

Belief in the power of organized activities as an antidote to delinquency is based on some misinterpreted research. Numerous studies have clearly shown that those who participate in school sports (or organized school activities of any sort) are less likely to be delinquent than nonparticipants. Such statistics are misleading, however. They ignore the fact that organized sports attract conforming-type boys and girls, the ones who are willing to abide by rules and rigid training routines. Almost by definition most of the delinquent-prone population is eliminated.

Youths who actively participate in any organized community activity—Boy and Girl Scouts, 4-H Clubs, Hi-Y, and so forth—are also less likely to be delinquent. (The public is continually reminded of this. I shudder every time I hear the speaker at a fund-raising dinner quote a judge who declared he'd never had a Boy Scout come before his court.) But such programs usually have little appeal to delinquent-prone youths, and rarely do scoutmasters attempt to recruit "bad" boys. Instead, most give a sigh of relief when they succeed in easing out the troublemaker.

Walking down Fifth Avenue in New York City, I saw a graphic

demonstration of the disdain the "bad" kids have for organized programs. A troop of neatly uniformed Scouts were marching two abreast down the street on their way to visit the Empire State Building. Idling on the street corner were five boys who matched what was at the time the stereotype of a delinquent. As the Scouts passed, the leather-jacketed boys, with their greasy ducktail haircuts, spontaneously broke into a finger-snapping, hip-wagging ditty:

> On my honor,
> I will do my best,
> To take all you'll give me,
> And steal the rest.

A Decade Too Late

Since sixteen is the peak age for official delinquency, most prevention programs zero in on potential delinquents in junior high school—just as they are about to enter the "dangerous age." Regrettably, program planners are more adept at reading statistics than they are at reading the literature on human development. They are years too late with their programs—at least a decade too late.

By the time children reach puberty (which today is usually shortly before junior-high age), most of their attitudes and behavioral habits—their self-concept, their emotional responses, their approach to problem solving, and their personality in general—have already crystallized. These can be altered only with considerable effort, a process usually requiring years of intensive, individual therapy. Delinquency programs in junior high school don't come close to having the artillery required to effect such a change.

The failure of no single program has saddened me more than that of one carried out during the latter part of the sixties in the public schools of Columbus, Ohio, under the supervision of Walter Reckless and his associates at Ohio State University. This meticulously planned program was the culmination of fifteen years of systematic research by one of the all-time great academic criminologists at the peak of his career. Reckless had identified a positive self-concept as the factor that insulates the boys in high-delinquency areas from becoming delinquent. The National Institute of Mental Health funded an eight-year project to utilize this finding in a school-based prevention effort.

Teachers and principals of inner-city schools were asked to nominate boys in the sixth grade who were headed for trouble. Those nominated were randomly assigned either to the research program or to a control group. The experimental boys were placed in self-contained classrooms as they entered the seventh grade. Male teachers, carefully selected as adult role models, were trained in special skills for building self-esteem. Curriculum plans, remedial reading programs, and supplemental materials were designed for the specific needs of these potential delinquents. The program was repeated in the sixth grade for three years in eight schools. In all, 1,726 students were followed.

Three years after the experimental boys had completed their year-long prevention program, they were compared with the controls who had attended conventional classes. *There was no significant difference between the groups*—not in the number of official police contacts, not in their self-reported behavior. I had to hold back the tears as I read the report.

There had been similarly disappointing results from many carefully planned efforts because they were initiated too late in the youngsters' lives. There were, for example, the four hundred New York City potentially delinquent high school girls randomly assigned to an intensive counseling project or a control group. After three years the girls in the experiment had no better records than the controls for truancy, pregnancy, or court appearance. And in a Kansas City inner-city high school there were the four hundred problem boys who were randomly assigned to a control group or a special work-study program designed to prepare them for the world of work. Those in the program were given part-time jobs while in school and help in finding full-time jobs afterward. The six year follow-up showed no decrease in arrests of these boys compared to the control group.

Flint, Michigan—Mecca for Planners

To its credit, the United States has tried harder than any nation in history to implement programs for the prevention of juvenile crime. In the heyday of Lyndon Johnson's War on Crime, the federal government had to establish a separate council just to coordinate the more than two hundred often overlapping federal youth programs. By 1972 more than 120,000 individual federal grants were being funded at an annual cost to the taxpayers of $11.5 billion. Everyone in government was trying to get in on the act. The Department of Interior sought to prevent delinquency by taking inner-city youths on fishing trips. Even the Postal Department was conducting street academies in five cities for delinquent dropouts.

Despite the massive efforts at federal, state, and local levels, despite the billions of dollars and countless hours of individual effort expended over the past half-century, the United States still has the world's highest delinquency rate. It is just possible that there is a perverse correlation between these two facts—an effect opposite to what was intended. There is considerable evidence to suggest that the greater the amount of money spent for delinquency prevention, the greater will be the incidence of delinquency.

If money for youth programs were the answer to the delinquency problem, Flint, Michigan, would be virtually crime-free. Nowhere in the world has there been such a concentration of delinquency prevention and youth development programs. Annual grants that reached as high as some $5 million from the Charles Stewart Mott Foundation and approximately $7 million from local taxes and other sources made possible the many-tentacled Community School system. While much of the effort was aimed at general community improvement, the main thrust remained the same as it had been back in 1935 when the first Mott Foundation grant of six thousand dollars was made for a summer recreation program to reduce juvenile delinquency.

At the peak more than fifty projects were being conducted. They ranged from Hamady House Stepping Stones (which enrolled over a thousand girls in clubs stressing positive phases of youth development), to the Police-School Liaison Program (placing a plainclothes policeman in each of the city's secondary schools as a counselor-friend to the students), to the Family Life Education Program (helping students and their parents understand human growth and development).

Understandably, Flint became Mecca for program planners and administrators. In retrospect it seems strange that apparently none of the pilgrims bothered to inquire about the delinquency rate in Flint. Everyone assumed that such an array of well-run programs would have a beneficial effect. But it isn't necessarily so. Look at the statistics.

There are five counties in Michigan with populations of over 400,000. Genesee County, of which Flint is the county seat and principal city, is fourth in size. According to HEW's Juvenile Court Statistics published in 1975 (during the heyday of the program), 31.25 out of every 1,000 youths aged ten through sixteen were brought before the juvenile court—a rate over three times as high as the 9.48 per 1,000 average of the other four counties, including Detroit. Furthermore, it was 50 percent higher than the rate in the nation as a whole.

Undoubtedly some, or even many, of the individual programs had a positive effect. But there were so many programs that the nets had to be spread wide to capture enough juveniles to justify their existence. And it is possible that in the process more and more youths were negatively labeled, damaging their self-concept and inviting social discrimination from outsiders.

Admittedly there are differences in the way juveniles are referred to and processed through the court in various cities. And statistics frequently are not altogether reliable. But a difference of three times as great cannot be lightly explained away. Since juvenile delinquency is the training ground for adult criminals, perhaps the real measure of effectiveness is the adult crime rate. Despite decades of comprehensive delinquency prevention efforts, Flint has one of the highest crime rates in the nation.

All of this is devastating to those who put faith in delinquency prevention programs. It is devastating to have to admit that all those years of intensive effort in Flint, all the millions of dollars invested in youth, all the experimentations with virtually every conceivable type of program, all have been losing battles in the war against juvenile crime.

When I first looked up these statistics I concluded that they were verification of a principle that I facetiously had called "Baker's Law of Delinquency"—namely, *the number of official delinquents in a community will expand to fill all available slots in the community's programs for rehabilitation and prevention.*

After nearly six decades of America's experimentation in delinquency prevention, there are few encouraging results to report. But two explanations for the failures stand out:

1. Most efforts at prevention have been instituted far too late in the juvenile's life.
2. Most efforts have been narrowly aimed at "curing" individuals rather than at correcting the physical, social, and educational conditions that eventually will push those individuals into delinquency.

Chapter 5

THE PUBLIC SCHOOL AS VILLAIN

No factor correlates with delinquency so closely as does lack of success in school. One can go back almost a half-century to the Gluecks' classic study[1] of five hundred white delinquent boys brought before the Boston juvenile court. Two-thirds were two or more years behind in grade level, and 85 percent had school behavioral problems. Nothing has changed. Today a boy with poor grades in high school is more than six times as likely to be in trouble with the law as is the youth earning above-average grades.

The correlation applies not only to individuals but to entire school populations. In a study made for the Louisville public schools I found that those areas of the city where the achievement level of the schools was the lowest also harbored the highest concentration of delinquents. In the system there were twenty-four elementary schools where the sixth-grade students were on the average two or more grade levels below the national norms. The delinquency rate in the areas served by those schools was nearly five times that of the remainder of the county. Although these areas contained only one-sixth of the total juvenile population, they produced more than two-thirds of the habitual delinquents.

School performance is by far the most significant single predictor of delinquency and future criminality—more accurate than race or economic level or social class, more accurate than any of the sociological variables commonly considered to have an effect on the rate of delinquency.

Take social class. It is generally conceded that lower-class youths tend to be considerably more delinquent than middle- or upper-class juveniles. But when one delves deeper into the characteristics of delinquents one discovers that what appears to be obvious is not really so clear-cut. The higher rate of delinquency among lower-class youths may merely reflect the fact that they are, on the average, far less successful in school.

In a midwestern town of fifty thousand the rate of delinquency among schoolboys from white-collar and blue-collar homes was compared. Among high-achieving students, those with a grade average of A or B, delinquency was virtually nonexistent for both white-collar boys and blue-collar boys. C-average students in both categories had considerably higher juvenile court records—11 percent of the more affluent and 12 percent of the less affluent. At the D and F levels delinquency increased rapidly for both groups—20 percent of the white-collar boys and 27 percent of the blue-collar boys.[2] Clearly, delinquency was a correlate of school achievement—not social class.

The same relationship exists between academic achievement and race. *Blacks have a higher delinquency rate than whites. But there is virtually no difference between the illegal activity of blacks and whites who are making the same grades in school.*

With findings such as these, it is easy to jump to the conclusion that delinquents just are not as bright as nondelinquents. But not necessarily. Delinquency seems to be a product of underachievement rather than a lack of innate intelligence.

This correlation between delinquency and academic failure continues through adulthood. According to the Bureau of Justice Statistics,[3] a recent survey of state prison inmates found 72 percent of the males had not finished high school, whereas in the general population of males aged twenty to twenty-nine only 15 percent have not done so. Stated differently, the dropout was five times as likely to be in prison as was the high school graduate.

Among repeat adult offenders surveyed in a California prison (three-fourths had served two or more prior terms), most had not even entered high school. Yet four-fifths of these early dropouts had intelligence levels of normal or bright-normal. Researchers found that of all the many variables considered for these repeat offenders, including broken homes and lower economic status, underachievement in school was their *only* general characteristic.

In all major standardized tests of basic educational achievement—from the National Educational Testing Service to the Armed Forces Qualification Test—minorities and the poor have been heavily concentrated in the one-fifth making the lowest scores. On the average the scores of blacks and Hispanics have been only 70 percent of scores made by whites.[4] Thus, it should come as no surprise that these same youths are also concentrated in the delinquency statistics.

The Chicken and the Egg

There is little question that this correlation between school failure and delinquency exists. But which came first? It is the old chicken-and-egg controversy. Is delinquent behavior a cause of school failure? Or is school failure a cause of delinquent behavior?

Most school administrators like to claim the former—placing the blame on the juveniles and their parents and friends and everything else besides the school. But a look at the post-dropout careers of delinquents places the blame squarely on the school system.

Each year at least a million youths quit school before graduation from high school. This includes nearly half of all students in the New York City, Chicago, and Detroit systems. In some poverty districts over two-thirds will quit. A few are forcibly expelled; many others drop out illegally. Most do it legally when they pass the age for compulsory attendance—sixteen in most states. But contrary to the popular myth, dropping out of school *does not* always increase antisocial behavior.

Usually dropping out of school reduces it!

Four major research projects, spread over a long period of time and focused on various sections of the country, have monitored the delinquent activity of thousands of students before and after leaving school.[5] All have shown that bouts with the police were more frequent just *before* dropping out of school. *After* dropping out delinquent behavior dramatically decreased.

Although not the most recent, the most detailed study was done by Marvin E. Wolfgang and his associates, who followed all 9,825 boys born in 1945 who attended school in Philadelphia. Over one-third dropped out before graduation. Not surprisingly, half of these drop-outs had official delinquency records *before* they left school. But it is startling to discover that only one out of seven—only 14 percent—had an arrest record *after* quitting school. (This one juvenile out of seven then went on to become the serious criminal who terrorized the public.) For many of these pre-dropout delinquents, quitting school was a therapeutic act. They were "cured" of delinquency.

This would indicate that there is something inherent in the school system that provokes many juveniles into antisocial, illegal behavior. Frustration and embarrassment at continual failure propel them into other activities where they can achieve success and restore some measure of self-esteem. Frequently these activities are delinquent or gang-related. Rather than meaning the youths are "bad" individuals, school failure may simply reflect their inability to adapt to an institution geared to college-bound, middle-class students. When the school fails to place these individuals in programs where they have some hope of success, dropping out may be a healthy decision.

This decision to drop out is seldom made on the spur of the moment. With few exceptions it began to form during the primary grades when the seeds of failure were first fertilized. Herein lies the absurdity of the run-of-the-mill dropout prevention program promoted as a delinquency prevention measure. Too often it does little except exert pressure on the failing youth to remain in school or to return to school. The cause of the academic failure is ignored.

This was impressed on me in Louisville by a black paraprofessional who I was told had served time in prison for the murder of his wife. His missing right hand had been replaced with a steel hook, which he waved menacingly when making a point. His keen knowledge of the ways of the street had qualified him as a counselor in a federally funded dropout program. He barged into my office with two teenagers in tow. They were his most visible success story—two long-failing dropouts whom he had persuaded to return to school after release from the state reform school. He personally had seen that they were in classes each day. Now, six weeks after graduation, neither the graduates nor their mentor had been able to find them jobs.

"You damn honkie school bastards lied," the recruiter said, shaking the steel hook in my face. "You promised these boys if they ate shit in your school long enough to graduate they'd get a high-paying job.

Well, they done ate buckets of that shit, and they still can't get no fuckin' job."

He was deaf to my protests that I had nothing to do with the program. Instead, he became more menacing. "Now, by God, you're gonna hire them right here. You give them a job, or you ain't gonna lie to no boys again." With that he banged the hook down on a pottery ashtray on my desk, sending fragments flying across the room.

Somehow I managed to get them out of the office without fainting from fright. In retrospect I was more saddened than angered. At a considerable financial expense to the program, the boys had been kept glued to a classroom seat, which had not guaranteed that learning would take place. Quite likely they had been awarded diplomas to get them out of school rather than to certify any academic achievement. The diplomas were inadequate to overcome any employer's bias against hiring former institutionalized delinquents unable to fill out a job application without help.

Perhaps the boys *had* been lied to.

The New York City schools have just completed a four-year dropout program in junior and senior high schools at a cost of $120 million—$8,000 per student. Automatic dialing machines alerted parents to absences, guidance counselors pleaded with the students, neighborhood workers went into the homes to provide job training and other support.

And the results?

"Disappointing" is the most charitable evaluation. Most of the students improved neither their attendance nor their academic achievement. By the third year over half of the participants had already dropped out. The crowning insult was that those youths who were in the program for only one year did as well as those who received the four-year treatment.

How many hundreds of projects must be tried, how many millions of dollars must be wasted before administrators finally admit that junior and senior high school is far too late to become concerned with a failing youth?

Protecting Society from a Dangerous Truant

One afternoon while I was director of juvenile studies for the Kentucky Crime Commission I was laboriously tabulating data regarding the "success" rate of the various delinquency institutions in the commonwealth. Suddenly one card jolted me to a wide-awake disbelief. Here was a boy, not yet twenty-one years old, who during the previous seven years had served three terms in juvenile correctional institutions and was now on his second two-year sentence in an adult prison. Any researcher worth his salt would be curious as to the background of such an incorrigible criminal.

At the state child welfare department I read through his voluminous file, then visited him at the penitentiary. He turned out to be not the monster I had anticipated but instead a meek, quiet young man. Until he was thirteen Billy had been a rather normal, all-American boy—interested in athletics and his Scout troop and just beginning to decide that maybe girls were not all bad after all. Then his father, a skilled construction worker, moved the family to a western Kentucky town. In the new school Billy's seventh-grade teacher discovered he was barely reading on the third-grade level.

The teacher was rightfully concerned. She devised a plan to motivate the newcomer to improve his reading. Each day she had him stand in front of the class and read aloud. As he stumbled over words a nine-year-old should know his new classmates snickered loudly. Someone coined a nickname—Birdbrain—and it stuck. Juveniles can be cruel. In the hall between classes he would hear someone call out, "Hey, Birdbrain, seen any 'wa-ah-waas' lately?" Finally Billy could take it no longer. He began skipping school rather than face the daily taunts.

The scenario picks up speed. School officials warned him of the penalties for truancy. No effect. His parents were summoned to school. Still no effect. The juvenile judge threatened him with institutionalization. Now for a few days he did attend school, but soon Billy was truant again. Another ineffective judicial warning. And finally in desperation the juvenile judge committed him to a camp for thirteen- and fourteen-year-old delinquents.

The night before he was to leave Billy attempted to slash his wrists with a razor blade. It was more a symbolic gesture than a serious attempt. The emergency room at the hospital put Band-Aids on his wrists, and the next day he was sent to the camp. There, in therapy sessions—Guided Group Interaction—he and the other boys worked on his "truancy problem."

He was released as "cured" some five months later—three weeks after the school's fall semester had started. The timing put him far behind his classmates, a virtual guarantee of failure. One boy composed a hilarious ditty: "Birdbrain is a jailbird." In November he was again institutionalized for habitual truancy, this time serving seven months at Kentucky Village, the state's large institution for serious delinquents.

The scenario repeats itself like a broken record. The third time he was institutionalized for truancy he became desperate. A few days after arriving he went AWOL, appropriated a car for transportation back home a hundred miles away, and then left the car abandoned and undamaged on the main street of his hometown. For this crime, a felony, he was sentenced to two years in the penitentiary. He didn't have a chance. The judge and the prosecutor knew that a three-time reform school inmate was a no-good cookie.

At the penitentiary he made some interesting new friends. With them when on parole he broke into a number of country stores, was caught, and was sentenced again to two years in prison.

So there's the story of Billy, at thirteen an all-American boy, but before he was old enough to buy a glass of beer at the neighborhood tavern he had served time behind bars five times. The facts would make the synopsis of a documentary film: *How to Protect Society from a Dangerous Truant.*

Consider the people and institutions who contributed to the almost total destruction of a human being:

- There's the original school and its teachers, guilty of letting a boy of average intelligence get to the seventh grade without being able to read adequately.
- There's the seventh-grade teacher, guilty of being untrained in techniques of remedial reading and, more serious, of being totally insensitive to the emotional feelings of an adolescent.
- There's the school system, guilty of trying to solve a truancy problem by turning it over to the juvenile court.
- There's the juvenile judge, guilty of having a distorted idea of what a delinquency institution can accomplish in the area of re-habilitation.
- There's the staff of the juvenile camp, guilty of not bothering to try to find out Billy's problem and, instead, believing that five months of Guided Group Interaction would cure him of his desire to play truant.

And there's Billy. After seven years of treatment, counseling, and punishment, he still can't read beyond the third-grade level. No one ever took the trouble to get at the basic cause of his trouble. He had a reading problem. He still does.

In the first chapter it was noted that all too often the adult criminal is the juvenile delinquent grown up. Now this can be carried still further back. *All too often the adult criminal is the child who early in his school career was, for a variety of reasons, unable to keep up with others in the class.*

Frequently this early failure has its roots in the intellectual famine experienced in many homes of low socioeconomic status. But, as in the case of Billy, not always. Fifty years ago Frank Tannenbaum, a pioneering sociologist, enumerated some of the conditions out of which school failure can arise:

> . . . from lack of good hearing, from poor eyesight, from undernourishment, from being left-handed, from dislike for the teacher because of favoritism, from being taken away from playmates because the family moves, from lack of interest in intellectual pursuits, from being either too big or too small for the grade, from undue competition with other children within the family, from a desire for excitement which the school does not provide, from having poor clothes and being ashamed to go to school, from a too rapid maturing, from a too slow development, from losing a grade because of illness, or from any number of other causes.[6]

Little has changed in fifty years. These problems still occur across all economic, racial, and social strata.

Once a child has fallen behind early in school, no matter the reason, once he has been berated, scolded, and even punished for his poor performance, he is catapulted onto a treadmill of failure. The end product is delinquency almost as certainly as college is the end product for the youth showered with praise for his achievement.

This chapter is not intended as a total critique of the American educational system. For many fortunate enough to fit into the groove, it provides exceptional educational opportunities. Exceptionally talented or brilliant students may also be cheated by the system. But here the concern is only with those policies and practices which lead to delinquency. In general, anything the schools do, or fail to do, that contributes to academic failure can in time play a critical role in the making of a delinquent.

In this regard, seven charges must be leveled against schools for practices found in many communities.

CHARGES AGAINST THE SCHOOL SYSTEM

1.   Many school personnel believe in the myth of the limited intellectual capabilities of disadvantaged children.

Thousands of children become victims of the prejudgment of school personnel. The myth of a ghetto mentality declares that socially disadvantaged children and those from racial minorities are incapable of learning very much. Spending a lot of time and effort is really a waste . . . like fertilizing an already dead tree. The prejudgment becomes a self-fulfilling prophecy.

Using this myth as an excuse, administrators with clear conscience give these children inferior teachers, inferior curricula, and inferior facilities—give them an education befitting their inferior status. Because the disadvantaged have little political clout, few rise up in their defense. It is easier for school officials to cater to the more vocal, more powerful middle class.

And since these "inferior" children are assumed to have a low potential, little is expected of them. Even less is demanded. So they flounder along, seeing little relevance in what they are doing, and in despair finally drop out. In the worst districts of Detroit only one out of five of those entering school finally collect a diploma.

In the middle of the nineteenth century the educational revivalist Horace Mann preached that education was "the great equalizer of the conditions of men—the balance wheel of the social machinery." Thus, free universal education was established in America. But if Horace Mann could return today he would be crushed to discover what happened to his vision. *Instead of being an "equalizer," schools have become the institution that screens out the social underdogs.*

Just how schools accomplish this was dramatically documented by a study reported in the *Harvard Educational Review.*[7] The classroom experiences of a single class of all black children in an urban area were carefully recorded from the first day they registered for kindergarten on through the second grade. On the eighth day the kindergarten teacher permanently assigned each child to one of three tables—one each for the blue birds, the red birds, and the yellow birds. The teacher explained that the assignments had been made on the basis of readiness to learn.

What the teacher had to go on was the child's registration form, which listed the address and occupation of the father (if there was a father at home), whether or not the family was receiving welfare, and any notes from brief interviews with mothers at registration. In addition, the teacher had observed how well the children were dressed and how well they had been taught middle-class values such as properly saying, "Yes, ma'am." Thus the teacher, in all her omnipotence, was able to determine the learning ability of each child after only seven half-days of kindergarten.

As the year progressed the research observers recorded that the teacher devoted 65 percent of her time to the table of children she had predetermined to be the most advanced, 25 percent to the middle table, and only 10 percent to the last. In some periods of over an hour the only teacher contact with the two lower tables was to tell a child to sit down. Although the blackboard extended parallel to all three tables, classwork such as numbers and letters was put on the board in front of the blue birds, the number-one table. Many times the yellow birds—the number-three table—could not even see the material. And it was children at the first table who were called on for recitations and activities. To give a Halloween report, for example, seven were called on from Table 1, one from Table 2, and none from Table 3.

The yellow birds at Table 3 may have been slow, but they were sharp enough to soon realize that "yellow bird" spelled "d-u-m-b." The other pupils did too. The blue birds were the in group, a group from which the inferior yellow birds and red birds were socially excluded. At playtime the yellow birds went off by themselves.

It should come as no great surprise that at the end of the kindergarten year the children at Table 1 had made by far the greatest progress. Just as the teacher had predicted! But regardless of their progress *all were sent on to the first grade* to compete on equal footing. The original gap (if one actually existed) had now vastly widened.

At the end of the second grade the same clear-cut division in achievement still existed. Now, however, the children who had been at Table 3, and to a certain extent several from Table 2, no longer tried to get the teacher's attention. Instead, they just sat or found disruptive ways to amuse themselves. In time, as future teachers reacted negatively to their inattention and disruptive behavior, they would know that they were not only dumb, they were also bad.

Because of the prejudgment of a teacher, these children's academic future had been ordained on their eighth day of kindergarten. And likewise their self-concept. For them the race was over. Jonathan Kozol calls it "death at an early age."

A recent newsletter of the Harvard Graduate School of Education notes that in a study of twenty thousand high school seniors, "low-ability students who did one to three hours of homework a week reported grades as high as those average-ability students who did no homework."[8] Yet teachers widen the gap by demanding little or no outside work from lower-class students. (In many schools they are not even allowed to take textbooks home at night—they might get damaged.) On the other hand, college-track students are given at least an hour a day more instruction in academic subjects than are those inferior students.

One might conclude that schools are dedicated to the task of keeping lower-class children in their place.

2.   *Despite their greater need, less money and concern are spent on underclass children than on their affluent counterparts.*

School districts usually send their least qualified, least experienced teachers to slum area schools. Here, in deteriorating buildings, these soon-to-be-frustrated teachers find educational materials, books, and equipment in short supply, or totally lacking. It requires no stroke of insightful brilliance to recognize that the American educational system is living in an Alice-in-Wonderland world of topsy-turvy values. Children needing the most help are given the least.

This tragic condition further deteriorated in the Reagan years as meager funds for compensatory programs were slashed. An estimated one and a half million underprivileged children, for example, had to be dropped from the federally subsidized school lunch program. Without more compensatory help than is being given today, under-privileged children have little chance of overcoming the cultural and educational deficits they have accumulated before knocking at the schoolhouse door. (For many Hispanics, language is part of the handicap.) Seldom does the child who began behind ever catch up.

Because many districts have given up on their neediest children, we find a two-tiered educational system. One, incorporating high expectations for its youths, is found in affluent and stable areas. Here parents are able and willing to meet the costs. The other tier is found in many poverty areas of the inner cities where student violence and failure are the norms. Here we find astronomical dropout rates and graduates unable to read.

The Supreme Court in ruling that "separate but equal" facilities are not equal forced desegregation of the schools. But the Court failed to rule on a more critical issue—that of economic equality between school systems. Thus, we find districts able to spend less than two thousand dollars per year on a student, and others spending four times as much. Certainly money is not the sole criterion for providing meaningful education. But in no way can a policy of spending more on the advantaged and less on the disadvantaged bring about equality in education. (Fortunately, as will be discussed in Chapter 11, many state courts are now facing up to this problem that the federal courts have refused to consider.)

As a consequence of having two unequal school systems, the gap between the haves and the have-nots steadily widens. One out of every three students in urban high schools will eventually be on welfare. Alarmingly, the specter of a permanent underclass becomes more of a reality. And greater and greater numbers of uneducated, unemployable, bitter youths will fan out across the city to mug and rob those more fortunate.

Poor old Horace Mann and his vision of equalizing the conditions of men!

3. *Schools are structured to produce losers.*

There are valedictorians, the top 10 percent, the honor roll, the above average, the college-prep track—all are trophies for the winners in the competition for grades. But they say nothing about how seriously the youth tried, nothing about his or her character, nothing about how relevant the material was to his or her needs and goals. Unfortunately, a system designed to produce winners must by definition also produce losers. When children are rank-ordered it is axiomatic that some must be placed at the bottom. From among these losers delinquents are recruited.

Comparative grades heap praise on the easy learner and punish the slow, plodding learner. At the same time the educational system relies on grades almost solely to motivate students. But grades are a motivation only for those who think they have a chance of winning. Those who know they have no chance—the "yellow birds" whom the schools have told in hundreds of subtle ways that they are inferior human beings—have quit trying.

An F becomes one more self-fulfilling prophecy. Instead of being a motivation for improvement, all too often it is a signal to quit trying: Why bother? I'm dumb and won't get anywhere anyway.

Psychological studies have repeatedly shown that low self-esteem is rampant among delinquents, that in many instances it may be the precipitating factor for antisocial behavior. While low self-esteem stems from many sources, nowhere is it more likely to be generated than in school failure. When grades are the measure of a student's worth, failing marks quickly tell youngsters how no-good, how second-rate they really are. But in the company of losers the grade card with the most F's or the most days absent may become a macho status symbol.

The pressure for grades is also a motivation for another activity—cheating. Some slow learners manage to stay in the race by various forms of dishonesty. For those who are skillful, cheating permits an escape from the stigma of failure, and they may avoid the delinquency route. Instead, they may grow up to become business tycoons with no qualms about falsifying invoices for work on government contracts or overbilling for treatment of Medicare patients. (Pollster Louis Harris at the Commonwealth Club in San Francisco in 1987 declared that "a majority of yuppies admit that they do their own tax returns so they can cheat—no CPA would sign their returns.")

All students, the good and the bad, in the long run suffer because of the grading system. In pleading for the abolition of grades, America's venerable child care doctor Benjamin Spock points out that "they corrupt students into memorizing instead of understanding and analyzing."

4. Schools fail to diagnose and correct the causes of early failure.

Early difficulties at school largely go unnoticed until the youth becomes a serious behavioral problem and starts tearing up the classroom. At this stage concern is long overdue, perhaps even too late. A child who has not learned to read by the third grade is likely destined to a history of spiraling failure. Seldom can it be reversed.

Most children of the ghetto suffer not from lack of innate abilities but from the mental atrophy caused by starvation for those hundreds of stimuli which middle-class children receive in the normal course of the day. Perhaps the greatest deficiency comes from having mothers who never read to them. Not once. The mother couldn't read. Not having learned the excitement to be found between the pages of a book, these children have no motivation to learn to read. The cycle of illiteracy is perpetuated. Certainly schools are better qualified to supply programs to overcome cultural and cognitive deficiencies than is the juvenile court years down the road.

The basis for learning difficulties is often physical. Faulty nutrition and ill health can sap a youth's attentiveness. In one examination of three hundred delinquents, 24 percent failed a simple hearing test. And it is a national disgrace that children with correctable vision problems are still encountered in schools where they are rapidly falling far behind.

When I was visiting a seventh-grade class for the educable mentally handicapped, the teacher instructed the students to copy the days of the week from the blackboard. One boy picked up his chair and moved it to within a foot of the board. To my horrified comment that the boy obviously needed glasses the teacher replied defensively, "Yes. I sent a note to the counselor about it last month." (As this was in February, it meant that it had taken the teacher four months to recognize the disability.)

I couldn't believe it! A boy, possibly of normal intelligence, had been labeled mentally retarded because of uncorrected vision. Had it taken one of the state's leading school systems eight years to discover this disability? I checked his permanent record file. The need for glasses had been discovered in the first grade and the parents notified. But his parents had not wanted the child to wear glasses. Their son was perfect the way God made him. The school let the matter drop. Then, after being required to repeat the second grade, he had become disruptive and the teacher had him tested by the school psychologist. He was found to be "mentally retarded" and transferred to a special-education class. At this time no mention was made of his defective vision.

A major contribution of the schools to the making of delinquents is their failure to diagnose learning disabilities, which are variously labeled minimal brain dysfunction, dyslexia, specific learning disability, specific perpetual motor disability, neurological learning-disability syndrome, and other less familiar names. A gremlin in the brain's computer garbles the messages. The child may know the answer to a question but is unable to write it down. Often this is the child of whom the teacher says, "He seems bright enough but he just doesn't try."

Between 2 and 5 percent of children in the general population are affected by this condition. *Yet between 30 and 50 percent of all delinquents have some form of learning disability.* Had these delinquents been diagnosed and treated early enough, most could have been helped to compensate for, or even to overcome, the difficulty. With specialized help more and more dyslexics are making it through college and graduate school. Individualized help can be expensive—but not as expensive as later paying fifty thousand dollars a year for room and board in a delinquency institution.

When the New Jersey Supreme Court ruled last year that the state must equalize the financing between the richest and poorest districts, the case was named *Abbott v. Burke.* Although Raymond Abbott experienced early academic difficulties in the Camden schools, he was not diagnosed as learning-disabled until the age of fifteen. His teen years have been all too typical of similar youths who have gone undiagnosed and untreated: he went from truancy to being a runaway and then on to dropping out of school, drug addiction, and burglary.

In this day of multimillion-dollar lawsuits brought at the drop of a hat—malpractice, accidental injury, defective products, sex discrimination, and so on—it is a wonder that some parents (and sharp attorneys) aren't bringing suits against school boards for having failed to teach their children to read.

5. Lack of alternative programs locks many youths out of the educational system.

We have noted that schools designed for some to win and some to lose are great for the winners. But most schools offer few opportunities to the losers. It is generally assumed that opportunity is satisfactorily provided by permitting every child to have a seat on the bus; it matters not that the bus's destination is college and graduate school with no intermediate stop at the world of work.

Regular school programs are not for everyone. Among popular examples: Thomas Edison was thought to be so dull-witted that he was asked to leave school. Albert Einstein flunked math. Pablo Picasso's art work failed to meet the standards of his elementary school teachers. But the genius is not our primary concern here (though one can't help wondering how many would-have-been geniuses have had their spirits massacred in schools that demand conformity). Regretfully, most systems fail to provide for youngsters with intellectual, emotional, or cultural handicaps. To them school may not only seem irrelevant, it frequently *is* irrelevant. Boredom, rebellion, truancy—and delinquency—soon set in.

Typically it is the disinterested, failing students who are blamed, not the school. They are told, "Shape up or ship out." Since the law will not permit them to ship out physically, they ship out mentally and emotionally. On days they are not truant they sit disinterested and disruptive. Alternatives have always been available to children whose parents are financially able to send them to private schools—everything from Montessori schools to military academies. But for their less fortunate counterparts, frequently the only alternative has been reform school.

"Vocational education" in many schools is a pitiful effort to occupy the time of non-college-bound youth. Often it's a joke. In "shop" the student makes a magazine rack to take home, where there aren't magazines to put into it. Unfortunately, the job market is rather limited for magazine rack makers. Many vocational programs are too job-specific for a rapidly changing technological society. A youth is locked into a field that may soon be obsolete, if it is not already. He may, for example, have been learning to operate outdated machinery that has been magnanimously donated by a company in order to take a tax write-off.

Instead, most of these students desperately need skills they are not receiving—a working proficiency in reading and basic math, a foundation that would permit them to understand on-the-job training as the occasion arises. They need a practical grasp of the operation of government and of business. They need to know the responsibilities of sexual conduct and the ultimate costs of drug experimentation.

A high school diploma should mean far more than it does in many schools today. It should certify that for twelve years the school system has employed every means available to help a youth achieve his or her maximum potential. For some that may mean understanding nuclear physics; for others, merely being able to read the daily paper and fill out a job application.

6. Discipline is so lax in some schools that learning is virtually impossible.

After receiving a low grade, a thirteen-year-old in Clearwater, Florida, threatened to kill his social studies teacher. When arrested he was carrying two pistols and a box of bullets. In Portland, Connecticut, after an eighth-grader was suspended from school for refusing to remove his hat, he brought an assault rifle to school and killed the janitor and wounded the principal and his secretary. These were among the nearly 3 million crimes committed each year inside the nation's public schools.[9]

When both students and teachers justifiably fear for their safety, when school corridors are crowded with drug pushers, muggers, and at times even rapists, when administrators throw up their hands and surrender to a philosophy of permissiveness for gun toters, knife swingers, and gang recruiters, then there is little hope that learning can take place even for those who are desperately trying.

This is the saga of many schools today, particularly those within the ghettos of major American cities . . . schools totally out of control. Even the buildings and equipment are being torn apart as students commit a half-billion dollars' worth of vandalism each year. On any day up to half of the entire student body may have decided to skip school. For over two decades the public has been repeatedly warned that this "blackboard jungle" exists. But the bedlam has steadily increased.

Such conditions are not inevitable. Here and there in ghettos throughout the nation dedicated administrators have been able to tame the inhabitants of these academic jungles. Principal Joe Clark became a national celebrity with a cover story in *Time* magazine when he brought order to a 3,200-student high school in Paterson, New Jersey. The ultimate accolade was a movie. While some of his techniques were questionable and failed to increase achievement dramatically, he did the education industry a major service by bringing to the public's attention the conditions that exist. And he demonstrated that drastic disciplinary action can regain control of a school.

In some schools it has been necessary to declare total bankruptcy and start over from scratch. This has required the transfer of old, disillusioned administrators and teachers, along with the institution of rigid new rules of discipline—rules that prohibit drugs and drug pushers on the premises, that demand order in the hallways and classrooms, that require regular and on-time attendance . . . *and rules that permit the expulsion of youths who refuse to accept the rules.* This latter is sad but absolutely necessary.

It is a tragic fact that these bored, bitter, disruptive, and frequently violent students are not learning anything during their attendance required by law. They drop into school now and then as the mood strikes them—drop in to socialize and hassle those who want to study. While one may legitimately weep for these disruptive students whom society has failed, it is better to save those who are trying to make an effort than to let concern for a group of hoodlums destroy the opportunity for everyone. And with their departure a major part of the school's problems with discipline and vandalism will evaporate.

Though many have loudly criticized a policy of expelling the most recalcitrant offenders, most of these critics have never experienced olence of some inner-city schools. It is all too easy to say that expulsion "pulls the plug" on the youth being kicked out. But it is not the policy that is pulling the plug. That was done years earlier. It was done by the inadequate schools that from kindergarten permitted these disadvantaged youths to drift into hopeless failure.

Contrary to popular myth, most disadvantaged youngsters yearn for order and discipline. The first time I visited a class being taught by an idealistic new social studies teacher in a predominantly black junior high, the room was in chaos. The young teacher confused permissiveness with love and concern. Several students were literally asleep, their heads down on the armrests of their chairs. One boy was thumping spitballs at his classmates. In the back row two were playing a card game. Two girls were absorbed in watching a tall lanky classmate; he was nonchalantly stroking the crotch of his pants, which covered an obvious erection. The teacher pretended not to notice and went on with his lecture.

I met a number of times with five of the most disruptive students. Among them was one who during class would regularly jump out the first-floor window and reappear at the classroom door. He summed up the situation to me: "Greg, he don't care enough about us even to make us behave." A couple of the others chimed in, "Yeah, he don't."

Constructive punishment can take many forms—special academic assignments, needed repair work around the school as a penalty for vandalism, requirements to remain in study periods after school. No punishment, however, is so foolish and so devastatingly counterproductive as the one that is most widely used—temporary suspension. It thrives because it doesn't require any effort or imagination on anyone's part. Just kick the kid out for a few days. Centuries ago the legal penalty for attempting suicide in England was to be "hanged by the neck until dead." This same logic dictates the school practice of suspending troublemakers for several days. The misbehaving youth is forced to do what he or she wanted to do in the first place—escape from an intolerable classroom situation. The punishment is a reward. A bittersweet reward. Upon returning, the youth is further behind. Catching up is now an even more hopeless dream.

7.   *Academic standards are meaningless . . . or missing.*

A diploma from an inner-city school may mean nothing more than that the graduate was enrolled in the school system for twelve years—not even that he or she kept a seat warm most of those days. Social promotions—passing a youth along to the next grade regardless of whether or not any of the skills projected for the year have been achieved—are the line of least resistance for apathetic, frustrated teachers. Because of this lack of real standards, thousands of students are graduated each year from high school unable even to read comic books, certainly unable to read a bus schedule or fill out a job application.

The New York Telephone Company in 1987 had 57,000 applicants for job openings. Of these, only 2,100 were able to pass the basic employment exam. Four-fifths of the job applicants at Motorola were unable to pass an entry-level exam requiring seventh-grade English and fifth-grade math.

America could afford to permit such educational apathy in years past when there was a surplus of jobs requiring little or no skill. But these jobs have dried up. Simultaneously the demand by business and industry for skilled, educated workers has skyrocketed.

Obviously not all schools are the disasters suggested here. Far from it. In upper- and middle-class areas there are many, many school systems providing superior education, and even some inner-city schools have found ways to overcome the shortcomings enumerated here. Many diverse publications, such as an encouraging book, *Within Our Reach* by Lisbeth Schorr, numerous educational journals, and the U.S. Department of Education's *Schools That Work*, list dozens of approaches that have proved effective. Television has run numerous heartwarming documentaries about inner-city schools that have beaten the odds. This is both good and bad.

The good: We have learned how to educate the disadvantaged.

The bad: We have been too shortsighted to spend the necessary money to do so.

In many areas parochial schools have taken the lead in proving that disadvantaged children can be given a full education. One was featured in a PBS television series *Learning in America* with Roger Mudd—the Holy Angel School on the south side of Chicago. Although the students come from the lowest socioeconomic area in Chicago, they are performing at the national norms in all academic disciplines. The success has been the result of:

1. Strictly enforced discipline
2. Parent participation (parents must agree to take part in activities)

3. A large proportion of male teachers to serve as role models (most students come from mother-only homes)
4. A twelve- rather than nine-month school year
5. Maintenance of a high standard of performance

But many public schools are just muddling through. They are providing a passable education to many but leaving behind millions who will eventually drop out and add to the ranks of the unemployable in a modern technological society. And add to the ranks of drug addicts and delinquents.

Reform is long overdue.

Later, in Part II, we will consider ways to restructure a nineteenth-century educational system to meet the twenty-first-century needs of disadvantaged children as well as of the advantaged.

Chapter 6

PUNISHING THE VICTIM: STATUS OFFENDERS IN THE JUVENILE COURT

If Lewis Carroll's Alice should wander into the juvenile court she would discover an establishment as weird and as topsy-turvy as Wonderland. She would find a court where often the prosecutor is actually the criminal and the one being punished is the victim. The inhabitants of this topsy-turvy world are the status offenders—that special class of children who have violated no criminal law but who someone *thinks* might turn out to be "bad" in the future. They have committed acts that are illegal only for children. More often than not, it is irresponsible adults who are at fault, not the juvenile being condemned.

Most delinquency statutes have been painted with such a broad, moralistic brush that virtually any child at some time could have been hauled into court because of what someone—parent, neighbor, school official, social worker, policeman—considered to be improper behavior. The reasons have been countless, frequently trivial, and sometimes bizarre—everything from a boy hanging around a video arcade during school hours to a girl refusing to take her birth control pills, from inappropriate dress and hairstyles to the use of vulgar language around women. Because of the vagueness of the law, it becomes possible for the judge to impose his personal code of proper behavior on the hapless youth brought into court.

The most frequent charges are truancy, being beyond parental control, and running away from home. In most states youths committing these noncriminal offenses make up 20 to 40 percent of all juveniles coming before the court.

Once there, status offenders are not treated lightly. They are more likely to be locked up while awaiting their hearing than are those charged with criminal offenses. Strangely enough, they have the same, if not higher, probability of being committed to a reform school as do juveniles guilty of serious crimes. And when institutionalized, these status offenders are frequently held longer than those guilty of aggravated assault, rape, and other felonies classified as FBI Index crimes.

It is, indeed, a topsy-turvy court in a topsy-turvy world.

All of this might be palatable if being processed by the court actually helped these youths solve their problems or deterred them from turning to crime. But as noted in the chapter on the myth of rehabilitation, instead of being a cure the treatment usually escalates the worrisome behavior. Gordon Gonion, a San Diego probation officer, points out that there is no evidence that truants are any less truant as a result of their court experience, or that runaways are any more compatible with their home situation, that teenage girls have any fewer illegitimate babies, that "problem" children are any less likely to become adult thieves and robbers.

The assumption has been that self-destructive behavior can be stopped by legal sanctions. It is a false assumption. In the adult world legal sanctions have not stopped excessive drinking or gambling or prostitution or drug abuse or adultery or any of the many foibles of mankind. Why should adults think sanctions would work with a rebellious teenager?

Good Intentions That Backfire

Because of the stigma attached to court intervention, even for noncriminal behavior, a youth who has appeared there finds it increasingly difficult to pry open the gates to social, educational, and economic opportunities. In an attempt to avoid this stigma, the court system frequently gives euphemistic labels to status offenders—PINS in New York, MINS in Illinois, CINS in Florida, CHINS in Colorado, and JINS in New Jersey, referring respectively to Persons, Minors, Children, and Juveniles in Need of Supervision. In California they are assigned a nondescript label, 601 Offenders. All is wasted effort. The public, social agencies, and the schools fail to differentiate between status offenders and criminal offenders. If a youth has been to court, *ipso facto*, he or she must be a young hoodlum.

Add it all together: the adverse effects of labeling, the youth's natural "reactance" (rebellion at being forced to do something), and the ineffectiveness of therapy. The sum total is a picture of good intentions turned sour. Very sour.

One longitudinal study is particularly revealing as to the effectiveness of the court in forcing a youth with a noncriminal problem to shape up. Lee N. Robins traced the adult careers of 524 people who thirty years earlier had been treated in a St. Louis child guidance clinic, and then compared them to 100 "normal" children of the same period. Of the treated children 30 percent had been referred to the clinic by the parents and doctors because of "neurotic symptoms." Seventy percent had been sent by juvenile judges because of antisocial behavior—in effect, they were status offenders.

For the neurotic children, the ones who were not under court order to participate, the treatment could be considered a success. As adults they resembled the control group. Both led reasonably well-adjusted lives, with only 3 percent having acquired serious criminal records. But the adult lives of the 350 status offenders were disasters. Their careers were demolished by frequent criminal arrests, drunkenness, divorce, and occupational instability. A staggering 44 percent of the males were arrested for serious crimes. The juvenile judges may have been accurate in identifying problem children. But they didn't have the solution. The suspicion is strong that a major factor in the status offenders' adult instability was having been forced into therapy by the court when young.[1]

Virtually all status offenders do need help. But not the help the juvenile court commonly offers—meaningless probation, coercive therapy, commitment to an institution, all designed to force a youth into compliance with what are often inappropriate adult rules. The help the status offender needs frequently means protection from adults—protection from inadequate schools, irresponsible parents, and intolerant neighbors.

The Truant

Consider truancy. Few youths are habitually truant just for the fun of it. School is where all their friends are, where all the action is. They are truant because they can no longer endure the frustration, the criticism, the humiliation of sitting day after day in classes where they can't possibly succeed, can't understand what is being discussed, and probably can't even read the assignment. There is no joy in being the perpetual class dummy.

Several years ago, while conducting a workshop on truancy, I placed much of the responsibility on school officials who put students in classroom situations where failure was inevitable. One irate principal, tired of hearing an outsider criticize the schools, stood up. "I'll tell you one thing," he said. "I'm plenty responsible. I try to get the judge to ship every damn hard-core truant off to the reform school. In my school they get what they deserve."

I naively thought I could win an emotional debate with logic. I pointed out that this didn't really solve the youth's problems and asked if he had ever followed up on what happened to those students after their release. "You're damn right I have," he answered as he stalked out of the room. "Those troublesome little bastards don't ever show up in my school again. I'm rid of them."

Several weeks later at a similar workshop in another city, a juvenile judge expressed a vastly different point of view. He told how a local school principal had pressured him to put a stop to an epidemic of truancy. "Okay," he had agreed. "I'll start committing every truant you refer to me."

The principal's joy was short-lived. The judge had added: "All you need to do is send me a statement indicating three things: first, that you have the youth enrolled in a class or program where he has some reasonable expectations of succeeding; second, that the program is meaningful to his personal needs for the future; and third, that you have some evidence that sending a truant to a reform school will somehow make him a better adult. You do this and I'll do the dirty work and I'll send the kid up."

The truancy petitions weren't filed.

The judge should have added a fourth stipulation: that the truant's parents were not the ones at fault. Many juveniles are held out of school to care for younger children or a sick parent, or to hold down a job to supplement the family income. At times the parent is just too unconcerned to insist the child go to school.

It would be redundant to repeat here the charges against the school system made in the previous chapter. Truancy and dropping out are primarily the end products of inadequate school programs. The problem likely began early in the elementary grades. After failing for years to meet the educational needs of many youngsters, the school system then asks the court to chain them to a classroom desk. And when the judge's threat fails to scare them into compliance, they are sent to an institution—as if locking them up will somehow solve their problem. (Recall Billy, the young all-American Kentuckian who was sent three times to a juvenile institution for truancy, but no one ever took the time to tutor him in remedial reading.)

The Runaway

Many parents are like those school officials who would dump their responsibilities on the court. "Beyond control" cases often reflect unreasonable rules and demands made by parents who themselves need counseling more than the youngsters. Even more of these charges reflect inadequate skills in parenting. For the judge to tell the unmanageable child to "shape up and mind your parents or I'll send you to jail" is the old story of punishing the victim. It merely exacerbates the parent-child conflict. Many of these parents are sincere in their concern about an insubordinate child. They could benefit from help in learning how to control the unmanageable behavior of their children.

Just as truancy is usually the end product of inadequate educational programs, running away is usually the end product of unresolved parent-child conflict.

Juveniles leave home for countless reasons. Some run away because of anguish over being an unworthy drain on the family budget. But most leave because of some form of parental abuse. Surveys consistently indicate that from 60 to 80 percent of all runaways have been physically or sexually abused at home. Workers with runaways estimate that four out of five of the girls found selling their sexual services on the streets have been sexually molested at home before running away. Nor do boys escape sexual molestation at home—by fathers, stepfathers, older brothers, mothers' boyfriends, even on occasion by incestuous mothers.

Physical abuse, at times sadistic punishment, frequently is associated with parental drug and alcohol problems. Psychologists have discovered that *most parents who abuse their children report a history of having been abused themselves as children.*

To sexual and physical abuse must be added a more subtle form—psychological abuse. It is particularly prevalent among upwardly mobile middle-class families. And it is among this group that teenage suicide is so prevalent. The youth is continually hounded at home to succeed—academically, socially, athletically—when actually he or she is not physically or mentally equipped to fulfill the unreasonable expectations of the family. Psychological abuse also takes the form of unwarranted restrictiveness by an overprotective parent. As the esteemed family psychiatrist Dr. Bruno Bettelheim observed, "It is a terrible burden to be loved too much."

For any of these reasons a youth may feel that the only means of escape is to run away. Contrary to a common myth, few of these juveniles are psychological heirs of Mark Twain's adventurous Huck Finn—runaways in search of fun and excitement. (But even Huck was trying to escape the clutches of an alcoholic, abusive father.) Most are searching for the love and understanding—and the safety—they did not find at home.

The Homeless

Out on the street these runaways are joined by throwaways and pushouts—homeless youths who have been abandoned or kicked out permanently for various reasons. These include insufficient money in the family budget to feed and clothe them, failure to live up to parental expectations, and, perhaps most of all, incompatibility with a new stepparent or live-in lover.

Then there are the kids who have been homeless all their lives. Abandoned by their mothers at birth or soon afterward, they have for years been tossed back and forth between a grandparent, an aunt or uncle, and even casual strangers, or between a series of unsatisfactory foster homes. These throwaways become convinced that no one really wants them. Running away is unduly prevalent among older teenagers living in foster care homes and among adopted children, particularly those who have been adopted at an older age.

Sasha Owen, a counselor for San Francisco's Larkin Street Youth Center, discovered that in 60 percent of the cases where workers have tried to send runaways home, the parents refuse to take them in! They claim their children are unmanageable.[2]

Too young to hold a job, these runaways, throwaways, and pushouts have four means of survival: panhandling, stealing, hustling drugs, and selling their own bodies. By the time they have existed on the street for a month their outlook on life, their hopes and aspirations drastically change. This was dramatically related to me by three juveniles—two males and a female—who were among the dozen or so young prostitutes I spotted on Polk Street in San Francisco one afternoon during the writing of this chapter.

One of the two males was a runaway, escaping physical abuse. The other was a pushout, having failed to live up to parental expectations. I asked them, "If you had the ear of the governor, what would you ask him to do to help young people living on the street?"

The difference in their replies was revealing.

The runaway, who called himself Ralph, had been self-supporting since he ran away at thirteen from a sadistic vice-squad policeman father in Florida. The father had discovered that the youth was gay, and his response was to violently whip his son each night in an effort to force him to change. Ralph has had no contact with his parents since the day he left. "I don't want to," he said. "The memory is too bitter." At first he survived by getting drugs from an aunt and uncle and peddling them at his junior high school. When his aunt and uncle were busted, drying up his supply, he turned to prostitution. "Working" nights, he put himself through the eleventh grade. The summer he was seventeen he decided to try California and bought a plane ticket to San Francisco.

Being good-looking and an old pro at the business, Ralph makes big money—depending on the sexual services requested, up to a hundred dollars or more for an hour date, never less than thirty dollars just for letting the customer give him a "blow job." On weekends he is on the street working night and day, gobbling amphetamines to stay awake. Despite his claim to have earned twenty thousand dollars last year, he admits that he is desperate at times for food and has never saved any money. But he lives high, usually eats well, spends a considerable amount on "easy" drugs ("no hard stuff"), wears expensive designer clothes, and stays in a nine-hundred-dollar-a-month apartment which he shares with two other boys and a girl.

These three are his street family. Like most homeless youths they have banded together in a quasi-family group, desperately clutching for the love and concern they never had. When Ralph has money he freely shares it with any of his "family" in need. He is extremely protective of the girl, particularly when, as is often the case, she is too exhausted or sick to go out soliciting. Another boy who lived with them had just disappeared one night a couple of months earlier—"left all his stuff and everything." They are worried about what happened to him but are afraid to contact the police.

Ralph fantasizes that "Diamond Daddy" will come along and permanently support him in a life of luxurious leisure—a fantasy common among boys on the street. But now that he is past eighteen, he has begun to worry about the rapidly approaching time when he will be too old to be attractive as a male prostitute. (It's young boys who most readily "turn on" customers.) He's thinking about getting his G.E.D. and then going to city college to learn a skill for a "high-paying job." Whether he follows up on this remains to be seen, but the odds are that the lure of some illegal activity will win out and he will join the ranks of adult criminals.

When asked what he would have the governor do to help young-sters living on the streets, Ralph was quick with his answer: "Make prostitution legal. Then we won't have to waste so much time dodging cops."

Sixteen-year-old Chuck has been on the street just over a month. Trim and muscular, he was always more interested in sports and partying than academics. This year he failed all but one subject in high school and his father ordered him to get a job or get out of the house. He was unable to find employment in the small town where he lived and under threatening pressure from his father decided to try San Francisco, some sixty miles away. He went to the Larkin Street Youth Center, where he received food vouchers for two meals, advice to return home, and referral to a shelter house for job counseling. When he was unsuccessful in finding a job and his time limit at the shelter house ran out, he took the advice of some other runaways and started hustling sex on the street.

He is disgusted with his work. (Ralph is gay, so his "work" isn't as abhorrent to him.) "But," Chuck says, "if you are hungry enough you'll gladly let some fat bastard undress you and slobber all over you. You even get where you can slobber over him without gagging." Asked about AIDS, he shrugged. "Sure I'm scared, but I know about safe sex. And they [the Larkin Street Youth Center] give us these." He pulled a handful of condoms from his pocket.

He has no plans other than hoping a job will turn up. He believes he can't go home, and claims that neither of the two youth centers he visited tried to intercede for him with his out-of-town father. He is living day by day, at the moment crashing in an abandoned building with some other runaways. He doesn't like them very much—they are pretty heavily into drugs.

When I asked him what he would have the governor do, his reply was vastly different from streetwise Ralph's. "Get us a decent place to stay when we are dead broke," he said, "and get us a job. I'm big enough to hold down a real job. Anything would be better than this fuckin' thing I'm doing."

Chuck has not emotionally joined the runaway counterculture. Not yet. There is still hope that he will find a job or manage some reconciliation with his father before it's too late.

I managed a conversation with only one runaway girl that afternoon, a heavily made-up fourteen-year-old in high heels, a tight miniskirt, and a bright red blouse revealingly opened down the front. As I leaned against a building on Polk Street she came up and asked for a match. After I supplied the light and a friendly smile she added, "Thanks. I'm Marie. Ya wanna quick job?" I countered with an offer of coffee and ten bucks just to talk for a few minutes. It was okay with her, if I paid first.

She told me that she had left her home there in the city two months earlier when her antagonistic mother refused to believe that she was being regularly molested by her "stepfather." Her mother helped her pack. For a couple of weeks she had stayed with a former girlfriend who several months earlier had also left home. Now Marie was living in an apartment with an "older man"—twenty-six—who accepted sex in lieu of rent. While she had "tried everything," she specializes in oral sex. It is quicker, and fellatio can be done right there in the guy's car. Twenty dollars for a ten-minute trick! She'd gotten as many as eight jobs in a single night.

I didn't get to ask her what she would have the governor do because she abruptly left. Apparently she thought I was trying to pressure her into going to a youth center for help, and she was "happy with things just like they are." She has been luckier than most. So far she hasn't been busted and she has escaped enslavement by a pimp. Her health is still moderately good. But in just two months she has already adapted to the underground. Her life, she thinks, is now much better than living with a "bitch of a mother" and her sexually abusive live-in lover.

A "Benevolent" Court Steps In

The fact that running away is a status offense escalates the problem in two dimensions. First, most courts take a very simplistic approach. Runaways are bad boys and girls—always at fault. Because they have broken the law they are routinely returned to the unsatisfactory home situation from which they ran and are threatened with institutionalization should they run again. Seldom is an effort made to mitigate an abusive situation or to ameliorate friction in the home.

Even more critical, since runaways know they will be arrested and sent back home if caught, they are forced into the underground, becoming invisible to police and other authorities. Consequently, only one in every four or five runaways either is caught by the police or comes to the attention of those who could be of help. Most are afraid even to seek aid at the runaway shelters that do exist, fearing that they will be turned over to the authorities.

For the past two decades criminologists and youth advocates have recognized the damage that can be done by the court's handling of runaways and other status offenders. As far back as 1967 the President's Commission on Law Enforcement and Administration of Justice cautiously proposed narrowing the juvenile court's jurisdiction over noncriminal matters.

In 1975, after much agonizing, the board of directors of the nation's most prestigious group dealing with the problems of crime, the National Council on Crime and Delinquency, proposed a 180-degree about-face from its long-held philosophy. No longer did it believe the juvenile court should intervene in the lives of children because of noncriminal behavior. A policy statement was issued calling for the total removal of status offenses from the jurisdiction of the court. Since then, most youth advocacy groups and students of the problems of delinquency have taken similar stands.

The National Juvenile Justice Assessment Center studied the problem under a grant from the Law Enforcement Assistance Administration. After extensive research, its 1980 report summarized the need to remove status offenders from the court:

1. The court is ineffective in changing undesirable behavior of youthful status offenders or in meeting their needs.
2. It unnecessarily criminalizes noncriminal behavior of juveniles.
3. The process labels or stigmatizes these youths as criminals, endangering their future careers.
4. Many status offenses are part of the normal socialization and maturation process; and while their behavior may not be desirable, it does not predict future involvement in serious delinquency.
5. Status offenses do not threaten the public safety, social order, or even necessarily the welfare of the child; thus the needs of neither the child nor society are being met.
6. The juvenile justice system is overburdened with status offenders, impairing its ability to deal with criminal youths.

It is true that some status offenders do eventually turn to crime. If they should, then that is the time for the court to deal with them. But to punish all status offenders because a few may in time commit criminal acts is indeed a miscarriage of justice and a counterproductive policy. In a study of 1,222 violent juvenile offenders in Columbus, Ohio, researchers concluded that status offenders are not headed down a path to criminality. They found that the criminal careers of fewer than 10 percent had begun with a status offense.[3]

But Some Disagree

Not all persons agree with this reasoning. Prominent among those opposed to decriminalization have been some juvenile judges and, as could be expected, some whose livelihood depends on the "rehabilitation" of these nonoffenders—social workers, probation officers, and institutional employees. It is not solely the salary. Human nature rebels at being told that one's work is of no value.

While I was with the Kentucky Crime Commission, we invited the governor, Louie Nunn, to give the welcoming address at a seminar on crime. The governor had previously been a county judge, which in small Kentucky counties included the role of juvenile judge. In his speech he reached back into his experience for an illustration of the need for the court to deal with status offenders. In this instance the governor had decided that the unmanageable behavior of a youngster stemmed from his mother's unwillingness to administer proper discipline. So the judge had removed his own belt and handed it to the mother, instructing her to give the boy "the whipping of his life" right there in the courtroom. As the youth cried out from the lashings the judge insisted that the mother whip harder and harder.

"That was a whipping that boy never forgot," the governor exclaimed proudly. For a moment he paused in his speech, seeming to revel in the memory of how wisely he had dealt with this unruly status offender.

The governor should have quit while he was a winner. But he went on. "I *know* he never forgot. Last year while I was touring the state prison, a young man rattled his cell door and beckoned to me. 'Governor,' he said, 'you probably don't remember me, but I'll never forget that whipping you had my mom give me in your court.' "

Because of the pressure of advocacy groups a number of states have passed laws making it illegal to put status offenders in jails or institutions. But juvenile judges have found ways to play games with the law. For example, the judge can order a truant to attend school and when he or she fails to do so can have the truant locked up for violating the terms of probation. A Hammond, Indiana, judge sent four boys to jail for sixty days for having received D's and F's on their report cards in violation of his court order to improve their grades.

During the administrations of Presidents Nixon, Ford, and Carter, progress, albeit slow, was made toward a more positive approach to the handling of status offenders. In 1980 the Judiciary Committee of the U.S. Senate, after holding hearings which documented the seriousness of the runaway problem, published a 256-page report, *Homeless Youths: The Saga of "Pushouts" and "Throwaways" in America.* An abstract of the report stated:

> As the size of the homeless population grows, there will be an even larger underclass of bitter, defeated, or angry people in this country. Out of loneliness, boredom, and need for love, homeless youths are producing another generation of youngsters whom they, in turn, will abuse and abandon. The next generation will take their parents' place, swelling future costs of public assistance, increasing the loss of taxes and revenues, and increasing involvement with the juvenile and criminal justice systems. It is far less expensive to aid homeless youths now than it is to build bigger prisons and institutions to house them and their children in the future.[4]

Instead of heeding that challenge, President Reagan's appointee to head the Office of Juvenile Justice and Delinquency Prevention (OJJDP), Alfred S. Regnery, galloped off in the opposite direction. He crusaded to make it easier for the court to lock up runaways. Having the juvenile court punish them and forcibly return them to their homes was his simplistic solution. Financial support to state programs attempting to help runaways and keep them out of jail was slashed. Consequently in just one year, 1984–85, detention of runaways increased by over a third.

The tragic fallacy of such an approach has been documented in many studies, some of which Regnery himself, ironically, reported.[5] One was the Wisconsin Juvenile Offender Study Project, which found that among girls who had again run away two or more times *after* being returned home by the court, 72 percent had attempted suicide. Nearly three out of four! Regnery used this statistic to "prove" that runaways are "deeply disturbed and incapable of caring for themselves." He was blind to the fact that a home environment can be so unbearable that if a girl is repeatedly frustrated by the court in her attempt to escape, suicide may seem to be her only option.

It is incredible that anyone holding the highest office of child advocacy in America could have been so lacking in understanding. To advocate forcing a youth back into an abusive home without attempting to ameliorate the conflict is in itself child abuse. It is also incredible that Reagan could have appointed to this high post a man who had absolutely no prior training or experience with juvenile justice matters and whose only apparent qualification was that he was a reactionary conservative who had been defeated in a race for district attorney in Madison, Wisconsin.

During the Senate confirmation hearings, when questioned about his total lack of experience or qualifications, Regnery claimed to have done considerable reading about juvenile problems. But he was unable to name a single book, article, or author. The appointment of someone so grossly unqualified, however, fit into Reagan's sly effort to do an end run around Congress. With the strong support of youth advocates and juvenile justice professionals, Congress had rejected the President's request to zero out of the budget the Office of Juvenile Justice and Delinquency Prevention. So Reagan set out to destroy OJJDP from within.

Regnery was the right man to sabotage the intent of the Juvenile Justice and Delinquency Prevention Act of 1974 (and amended in 1977), which had been written after six years of exhaustive study by the Senate Committee to Investigate Juvenile Delinquency. It had been signed by President Gerald Ford after passing the House of Representatives by a vote of 329–20 and the Senate with a single dissenting vote. Regnery devoted much of the energies and budget of the Office to attempt to discredit OJJDP activities and programs of the previous administration, policies that had been mandated by Congress.

One of the more blatant pieces of propaganda was the 1985 *Juvenile Justice Bulletin* dealing with runaway children. In page after page the sexual exploitation of many runaways was described in lurid detail— enough to make anyone with even a modest concern for young people cringe. But the bulletin naively placed the blame for all these tragedies on the Office's expenditure of a paltry $120 million between 1975 and 1980 on programs to keep status offenders out of jails and correctional institutions.

How simplistic can one be?

It is not the intention here to give the impression that runaways or other status offenders are all nice, sweet little kids who have been mistreated. Many are cold, hardened, and bitter youths, unable to communicate with adults and wallowing in the depths of low self-esteem. Many are mean and difficult to deal with. Their experiences have made them so. The issue here, however, is the effect of the court's intervention in their lives. It must be concluded that rather than in locking them up, if solutions to their complex problems are to be found, they will be found in services and organizations outside the juvenile justice system.

Chapter 7

CULTURAL ROOTS OF DELINQUENCY

In England, Japan, Sweden, and most other civilized nations the rate of juvenile delinquency is only a fraction of the rate in the United States. An American youth, for example, is some twenty times more likely to be delinquent than is a youth in Sweden or Japan.

And since juveniles are guilty of a disproportionately large share of all crime, coupled with the fact that adult criminals, by and large, are merely youthful offenders grown up, the United States is also one of the most crime-ridden nations in the world. Consider crimes of violence. An American is 13 times more likely to be murdered than is a person in England, Greece, or Holland; 9 times more likely than one in Australia, France, Germany, or Japan. The rate of rape is 15 times that of England and a whopping 180 times as high as in Japan. And robbery? Americans are roughly 9 times as likely to be robbed as their European counterparts. And in Japan? Our rate is a staggering 128 times as high.[1]

These statistics are a mind-boggling indictment of America.

But why?

Are Americans really this much more violent, this much more criminally inclined than other civilized peoples? Is it a genetic defect?

Are we born to be bad? Surely not. Then why? If it is not innate, then it must be something within our cultural history, something within the American way of life that spawns delinquency. We consume more drugs than the remainder of the civilized world combined. Does our culture drive us to attempt a chemical escape from life?

Many cultural traits peculiar to our American culture make us the delinquency champion of the world. To try to reduce juvenile crime without considering these factors is like trying to empty the bathtub without turning off the spigots.

The Top Dog Syndrome

A cursory glance at history reveals how cyclical is the story of the rise of great empires to a place of dominance, only to fall and be replaced. Only seventy years ago, after Europe had been decimated by World War I, did the United States begin to replace Great Britain and become "number one." Since then we Americans have reveled in that distinction, refusing to believe that we could ever be anything but tops in any measure of accomplishments.

Pride in this achievement has caused Americans to become obsessed with being top dog, individually and collectively—obsessed with being the finest or the biggest or the smartest or the richest, anything with an "est" on the end of it. Everyone seems to be driven by a need to feel that in some measure he or she is just a little bit better than all others. *The Guinness Book of World Records* is a testimony to the bizarre extremes an individual will go to in order to achieve self-esteem by being tops in something. Winning is what is important. It does not matter how it is achieved, fair or foul, legal or illegal.

Even superlatives with negative connotations—meanest, toughest, drunkest—can indicate a measure of success. If you are going to be bad, take pride in being the "baddest."

As we noted in the previous chapter, parents often inflame this top dog syndrome. They put undue pressure on the child to win in whatever they themselves consider to be important—grades, sports, the social scene. When these parental demands are unrealistic, particularly in middle- and upper-class families, a youth's self-esteem may be shattered. A survey sponsored by "Who's Who Among American High School Students" found that 31 percent of high-achieving teenagers have contemplated suicide and 4 percent have attempted it.

Suicide, the second most common cause of death among fifteen- to nineteen-year-olds, has tripled since 1950.

But delinquency is a far more frequent youthful response to failure to be tops. One delinquent youth I came to know intimately was the son of a highly successful doctor. Larry was scrawny for his age and not very attractive. Shy. And it was readily apparent that he was not too bright—not retarded, simply just not too smart. Yet his high-achieving parents demanded the impossible. "Why don't you try to be like your brother and sister?" they hounded him. The older brother was captain of the high school football team; the sister had been valedictorian the year before. But Larry wasn't even good enough to play in neighborhood games on the corner lot, and barely managed to pass in school each year.

Like the vast majority of delinquents, Larry had experienced failure all his life—socially, athletically, academically. So he was forced to make his own definition of success. He became the best car thief in town. His eyes sparkled as he told me how he had taken twenty-seven cars for joy rides and had been caught just twice (and then only because in his desire to share his success with others he had talked too much). He always left the cars unharmed. Sometimes he even put gas in them. With real pride of achievement he explained to me how he could hot-wire almost any car.

Whenever there are top dogs there are also bottom dogs. In the ghettos most youngsters are losers. From the losers, no matter whether poverty-stricken or affluent, delinquents are recruited. No one wants to be a failure all the time. A youth may succeed in becoming the greatest beer guzzler or the hottest hot-rodder or the most successful purse snatcher . . . or the most successful drug dealer driving the most expensive car.

A Heritage from Our Brief History

Three influences from our brief history have been particularly significant in making America the world's leader in delinquency.

One developed during the early days of the settlement in the wilderness of the New World. It laid the philosophical foundation for a Calvinistic bias against the poor—an undercurrent that has persisted throughout the years and resurfaced with fresh vigor in the Reagan eighties.

A second grew out of our history of slavery, which caused a large segment of the population to consider blacks not as persons but rather as chattel property. Created by God as inferior beings, they neither deserved nor were expected to share in the good things of society.

The third facet was the great expansion into the wide, wild western reaches of our continent where one lived by the gun, died by the gun. The trails were long and the days were lonely, relieved often by sporadic outbursts of violent activity.

1.   A Violent Society

Evolving out of this heritage is a fact that must be faced. Ours is a violent culture, far more violent than other long-settled "civilized" countries. We love violence, approve of violence. Television and the movies are filled with scenes of violence. Rambo is a folk hero. It is not that producers are fiendishly depraved but simply that the public demands it.

We pay hundreds of dollars for ringside seats to savor the pleasure of seeing two men pummel and bloody each other. While it is illegal to watch animals doing the same, we hold clandestine dogfights and cockfights, and at auto races we feverishly await the orgasmic rush of adrenaline that comes with each flaming crash.

While Western European countries and most of Latin America have abandoned the death penalty, Americans remain fascinated with the idea of legal, public murder. Etched in my memory is the carnival scene that erupted in my small western Kentucky town when thousands of people from all over came to watch the hanging in the jailhouse yard of a convicted rapist.

President Bush's approval rating jumped to the highest ever known at the time for a president when he flexed his muscle in the bloody and illegal invasion of a small nation to capture a formerly friendly drug dealer. (The approval rating later went off the chart when with clanking sabers he galloped off like a knight in shining armor to hold down the price of oil.) The President didn't have to worry about public reaction to the death and injury of hundreds of American soldiers (many of whom were victims of our own ill-planned and unnecessary spraying of bullets) . . . or the far greater loss of Panamanian lives and the indiscriminate destruction that left eleven thousand homeless.

Bush had learned from his predecessor's experience. Reagan's popularity had likewise soared when he made a military assault on a tiny island. By contrast, President Jimmy Carter was defeated for reelection in large measure because of the public's disapproval of his use of diplomacy instead of brute force to gain the release of a handful of American hostages: He was a wimp. President Bush proved he wasn't.

In frontier days a gun was a necessity. It was virtually an extension of one's body. It meant protection when protection was a foremost need—protection against Indians and later against roving outlaws. But today, when the gun is more of an invitation to disaster than a protection, the love affair persists.

Not only is the crime rate in America greater than in other industrialized nations, the degree of violence is almost incomparably greater. During 1985, 35 people in Japan were killed with handguns, 8 in Great Britain, 6 in Canada, 7 in Sweden, 10 in Australia—and 33,000 in America!

Few of the 33,000 persons who fired those guns were doing so in defense of themselves or their homes. An account in the *New England Journal of Medicine* says that a gun purchased to protect the home is twenty-seven times more likely to be used against a member of the family than against an intruder.

This love affair filters down to the young. We noted earlier that elementary school children are now using guns to settle petty disputes, killing each other because of insults or even just for the thrill of it. An estimated 135,000 boys carry a handgun to school with them each day. Joseph McNamara, police chief of San Jose, California, declares that of 400 California children killed in 1988 by gunfire, 90 percent were shot by another kid under nineteen years of age, 70 percent by killers under sixteen.[2]

Chief McNamara further points out that a person can be arrested in California for carrying Mace, a blackjack, or a billy club without a license. Such a person is guilty of a felony. But because of our love affair with guns, it is perfectly legal to carry an AK-47 assault rifle. That's getting our priorities straight!

By the age of eighteen the average American child will have spent 50 percent more time watching television than attending school. He or she will have internalized a massive dose of violence, having watched according to one study 32,000 murders and 40,000 attempted murders. Even in "comic" pages children are socialized to accept violence. They are taught to laugh when Sarg whacks poor old Beetle Bailey into oblivion and Garfield, the best-seller-list cat, strangles Odie, his not so bright doggie playmate.

Small wonder so many juveniles turn to violence—even murder—when frustrated.

Another root of delinquency from our frontier heritage is our extremely punitive response to crime, particularly to petty property crimes. "What's mine is mine, and I'll hang you if you try to take it." Out in the West before the days of courts and prisons and probation officers, justice was delivered by a gun or at the end of a rope. This punitive attitude toward criminals continues, although now that we are "civilized" long prison sentences are usually substituted for the sudden-death penalty. But whereas the frontier justice was permanent, today's thief eventually will be released back into society. Because of his prison experience he most likely will be more dangerous than ever.

Many people in the United States find it difficult to believe how extremely mild the sanctions against adult criminals are in most European countries. In the Netherlands the majority of prison sentences are for less than one month, and fines start at fifty cents. And yet these slaps on the wrist there and elsewhere in Europe, particularly in the Scandinavian countries, have proved to be successful in maintaining a lower crime rate than have the harsh sentences levied in America.

America makes a gallant effort to be less punitive toward youngsters because of their age. Nothing is done either *to* or *for* most young offenders, even serious ones, until they have made repeated trips to the court. Then, after the seriousness of the delinquency has escalated, the court's patience explodes. In the end punitiveness wins out. The youth is clobbered. The result: America locks up more of its youth in jails and reform schools and for longer periods than any other nation.

Contrast this to countries with extremely low crime rates among both adults and juveniles. In Sweden, for example, juvenile crime is considered to be largely a family or economic problem. Consequently, an erring youth up to the age of fifteen or a status offender of any age is not taken to court but is handled by welfare authorities; even most older delinquents are referred to social agencies. A youth's problem is not exacerbated by being placed in "rehabilitative" programs or institutions. Instead, emphasis is placed on finding out what needs to be done *for* the unsocialized youth. Only seventeen Swedish youths under the age of eighteen were committed to training schools and an additional eleven to prison in a recent record year.[3]

2. A Legacy of Slavery

Few factors have been more responsible for delinquency in America than prejudice against blacks. In the time sequence of history, it was only yesterday that slavery was an accepted fact of life. Our culture has not yet wholly cleansed itself of the attitude that blacks are not fully persons, that they deserve only inferior homes, inferior schools, inferior services—if they deserve them at all. Furthermore, they should be subservient—gladly step off the sidewalk while the white man passes.

The result of this prejudice is highly visible in our prisons. For example, New York State's substance abuse agency has estimated that in 1987 more than 400,000 New Yorkers illegally used drugs at least once a week. Of these, two-thirds were white. But 91 percent of those committed to the state prisons on drug charges were black.[4] The war on drugs has in reality become a war on minorities in the inner cities. The prejudice against black juveniles is becoming even more blatant. Of the record increase in the number of juveniles being locked up in detention since 1985, only 1 percent has been white. But there has been a 30 percent increase in the number of blacks and Hispanics.

The effect of racism in the juvenile justice system was explored in the chapter on the myth of the juvenile court. Blacks are far more likely to be arrested for crimes that are overlooked in white youths, more likely to be locked up in detention while awaiting trial, and more likely to be sent to a juvenile institution. They emerge bitter and vindictive, ready to commit more serious crimes against an unfair society that holds them in contempt. And we saw that as a result of racism in educational practices, blacks are more likely than whites to leave school illiterate and unemployable.

In the days after the civil rights movement America made steady progress in ridding itself of the emotional relics of the years of slavery. But suddenly, with the Reagan administration's leadership, progress went into reverse. Racial hatred broke out among students on college campuses that once had been in the forefront of the struggle for equality. Violent groups like the skinheads and the Ku Klux Klan suddenly began to gain strength and attract new recruits, particularly young ones.

The message had come down from the top levels of government that we had gone too far in trying to overcome the legacy of slavery. It was really all right to discriminate against blacks *just a little bit*. The Justice Department worked feverishly to nullify affirmative action programs and succeeded in persuading the Reagan Supreme Court to weaken those statutes which sought to guarantee civil rights. Hope that a change in administrations would reverse this message was dashed early on when Bush blatantly appealed to the hidden prejudices of Americans in one of his more powerful TV campaign spots. It bodes ill for the future of underprivileged black children.

3.   The Puritans Leave Their Mark

The philosophical tenets of Calvinism brought to the New World by the Puritans and other religious groups quite possibly account for how rapidly the early settlers in America were able to conquer the wilderness and turn it into a thriving economy. In a cold, hostile environment the frugality, self-reliance, and industry demanded by the Protestant ethic made it possible to succeed against unfavorable odds.

Here, however, our interest is in that part of the Calvinistic doctrine which became woven into the fabric of our social structure: Amassing great wealth was a sign of being in God's favor—one of the elect. So the wealthy were held in high esteem. Being poor indicated being outside of God's favor. In the Protestant ethic this was translated into meaning that it was sinful to be poor and, by further refinement, that if people were poor it was their own sinful fault.

Calvinistic religious doctrines lost favor in America but a number of attitudes survived quietly below the surface. One is that the richer an individual is, the more revered he or she should be. So the railroad tycoons of the robber baron era and the Donald Trumps of the present were all set upon a pedestal. Because of their ingenuity and brilliance, certainly they deserved all the wealth they could accumulate. And likewise the poor deserved their status—they brought it on themselves.

Because of this attitude, it is not too surprising that the punitiveness of our justice system is overwhelmingly aimed at the poor. In ancient Greece and Rome two sets of laws governed criminal behavior, one for free men and one for slaves. While such a dual system—one for the rich, one for the poor—does not officially exist on the lawbooks in America, it is blatantly apparent in practice.

In "The Rich Get Richer and the Poor Get Prison" Jeffrey Reiman, a professor at the American University School of Justice, points to the preferential treatment given white-collar criminals.[5] The average prison sentence for burglary is forty-seven months, while it is less than half that much, twenty-two months, for embezzlement. Yet the dollar magnitude of the embezzler's crime may be several hundred times as much as the burglar's and may involve the life savings of thousands of retired or widowed investors. To top it off, most embezzlers, if they serve time at all, serve it in minimum-security facilities, commonly referred to as country club prisons or "Club Fed."

It is a high-level sin to steal only if you are poor.

On the day this was written, the *Wall Street Journal* featured the saga of David L. Miller, who rather than prison garb was sporting monogrammed shirts and gold cuff links. The previous year his superiors at Associated Communications Corporation discovered that he had embezzled $1.3 million. Instead of being prosecuted, however, he was quietly dismissed after he promised to repay "part" of the stolen money.

While charges frequently are not pressed against white-collar criminals, Miller's story was exceptionally gross. He had been a successful embezzler over a period of twenty years, having stolen from six former employers—*and had never been arrested*. Each time, the scenario was the same. He escaped prosecution with the promise to make some restitution out of pay from his next job. (In most cases he did repay part—by embezzling from the next employer.) Because of this promise, the companies had been "less than forthright" in reporting his dishonesty to law enforcement officers *or* to other companies interested in hiring him. Money comes before ethics for many of the not so poor.

The annual take from white-collar crime (embezzlement, bribery, illegal kickbacks, fraudulent products, crooked investment schemes, illegal price-fixing, insurance frauds, and so on) is at a minimum estimated to be over ten times greater than the total from all juvenile and adult property crimes (robbery, theft, burglary). Yet there is small disgrace for being a well-to-do crook—frequently there is even admiration. A bestselling book may be in the offing. Reactionary conservatives scream loudly about "coddling juvenile criminals." But if any group of criminals is coddled in America, it has to be white-collar criminals.

This bias against the poor carries over to juveniles in the court system just as does the bias against blacks. (Thus many blacks are doubly exposed.) The underprivileged face discrimination at each step of the way, from arrest to incarceration. The son of well-to-do parents is given a slap on the wrist for committing the same offense that often sends the son of a welfare recipient off to a juvenile prison. Once he is there it can take two years in the institution to "rehabilitate" a lower-class, uneducated, unemployed youth caught shoplifting at a grocery store when he was hungry. This policy has accelerated. The crackdown on delinquents is aimed increasingly at the poor among minority groups.

The Relative Worth of a Human Being

America is also indebted to the Calvinistic heritage for the definition of an individual's worth—a measure often quite different from that used by other civilized societies. The measure is not wisdom or piety or good works or scientific contribution or artistic achievement. The measure of a person's worth in America is money. How much you got? How much you paid? (It was not artistic talent that caused most Americans to elevate Picasso to the heights of greatness even though they didn't like his art. It was the fact that he could command thousands just for doodles on a paper napkin.)

Consequently, there is an incessant demand for higher and even higher salaries, all to prove just how great these individuals really are. The top executive gets his name and salary listed in *Forbes* magazine. (No one publishes the young crack dealer's worth, so he has to publicize it with heavy gold necklaces and the Ferrari or Jaguar he drives.)

And up and up the salaries keep going, piggybacking over each other. . . . But even Wall Street was finally shocked when junk bond writer Michael Milken was indicted and the discovery made that he had been paid $550 million in 1987, and over a billion in a four-year period. Perhaps the quote of the century was made by Donald Trump, the New York developer whose net worth was for a time estimated to be over a billion. "You can be happy on a lot less money," Trump said. As Trump feverishly continued to wheel and deal, one wondered how many billions it would take to make him happy.

The self-made man is an idol worshiped by Americans. But the self-made man is a mirage. There is no such thing. All of us—the rich and the poor—are largely products of the innate intelligence God gave us, the genes we inherited, and the care we received long before we began fending for ourselves. What each of us contributes individually to our success pales in comparison to what is showered upon us through no effort of our own.

Only the most extreme doctrinaire communist would claim there should be no difference in the material rewards given to individuals regardless of their skills or their contribution to society. Communism has collapsed trying to deny that the incentive of personal reward is necessary to move the wheels of progress. But it is legitimate even for a noncommunist to question the size of the difference in rewards.

When putrid odors engulf a city and disease is spreading rampantly because rotting garbage has piled up in the streets, it might be fair to ask if the doctor's contribution to the overall health of the community is really twenty or forty times that of the garbage collector's. The services of both are necessary for society's survival. On a global scale the garbage collector is possibly a little more important in preventing plague and pestilence.

Or consider two young friends who played basketball together in a New York ghetto school. They were similar in background and intelligence, similar in habits and ambition, similar in all ways except for one small detail. The genes of one happened to cause him to grow four inches taller than the other. Because of this gift of fate he was able to make it to the pros and eventually demanded a salary of a million a year. The friend struggles at a minimum-wage job sweeping out the Coliseum. Is it really fair that such a vast difference exists in our rewards system? As Donald Trump might ask, does it really take that much to make the pro happy?

Michael Jackson is reported to have made an estimated $65 million last year. This is almost as much in an average day as the salary of the President of the United States for an entire year. Is any person really worth that much? Apparently President Reagan thought that such an inequity should be preserved and even increased because he engineered a tax schedule to slash the taxes of the ultrarich. It seems incomprehensible that including Social Security taxes, the Michael Jacksons and Donald Trumps of America are in a *lower* tax bracket than is a middle-class individual with a net income of only $45,000. And by proposing cuts in capital gains taxes, President Bush would lower taxes for the wealthy even further.

When history reviews the Reagan administration, perhaps its greatest legacy will be that Reagan restored respectability to the concept of personal greed. Compare "Ask not what your country can do for you . . ." with the Reagan reelection slogan, "Are *you* better off than you were four years ago?" Not "Is the country as a whole better off?" Not "the poor and disabled," not anyone or anything except just *me*. (And one could also compare ex-President Reagan's $2-million personal appearance fee to promote Japanese industry with ex-President Carter's hands-on work with Habitat for Humanity building houses for the poor. It's a matter of personal priorities.) So greed came to dominate the highest levels of government and business and to color all our thinking about the poor and disadvantaged.

It is fine to talk about education and training disadvantaged youths to qualify for higher-paying jobs. A commendable humanitarian goal! Quite typically, a spokesman for the disadvantaged declares that "what we need are careers, and selling hamburgers isn't a career." But this is tunnel vision. It ignores the fact that someone has to sell hamburgers, that someone has to do any one of the hundreds of seemingly unimportant, low-status tasks that are necessary if society is to function. There always will remain the dull, dirty, dead-end jobs that must be filled by those at the bottom of the social ladder. And there always will be crime and delinquency as long as society refuses to reward such workers with sufficient pay to provide a decent standard of living. *By demeaning the value of the lower echelons of our society, we invite costly reprisals.*

Economic Imbalance and Delinquency

It is not poverty per se that results in crime but the vast inequities that exist. (Wrenching poverty exists in Appalachia but little delinquency—most everyone is poor.) If none of my friends has a bicycle, I'm not likely to steal one. But if every boy but me on the block has one, I'll likely steal one if I have the chance. Delinquency is fomented in the vast economic gap between the middle and lower classes. Thus it has roots in another cultural attitude—the willingness to close our eyes to those inequities existing side by side in our society.

Reagan was the high master of this blindness. He couldn't see the hungry, couldn't see the homeless, couldn't see the children being raised in deprivation. Consequently, there was no reason to spend money on these persons who didn't exist.

By contrast, consider the case of Sweden which, as has been noted, has an extremely low rate of crime—both juvenile and adult. This is not the result of a tough legal stance but rather the absence of most of the conditions that breed crime.

The nation has no poverty, no illiteracy. The gap between the rich and the poor, by American standards, is virtually nonexistent. It is generally accepted that the salary of a company's chief executive will be no more than five times that of the lowest-paid worker; in the United States the ratio has soared from forty to one in 1980 to ninety-three times as high in 1989.[6] Health and life expectancy are higher in Sweden than in the United States. Instead of a punitive attitude toward those few who do break the law, particularly juveniles, there is a vigorous effort to ameliorate the condition that precipitated the crime.

Conservatives dismiss this extraordinary social accomplishment by smugly calling the government "socialistic"—as if a label somehow turns a contented, peace-loving nation into a dangerous ogre. And critics argue that steeply progressive taxes imposed to distribute the wealth more evenly stifle ambition and destroy the work ethic. Yet the per capita income in Sweden is considerably higher than that in the United States. Someone there must be working instead of sitting around waiting for welfare handouts.

Ironically, it was only with the assassination of Swedish Prime Minister Olof Palme in 1986 that most Americans became aware of how virtually crime-free Sweden is. Americans could hardly believe that a head of government would feel safe enough to roam the streets of the nation's capital at night without bodyguards.

It is interesting to note that Palme developed his political philosophy while in the United States. The son of a wealthy, conservative Swedish family, he spent a year at Kenyon College in Ohio obtaining a liberal arts degree. Then in the summer he hitchhiked around the country, picking up odd jobs along the way. He later recalled, "For the first time, I saw real poverty, and it gave me strong feelings about social injustice." He disavowed his conservative stance and upon returning to Sweden became active in the Social Democratic party, determined not to permit such injustices to develop in his own country.

Those who would shrug off the example of a "socialistic" country might consider Japan. Few will deny it is democratic and very, very capitalistic. Because of the citizens' devotion to the work ethic, their belief in saving their money, and their strong defense of capitalism, they (with Reagan's help) were largely responsible for changing America from the world's largest creditor nation into the largest debtor nation. Yet, with the exception of Sweden, Japan has the most equitable distribution of income in the industrialized world. There is little teenage unemployment. Only 1 percent of Japanese babies are born to teenagers out of wedlock, versus nearly 20 percent in the United States. There are few Japanese slums and little economic stratification of neighborhoods.

And what does all this have to do with delinquency? A lot!

Because the conditions that foment delinquency are largely absent in Japan, teenage alienation and crime are extremely low. Actually, the Japanese are beginning to worry about delinquency. More inequities in income are starting to show up, and economists warn that this could cause social alienation like that in the United States. They see an alarming increase in juvenile arrests—*now at one-twentieth the rate in the United States!* In America approximately seventy-nine out of a thousand youths are arrested each year. In Japan it is four.

Since juvenile delinquency is usually a precursor of adult crime, Japan's overall crime rate is but a fraction of America's. Consider the two largest cities. In New York City during an average year some 75,000 robberies are reported. Although Tokyo is somewhat larger, the figure is around 500—less than 1 percent of the New York rate.

Some have credited the low crime rate in countries like Japan and Sweden to the racial homogeneity of their populations. Such an explanation is a cop-out—a crutch used by those who refuse to admit there just might be a flaw or two in our society. It is homogeneity all right. But most of it is *economic* homogeneity.

It can be considered a sociological axiom that in a democratic country, the greater the gap between those who have and those who have not, the greater will be the delinquency rate.

Throughout world history when the rising expectations of downtrodden individuals or groups or nations are suddenly smashed, rebellion or even revolution is often the result. Such a collapse occurred in the United States a few years after passage of the Civil Rights Act. Black youths thought that the long journey from slavery to the promised land had finally ended. Reality dashed that dream. The legislation afforded only a glimpse of the promised land, not a ticket for admission. High-salaried jobs were not suddenly available. Attendance in white schools did not automatically increase academic achievement.

When impoverished young blacks discovered that their hope of immediate participation in the good life was phony, an orgy of rioting and looting swept the ghettos. "Burn, baby, burn!" And ever since, for those who are unable to climb out of the ghetto, crimes of violence have remained an appealing option. Many believe it is their only option. Rhetoric about equal opportunity, affirmative action, and trickle-down economics has failed to keep hope alive. The graffiti that attempt to cover up all that is beautiful in our cities are a very visual symbol of the bitterness and hate manifested by frustrated have-nots.

The Delinquent Child of Poverty

Because the poor are viewed as not fully worthwhile human beings (it's a sin to be poor), an affluent America has permitted vast ghetto areas to develop. Here despair, alienation, and bitterness are nurtured. Uneducated, untrained, unemployable youths roam the streets. And here most of the violent delinquency of the city is generated. Unmet material needs—food, clothing, and shelter—will, of course, trigger delinquent behavior. The universal need among American teenagers to possess "things" as status symbols—designer jeans and chrome-decorated boom boxes—is smothered by the youths' inability to qualify for a job even if they could find one.

But poverty stifles other, more basic needs. For the child of poverty, normal physical and mental development is crippled by inadequate nutrition, both before and after birth, by inadequate health care, by insufficient intellectual stimulation. With this start school failure is virtually assured. It is difficult to feel loved and wanted in a family whose energy is drained by a daily struggle to survive. Building self-esteem is nigh impossible for the youth failing in school, living with an illiterate parent in a crowded, vermin-infested room that is devoid of all the luxuries dangled before him or her on television.

To the youth for whom the American dream is only a nightmare, crime is a seductive solution. It is easy for people who are basking in affluence to say that those youths who turned to crime could have found legitimate solutions if they had tried. Yes, it is easy for those who don't understand the debilitating effects of poverty.

One of my most painful memories is of the evening after Martin Luther King, Jr., was assassinated. I was at a large dinner party in Kentucky where at the hors d'oeuvre table a woman greeted me with, "Thank God they finally got that nigger. Now he won't be stirring up all those young punks too lazy to work." I suggested that maybe those "punks" couldn't find jobs. "Hell!" she retorted. "If they hadn't been so trifling after the war they could have gone to college on the GI Bill, just like my husband did. He didn't sit around crying for a handout. He applied himself and amounted to something."

I walked away without asking if she thought that most of those "punks" had as children received the same educational and cultural advantages as had her husband, raised in an affluent home and handed a prosperous family business.

The child of poverty contemplates crime and with a shrug decides,

"What have I got to lose? It's unlikely I'll be caught. If I am, the court probably won't do anything to me, at least for the first half-dozen times. And if the court should send me up I'll have a warm bed, regular meals, and some pretty good recreational facilities. Crime? Why not? I can't lose."

The Widening Gap

Sadly, the gap between the affluent middle class and the poor is growing into a canyon. This foreshadows increasing crime in the years down the road— a ticking crime bomb. America will be unable to build prisons fast enough to protect the affluent from those who have been cut off from the mainstream of American life.

Some twenty years ago the Kerner Commission (appointed by Lyndon Johnson in response to the long, hot summer of 1967) warned, "Our Nation is moving toward two societies, one black, one white— separate and unequal." With the weakening of the federal antipoverty programs in the 1980s, that time has arrived. Ghettos have become even more entrenched. But now the blacks have been joined by a rainbow coalition of the poor.

Under Reagan programs for the poor were slashed so that taxes for the rich could be reduced from a top bracket of 70 percent to just 28 percent. The income of the top fifth of the nation's families jumped by 11 percent, and 32,000 new millionaires were created, an 825 percent increase over 1980. But this increase came largely at the expense of the families in the bottom fifth, where the annual income declined by 6 percent. The gap is at an all-time high. As Hodding Carter III warned in the *Wall Street Journal*, "We are structuring a country in which Third World conditions coexist side by side with prosperity."[7]

The United States may still be the wealthiest nation in the world, but last summer the Commission on the Skills of the American Workforce, headed by two former secretaries of labor, provided a different warning. America's great wealth is becoming more and more concentrated at the top. *Already a dozen countries provide higher average wages than does the United States.*

The poverty line is defined by Congress as the minimum cost of a basket of groceries containing an adequate diet for a family *plus* twice that amount. Thus, an amount just two times the allowance for food is expected to take care of rent, clothing, health care, and all other necessary and emergency expenses—a feat demanding a skilled magician. Certainly there is no spare pocket money for juveniles in the family. So low welfare payments virtually force these youths into crime. The most affluent country in the world has created the most miserly welfare system of all advanced nations. And we remain the only industrialized nation that does not give governmental assistance to virtually every poor family with children.

Today over 30 million Americans live below the poverty line—50 percent more than the total population of Central America excluding Mexico. Two out of five of these are children, the fastest-growing segment of the poor. Think of what this portends! Over one-fifth of all American infants and children are now suffering the debilitating effects of being raised in poverty. Last summer the National Commission on Children stated that *more than any other factor* childhood poverty places young Americans at risk for a range of long-term problems, including poor health, failure in school, teenage pregnancy, crime, and drugs. Here is the fuse of the crime bomb, burning short.

Reagan bragged about the 8 million new jobs that his administration created. He failed to report that over half of them (in fact, 62 percent) paid less that seven thousand dollars a year, leaving most of these workers still mired in poverty. With these minimum-wage jobs a family of four requires two workers in order to have enough after Social Security taxes to barely squeeze across the poverty line. A one-parent or one-worker family just can't make it.

Because of these low wages social workers are discovering a phenomenon never before seen in America—thousands of homeless persons who are holding steady jobs. Some surveys place these working poor at one out of five of all those presently homeless. According to a Congressional Budget Office report based on 1989 U.S. Census Bureau statistics, nearly two-thirds of the nation's poor have to pay more than half of their income for rent. This leaves them teetering on the brink of having to join those living on the streets and in abandoned cars. Many are mothers with small children.

Many children are being penalized even before birth because low Medicaid payments are making doctors increasingly unwilling to give prenatal care to low-income mothers. Among industrialized nations only the United States and South Africa do not have a national health program. In Mississippi a family of three is denied Medicaid if the annual family income exceeds $1,152—$22 a week for the entire family! Thirteen states provide Medicaid for less than one-third of their poor.

Admittedly, America's welfare system has not been very successful. It is rightfully assailed by liberals and conservatives alike. But it has at least warded off any revolutionary movement and, except for a brief period in the late 60s, has largely prevented wide-scale rioting. Even coldly calculated self-interest should argue against welfare cuts to the poor *unless* some other approach to the problem is offered.

Delinquency has its roots in all of these—our bias against minorities and the poor, our punitive attitude toward those who commit petty property crimes, our love of guns and violence, our obsession with winning and being number one. These are attitudes deeply embedded in the American psyche and they greatly affect the crime picture. Community planners cannot realistically hope that some $2-million, three-year delinquency prevention program will make even a slight dent.

It is difficult to refrain from discussing in humanitarian terms the personal tragedy of youths raised in poverty and ofttimes in ignorance—the human grief caused by overcrowded housing and rubble-strewn streets, by cockroaches and rats, by malnutrition and debilitating ill health, by gang-ruled neighborhoods where strutting pimps and drug pushers are the only role models. But that is another story. This book is a pragmatic proposal addressed to the movers and shakers of our society. Its basic thrust is enlightened self-interest— the need for self-protection through the reduction of juvenile delinquency and ultimately a reduction of adult crime.

Few will disagree with the proposition that juveniles should be held accountable for their actions. They must be taught by parents or schools or, as a last resort, the courts to accept responsibility for what they do. There is, however, less enthusiasm for the other side of the ledger, which demands that society be held accountable for its role in the making of these delinquents. It is this dual-accountability model that will be explored in the remaining chapters.

PART II

The Ultimate Hope:

PREVENTION RECONSIDERED

Chapter 8

DISCARDING FALSE ASSUMPTIONS

The evidence presented in Part I indicates that *the juvenile justice system, as it exists in most places, is a sham. It neither deters nor rehabilitates. Nor does it protect society from an increasingly dangerous segment of the youth population.* With an arrogant disdain for the constitutional rights of its juvenile clients, the system selects certain youths for cruel punishment and closes its eyes to the wrongdoings of others. It is a justice system that is not just, a social experiment that failed to live up to its noble expectations.

Many critics lay the blame on insufficient money, insufficient staffs, insufficient community concern. But the truth is that even if each of these were greatly increased, the court would still be ineffective. It would be ineffective because failure was the inevitable consequence of building a juvenile justice system on faulty assumptions. The fact that often these assumptions contradict each other reflects the shallowness of the philosophical foundation of the court. Already considered in the previous section, the more relevant may be summarized as follows:

FALSE ASSUMPTION #1: *Rehabilitation, not punishment, is the function of the juvenile court, because by serving in the role of sur-rogate parent the court can step in and forcibly retrain a wayward child.* Because of this assumption, the courts have been given virtually absolute power to intervene in the lives of juveniles. But as has been repeatedly documented, rehabilitative therapy under coercive conditions as ordered by the court has almost invariably failed and has frequently caused irreparable damage to the youth.

FALSE ASSUMPTION #2: *While status offenses—truancy, running away from home, being beyond parental control, and so forth—are not actually crimes in the adult sense, the court should intervene in the lives of these offenders before their behavior escalates into real crime.* But seldom are status offenses the forerunners of criminal behavior. And instead of having a preventive effect, official action is most often counterproductive, pushing the juvenile into a delinquent career. Instead of helping, this legal response to noncriminal behavior labels the child as a delinquent. This in turn causes these youths to be rejected by law-abiding society, forcing them to turn to delinquent friends, and seriously eroding their self-concept. Actually, most status offenses are the result of failure on the part of irresponsible parents, schools, or society in general.

FALSE ASSUMPTION #3: *A juvenile who commits a delinquent act will increasingly become a more serious delinquent and adult criminal if the court fails to intervene.* Surveys indicate that virtually all juveniles at some time commit delinquent acts, frequently quite serious ones. Yet the vast majority of those who are not caught do not subsequently embark on careers of crime. As they grow older they seem to tire of sowing wild oats, and maturational reform takes place. Ironically, this natural reform is greater among those who have not received the "services" of the court than those who have.

FALSE ASSUMPTION #4: *Because of their youth and immaturity, juveniles should not be held fully responsible for their criminal acts.* Try telling that to an elderly woman whose hip was broken in a fall when a juvenile grabbed her purse, or to a young girl psychologically scarred for life by a juvenile gang rape. This assumption was faulty from its inception. Most parents have always known that punishment for improper behavior, along with rewards for proper behavior, is an essential part of the socialization process. Today youngsters mature physically, mentally, and sexually far earlier than in previous eras. Because of easy mobility, television, and increased leisure time, they now become streetwise and ready for crime at an early age. They should be held responsible and punished for doing wrong . . . not continually put on meaningless probation.

FALSE ASSUMPTION #5: *Because the emphasis is on rehabilitation instead of punishment, nothing should be done with the repeat offender until all noncoercive efforts—such as stern warnings by the judge and counseling by probation officers—have proved to be ineffective.* This concept gave rise to the do-nothing court. The child's wrist is slapped and, as is the case with young drug runners, he is told, "Don't do that any more." Usually not until the juvenile has come before the court eight, ten, or more times does the judge sentence the youth to anything more restrictive than mere probation. The juvenile either interprets this message as meaning the court really condones his delinquent behavior, or concludes that he's much too clever for the stupid court. In the meantime the delinquent behavior and attitudes have been allowed to become firmly entrenched.

FALSE ASSUMPTION #6: *The juvenile court should usually ignore very young offenders (those aged twelve and under) because they are not capable of fully understanding right from wrong, and instead should concentrate on older delinquents.* Just the reverse is generally the case. Those who are older when they appear in the court for the first time will likely mature out of their delinquent ways. Many are merely rebelling against adult authority as part of the growing-up process. Those younger (ages nine through twelve) have the potential of becoming extremely dangerous juvenile and adult criminals. Their early delinquency reflects deep psychological disorders and/or serious family dysfunctioning.

FALSE ASSUMPTION #7: *Various instruments including psychological tests and sociological profiles can accurately predict which youngsters will become delinquent, and can determine when those in therapy have been successfully rehabilitated.* This is false on both counts. Predictive testing is so inaccurate that far more damage is done to those who are improperly labeled than any possible good. And because of the false assumption, juveniles are committed to institutions for an indeterminate length of time, supposedly until such time as they have been rehabilitated. Thus, vast injustices can occur because staffs are grossly unable to predict which juveniles will or will not get into further trouble.

FALSE ASSUMPTION #8: *Most delinquency prevention programs*

should zero in on juveniles in junior high school because this is the period just prior to the highest rate of delinquent activity. Such programs are years too late. By this age most attitudes and behavioral patterns that generate delinquency have been firmly established and are now extremely difficult to alter. To be effective, preventative programs should be instituted at least by kindergarten or the first and second grades. Preferably they should begin in the homes of disadvantaged children at the time of birth.

FALSE ASSUMPTION #9: *When juveniles reach eighteen, they should be legally forgiven for all childhood crimes and their records sealed so that they can make a fresh start in life.* Yes, so that all the serious and violent young criminals can with impunity go right on harassing the public. Young men who have been arrested twenty or thirty times for serious crimes now show up in adult courts as criminal virgins. Because of this false assumption, many violent criminals are prowling the streets during their most dangerous period—from age eighteen to twenty-two—while the adult court is concentrating on older criminals who actually are phasing out their criminal careers. Records should be sealed only for former delinquents who get into no further trouble with the law.

All this suggests that instead of doing more and more of the same things that have not worked in the past, America must seek a new approach. Assumptions that have proved faulty must be reevaluated. Myths that have hidden our failures must be exposed. When this is done, there is hope that an effective system can be devised.

Twenty years ago the President's Commission on Law Enforcement and Administration of Justice consulted the foremost criminologists in America. After a year and a half of extensive study the Commission concluded that the best hope lay in prevention. It said:

> Once a juvenile is apprehended by the police and referred to the Juvenile Court, the community has already failed; subsequent rehabilitative services, no matter how skilled, have far less potential for success than if they had been applied before the youth's overt defiance of the law.

Despite that report, however, both private and public efforts have continued to be geared primarily toward doing something *to* a youth after he or she has become delinquent.

Because of the proven failure of this approach, the recommendations of Part II are targeted at prevention. They will not be focused narrowly on delinquency per se, since *any problem—physical, mental, social—if left unresolved can be the precursor of a delinquent career.* Delinquency is but one manifestation of a matrix of social ills that consume many of today's youths. Included with delinquency are such ills as school failure, unemployability, teenage pregnancy, and drug abuse. The process of establishing an immunity to one will most likely reduce the risk of falling prey to the others.

In its broadest sense primary prevention means the eradication of the canker spots in the social structure that breed these ills. Poverty and discrimination are the most festering. Victims of either or both are seriously crippled in their effort to satisfy basic human needs, particularly the need for self-esteem. Those who feel that social justice does not exist for them will have little incentive to conform to the laws of what they see as an unjust society.

"Liberty and justice for all" must go beyond mere flag waving. Achieving it will bring a payoff for everyone. Increasing justice for all will simultaneously increase safety from violence and crime for all. *But justice cannot be achieved by merely doling out a few more dollars to keep the unfortunate from starving. That hasn't worked in the past. It isn't working now. Justice will come from breaking the cycles of poverty and illiteracy and crime.* Justice means providing training and opportunities whereby an individual can avoid becoming enmeshed in those cycles.

It is to this problem of society that we next turn. Focus will be on those measures which will best prevent our nation's young people from turning to delinquency. Finally, in Part III we will consider what should be done for and with the juveniles whom these measures fail to reach. But it is hoped that if the proposed prevention measures are implemented, there will remain few juveniles whom society must deal with in a court of law.

The prevention and control of delinquency will be no simple task. Nowhere has this book suggested otherwise. The causes of delinquency are complicated and multifaceted. Those who would look only for quick, easy solutions will not find them here. The proposals that follow are neither quick nor easy.

Chapter 9

DELINQUENCY AND THE POVERTY CYCLE

A Failed Welfare System

Contrary to a popular misconception, fully half of those on welfare rolls are there only temporarily, the consequence of some onetime misfortune. Many are victims of changing technologies and changing product demands that make their jobs obsolete. With a little help to tide them over they will rejoin the work force in a few months, or a year or two. Others are there because of ill health, divorce, or other transitory personal difficulties. Most are as anxious to get off welfare rolls as critics are to push them off.

Our concern is not with these temporary public assistance recipients but rather with the other half, which includes the millions permanently trapped in welfare dependency, some now in the third generation. The vast majority first joined the ranks as unmarried teenage mothers. Most of these who turned to welfare remain on the rolls for a decade or more. For them welfare proves as addictive as crack . . . and the addiction is passed on from generation to generation.

They are the underclass, a designation that encompasses far more than mere poverty. The underclass is a culture of despair, a ghetto culture where unmarried teenage pregnancies are the accepted norm, where school dropouts and illiteracy are the rule, where unemployment and crime and drug addiction are rampant, where pimps and gang leaders and drug lords are the successful role models. It is a culture largely financed by welfare—or crime—in which most long ago gave up any thought of escape. The value system that has evolved is incomprehensible to mainstream America. Social responsibility and the work ethic are foreign to most. Money is something that comes in the mail each month, not something that bears any relationship to work.

Isolated as alien to the rest of the nation, the members of the underclass are creating a "Third World" island within a sea of affluence. Most of them are clobbered by a double whammy of prejudice: the prejudice Americans have against the poor and the even greater prejudice against minorities.

Within this culture is spawned a major portion of the most serious and violent juvenile crime in America. A 1988 survey of inmates of state-operated juvenile institutions published by the Department of Justice reveals how closely the composition of this population parallels that of the underclass:[1]

- Three-fourths grew up with only one parent.
- Two-thirds are from minority groups.
- Over half report at least one close family member who has also been institutionalized.
- Well over half dropped out of school long before even entering high school.
- More than 60 percent used drugs regularly, about half of them having begun before the age of twelve.

To attempt to reduce delinquency without attempting to eliminate this major breeding ground is to be blind to the problem and its causes.

The eradication of the roots of this permanent underclass is essential if the America we know is to survive. As the members continue to multiply, their social and economic costs will pyramid so rapidly that sooner than we think they could bring democracy crashing down.

There will be the mounting expenses to protect law-abiding citizens and the escalating losses from drug addicts' robberies. There will be the multibillions needed for new jails and prison cells. Increasing at an incredible exponential rate will be the medical dollars required to care for defective infants born malnourished from inadequate diets, brain-damaged by the mother's crack and alcohol addictions, or carrying the AIDS virus bequeathed by a needle-sharing parent. Larger and larger welfare appropriations will be needed to provide subsistence for these children as they grow into adulthood and clone yet another generation of the underclass.

It is hoped that before it is too late we will agree to massive institutional reform on three fronts: the welfare system, the public school system, and the juvenile justice system. Each of these three "service" institutions plays a major role in causing the United States to have the highest rate of crime in the industrialized world. The public school system and the justice system will be considered in succeeding chapters. But the welfare system must take priority as the front line of attack.

After more than a half-century of federal experience with welfare it has become unarguable that not only is the system not working for many, it most likely has exacerbated the very problem it sought to solve. Even during the Reagan "prosperity" era the number needing assistance steadily increased. Trickle-down economics could not penetrate the invisible walls that seal off the enclaves of the underclass.

When Aid to Families with Dependent Children (AFDC) was begun in 1935, the number of mothers receiving subsistence payments was quite small, primarily widows and wives with disabled husbands. At the time an unmarried mother was a rarity, indeed a scandal. Even as late as 1950 only 4 percent of the children in the United States were illegitimate.

Somehow AFDC has aided in making illegitimacy respectable. Today 40 percent of all first children of mothers under thirty are conceived out of wedlock. For teenagers the number jumps to 60 percent. Among blacks the figure rises to 79 percent. Most of these mothers are candidates for welfare instead of marriage. Over half of their children are destined to grow up in poverty. What began as an emergency measure has for a dangerously large segment of the population become a way of life—devastating for them, costly for the rest of society.

In recent years the unofficial policy has been to make welfare so inadequate that there would be a strong incentive for recipients to stop loafing and go to work. This approach has had considerable popular appeal because of the stereotype of the AFDC recipient as a cheat—a lazy welfare queen making a career of having babies and supporting her unemployed boyfriend with her welfare salary. While this picture is true in some instances, as a stereotype it is grossly unfair to the vast majority who are on welfare through no deliberate personal choice. Furthermore, this false stereotype gets in the way of constructive criticism of the system.

The most pressing welfare concern is not that there are cheats, or that it is more costly than an affluent society can afford. The legitimate concern is that *it has permitted—yes, at times even seduced—an increasingly large number of individuals to be permanently enmeshed in the cycle of poverty.*

Unanswered "Help Wanted" Signs

Welfare critics claim that thousands among the permanent underclass refuse to take menial jobs when they are available. They point to the many "help wanted" signs that now decorate the windows of small shops and fast-food outlets. Want-ad columns offering jobs have steadily lengthened. "Those able-bodied loafers," the critics protest, "don't want to work. Let them get hungry enough and they'll quit goofing off."

There is, of course, much truth in this. Many minimum-wage jobs are not being taken. But before dismantling the welfare system in order to punish the "cheats," we need to ask why so many among the underclass fail to take these jobs.

1.   Many are functionally illiterate, unable to read, write, or add well enough to be employed in available jobs. They are unemployable. Since the disappearance of smokestack industries from the inner city, jobs requiring brawn and little else are decreasingly available. The problem is not a shortage of jobs but the growing mismatch between job requirements and the skills that children of the underclass have achieved. With no skills and no experience the underclass members have received rebuff after rebuff. Many, perhaps most, have given up even applying.

2.   Available jobs are often temporary, and from painful experience many have learned that once they are off the welfare roll it is a long hassle to be reinstated. When layoffs come it will be the uneducated, poverty-raised individuals who will be first to go. Play it safe. Don't take the job.

3.   Welfare rules virtually prohibit many from accepting low-paying jobs. While a minimum-wage job may support, albeit margin-

ally, a single individual or become a middle-class teenager's summertime bonanza, it will provide far less than the subsistence level for the millions of families with only one wage earner. *After paying for transportation to the job, necessary clothing, health care, baby-sitting expenses, and Social Security taxes, the net return to a single woman with children will be sharply less than the meager check being delivered by the postman.* While it might raise one's self-esteem to get off welfare, survival is a more urgent priority.

Eliminating the first of these reasons, the illiteracy of teenagers, is a difficult, long-range project, which will be explored at length in the chapters on school reform. The second and third reasons could be eliminated, or at least greatly reduced, by changing shortsighted regulations. Instead of making it a losing proposition to take a low-paying, possibly even temporary job, the rules should make it possible for welfare recipients to better themselves by accepting entry-level jobs. The promise of more money is the incentive that greases the wheels of the American economic system. Why deny this incentive to welfare recipients?

Until the total family income, *including welfare,* reaches a pre-scribed amount for the family size (certainly at least 100 percent of the federal poverty level), the new wage earner should be permitted to keep the income from a regular or part-time job. This would cost the system not one penny more than it now does when the recipient cannot afford to take a job. After this maximum combined-income level is attained, the recipient's welfare payments could be *gradually* reduced. Finally, when the family income reaches a minimally respectable sum, perhaps 140 or 160 percent of the poverty level, support could be totally withdrawn.

Instead of the present penny-wise, pound-foolish system, such a change would quickly become cost-effective, restore respectability and self-esteem to those who escape the squalor of the underclass—and radically decrease the number of future delinquents growing up in those households.

Children Playing "Mama"—for Real

Nowhere is an overhaul of the welfare system more essential than in the treatment of unmarried teenage mothers. This is the number-one spot for a long-range attack on crime and delinquency. (In New York City 80 percent of the juveniles being held in detention centers were found to have been born to mothers who first gave birth as teenagers.) Proponents of a more enlightened welfare policy point out that every other industrialized nation provides far more adequate financial aid and services to indigent teenage mothers. Yet despite this largesse they have far lower rates of teenage births.

America has pursued a foolish policy. The stipend is sufficient for bare survival but inadequate to provide the child with the physical and cultural advantages needed to escape the ghetto. With total disregard of the child's future, the Scrooge in us says to the mother, "You've made your bed, now sleep in it."

More than a million American teenagers, *80 percent unmarried,* become pregnant each year. The rate is two to three times that of Canada, England, France, and Sweden. It is nearly seven times that of the Netherlands despite the latter's quite permissive attitude toward unmarried teenage sex, and ten times that of Japan. Whereas having a child out of wedlock was formerly considered taboo in America, it now has become a rite of passage in the ghettos. At Los Angeles's Jordan High in the heart of Watts, one-fourth of the girls have babies each year.

The total annual cost of welfare and Medicaid as now structured for these teenage families comes to nearly $20 billion.

PACE (Policy Analysis for California Education, located at Stanford University and the University of California in Berkeley) has recently addressed the problem of the public costs of these teenage pregnancies. Their research places the social cost in 1985 of California families begun while the mother was a teenager at $3.08 billion. Had these births been delayed until the mother was twenty years old, 40 percent—nearly $1.25 billion—would have been saved in 1985 alone.

Despite the fact that the one-parent family is six times as likely as a two-parent family to be living below the poverty level, welfare policies have been destructive of family cohesiveness. Many states deny welfare payments if the father hangs around even if he is unemployed. So he skips out, escaping all responsibility.

Raising a child single-handedly is not always disastrous. These parents often do a superb job—provided they have sufficient resources, both emotional and financial, to draw upon. Unfortunately, few unmarried teenage school dropouts have such resources. The children they raise are much more likely to become school dropouts too, more likely to be abused (by the mother or her boyfriend), more likely to use drugs, and more likely to become delinquent than those raised either in two-parent homes or by single parents under more affluent circumstances.

Twenty years ago Daniel Patrick Moynihan warned of the breakdown of the black family caused by soaring rates of illegitimate births. At the time his warning was largely disregarded and was called racist. Now, however, most black leaders regret that early attention was not paid to the problem. The black family has continued to deteriorate.

In San Francisco, possibly the most integrated city in America, where no race is a majority, black children make up only 20 percent of the under-eighteen population. Yet they represent 70 percent of the children in the welfare system—three and a half times the expected ratio. And reflecting the correlation between welfare and delinquency, this same 20 percent of the youth population accounts for more than half of all juveniles referred to the courts by the police.

In his more recent book, *Family and Nation*, Senator Moynihan sounds the alarm that the crisis is no longer restricted to poor black families. It now affects the poor of all races. The rate of teenage pregnancies among whites has rapidly increased until it is now half that of blacks.

Two further statistics are significant for understanding the source of the permanent underclass: A comprehensive study found that 82 percent of the girls who gave birth at age fifteen or younger were themselves daughters of teenage mothers. And nearly three-fourths of all women under thirty who are drawing AFDC had their first child as a teenager.

The Why of Getting Pregnant

Why do unmarried American teenagers become pregnant so much more readily than their peers in other developed nations? Are they so much more promiscuous? Youngsters in the United States are more sexually active than they were a generation ago and they start at an ever younger age, frequently even in grade school. But their activity is believed to be much less than in many countries where teenage pregnancies are less frequent.

Most pregnancies occur because of ignorance and/or unavailability of birth control methods. Surveys indicate that less than a third of all sexually active teenagers use any contraceptive regularly. Others are inept and careless. Myths, such as "You can't get pregnant the first time," are rampant.

While a counselor in an all-black junior high school, my wife insisted that one of her students have a pregnancy test. Mystified by the results, the girl protested, "We just did it a little bit." A fourteen-year-old delinquent boy boasted to me that he never got any of his girls "with babies" because he knew how to prevent it. This turned out to be: "Don't touch her tits while you're doing it." He didn't know what a condom was.

Some pregnancies are a deliberate act of defiance against an unyielding parent. Middle-class parents may refuse to permit their young daughter to date an "unworthy" or older boyfriend. The girl believes that if she becomes pregnant her parents will be forced to accept him. (The "great love" usually takes off like a scared rabbit when he discovers she is pregnant.) At the other end of the economic continuum, a teenager angry with her mother who draws AFDC may decide that if she has a baby she can collect the welfare money herself and her mother will be cut off. At the Teenage Parents Program in the Louisville schools, I was amazed at how many would openly admit this vindictiveness.

Consider a girl in a crowded, rat-infested, two-room ghetto apartment, worn out with never-ending family arguments, continually hassled in school where she is failing, tired of never having spending money, knowing no boyfriend who could support her, and unable realistically to see a job in her future. Such a girl may know that a welfare check will not be a magic carpet to transport her to the land of milk and honey. But she may very well believe that it can take her as close as she will ever get. And a baby will give meaning to her life—someone to love, someone to return her love.

So begins another generation of the welfare-trapped underclass.

But it takes two to make a baby. The males of the species must share the responsibility. Many inner-city counselors have found by sad experience that condoms can be successfully promoted to boys only to prevent venereal diseases and AIDS, not for birth control. The number of babies a youth has made becomes a macho status symbol in the ghetto. When Ed Koch was mayor of New York he admitted that his compassion for the downtrodden was sorely tested with the discovery of thirty-one-year-old welfare recipient Calvin Watkins. At last count he already had nineteen children—ranging in age from fifteen down to a few days—by four different women living in two Manhattan welfare hotels and a Harlem apartment.

News reporters had learned about Watkins when fourteen-year-old Calvin Junior was arrested for burglary about the same time that son James was nonfatally stabbed fourteen times. When found, James had on him a quantity of crack and a thousand dollars in cash. Yet welfare was providing free shelter and subsistence for him—as well as for his eighteen brothers and sisters, their four mothers, and his father. At age thirty-one, Calvin Senior is far from the end of his productive years for baby making. He's good for many more. And his delinquent sons can look to him as a role model.

Mayor Koch was painfully forced to conclude that "there is only so much that government can and should do for those it seeks to help." Without some measure of personal responsibility there must be limits to an individual's rights.

As I read about Watkins I was reminded of a conversation with the fifteen-year-old partner of a girl in the Louisville school for pregnant students. I was attempting to persuade him to use contraceptives in the future. His response: "Skin to skin. Man, that's the way. I don't want no piece of rubber getting in the way of how good it feels." When I reminded him that the girl could become pregnant, he shrugged. "That's tough titty for her. Not me! Hell, if she gets knocked up like Crystal did I can always find me another bitch. There's plenty good ass around."

His size stifled my urge to strangle him on the spot.

In far too many instances these baby-making males are in effect prostitutes. They scheme to get one or more women pregnant. Then, in return for continued sexual attention, they force the women to share their welfare money.

Laws permit welfare departments to demand that fathers of illegitimate babies contribute to their support. But seldom are the laws pursued. It is easier for the department to pay for the support than to make the time-consuming and expensive effort to track down the father, prosecute him, and then try to collect the money every month. This do-nothing policy sends a strong message to the studs in the ghetto: "You really don't need to be responsible for all those babies you father. The taxpayers will take care of them."

The Cycle of Poverty

There are a number of significant factors in the relationship between teenage pregnancy and the cycle of poverty:

1.   Few of these girls receive any prenatal care. Their unbalanced diet is highly inadequate. They deliver millions of babies with malnourished brains and bodies, already seriously crippled in any effort to climb out of the ghetto. When these babies grow up their reserved seats at the welfare office are waiting for them.

Fortunately, the 1988 Medicare Catastrophic Illness Act tackles this problem by providing Medicaid coverage to all pregnant women living in poverty. But implementation of the Act on the state level and assurance that quality care is actually delivered remain a massive unfulfilled undertaking. Increasingly, competent doctors—as many as a third of all obstetricians—are refusing to take welfare patients because of the low reimbursement for what frequently turn out to be unduly complicated cases.

2.   As the typical new mother from the underclass is unmarried, undereducated, and unskilled, all the debilitating effects of poverty are brought to the new family. She becomes bored, disheartened, envious of the wealth she sees on TV, malnourished from the effects of junk food, exhausted from taking care of an ever-demanding baby. She succumbs to the helplessness that permeates the underclass. Senator Moynihan reports that over half of the welfare recipients in New York City have never had one day's work in their lives.

3.   She is likely to remain unmarried and drawing AFDC because the baby's father and other males she knows are likewise undereducated, unskilled, and undisciplined—unable to offer her even the menial security promised by welfare. The child grows up knowing a man not as a wage earner but as someone who shows up on Saturday nights, possibly drunk, molests the mother, and eats up all the good food before disappearing again.

4.   Child abuse, a major contributor to the making of a delinquent, is common among young unwed mothers. Without money for entertainment and recreation, or a husband for emotional support, the girl becomes bored with being handcuffed to a squalling infant. Frustration is vented on the child. And the boyfriend jealously swats the baby who competes for his time. The abused child tends to grow up socially maladjusted—and delinquent—and is destined, in turn, to abuse his or her own children.

5.   Longtime advocate of educational reform Jonathan Kozol warns that among adults, 16 percent of all whites, 44 percent of blacks, and 56 percent of Hispanics are now either totally or functionally illiterate. Herein are the members of the underclass who were themselves born of illiterate parents. Now they in turn are unable to read to their children, too poor to provide cultural advantages, too ignorant to offer mentally stimulating activities. The children arrive at the schoolhouse door ill prepared to compete in the educational race. In time they will become discouraged and drop out and have babies. And the cycle of one illiterate generation to the next is perpetuated.

It is well and good to argue that all this is a moral problem—that unmarried teenagers shouldn't engage in sex. Maybe they shouldn't. But that is a naive stance. No matter who wins the morality debate, today's teenagers are going to engage in sexual activity . . . and many are going to become pregnant.

The realistic moral stance is to work toward preventing these unwanted pregnancies. This effort has been thwarted by many who are blinded by their own self-righteousness. The Moral Majority, the right-to-lifers, and their fellow travelers in the Catholic Church would put a stop to sex education, put a stop to making contraceptives available to unmarried teenagers, put a stop to legal abortion. It might be possible to feel a little sympathy for these chest-thumping, self-proclaimed moralists if they were equally concerned for the welfare of all those unwanted babies they would bring into the world . . . concerned that these infants would not be abused, unloved, undernourished, or permanently crippled in the culture of the underclass.

But no. With righteous indifference many choose to ignore the plight of those children they have "saved." Few have recognized the tragic irony in this "moral" stance as did a judge last year in Fremont, California. He sentenced ten antiabortion protestors to give a home for three weeks to homeless children, products of unwanted pregnancies.

And So . . . What to Do?

The most obvious starting point is to greatly increase the availability of the very things these self-appointed guardians of the public morality would prohibit. Heading the list is sex education. (The tragedy of AIDS has forced many to rethink their stance. As Harvey Fineberg, dean of the Harvard School of Public Health put it, "Sex education is no longer a matter of morals— it's a matter of life and death.") Recent national polls indicate that 85 percent of American adults now favor such instruction. Nevertheless, schools are so harassed by the militant minority that most programs are highly inadequate.

There is nothing wrong with the argument that home is the proper place for sex education—nothing wrong except that it seldom occurs. Over half of America's teenagers have received no sex education at school or at home. Most parents are too embarrassed or too incompetent. Sex education needs to begin long before puberty, needs to begin early in the elementary grades as it does in European countries where unwanted pregnancies are at a minimum. Waiting until high school, even junior high, is locking the safe after the jewels have been stolen.

Moral education and counseling are needed. It is just as essential to learn the social and economic disadvantages of having a child outside marriage as it is to know how to prevent pregnancy. Girls should be taught that it is morally wrong to have a baby, regardless of marital status, until they are mature enough and financially able to raise it. They should learn that instead of solving problems, becoming a parent compounds them.

Realism dictates that contraceptive counseling clinics be available to all teenagers. Where advisable, particularly in the inner city, satellites of the clinics should be based either in or near the schools. Most sex education programs have proved inadequate unless contraceptive devices and the Pill are made readily available—available without parental consent. No strings attached.

In indigent areas contraceptives should be free. The relatively small expense of such a program should be of no concern. *In view of the cost of medical care and AFDC payments for these teenagers and their babies, free contraceptive clinics could be society's most cost-effective single program.* Some clinics have already been established at or near schools at high risk. But the openings have typically brought picketing and protests by Catholic clergymen and antiabortion groups who claim that distribution of birth control devices promotes promiscuity.

The facts do not back them up.

A recent three-year study by researchers at Johns Hopkins University involved over 1,700 inner-city Baltimore students.[2] An intensive sex education program, which included free birth control centers next door, was carried out at both a junior and senior high school. A comparable junior and senior high offered only the watered-down sex education courses required by Maryland law. Girls in the schools without the intensive program had a 57.6 percent *increase* in pregnancies during the three years. Schools in the program showed a 30.1 percent *decrease!*

Similar results have been recorded in smaller, less fully documented studies. Records from St. Paul indicate that birth rates fell by 40 percent in the four high schools where clinics were established. Significant in this study was the effect on another phase of the problem—the frequency of repeat pregnancies. Among teenage mothers who used the services of the clinics after the birth of their first child, 80 percent remained in school, and a second teenage pregnancy was virtually eliminated—less than 2 percent.

The Baltimore study is also relevant to the morality debate. Contrary to the argument that sex education promotes sexual activity, hard data prove otherwise. Girls in the demonstration group remained virgins about seven months longer than those not in the program, and sexually active fourteen-year-olds decreased by 40 percent. An analysis of nine sex education programs done by Mathtech, Inc., likewise found that those who participated were less permissive about premarital sex than controls who did not receive the instruction.

Again the right-to-lifers must be held responsible for much of the problem. Contraceptive methods commonly available in the United States are often difficult or inconvenient to use—and have a failure rate of 3 to 26 percent. (Condoms, diaphragms, and cervical caps have a failure rate of 12 percent or more.) Because of the highly vocal protests of a small minority, far more effective and simpler methods available in other countries are prohibited here. For example, an injectable contraceptive lasting for two months has only a 2 percent failure rate, and a removable implant of progestin under the skin on the inside of the arm can provide 99 percent protection for up to five years. The RU-486 pill, subsidized by the French government, can safely interrupt a pregnancy up to six weeks after a missed period.

All this, however, will have little effect on the one in five unmarried teenagers whose pregnancy was a deliberate decision, even when she had no means to support the child. If this growing trend is not reversed the weight of the permanent underclass will in time sink the entire welfare program . . . and more and more delinquents will rise out of the morass. For these and for those unreached by sex education, drastic means are needed. No longer should having a baby be a free meal ticket for the mother to sit around and do nothing.

The outdated welfare system must be restructured to emphasize breaking the cycles of delinquency, illiteracy, and welfare dependency. To do this a two-pronged attack is proposed in the next chapter. One is aimed at the youthful mother, the other at the child.

These will be expensive, as are many of the other proposals to be made. But as the Ford Foundation's project Social Welfare and the American Future puts it:

We can pay a little now to try to prevent blighted childhoods or we can pay a lot later for the consequences. In other words, money for decent prenatal care, or more than three times as much to deal with low-birthweight infants; several thousand dollars for a good preschool program to open the mind of a ghetto three-year-old, or tens of thousands of dollars to cope with a hardened teenage criminal.[3]

Chapter 10

ESCAPE FROM THE SYMBIOTIC CYCLES OF DELINQUENCY, ILLITERACY, AND WELFARE DEPENDENCY

ESCAPE PLANS FOR WELFARE MOTHERS

As previously noted, AFDC payments need to be sufficient to provide for proper growth and development of the child—physically, mentally, emotionally. Providing less has proved to be self-defeating. Many liberals err in believing that merely throwing more money at the problem will solve it. But no! Increased no-strings-attached payments will only add to the attractiveness of becoming or remaining a welfare mother. The strings must be sufficiently strong to pull welfare-dependent mothers out of the underclass. For most either "learnfare," "escapefare," "workfare," or "rehabfare" should be required.

1. Starting Date for Participation

Legislators have traditionally shown a misguided allegiance to the sacredness of motherhood. Consequently, they have made few demands upon the welfare mother as long as she has an under school age child at home. Most state experiments in workfare have excused those with children under six. Even the Family Support Act of 1988 was such a timid approach to breaking the poverty cycle that a mother with a child under three continued to get a free ride, escaping even the mild demands of the new act.

Such a concept is so out of step with the realities of modern society that it is ludicrous. No longer even among "respectable" families is it considered improper for a mother to return to her job only days after giving birth. Television celebrities do it routinely. Among married mothers *not drawing AFDC*, 72 percent choose to work. According to the U.S. Census Bureau, as of March 1988, over half (51.1 percent) of all married women with newborn children had joined the work force before the baby's first birthday. Most commonly they returned to work within two or three months. But we have subsidized AFDC mothers to sit idly at home just because they have a child under six. It is critical to note that 47 percent of teenage mothers now have a second child within three years. It doesn't require too much planning for a woman to remain exempt from any welfare demands until she is well past the childbearing age.

Obviously the problems involved when a new mother mired in poverty tries to leave home for a job are vastly different from those of the television celebrity able to turn her child temporarily over to a well-educated nanny or a well-planned, well-equipped nursery program. But only a topsy-turvy sense of values would declare that whereas it is not necessary for a highly educated, highly competent mother to remain home twenty-four hours a day to personally nurture and train her child, it is essential that the functionally illiterate, untrained teenager remain a full-time mother. To a large extent, this policy ties the welfare mother to her ghetto home but provides no assistance in the developmental care and training of her child, thus keeping the poverty cycle walled in with concrete.

Instead the AFDC mother needs to be offered specialized nursery care designed to give her infant the physical attention and stimulation so often missing in the homes of the underclass. When this essential ingredient is added to the welfare agenda, it will become possible for this mother to be away from home to pursue a program of self-improvement, a program that will help her break out of poverty, be it by continued education, employment training, or work—along with a steady diet of counseling in becoming an effective parent. Such an opportunity is now available in a few places. Some two hundred schools now have day-care programs (of varying quality) for student mothers. There is, for example, Albuquerque's very successful New Futures School for teenage mothers, where most students take off only two weeks following delivery and then bring the baby with them to the school's nursery. But today such opportunities are indeed rare.

As the first step in restructuring an antediluvian system, compulsory participation in one or more of the programs being proposed would be *required* for all physically able mothers with children over the age of one. Voluntary participation would be strongly encouraged when the infant is four weeks old. After a doctor has certified the mother's physical readiness, she would be enticed, even bribed, with special benefits and financial allowances to waive the permitted year of nonparticipation.

2. Guaranteed Family-Income Maintenance

In return for participation additional allowances and benefits would make self-reliance more attainable: cost of transportation to and from either a school, a job-training program, or an actual job; medical care for mother and child; nursery and day care for the child. The basic allowance would be increased by up to 20 percent if this much could be collected as child support from an absent father. Any monies collected beyond this 20 percent would be deducted from the mother's allowance.

No increase in the basic AFDC allowance would be made for a second child. Such a policy may seem uncaringly harsh. But it is critical to strongly discourage the birth of additional children while the mother is trying to become self-sufficient. Although the mother would not receive any additional maintenance and spending money, the new child would receive all the supplemental services provided to the first. This would include health insurance and nursery care, where the child would receive two nourishing meals each day. Thus, the child would not suffer even though the mother would not benefit.

3. Learnfare for Those Under Twenty

More teenagers are shackled to welfare dependency by lack of education than possibly any other condition. Consequently, finishing high school or obtaining a G.E.D. certificate would be the top priority for those capable of satisfactory academic work. To achieve this, a built-in nursery care program is essential in all schools. In Chapter 13, dealing with alternative schools, a proposal will be made for a special school to which a student nursery, largely subsidized by AFDC, would be attached.

Research has shown that the best predictor of how far a youth will go in school is not his or her IQ score, not even the quality of the educational program, but simply how far the parents went. Thus learnfare would help two generations escape the ghetto—the mother and her children.

Those eighteen and younger whose past academic failure puts them beyond reasonable hope of success would be required to attend a vocational school or special job-oriented training program operated either by the school or by some department of government. (In the proposals made in Chapter 13 for restructuring the school system, this would be in the Alternative School Career High.)

4. Escapefare for Those Over Eighteen

All able-bodied AFDC recipients over eighteen *and not in school* would be required to meet with a career counselor for an assessment of their abilities. An individualized plan would outline the steps needed in the journey toward self-sufficiency. AFDC recipients would be required to sign a contract agreeing to the plan calling for either advanced schooling, training for a job, or working at a job in either the private or the public sector. The state would provide day care for the child, health insurance, and transportation.

The heart of the program would be three to six months of training in a job skill determined to be suitable for the trainee and in demand in the community. The staff would be alert to creating new areas of employment—for example, elder-care attendants for sick or frail persons in their homes. The need for trained workers in day-care centers is insatiable.

Those ready to seek employment in the private sector would be assisted in job hunting. As previously suggested, AFDC would supplement the pay on a diminishing scale and continue medical insurance until the family income reached 140 or 160 percent of the poverty level.

5. Workfare for Those Without Jobs

Being unable *or unwilling* to find employment should not be a viable excuse to escape the welfare requirements. A reasonable time after training, the government would become the employer of last resort and provide work to those physically able who failed to find employment. Assignment to a public service job would, as far as possible, be based on individual interests and abilities. The welfare check would be the payment. Those failing to show up for work without a verifiable, legitimate excuse would be docked as are workers in private jobs. Continued employment would be contingent upon performance compatible with the individual's abilities.

No longer would the choice be between work or welfare. For those unable to hold a public sector job, the choice would be either working at a subsidized public job or finding a way to survive without welfare. With the latter option, if the loss of welfare payments endangered the health and security of the child, the case would be handled as any other instance of parental child abuse. If no solution could be found, the child would be removed from the incompetent, abusive mother.

Workfare would in itself be job training, particularly as to work attitudes, and would be an incentive for the recipient to find a better-paying private sector job. Safeguards would be necessary to avoid undue hardships and to prevent unfair treatment due to prejudice or bad judgment by the staff. A method must be available for any worker to appeal the job placement to which she was assigned.

6. Rehabfare for the Addicted

The number of drug-addicted women becoming pregnant has reached crisis proportions. In some inner-city hospitals as many as half of the women having babies are testing positive for drug use within seventy-two hours of delivery. Many of the babies have serious defects of various kinds and even brain damage. At the same time, child welfare agencies are being overwhelmed with abuse and neglect cases related to the mothers' use of crack. For the future of these children and for any hope of eliminating the permanent underclass, two measures are needed.

First, there must be greater commitment to therapy for drug-addicted pregnant women. More residential slots must be made available. Widespread public education must publicize the extreme physical danger to the fetus from the mother's use of drugs. All pre-natal clinics should encourage women testing positive to enter therapy programs.

Second, any new mother testing positive at the time of delivery would automatically be charged with endangering the life of another and subject to a six-to-twelve-month sentence. Based on the report of a medical social worker's investigation to determine the type and severity of the illegal drug use, the judge could offer probation contingent upon either remaining negative in biweekly drug tests, or agreeing to serve the time in a voluntary residential drug therapy program. In this latter alternative, the baby would remain with the mother in the residential program. In both instances custody of the child for two years would depend upon the mother's remaining negative in random drug tests.

Refusal to enter the voluntary therapy program or failure to remain clean during the probationary period could be considered strong grounds for suspicion of parental unfitness, calling for investigation by the court staff. Ultimately this could lead to neglect proceedings to permanently sever custody of the child.

Again, these terms may seem unduly harsh. But the severity of the problem, which threatens to cause both the health delivery system and the welfare system to come crashing down, demands draconian measures. The charge of endangering the life of another is far more serious than mere drug addiction.

While education and/or job training would be incorporated into the therapy, for addicted mothers rehabfare would take precedence over both learnfare and escapefare.

7. Training in Parenting Skills

No matter how irresponsible many mothers may be, most desperately want the best for their children. But they may need help to determine what is best. Those not enrolled in other programs offering training in parenting skills—such as public schools for teenage parents—would be assigned to a special three-hour weekly class. Its contents would be patterned after the successful classes conducted for the past fourteen years for low-income Hispanic mothers in San Antonio, Texas. That program, called Advance, serves some 1,300 families at four locations each year. Mothers are taught how to nurture, educate, and discipline their infants.[1]

The first hour of the weekly session is spent making toys designed to stimulate the child's learning experiences. The second hour is devoted to learning basic parenting skills: how to give positive reinforcement to the child, how to handle discipline and encourage socialization, how to provide mental and emotional stimulation. The third hour deals with practical household problems in coping with poverty and includes discussion of videotapes of mothers dealing with their children.

8. Making Fathers Responsible

The reprehensible role that irresponsible males play in perpetuating the cycle of poverty and delinquency has already been mentioned. The problem is how to make them responsible.

The first step obviously is to identify these absent fathers. Admittedly this can be difficult. The mother may not know which of several males is the father. A greater number of mothers may refuse to reveal the name out of either fear of reprisal or misplaced loyalty. And many of the fathers have simply disappeared. As a result there are over 4 million children today for whom paternity cannot be established, thus making it impossible to assess child support payments. According to a 1986 Census Bureau survey, only about one-third of all mothers living alone receive any child support payments from fathers.

Requiring the Social Security number of both parents on the birth certificate helps. Fortunately, the 1988 Welfare Reform Act mandates that states attempt to do this, and also that they increase efforts to establish paternity. But, again, this is not easy. In many states laws are needed to permit the use of blood tests in determining paternity.

Perhaps the most promising approach would be to advise the new mother of a proposal made here—that she would be able to increase any welfare allotments by 20 percent if payments could be collected from an absent father. (Sex education classes should alert girls and boys to the need for child support.)

Next comes the task of collecting support payments from the absent father. The Census Bureau survey found that less than one-fourth of the mothers who had been awarded support by the court were actually receiving the full payments. Back in 1975 the federal government ordered states to establish child support enforcement offices and offered to pay 70 percent of the administrative costs (raised to 90 percent by the 1988 act). Wisconsin has taken the lead. In 1979 the state began withholding the amount of court-ordered support payment from a delinquent parent's paycheck. (The legislature also made the admission of blood tests legal in paternity cases.)

Finally, in 1987, after a four-year trial in ten counties, Wisconsin began to automatically withhold payments from all fathers' paychecks, delinquent or not, after the court had entered a support order. A mandatory schedule of payments was established: 17 percent of the father's gross income for the first child, 25 percent for two, and 34 percent for five or more. In the first year collections increased by over one-fourth. Following Wisconsin's success, Congress in 1988 adopted similar features for a mandatory schedule of payments to become effective over a six-year period.

One of the most efficient methods for collection would be to make child support part of the Social Security system. Court-ordered payments would be deducted from the paycheck along with Social Security payments. These collections would be credited to the AFDC account or, for nonwelfare mothers, forwarded directly to them.

Tactics such as these, however, will not touch fathers with no visible income. Here, again, draconian measures are required. Any able-bodied father who refuses to pay court-ordered support should be declared in contempt of court and after sufficient warning would be subject to jail on the first conviction, prison on the second. If he is unable to find a job, the welfare department or the state employment office would be instructed to find one for him. As a last resort, a public service job would be provided similar to workfare. If he refuses to take the job or give satisfactory performance, he would again be in contempt of court with jail in the offing.

Civil libertarians will cry "Debtor's prison! Jail for not paying a debt!" But our society condones prison for a man guilty of child abuse. Is not refusal to support a child one has fathered also child abuse of the most basic order? Collecting support payments in this manner would not in itself be cost-effective. But it would send a strong message to those males who now so cavalierly dismiss responsibility. It might even convince the fifteen-year-old I counseled in Louisville that he should forgo a bit of his "skin-to-skin" pleasure and wear a condom.

The problem of child support from underclass fathers is not a problem in isolation. Many of these fathers who are "just doing what comes natural" are unable to be financially responsible, even if they want to be. They are too uneducated and too unskilled to hold a job. Making them responsible involves the problems of education and job training to be discussed later. Providing them with the skills to become employed will ameliorate many welfare problems. Studies show that employed fathers are twice as likely to marry the girl they get pregnant as are the unemployed. Similarly, how far the father went in school is an important variable in whether he marries.

Timid Beginnings

Much of the program presented here is philosophically akin to the 1988 revision of the welfare laws. But because of the threat of a presidential veto, the election-eve compromise bill was so watered down that there is virtually no substantive similarity. The 1988 Welfare Reform Act may actually be counterproductive insofar as it creates the illusion that something has been done. The bill is so timid that it has little chance of breaking the cycle of dependency. Few mandatory features are included. Although the states are required to establish a Job Opportunities and Basic Skills Training Program, they were required to enroll only 7 percent of the *nonexempt* AFDC recipients (those with children under three are exempt) by 1990 and only 20 percent by 1995.

This ridiculously small number means that participants will be drawn almost entirely from the 50 percent of recipients who normally manage to leave welfare within a year or two anyway. The illiterate, unmotivated, hard-core recipients will not be even remotely involved. The bill's shortcomings are legion. Perhaps the greatest is the failure to provide a subsidy so that a welfare mother would be able to accept a minimum-wage job that nets her considerably less than her already inadequate welfare check.

A number of workfare programs sprang up after Congress in 1981 *permitted* states to require welfare recipients to participate in unpaid community service work in exchange for their monthly checks. A few of these experimental programs, when coupled with job training or help in finding a job, have been promising. The Manpower Demonstration Research Corporation, which conducts independent studies of social policy issues, looked at experimental job-training programs in four states: Arkansas, Maine, Maryland, and Virginia. The gains in employment and earnings were found to continue for at least three years and in most cases could be called cost-effective. But the success was not of a magnitude to make significant inroads into the problem of welfare dependency.

Generally the programs have been niggardly funded, most have not been mandatory, and they have applied only to women without a child under six. The hard-core have been left untouched. The most successful state program has *not* been a workfare program. This is Massachusetts' Employment and Training program, popularly called ET. Unfortunately, it became involved in the rhetoric of the 1988 presidential campaign and its merits were seriously distorted. But it has proved that a visionary investment of a substantial amount of up-front money can produce big dividends.

As is being proposed here, ET pays not only for training costs but also for the extra expenses of the trainee, including transportation and child care. The latter, necessary for the program to work, has required half of the program's budget. For up to a year after the trainee is employed, the state continues to supply child care vouchers and provide health insurance for both mother and child. These provisions make it feasible for mothers to accept entry-level, minimum-wage jobs. In 1984–85 over 23,000 former welfare recipients were placed in permanent jobs, primarily in the private sector, with the result that for every dollar invested the state showed a saving of two dollars in reduced welfare benefits and increased tax benefits.

Although ET is a highly encouraging start, it, too, is quite timid. Only the initial step of the program is compulsory, and it applies only to mothers with children over six. Nonexempt recipients are required to meet with a counselor to develop an employment plan based on identifiable skills. Available support programs are then explained, and the recipient is given the *option* of enrolling or refusing. Approximately 80 percent opt to participate.

Among ET's available components are (1) *job placement*, which includes learning to write résumés, practice in interview skills, and use of the state's computer job bank, (2) *supported work*, which is subsidized on-the-job training for those with little or no work experience, (3) *skills training*, where three to six months of specialized training is given for occupations such as office work or electronics assembly, and (4) *education*, which includes any form of education from learning English as a second language and studying for a high school equivalency diploma on up to college work at state schools.

Political critics of the program charge that the success was largely the result of Massachusetts' strong economy and low unemployment rate in the late eighties, making jobs readily available. This is partially true. But the American Friends Service Committee, which has made the only in-depth, independent analysis of the program, makes a significant point. In the six other states where unemployment rates also dropped during this period, AFDC caseloads rose. Welfare dependency continued to increase despite the improved employment picture.

In depressed areas the community and state will have to provide "made work." Call it workfare if you wish. Contrary to an elitist attitude, there is nothing wrong with creating jobs by developing public facilities and providing needed services. The parents and grandparents of many of today's affluent citizens managed to survive the Great Depression and keep their families intact because of made work in the WPA, the PWA, and for younger citizens, the

CCC. Far better that welfare be managed this way than in debilitating handouts.

THE OTHER PRONG—PROJECT EARLY START

Programs aimed at helping mothers escape from welfare will, at best, address only half of the problem. If the cycles of poverty, illiteracy, and delinquency are to be broken, massive and early attention must be directed to those children born in poverty.

In his flowery but nonsubstantive 1990 State of the Union address President Bush proclaimed that every American child must by the year 2000 start school prepared to learn, sound in body and sound in mind. Bravo! A truly visionary goal. But he offered no road map for getting there, no provisions to pay for the gasoline needed for the long, expensive journey. Instead, he offered cost-free nostrums that were an insult to those Americans who truly care about the children of the underclass. ("Read to your small children"—valuable advice to mothers who can't read.)

What Bush's goal must encompass is the second prong of the attack, Project Early Start. Here the concern is with the health care, training, intellectual stimulation, and early education needed to provide these children with the physical, mental, and emotional abilities for joining mainstream America. Will this be expensive? Yes. But as the National Alliance of Business recently declared, "Every $1 spent on early prevention and intervention can save $4.75 in remedial education, welfare and crime costs further down the road."[2]

Several stages are entailed in Project Early Start: (1) prenatal and neonatal health care, (2) developmental day-care nursery (birth to three years), (3) early-start education (ages three to five), and (4) school-based day care (ages five through twelve).

1. Prenatal and Neonatal Health Care

Some 6 million American children and adults are labeled as being retarded. Most languish in special-education classes until they finally drop out of school. Yet 80 percent have no detectable abnormality of the central nervous system. Psychologists are now discovering that for many, perhaps for most, the condition arbitrarily termed "mental retardation" is not the result of inferior or defective genes. Rather, it is often due to prenatal and neonatal malnutrition and severe sensory deprivation during the first two years of life. The mother's use of alcohol or drugs greatly compounds the potential neurological damage.

Consequently, an infant's first contact with Early Start should be while it is yet unborn.

This year some 4 million American women will have babies. Nearly one-third will receive little or no prenatal care. Others will be unscrupulously defrauded in Medicaid factories where patients are seen for as little as two minutes each. Many will not even see a doctor before being wheeled into the delivery room. One way or another society pays dearly for this lack of attention.

Investigative reporter Sonia Nazario tells in the *Wall Street Journal* of a recent Los Angeles case where frustrated doctors say a twenty-dollar penicillin shot would have wiped out the syphilis that led to the patient giving birth to a baby with cataracts, liver and heart problems, and rickets. Medical bills mounted to seventy thousand dollars before the infant finally died a month later.

Because of inadequate prenatal care and nutrition in the United States, we have higher infant mortality rates than twenty-one other industrialized nations. Our rate is even worse than that of some developing countries. As shameful as this statistic is, it is not as socially destructive as the quarter-million low-birthweight babies who manage each year to survive . . . but barely. Defined as below five and a half pounds, low-birthweight babies generally require expensive long-term, high-tech hospital care and after discharge are subject to frequent illnesses and rehospitalizations.

These problem infants strongly correlate with four factors: poverty, low educational attainment of the mother, lack of adequate prenatal care, and maternal use of alcohol and illicit drugs while pregnant. Studies are conclusive in their findings that these babies are at far greater risk of developmental, medical, and behavioral problems than are their more robust counterparts. They are, for example, three times as likely to be mentally retarded.

There is a brighter side to this story. An exciting piece of research was reported in the *Journal of the American Medical Association* of June 1990.[3] A total of 985 premature, low-birthweight infants were divided into two groups for a study done at the Albert Einstein College of Medicine in New York and in satellite programs in seven other major cities. Parents in the special intervention program met for group counseling every two weeks, and the researchers visited each home every week, providing health and developmental information as well as games and activities to stimulate the infants' cognitive and social skills. In the second and third years they were put into a developmental day-care center.

At the end of three years the children in the program had IQ scores averaging 13 points higher than the control group. (Smaller studies had shown gains of up to 16 IQ points.) This is not a minor difference but instead a major improvement destined to profoundly affect these children's future. Dr. Ruby Hern, a vice president of the Robert Woods Foundation, who conceived the study, modestly reported, "The very encouraging thing is that by intervening early and frequently we were able to make substantial differences in the children."

Despite the vast benefits to be gained by prenatal care, Congress and the administration for years foolishly indulged in penny-pinching until the fall of 1988. It remains to be seen whether the provision of the Medicare catastrophic illness legislation making more indigent women eligible for prenatal care through Medicaid will adequately address the problem. Unquestionably it is a major step forward. But early indications are that the services may not be broad enough. Many mothers-to-be have become bogged down in eligibility red tape, and many others have not been made aware of both the need for and the availability of the services. In addition, the nearly 2 million children with mothers working full-time but living below the poverty line may fall through the cracks and continue without any form of health insurance after age one.

The state of Washington in January 1989 began a five-year pilot project to determine if a state can and should provide low-cost health insurance to families whose income is below *double* the poverty level. Based on a sliding scale, some thirty thousand Washingtonians will pay from $7.50 to $38.00 a month for the costs of health care. New Jersey in 1990 also decided to offer on a generous sliding-scale fee a full range of prenatal health services to every pregnant woman.

In the Scandinavian countries, where infant mortality is among the lowest in the world, health insurance automatically covers all citizens. A nurse begins visits to each home at least two months before the birth and continues as needed after delivery. Yet such assistance is not needed in these literate countries nearly as much as among America's underclass. Programs such as one in Elmira, New York, have demonstrated the spectacular health gains that can be made by the babies of fourteen- to sixteen-year-old indigent mothers-to-be who received twice-monthly home visits from a child development nurse.

2. Developmental Day-Care Nursery, Birth to Three Years

Back in 1971 Congress passed a child care bill that with the strong backing of President Nixon had been proposed by Dr. Edward Zigler, then the director of HEW's Office of Child Development and a principal architect of the Head Start program. The intent was to provide child care for mothers getting off welfare and going to work. But Nixon was inundated with mail from the evangelicals and the far right charging that the bill would "Sovietize" American children by raising them in state-controlled centers rather than at home with their mothers. So Nixon capitulated and vetoed the bill, calling it the "most radical piece of legislation" to come out of the Ninety-second Congress.

And for the next twenty years the lack of child care has continued to shackle many to the welfare system.

But times change. As more and more middle-class mothers have entered the work force, readily available, quality day care has become a visible major need. Child care has become big, big business. One consultant to venture capitalists advised that in some areas the need is so severe, "you can do anything and make money." On the eve of the 1988 elections, to show the people back home that they were listening, congressmen feverishly introduced over seventy child care bills.

It is estimated that today there are over seventy thousand for-profit day-care centers in the United States, with the number increasing daily. Inadequate and often poorly enforced state regulations have permitted undesirable and dangerous conditions to exist. Frequently, unqualified, underpaid, and overworked employees supply the care. In the fall of 1987 America poured out its heart to little Jessica Mc-Clure as television cameras captured townsmen in Midland, Texas, working around the clock for days to rescue her from the narrow well into which she had fallen. But scant attention was paid to the fact that Jessica's accident occurred while she was in an unregulated, unlicensed child care facility. Attempts to get Congress to mandate minimum standards, such as a maximum of three infants per adult worker, have regularly failed. Only Kansas, Massachusetts, and Maryland meet this standard.

Generally speaking, the poorer the mother, the poorer the quality of care she is able to obtain. It is yet another force widening the gap between the haves and the have-nots.

Despite the overwhelming need for quality child care among all classes, our primary concern here is helping welfare mothers break the cycle of dependency. Echoing the words of Dr. Zigler eighteen years ago, Senator Christopher Dodd maintains that the major reason people do not get off welfare and go to work is the absence of any kind of child care program. But the need is far more inclusive than mere baby-sitting.

Developmental psychologists maintain that the first two years are the most critical in the whole learning process. This period is particularly vital to children of the underclass who too often exist in a mind-starving environment. Congresswoman Pat Schroeder, long a proponent of using child care time as an educational opportunity, suggests that the average child learns more from birth through three than even Einstein learned in the remainder of his life after three. Yet in this country, she charges, we pay more to the people who watch our cars in a parking lot than we do to those who watch our children.

In the proposal here, AFDC recipients continuing their education in the public school's program for teenage mothers would bring their infants to the school's nursery (see Chapter 13 on alternative schools). Others beginning a skills-training program or a job would take their children to a developmental day-care center. At both the real agenda is not baby-sitting, per se. Rather, it is to provide the intellectual stimulation and physical care so often absent in the homes of the underclass. Additionally, the infant's nutritional needs would be met with proper meals as required. When the enrollment includes children from homes where English is seldom or never spoken, the staff would help them become bilingual.

Depending on the state or local preference, the center could be run by a fully funded, quasi-public agency (similar to the public schools), or the mother could be given a voucher to be used at a privately operated, *state-licensed, and carefully monitored center.* As previously suggested, the developmental center should be available free to working or student mothers as long as they are drawing AFDC, *and* after they have obtained a job until their income reaches 140 percent of the federal poverty level. After that the fee would be based on ability to pay.

The efficacy of such a program of early intervention has long been proven. Back in the seventies, two psychologists, Rick Heber and Howard Garber of the University of Wisconsin, suspected that part of the reason retarded mothers were likely to have retarded children was not defective genes but the conditions under which the children were raised. From a ghetto of Milwaukee they recruited retarded mothers with newborn babies. Twenty were randomly assigned to an experimental group and twenty to a control group.

For the experimental group, the retarded mothers were taught homemaking and infant care skills. When they were three months old the babies were picked up each morning and taken to the Infant Education Center where they were bathed, fed, and taught by "stimulation teachers." At four in the afternoon they were returned home. When the children were one the program changed to more typical nursery school activities. The Center continued to work with the mothers in effective child care techniques. Five years later at kindergarten age the children in the program had an average IQ 30 points higher than the control group.

No, mental retardation is not always genetic.

Techniques for improving the future of underprivileged children are well known to developmental psychologists and educational specialists. Over the years dozens upon dozens of projects have been funded to design and test various models. Many have proved highly effective. But the grant money dries up and that is the end. The findings are buried in a scholarly journal. Money to replicate the model in other communities is seldom found.

The developmental day-care nursery program proposed here goes infinitely beyond President Bush's vote-getting proposal to give up to a thousand dollars to all poor mothers of young children, regardless of whether they are working or in school or watching TV all day. Intended for child care, the money could be used for anything—beer or crack or to entertain a boyfriend. It would not make possible the purchase of even moderately adequate child care, which usually costs a minimum of three thousand dollars a year. At best it would purchase baby-sitting from a neighbor or relative who likewise would probably be unqualified to provide the intellectual stimulation necessary to equip the child to escape the ghetto.

Any child care planning today must address the problem of children exposed prenatally to crack. This threatens to be one of the most intractable problems facing the health care and educational systems in the present decade. A researcher in the problems of crack-exposed infants, Dr. Judy Howard at the University of California at Los Angeles, warns that within the next few years these children will make up from 40 to 60 percent of the enrollment in some inner-city elementary classrooms.

While the degree of brain damage is on a wide continuum, many crack babies are virtually unmanageable, being subject to seizures, violent temper tantrums, and mental retardation. Pilot programs have shown that intensive *and expensive* care can help these children lead normal, or almost normal, lives. But it is essential that the therapeutic attention begin early—from the day of birth. For these the developmental day-care centers will be an absolute necessity. High-risk areas will require centers solely to deal with this problem.

3. Early-Start Education, Ages Three to Five

For three- and four-year-old children, the proposed program would be day care with a purpose, a continuation of the developmental nursery program for infants birth through two. Games to promote mental and physical stimulation would be emphasized, along with experiences (videotapes, records, being read to, and trips) for cultural enrichment. Children as young as three can be introduced to the magic of computers, which can then help them build sorting, matching, counting, and prereading skills—skills that most middle-class parents normally teach.

A leading spokesman for programs to help break the cycles of poverty, illiteracy, and delinquency is the same Dr. Zigler who was one of the architects of Head Start and of President Nixon's vetoed child care bill. He founded the Yale University Center in Child Development and Social Policy and from there he shuttles back and forth to Washington to plead the cause of underprivileged children.

Dr. Zigler insists that in middle-class areas there is little, if anything, to be gained by exposing children under five to formal education. However, in low-income-area schools (the ones of greatest concern here) activities for three- and four-year-olds need to be similar to those used in Head Start and the Ypsilanti (Michigan) Perry Preschool Project. Overall, young adults who as children participated in Head Start have shown fewer adolescent problems, higher educational achievement, and less unemployment than their peers who did not have this experience.

The most convincing evidence has been developed by the Perry Preschool Project, one of the most carefully documented research projects dealing with this age group ever undertaken. For twenty-four years it followed the lives of 123 disadvantaged black children. They were selected in 1962 at ages three and four from an impoverished school district. Half were randomly assigned to the control group, the others to a culturally enriched early-education program. For two years the latter attended a two-and-a-half-hour preschool class five mornings a week. Teachers also visited each home for ninety minutes a week to help the mother learn parenting skills.

The program showed immediate results, but the most significant gains were in the long-term effects. A comparison of the two groups made when they were nineteen found that:

- Less than half as many of the experimental preschool group had at some time during their school years been classified as mentally retarded; thus, they required less time in more expensive special-education classes.
- Two out of three of the preschool group (67 percent) graduated from high school, compared to one out of two (49 percent) of the control group.
- Nearly twice as many of the experimentals continued their education after high school—38 percent versus 21 percent of the control group.
- The teenage pregnancy rate for the experimentals was 64 per 100. Because of multiple pregnancies the control group rate was twice as high, 117 per 100.
- At age nineteen about half as many of the preschool group were receiving welfare assistance—18 percent versus 32 percent.
- And as for crime and delinquency, the preschool group were less likely to have been arrested (31 percent compared to 51 percent), and they were arrested for the second time less than half as often.

Almost identical results were obtained in the 1960s by a five-year New York City project conducted by the Institute for Developmental Studies. Clearly, quality early education will help disadvantaged children overcome later problems—and will pay off to society in dollars and cents.

Today over half of all middle-class families have their three-year olds in preschool programs. But only a small fraction of the children of the underclass are receiving this training. Yet it is these latter who most desperately need the help. Thus, we see the gap between the advantaged and the disadvantaged continuing to spread, helping to create the crime bomb just waiting to explode.

The proposal to allocate an additional $500 million to the Head Start program was one of the few bright spots in President Bush's educational agenda speech. But that represented only a 27 percent budget increase and will fall far short of Bush's claim to make Head Start available to 70 percent of the 2.5 million who are eligible. While the program now reaches one out of five of these children, the proposed additional funds would raise the ratio only to one in four.

Top executives in the National Alliance of Business have since lobbied Congress to appropriate far more in order to provide an enriched program to service all low-income children. The Ford Foundation's project Social Welfare and the American Future has calculated that it will require at least an additional $2 billion to reach 80 percent of those desperately needing the early educational help.

Nevertheless, Bush's program is indeed a hopeful start.

New York City made a promising start in 1986 under Mayor Edward Koch with Project Giant Step, designed to provide a comprehensive half-day, preschool program for four-year olds from low-income families. Building on Head Start strategies of learning through constructive play, the project adds more staff training and a larger parent component. The family worker helps mothers obtain food stamps, assists in plans to get the child from the Giant Step location to afternoon day-care programs, and visits in the home. In addition, workshops are conducted on family planning, nutrition, and drugs.

A preliminary evaluation study with a sample from the nearly seven thousand participants indicates that the children may be showing as much as twice the cognitive gain of similar early-education programs. It is hoped that instead of becoming bogged down in New York City politics and inadequate funding, it will be able to expand to all disadvantaged children.

4. School-based Day Care, Ages Three Through Twelve

One of our seldom publicized scandals is that we permit upward of 5 million latchkey children, youngsters aged five and up, to return from school each day to empty homes. Unsupervised by adults, these children—crossing all social, ethnic, and economic lines—learn early the lure of delinquency, drugs, and promiscuous sex. A study of eight thousand eighth-grade students in Los Angeles and San Diego found that latchkey kids who spend more than ten hours a week on their own are twice as likely to smoke and use alcohol and marijuana.

Among one-parent families where the mother works at a minimum-wage job, the possibility of the occurrence of such problems is particularly high.

Of many proposals, the one showing the greatest promise in both quality and economy is the use of elementary school buildings for a dual function—formal education for part of the day, a child care center before and after school hours. The late Richard R. Green while chancellor of the New York City schools saw such programs as part of the modern mission of the public schools—schools that would even serve as surrogate parents when needed. "I see schools," he said, "as places that feed children, educate their parents, and provide early childhood education."

Again the principal architect and spokesman for this approach is Dr. Zigler. He would make neighborhood schools the nation's principal child care providers for children from three to twelve. Along with after-school care for elementary-school-aged children, the public schools would also provide half-day care for the three- and four-year-olds attending the proposed Early Start programs. Care would be provided by trained child care aides under the supervision of developmental psychologists. A few successful experimental programs in school facilities are already to be found throughout the nation.

In Louisville the Childcare Enrichment Program, a joint effort of the YMCA and the public school system, is in its fourth year. A safe, supervised environment is provided for both public and nonpublic school students at fourteen convenient school sites. Morning sessions are held before school from 7:00 to 9:00 A.M. and in the afternoons from 2:00 to 6:00 P.M. All-day care is offered during the summer and on days when schools are not open because of bad weather or vacations. Weekly fees, based on the family's ability to pay, cover transportation, breakfast, snacks, and tutoring. A wide variety of enrichment programs (drama, art, gymnastics, and dance) and field trips are scheduled with the cooperation of community agencies.

Unfortunately, most of the experimental projects have not addressed the need for day care for preschoolers.

Funding for the programs proposed here would come from three sources: local taxes, as the schools are currently funded; state and federal subsidies; and sliding-scale fees to parents based on ability to pay. Fees for mothers in one of the escape-from-poverty programs would be paid by AFDC until such time as their private sector jobs qualified them for the fees charged other parents. Since otherwise empty facilities would be used, a large capital investment would not be required.

A substantial federal subsidy would probably be needed in most states as the carrot to encourage matching funds at the state and local levels. But the amount needed probably would not be any more (and might be less) than the $3.7 billion now being spent on the present Dependent Care Tax Credit Program. This provides nonrefundable tax credits of up to $1,440 to parents of children under fifteen. Since income taxes are no problem for AFDC mothers and others struggling with a minimum-wage job, this tax credit is basically a subsidy of middle-class women who choose to have a second income for the family. It is highly discriminatory in that it is of no assistance in helping the poor meet their need for child care, a need that for them is far more severe than for those more fortunate.

As evidence of the need for and the popular appeal of the concept, some states and localities have grown weary of congressional waffling and have acted on their own. Indiana has just passed a half-cent cigarette tax to provide before-and-after-school care for all children. A $5-million bond issue in Seattle will permit the opening of sixteen centers at elementary schools to serve underprivileged infants and preschool children.

The two-pronged program proposed here—education, job training, and job procurement for the teenage mother and Project Early Start for her child—will go far in breaking the cycle of poverty and dependency. But . . .

I can already hear the loud wails of protest coming from two different groups. One is from fiscal conservatives concerned about the cost of such expensive programs for all those second-class people who really don't matter much anyway. The other equally loud protest is from civil libertarians who see the face of Big Brother hovering over the proposals.

The first should be dismissed as short-range, tunnel vision coming from those who resent spending pennies today to save dollars years down the road. The expenditures should be considered investing, not spending. The second protest needs to be taken more seriously. In defense of the program, it should be reiterated that a mother would not be forced against her will to participate. She always has the freedom of choice not to apply for welfare and thus to be exempt from the requirements. She may seek other means of support—her boyfriend, her family, private charities—or even go to work.

Admittedly there is some danger of Big Brotherism in the day-care centers. But actually this danger is little different from the danger inherent in the whole concept of public education. Both are given the same mandate—to provide the best training possible to help the individual achieve a personally rewarding and a socially and economically productive life. If this is achieved society is the big winner. And the people of America will be in far less danger from the future violence of embittered juveniles.

Chapter 11

INTERVENTION AT AN EARLY AGE: THE CHILD DEVELOPMENT SERVICES SYSTEM

Observe carefully children in the early grades of almost any elementary school in America. A discerning eye will quickly spot a few who don't seem to fit in—who somehow seem to be different in social behavior or learning abilities. In kindergarten, for example, there's Paul, who walks over to the table where four of his classmates are building a castle with blocks. He watches for a moment and then reaches over, knocks the blocks down, and saunters off. Next he goes over to a girl who is looking at a book and yanks it from her. He carries it away and sits down. After turning a few pages, he tosses it aside and again wanders around the room. Later when the teacher reads to his group, he sits fidgeting for a few minutes, then gets up and goes to look out the window.

In contrast, Marie sits listlessly while the teacher reads to her group. Her eyes are glazed and she shows no evidence of hearing the teacher. Out on the playground she sits down on a box in the shade and, unmoving, stares down at the ground. The teacher wonders if she is seriously retarded.

In the first grade there is Malcolm, who, to the teacher's despair, seems continually to need help—help to tie his shoelaces, to put on his jacket at recess, to get the coloring pencils back in the box, to find the right page in the workbook. By himself he never gets started on the assigned task. And there is Ralph, who, unlike most in the room, hasn't started to read, hasn't even learned his ABCs or numbers. He seldom raises his hand to answer a question because he "knows" he'll be wrong. Instead of trying to do his work, he now frequently tries to disrupt those who are working.

Billy, in the second grade, tries but just can't follow instructions, gets confused between right and left, even up and down. Earlier when the teacher told the pupils to put their papers in the box on her desk, he put his under the box. When shown a 9 he's as likely to call it a 6 as a 9, and he can't tell the difference between a *d* and a *b*. His friend Rickie, although apparently bright enough, has been absent so frequently that he's getting far behind and is losing interest.

Although their problems differ, these children have one thing in common. All have front seats on the bus to failure. By the time they reach the sixth grade, the most significant thing they will have learned is how to fail. And as they fall further and further behind, their frustration and bitterness will steadily mount to the explosion point. Dropping out—and very likely delinquency—looms in their future.

Increasingly, developmental psychologists are emphasizing the importance of early attention to behavioral difficulties in children. Johns Hopkins University, for example, has recently established the Prevention Research Center to examine these problems. The Center grew out of studies indicating that much teenage and adult abuse of drugs and alcohol, psychopathology, and delinquency stem from patterns of behavior and performance that can be recognized in the earliest days of school. Even easily observed behaviors such as excessive absences are warning signals, because those who later quit school had, on the average, twice as many days out of school in the primary grades as those who go on to graduate.

Rationale for a School-based Prevention Program

The first part of this book provided a litany of failure: failure of rehabilitation, failure of programs for prevention, failure of the schools to reach nonachieving and underachieving students. A panoramic view of these failures suggests a number of factors that should be considered:

1. *Any unmet need, any unresolved problem, can trigger unacceptable behavior that in time may evolve into delinquency.* A

child is not born "bad" but rather becomes that way in response to something that happens or fails to happen to him. Hope revolves around uncovering that something.

2. *Once a child has fallen into a pattern of academic failure, escape is virtually impossible.* Getting behind in the first or second grade builds upon itself, becoming more severe each year until truancy and dropping out are the end products.

3. *Most preventative and rehabilitative efforts are initiated far too late in the individual's life.* Despite our recognition of the pervasive influence of early childhood development, most programs—dropout prevention, remedial education, and so on—are basically "after the fact," after attitudes and behavior patterns have become firmly crystallized.

4. *Because of the need for early intervention, schools offer the most promising focus for efforts to prevent juvenile delinquency.* The school system is the one social agency that reaches all children at an early age. With their daily contact teachers can become an early warning system for evidence of child abuse, both physical and psychological. They can spot developmental difficulties—behavioral, learning, physical—before they escalate and become firmly established.

5. *The problem child cannot be treated in a vacuum, for the difficulties are a reflection of the total environment.* The amelioration of these difficulties may involve improvement in the family, the school, or the community. Because the school reaches all children, it is in a position to coordinate the fragmented services of many community agencies and civic organizations. Thus, it could help to eliminate duplicate and sometimes conflicting efforts and, even more important, see that the proper services are obtained when needed.

6. *Identification of a "problem child" most often also identifies a "problem family."* Any help or social intervention in the family to benefit one child may also benefit younger siblings and even those as yet unborn.

CDSS to the Rescue

These six concepts are the basis for the proposal to establish a Child Development Services System (CDSS) in kindergarten and the first and second grades of the public schools. Stated very concisely, the proposal calls for *the early identification of children with problems and the delivery of services to solve or ameliorate those problems before they pyramid and crystallize into deep-seated behavioral patterns.*

It must be emphasized and reemphasized that CDSS is not for the identification of delinquents, predelinquents, or potential delinquents. To permit such an unreliable and improper tag to be placed on a child singled out for help would become a self-fulfilling prophecy. It would be self-defeating. Instead, the concern is simply for those children who have a problem—any problem—that may be correctable.

Problems may be identified under four broad categories: (1) *medical* (including dental problems and malnutrition), (2) *behavioral* (aggressiveness, refusal to follow rules, and withdrawal), (3) *social* (family problems, cultural deprivation, and so on), and (4) *educational* (falling behind or inability to learn).

Difficulties related to any of these categories if left uncorrected can lead to academic underachievement, frustration, dropping out, social alienation, unemployability, and delinquency. In time an observed, correctable behavior may become disassociated from the original cause, taking on a more serious dimension. The need for glasses, for example, may be the cause of school failure which in turn may cause acting-out behavior, low self-esteem, and delinquency.

(Because of the importance of CDSS as an action program to reduce delinquency, considerably more detail is provided here than for many of the other proposals being made. Furthermore, it should be recognized that the results will not be apparent overnight. It will require a large expenditure of up-front money for as long as eight years before the payoff for early intervention will be evident. Only then can we expect a major decline in crime and an interruption in the cycles of poverty and illiteracy.

All of the money, however, need not be "new" appropriations. Much can be a reallocation of funds now being ineffectively used. For example, with an enlightened role for the juvenile court [to be proposed later], many of the social service workers now in the juvenile court could best be utilized in the school-based program. In the school system itself, many special-education teachers can be reassigned to CDSS because the early delivery of services will permit many youths to remain in regular classrooms. [Remember the youth labeled mentally retarded because he needed glasses?] Also, it may be possible to reallocate some monies and/or services of community resources, such as departments of public and mental health.)

Entry of a child into the system would be initiated by the kindergarten, first-, or second-grade teacher who observes some problem or is experiencing some difficulty with the child—virtually anything. At this stage the cause may be unknown. Frequent absenteeism, for example, could be due to the poor health of the child or of a parent, malnutrition, economic needs, lack of parental motivation, family instability due to drugs or alcohol, dislike of school, or fear of a teacher of a different race.

The teacher would submit a detailed written statement of the problem to the principal. After ascertaining the legitimacy of the need, the principal would then turn the case over to the child development coordinator, an individual with training in social service casework. As the child's advocate, the coordinator is the linchpin in the success of the entire program.

After consulting with the classroom teacher, the coordinator would visit the home for background information and solicit the parents' assistance and their permission to have the child tested. He or she would also determine whether the family is involved with other social service agencies that should participate. Next she would schedule tests by the diagnostic team.

The Diagnostic Process

The diagnostic team and the members' functions would be:

1. A *registered nurse* who screens for indications of health problems that might be a contributing factor in the child's difficulties. This includes the need for glasses, hearing aids, or dental care. Particular attention must be paid to evidence of child abuse. The nurse also determines whether medical tests should be done by the public health department or a private doctor.
2. A *clinical psychologist* who is concerned with behavioral problems and indications of neurological dysfunction. The possibility of emotional child abuse must be considered. The psychologist also heads up and supervises the training of the primary mental health team to be considered later.
3. An *educational diagnostician* who seeks to determine whether special tutoring is required and whether any learning disability

exists. The diagnostician decides upon the most appropriate corrective measures. Additionally, she works with the classroom and/or learning center teachers in carrying out the educational prescription.

While each elementary school would have one or more child development coordinators, the diagnostic team could serve a number of schools or, in some cases, the entire school system.

After all test results are available, including any outside professional tests and examinations, a *staffing conference* would be held. Attending would be the child development coordinator with his or her report on family conditions, the classroom teacher, members of the diagnostic team, and one or both parents. At this conference it would be determined what therapeutic action was indicated.

HEALTH SERVICES

The first concern would be health-related problems, which have consistently been shown to be a major cause of academic failure and, thus, later on to correlate with delinquency.

It would be absurd, for example, to embark on an extensive remedial-education program when the problem was simply that the child could not hear the teacher or see the blackboard. In Louisville a first-grader's unsatisfactory work magically improved after a nurse discovered a bean lodged deep in her ear. A child suffering from low energy levels, headaches, or other maladies may have difficulty in concentrating. Malnutrition should be considered. Studies in England suggest that the intelligence level of children who receive improperly balanced meals may be improved in just nine months by the addition of a multivitamin and mineral supplement. And excessive absences caused by ill health severely handicap even the brightest child.

CDSS would not deliver or pay for needed medical attention. But the coordinator would arrange for the services. Available means for payment would be utilized: family insurance, public health departments, Medicaid, public charities, medical school clinics, and in some instances, volunteer contribution of their time by doctors. Community service clubs frequently are willing to pay for hearing aids, glasses, and orthopedic equipment.

BEHAVIORAL PROBLEMS

Children needing psychological services would be identified by the diagnostic team. There are the shy, withdrawn youngsters as well as those so self-centered they are unable to make friends. And there is the first-grade bully, quick to start a fight. Psychologists have long believed that he is suffering from deep-seated feelings of inferiority and inadequacy; to compensate he attempts to dominate those around him. If undertaken early enough, minor interventions can often reduce these problems.

As many as 20 percent of first-grade males may exhibit some potentially damaging maladjustment. Studies consistently show that these early antisocial behaviors are frequently (but not always!) precursors of delinquency. Furthermore, highly aggressive elementary school boys are three times as likely as their nonaggressive classmates to show up later in juvenile court. In a high-crime area of New York City researchers found that three out of five of a group of seriously and/or habitually delinquent boys had been reported as having behavioral problems by their first-grade teacher.[1]

Because of the dangers of false labeling, it would be counterproductive to tag all maladjusted first-graders as predelinquent. But the correlation with delinquency and other later mental health problems is so powerful that high priority should be given to uncovering the reason for early behavioral difficulties, particularly undue aggressiveness. These children, predominantly boys, get into frequent fights because they are unable to control their anger. Others overreact to slights, teasing, and what they perceive as unfairness.

There are encouraging reports of success in teaching young aggressors how to handle their anger. Dr. Ronald Prinz, a psychologist at the University of South Carolina, believes that a boy's unruliness is learned behavior and, thus, can be unlearned. He works with parents of boys four to nine years old who are in danger of being kicked out of school. The frustrated parents have fallen into a pattern of spiraling anger and violent threats. They attempt to obtain obedience by destructive criticism and humiliation of the child.

Dr. Prinz first has the parents document the specific behavior that they want changed—lying, disobedience, stealing. Then the parents are taught a series of steps to take when this behavior occurs. The first is to make a clear request such as "Come to dinner." If the child complies he is praised for his good behavior; if he refuses he is given a calm warning of the penalty for continued disobedience. This might be the requirement to sit in a "time-out chair" for a specific period. Finally, if the warning doesn't work the penalty is actually carried out. Although this very simple process is regularly used by most parents, Dr. Prinz says that it is totally foreign to the parents who are referred to him.[2]

The fact must be faced, however, that it is a futile exercise in daydreaming to propose long-term professional psychological help for every elementary-grade child and its parents manifesting some abnormal behavior. There is no conceivable way a prevention program could obtain sufficient funds to carry it out—even if enough professionals were available, which is not the case. But because of the potential value of such help, a compromise must be made.

This compromise is to model the psychological component after the Primary Mental Health Project (PMHP), originally established nearly thirty years ago in the Rochester, New York, schools for children in kindergarten to third grade exhibiting moderate to serious school adjustment problems.[3] Overseen by psychologists at the University of Rochester, the program has demonstrated such great positive values that similar programs have been established in many schools across the country.

The key to PMHP is its use of carefully selected, *specially trained* paraprofessionals under the supervision of school mental health professionals. (Under the CDSS proposal this supervision would be done by the diagnostic team psychologist or in larger districts by a full-time professional.) These paraprofessionals (to be called child aides in CDSS) meet with problem children individually and in small groups at school as often and for as long as needed to effect a change.

Paraprofessionals in the PMHP programs have been successful—*and cost-effective.* By concentrating on early intervention and by using available professionals primarily to train nonprofessionals for specific tasks, the limited mental health resources of the community can effectively meet the needs of a much larger population.

Perhaps the most encouraging fact is that a 1984 study of PMHP students showed that the gains achieved are maintained for years after leaving the program. Samples of students who were seen two to five years earlier by PMHP for at least three months were drawn from three racially mixed urban schools. Assessments were made by the current teachers, by parents, by self-reporting tests, and by Metropolitan Achievement Test scores. The results were reasonably clear-cut. Not only had the gains been maintained, for several key criteria they had continued to increase.[4]

While the psychological component of CDSS would be carefully modeled after PMHP, any child whom the diagnostic team believed to be too maladjusted to be handled by the paraprofessional staff would be referred to a community mental health clinic.

SOCIAL PROBLEMS

No matter how inadequate a family may be, it will remain—for better or worse—the child's primary socializing agent. Frequently the most effective way to save a child is to first save the family. Potential family-related problems are manifold. Insufficient income may result in inadequate nutrition and health care for the child. Alcoholism, drug abuse, or the mental instability of one or both parents may be at the root of the child's problem. Many families of CDSS children would need counseling in marital difficulties, in the budgeting of money, in family planning, in health and sanitation, in legal difficulties with the landlord, or in dealing with a father who refuses to make child care payments.

CDSS would not duplicate existing social service agencies in the community. Through referrals it would depend on these and also volunteer organizations (everything from Alcoholics Anonymous to Big Brothers). Again, the child development coordinator would be responsible for seeing that the services are provided. In this role, he or she becomes an unofficial social services coordinator for the entire community, mobilizing the available resources at a critical period in the child's life.

A promising proposal from a state political arena was made in California by U.S. Senator Pete Wilson in his campaign for governor last fall. Recognizing that schools monitor all children, his first major policy proposal called for the integration of all social welfare services with the public schools. He pointed out that in California there are 160 state programs for children, administered by 45 different agencies. The result frequently is administrative chaos: many children fail to receive needed services, and duplicated and frequently competitive efforts lead to vast bureaucratic waste.

Senator Wilson proposed to make the schools a sort of social service brokering agency, as is being proposed here. By doing so he seeks to put more emphasis on prevention and less on reacting to the human disasters that occur when the needs of children have not been met.

Parents' School

Socialization of the child suffers when the parent fails to monitor the child's behavior, fails to provide proper discipline and rewards, fails to display adequate love and concern. "Remedial parenting" is necessary if CDSS is to reach its full potential.

Admittedly, many parents of children at greatest risk are difficult to deal with, recalcitrant, often bitter and unduly suspicious. But so critical is home environment that to ignore the family would be a tragic cop-out. Despite many shortcomings, these parents almost invariably want their children to succeed—"to have a better life than I've had." Their failure to supply the necessary support comes more from ignorance than from indifference.

Experience with parent education in Head Start and similar programs has shown that parents in impoverished areas are reluctant to attend formal meetings and when pressured to attend are too embarrassed to participate. Thus, in the first weeks after the CDSS staff had begun working with a child, a major thrust of the parent education component would be for a parent aide to go into the home and counsel the mother on a one-to-one basis.

This parent training might be modeled on the work of the Oregon Social Learning Center (to be discussed briefly in Chapter 19, on the constructive use of punishment). There the staff has been working with parents of children who fail to learn at school because of inattentiveness, children who are unduly aggressive, and those who manifest other disruptive and antisocial behavior. Eliminating patterns of deviant behavior in very young children has proved far easier than trying to rehabilitate older delinquents.

While significant progress has been made with as little as four hours of therapy, the average time for successfully teaching a parent how to monitor and change a child's undesirable behavior has been seventeen hours. A primary approach has been to persuade the parent to set firm limits for the child and to follow through with mild punishment (for example, being required to sit quietly for five minutes) when those limits are violated.

After the parent aide had established some rapport, the parent would be encouraged—enticed by whatever means available, even paid—to attend group classes at the Parents' School. Meetings could be made into social occasions with inexpensive refreshments and door prizes. These meetings would be scheduled at whatever time was determined to be most convenient in the community—afternoons, evenings, Saturdays, Sunday afternoons. It is essential that the budget of the school provide for "scholarships" for those needing help for carfare or baby-sitting expenses.

The school would rely heavily on volunteer professional help for programs in specific subject areas. Possible instructional programs might include:

Nonphysical Discipline
Building a Child's Self-Esteem
Health and Nutrition
Hygiene in the Home
Home Learning Experiences
Encouraging, Not Pressuring the Child
Safety in the Home
Home Economics
Family Planning

While the home visits of the psychological staff would be limited to parents of CDSS children, the Parents' School programs and meetings would be open to parents of all children attending the school.

Programs for family support as suggested here are not new. Many experimental programs have successfully operated on a smaller scale. One such program worth considering is the very successful Children's House program developed by the Yale Child Study Center.[5] This program has included home visits to help the mother with budget and nutritional problems and assistance in obtaining needed social services.

Child Abuse

Chapter 6, dealing with status offenders, painfully detailed the critical role that child abuse plays in the making of a delinquent and eventually an emotionally disturbed adult. We met many of these victims of child abuse existing on the city streets—runaways, throwaways, pushouts—children who managed to survive by selling their bodies, hustling drugs, shoplifting. In the much-needed war on child abusers CDSS would be on the first line of attack. No agency or group is so well situated as the school system to identify so many victims.

Yet, amazingly, most go undetected—or unreported—by school personnel.

(This failure was opened to public scrutiny recently with the death of six-year-old Lisa Steinberg, who attended a Greenwich Village [New York City] public school. A report by the city's board of education noted that before she was beaten to death, "Lisa's disheveled appearance [hair, fingernails and clothing]" had been observed by at least eight school personnel, and bruises on her face, forearms, and back had been seen by at least five of them. Yet despite a regulation that all child abuse cases be reported to the board's inspector general, no one did so.)

It will be noted that at each step of the diagnostic and remediation process, CDSS workers would be alerted to watch for physical signs of possible abuse or neglect. Furthermore, both the nurse and the psychologist on the diagnostic team would be trained to ask a series of medical and nonmedical questions designed to cover abuse that the child may be reluctant to reveal.

In many instances, the CDSS staff would be able to intervene with educational and psychological services for the parents. As many as 60 percent of child abusers can be encouraged to accept help in overcoming their hostile attitudes and behavior. The majority of these maltreating parents suffer from poverty-related problems rather than emotional disturbance. With many the CDSS staff could give short-term counseling and parent training in the home, arrange for homemaker services for ill or disabled parents, and contact social service agencies when needed. More serious cases would be referred to community mental health centers. At other times it would be necessary for CDSS to call on the protective services of the court.

LEARNING PROBLEMS

Because learning failure builds upon itself, becoming more critical each day, week, or year the failure is permitted to continue, the remedial-education component of CDSS may be the program's most important feature. It would provide special tutoring to normal children who have temporarily fallen behind because of unavoidable absences, and offer compensatory help to those who have entered school with social or cultural deficiencies.

These functions alone are sufficient justification for CDSS, but the diagnostic team would also be alert to far more critical individual learning problems. When appropriate an "educational prescription" would be written. In a Project Extra Help lab a remedial-education specialist, assisted by one or more paraprofessionals, would carry out the therapy indicated in the prescription. In many districts it might be possible to enlist volunteers to assist in this individualized tutoring effort. Most prescriptions would call for an hour a day after school for specific training. For those needing it, the lab would also be open on Saturday mornings.

Teachers and the diagnostic team would be particularly alert to reading difficulties indicating that the slow learner was suffering from one of a number of problems very loosely grouped under the term "specific learning disabilities." These are the children who for some reason have been born with a neurological defect whereby sensory messages become scrambled in the brain. It is difficult for them to learn, particularly reading and math. Most of the children we met at the beginning of the chapter may have had some form of this disability—definitely Billy, who confused right and left and letters like *d* and *b*.

The close link between learning disabilities and delinquency is indisputable. Delinquents are some ten times more likely to be suffering from a learning disability than are juveniles in the general population. According to various studies, the disorder is manifested by 30 to 50 percent of all youths appearing in juvenile court.

Recently the Foundation for Children with Learning Disabilities has been conducting a pilot study in the Brooklyn family court. Results show that 40 percent of the juveniles seen there have learning disabilities and either were failing in school or had dropped out. The majority had engaged in antisocial and criminal behavior ranging from robbery to drug-related murder. Among adult prisoners in the city the condition has been found to be even more prominent, with an estimated 60 percent suffering from such disabilities.

This difference indicates that whereas most delinquents outgrow their delinquent ways, many suffering from uncompensated learning disabilities do not. They more readily become adult criminals.

So strong is the correlation that one is tempted to single it out as the leading cause of delinquency. It is not, however, the disability itself that results in delinquency but rather the academic failure and low self-esteem it precipitates. The learning-disabled child, ridiculed and shunned by his peers, will often pay any price for acceptance, and if this includes the use of drugs or other antisocial activity, the price seems small enough. Later when he (most are boys) becomes a continual failure, all the dynamics in the making of a delinquent come into play.

In passing the Education for All Handicapped Children Act of 1975 Congress gave this definition of children with specific learning disabilities:

> . . . those children who have a disorder in one or more of the basic psychological processes involved in understanding or in using language, spoken or written, which disorder may manifest itself in the imperfect ability to listen, think, speak, write, spell or do mathematical calculations. Such disorders include such conditions as perceptual handicaps, brain-injury, minimal brain dysfunction, dyslexia, and developmental aphasia. Such term does not include children who have learning problems which are primarily the result of visual, hearing, or motor handicaps of mental retardation, of emotional disturbances, or environmental, cultural, or economic disadvantage.

Estimates of the number of learning-disabled children in the general population range from 2 to 12 percent, depending upon the rigidity of the definition used. This would mean that the average classroom contains between one and four such children.

Even today when much is known about these neurological disorders, most go undiagnosed. A learning disability is *not* a sign of mental retardation. An abnormally large percentage of these youths is in the genius levels. Yet the victims are often seen as those "not very bright" students who are always behind. In time they may be placed in inappropriate special-education classes for the mentally retarded. Sadly, in most instances the problem could have been overcome or compensated for had it been spotted and diagnosed early enough— spotted before the failure pyramided and the frustrated youth gave up.

Remedial efforts in CDSS would be aimed primarily at three treatable categories of disorders. As identified by Dr. Melvin D. Levine[6] of the Harvard Medical School these are:

1. Information-processing deficits, most commonly called dyslexia. Dyslexics may be unable to perceive the shapes of letters or remember the sequence of letters that make up a word ("on" for "no" or "god" for "dog" or *b* for *d*).

2. Attention deficits, to which the label "hyperactive" is frequently applied. The youth has trouble staying with a project until it is finished. He rushes through his schoolwork impatiently, not stopping to think. He may talk constantly. Frequently he is in perpetual motion, unable to sit still.

3. Memory and output disorders, which prevent a child from doing mental arithmetic or punctuating a sentence. The child may write laboriously and illegibly.

Techniques are now available for working with these children. One helpful approach is utilization of as many of the senses as possible. While the teacher repeats the name over and over, the child looks at a large letter of the alphabet on a card, then traces its outline on the card with his finger, paints the letter in the air with his hand, and says it out loud. Later this multisensory training will be done with whole words.

Hyperactive children require a more structured regime both at school *and at home.* They must learn to accept limits of behavior. Many learning techniques may be brought into play, including simple rewards and punishments for staying within those limits. Rigid consistency in enforcement is essential.

The drug Ritalin, an amphetamine, is effectively prescribed to slow down many hyperactive children so they can concentrate and control their disruptive impulses. Because the drug treatment seems to be an easy cure, it has become the dominant mental health intervention for children. But it has been grossly misused and overused in many schools and clinics. The *Journal of the American Medical Association* reports that its use has been doubling every four to seven years. In 1987 one in every seventeen elementary children in Baltimore County, Maryland, was being treated with the drug. Throughout the nation it is now being given to an estimated three-quarters of a million school children.

Ritalin does calm children suffering from an attention deficit disorder, making them more acceptable in the classroom. But the effect does not appear to be lasting and the drug is not without side effects. And by quieting some disruptive or inattentive children it may mask a primary problem such as a hearing loss. Nevertheless, with proper diagnosis and monitoring, drug therapy can be a godsend; it can control some children's attention span long enough for other treatment modalities such as behavior modification to be effective.

Regardless of the method used, learning-disabled children must be kept from becoming discouraged—three out of four learning-disabled youths now drop out or are kicked out of school—and their self-esteem and self-confidence must not be destroyed. In teaching them to compensate for their disability, parents and teachers need to create ways in which they can experience success. It is also important that they be made aware of the fact that they are not responsible for their disability and that they may need to accept compensatory help, perhaps throughout life. An increasing number of dyslexics, for example, are graduating from college and professional schools with high honors despite the fact that someone had to read the class assignments to them and they had to be given oral exams.

Other examples of highly successful people abound. Albert Einstein today would be diagnosed as learning-disabled because of his poor memory for words, his inattentiveness, and, ironically, his difficulty in solving mathematical problems in the traditional way. He invented his own method. Thomas Edison was probably dyslexic: he was never able to learn to spell or write grammatically. Always at the bottom of his class, he was finally taken out of school and tutored at home by his mother. President Woodrow Wilson, General George Patton, Leonardo da Vinci, sculptor Auguste Rodin, and Nelson Rockefeller are among the thousands who have proved that one can compensate for a learning disability.

Working with slow learners is not like performing a surgical operation that magically "cures" the patient for life. Rather, it is like physical therapy. Progress is often agonizingly slow. But as we have seen, with early diagnosis and help most victims can lead normal, productive lives.

Many affluent parents now send their slow-learner children to for-profit learning centers for tutoring. Most of these centers—successful in remedial help and very successful in making money—are franchised: The Reading Game, Sylvan Learning Corporation, and Huntington Learning Centers. They use certified teachers and the newest in educational and behavioral techniques; the teacher-pupil ratio is generally one to three. The charge is around twenty-five dollars an hour with the total individual cost running between one and three thousand dollars.

The service is well worth it—for those who can afford it. But it helps to perpetuate the educational advantage of the well-to-do, widening the gap between the rich and the poor. This private, for-profit service will help keep the poor "in their place." One center brazenly advertises, "Give Your Kids an Unfair Advantage."

CDSS would give this unfair advantage to all children who need it, regardless of economic status. And those children, in turn, might grow up not needing to rob and assault others who were more advantaged.

I find it difficult not to be exuberant over the potential of a well-run Child Development Services System. It could favorably influence virtually every facet of a disadvantaged child's future behavior and success. And as a delinquency prevention program it could nip in the bud many of those traits and conditions which propel a youth down the path toward the reform school and prison.

Chapter 12

RESTRUCTURING SCHOOLS TO MEET TODAY'S CHALLENGES

The strong correlation between school failure and delinquency—and later adult crime—is a fact interwoven throughout these pages. In Chapter 5, a critique of public schools, a number of serious charges were leveled against the school system for practices that turn schools into breeding grounds for delinquents. One was the failure to intervene at an early age in the social, physical, and psychological causes of a child's learning difficulties. In the previous chapter the Child Development Services System was offered as an answer to this problem.

Other concerns were incorporated in the charge that American public education has become a two-tiered system, one for middle-class students, and the other for disadvantaged children who are assumed to have limited intellectual capabilities. Little is expected of these latter youngsters, so they are given an inferior education befitting their inferior status. Pouring out of these second-class schools are long lines of functional illiterates, unemployable in today's society. Many of these schools have more dropouts than graduates, more students going to delinquency institutions than to college.

But the sad truth is that it is not only the disadvantaged who are being cheated. In varying degrees the system is failing virtually all students. In an effort to produce a homogenized student body with a homogenized curriculum, the needs of the top 20 percent and the lower 30 percent have been largely unmet. Content of courses has been watered down in an unsuccessful attempt to accommodate the lower 30 percent.

It has long been considered unpatriotic—like stomping on the flag—to be unduly critical of the educational system (unless you belong to the educational establishment). But smug Americans have been rudely shaken by recent revelations that U.S. students rank far below those of other industrialized nations. For example, the International Association for the Evaluation of Educational Achievement recently compared ninth-grade general science students in sixteen countries. The United States ranked fifteenth, outscoring only students from Hong Kong. High school seniors ranked twelfth out of fourteen in advanced chemistry. When the academic skills of American high school graduates are compared with those of their Japanese counterparts, the difference is so horrendous that it is more comfortable just to ignore the subject.

Our attempt to cram everyone—the gifted, the less talented, and the in-betweens—into the same academic mold has cheated all. So today we are hearing desperate cries from business and industry for workers who are even minimally qualified—cries being made at a time when thousands of unemployable juveniles are being forced into crime as a means of survival.

According to the National Alliance of Business, U.S. employers spend over $50 *billion* a year in remedial education necessitated by the failure of public schools to teach basic skills. The New York Telephone Company in 1987 had to test 57,000 applicants to find 2,100 qualified to become operators and repair technicians. As technology takes over our society even menial jobs will require greater literacy and skills. At the same time, for minorities and the poor the gap between *required* skills and *acquired* skills steadily widens.

In a 1990 Op Ed article in the *New York Times* Hodding Carter III issued a warning to those in power who selfishly ignore the educational needs of the powerless:

> If they [the public schools] do as bad a job over the next 25 years as they have over the past 25, all of us can kiss America's current position in the world goodbye, along with economic prosperity . . . Our allies and friends now include

ferocious competitors, all of whom are building their economic machines on firm foundations of well-educated and trained workers.

For a brief time last year there was a ray of hope when the Educational Testing Service reported that among seventeen-year-old black students there had been a steady and significant gain in reading proficiency during the years of the Reagan administration. In the same period the reading scores of white students remained virtually stable. The gap was finally closing! But a review of past scores dashed this hope. Earlier during the Ford and Carter years these same young blacks as nine-year-olds had also shown a steady and significant gain. But the seventeen-year-olds were not improving. In the Reagan era, however, the gainers were reversed. Now it was the older youths who were showing gains while suddenly the nine-year-olds started lagging behind.

The cause of this peculiar phenomenon is clear. During the Ford and Carter administrations underprivileged young children were offered an array of compensatory programs including free breakfast and Follow Through after Head Start. With this help they were showing substantial gains by the time they were nine. Then as these same better-prepared students moved on into high school during the Reagan years, their early advantages made it possible for them to continue their steady gain. But when Reagan slashed budgets for compensatory support the gains being made by the younger black students ceased.

This makes for a gloomy forecast. The steady increase in the spread between the achievement levels of middle-class and underprivileged youths, temporarily stopped, is resuming for these youths who were denied compensatory preschool and elementary help. Reagan was able to reduce taxes for the wealthy, but it was done at a great cost for the future.

Frustrated by the rise in youth crime and the quality of the labor force being produced by America's schools, thousands of businesses are desperately giving money to local schools, supplying volunteers, and providing countless Band-Aid efforts to shore up a failing system. A recent White House survey found 140,000 school-help partnerships. Major corporations are committing millions of dollars to set up experimental programs, even complete demonstration schools.

But other discouraged corporate leaders are calling for a total restructuring.

The basic format of the American educational system—six years of elementary school, two years of junior high, and four years of high school—was designed literally back in the horse-and-buggy days, back before the era of electronic and computer technology, back when it didn't really matter whether a youth received an education because there was a surplus of jobs available for the illiterate. Before we permit an antiquated school system to preside over America's slide into mediocrity (as the comparative international scores of our students foreshadow), it will be well to consider some blueprints for restructuring a nineteenth-century establishment to meet the educational needs of the twenty-first century.

IN THE BEGINNING THERE WAS MONEY

The 1990 report of the Economic Policy Institute revealed that of the sixteen industrialized nations studied, only Ireland and Australia spent less per pupil than the United States on primary and secondary education. Meanwhile fiscal reactionaries point accusing fingers at the schools for letting students in other nations get ahead of ours. But these same conservatives and spokesmen for the greedy pound their chests and sagely proclaim: "Money won't solve the problems of education." And right they are! Money won't. But the things that *will* solve the problems require money. Yes, lots of it. For this reason the question of finances is placed at the top of the list for restructuring.

For starters, there's the obvious need for money to pay teachers' salaries. It is sadly true that many teachers today cannot pass a competency exam even in the subject they supposedly teach. But the principal reason such incompetent individuals are employed is obvious. There just aren't enough qualified people willing to take on a tough job at a blue-collar wage. As sex bias in the workplace disappeared, unlimited opportunities opened up for women. No longer is their choice limited to becoming a secretary or a nurse or a teacher. The situation is also true of minorities: they can't be recruited. Opportunities for qualified blacks are now endless.

Thus, fewer and fewer individuals, black or white, male or female, are entering schools of education, and although it unfairly insults many dedicated teachers, it must be said that many of those who are entering come from the lowest levels of academic performance. There is new meaning in the old adage "Those who can't, teach."

Due to retirement and normal attrition, we will require around

175,000 new teachers in the coming decade. Under present wage scales there is no way that this need can be supplied.

Taxpayers who grumble about incompetent teachers interested only in the pay, teachers who put in only a six-hour day at work and get a three-and-a-half-month vacation, have a legitimate gripe. Holding salaries down, however, will not solve the problem. The situation will improve only when salaries are made comparable to those in other professions. It will improve only when competent individuals interested in helping children to learn can pursue that exciting career without too great a personal sacrifice. Only then will schools be able to pass up unqualified teachers and draw from a pool of professionals.

And this will take money! More at the local level. More at the federal level to serve as a catalyst for change.

The same holds true for dozens of other areas that require more adequate funding. Technological equipment is an obvious example. The specter of crack-exposed babies puts a dark cloud over the future financing of education. In Los Angeles it costs $3,500 a year to educate normal students, $9,000 for special-education students, *and for students in its pilot program for children who had been prenatally exposed to drugs, over $15,000.* The March of Dimes staff predict that by the end of the decade the number of these students could range from half a million to 4 million. The cost is mind-boggling.

Those who hoped that the election of the self-proclaimed "education president" would herald the start of desperately needed reforms have been sorely disillusioned. In the 1990 State of the Union address there was lofty rhetoric but no substance. Noble, indeed, were the goals proposed—things such as graduating 90 percent of all high school students by the year 2000 (as the Japanese now do) and making U.S. students first in the world in math and science achievement. Yes, noble—and expensive—goals. But then the American public was insulted by the niggardly proposal of only a 2 percent budget increase to achieve these lofty goals. (Bush failed to point out that in 1983 President Reagan in his rousing education speech had likewise called for the same 90 percent of graduates in the year *1990* instead of the 70 percent that was current also at that time.)

While a niggardly education budget can easily cause America to lose the race for competitiveness among industrial nations, it guarantees that America will continue to win the race for the greatest number of delinquents.

We know how to achieve Bush's education goals, but we are unwilling to pay the price. In Philadelphia, for example, a twenty-year-old program in partnership with local corporations, the Philadelphia High School Academies, has been recruiting eighth-grade youngsters in danger of dropping out. In return for participation they are guaranteed after-school and summer jobs at rates considerably above the minimum wage. With the enriched program, 93 percent of these *high-risk* students graduate compared to only 70 percent in the entire school district. Only 1,750 youths, however, can be offered this opportunity—less than one-third of the number the Academies hope to reach. *But* the $1.2 million needed to achieve this cannot be carved out of a public school budget faced with a $60-million deficit.

Efforts by corporate America to compensate for this two-tiered educational system, while commendable, have barely touched the problem. Comparatively few of the truly disadvantaged have been reached, and too often the funds have been wasted in short-lived, helter-skelter experimentations. The education of America's children is too important to be left to the whims of charity, even if there are a thousand points of light.

Instead of making charitable contributions, corporate America can do a far greater service to the cause of education by taking the lead in convincing Congress, state legislatures, and the public of the dire need for adequate funding for education. Politicians and voters will listen when executives of successful businesses speak out in favor of education reform that includes additional taxes.

Such an approach has already proved highly successful in one educationally backward state, South Carolina. There, in 1984, business executives led by the state's largest corporate employer, Spring Mills, pushed through the Education Improvement Act, which called for some seventy reforms including greatly increased pay for teachers— *and additional taxes.* Teacher morale has sharply improved, white students who fled the deteriorated public school system after desegregation are now returning, and most significant, since that time South Carolina has shown the greatest improvement in SAT scores of any state in the nation.

Equality of educational opportunity will never be achieved as long as the major funding comes from local taxation, and available state funds are distributed on a per-pupil basis regardless of need. In poverty areas schools are hard-pressed to come up with enough to spend two thousand dollars a year on each student; in affluent areas the sky's the limit—three, four, or five times as much. With the supreme courts in Texas and Kentucky leading the way in 1989, state courts have begun to rule that school systems are unconstitutional because of the "glaring disparities" between the education expenditures in rich and poor districts. It remains to be seen if the courts will be able to reverse the condition. But however it is accomplished, equalization of funds is a primary need in any comprehensive program to break the cycles of illiteracy, poverty, and delinquency.

THE SCHOOL DAY AND YEAR

The proposals being made for restructuring the school system are prompted by two goals: (1) to guarantee that no youth of even moderate intelligence leaves the public school system unequipped to function productively in today's society, and (2) to speed up the timetable for completing basic education so as to permit more time for either advanced studies or career-oriented education. The present twelve years of public education would be compressed into just ten grades.

This seemingly impossible timetable would be achieved in part by a radical change in the hours of the school day and weeks of the school year.

The present school calendar has evolved largely from the nineteenth century, when children had to be available for work on the family farm during the busy months. Today there's little reason for schools to sit idle three months of the year. Each fall teachers in ghetto areas must spend weeks reteaching lessons that students forgot during the summer. Youths desperately needing help to overcome past disadvantages would be better off spending part of the summer in school rather than hanging out on crime-ridden city streets.

American children go to school 180 days a year, European students 220 days, and Japanese 240 days. In addition, in most other countries the school day is longer; in Japan it is two hours longer. Thus, over twelve years of schooling Japanese students receive the equivalent of four more years of instruction than their American counterparts. It is reassuring to note that maybe the reason American students are so far behind those in other nations is not that they are less bright; maybe it is just that we don't demand as much of them.

(It is also important to point out the absurdity of the claim that American youths turn to drugs because of academic pressures placed on them. Japanese students have academic pressures so much greater that by American standards they should be considered cruel and inhumane punishment. Yet there is virtually no drug use or delinquency in Japan.)

With restructuring, the school year should become forty-five weeks instead of the present thirty-six. (This would still be four weeks less than Japanese schools.) The new calendar would have a four-week summer vacation and three other weeks of vacation scattered throughout the year. The schedule would call for an eighteen-week fall semester, an eighteen-week spring semester, and a nine-week summer semester. The summer semester would meet for only four hours a day, thus permitting youngsters to hold part-time summer jobs. In poverty areas a federally funded breakfast program would be offered at primary and elementary levels.

While the official school year would be forty-five weeks, students in kindergarten through sixth grade who had satisfactorily completed the work for their level would be exempted from the summer semester. For others this would be a compensatory review of the year's curriculum. The psychological ploy is important: students would be rewarded for having completed the expected work rather than slow learners being punished.

The summer semester would be required for all students above the sixth grade. At this level all subjects would be taught in self-contained units. Those who were not behind would take two new units for credit during the summer. Other students would take compensatory work in subjects in which they had received an "incomplete" in the fall or spring semesters.

Not only does the number of school days need to be increased for all, so do the hours of instruction for slow learners. This time for compensatory help can be provided either by a four-hour Saturday session or by an hour's extension on the regular school day. At levels K through six, individualized tutoring would be provided to all youths who have fallen behind in their work.

Many schools have been highly successful in recruiting volunteers to assist in remedial tutoring—high school and college students, parents, nonworking women from nearby middle-class communities, retired teachers and other retirees, all willing and anxious to have a part in giving a boost to disadvantaged children. A further source of tutorial help would be fourteen- to sixteen-year-old youths employed in the Community Service Corps to be considered in Chapter 15.

The same hour of compensatory time would be scheduled in the higher grade levels. Here one of the aids for slow learners would be a system of peer tutoring, which has proved successful in many schools.

THE FRAMEWORK FOR RESTRUCTURING

In the early part of the century any student who failed to pass the exams required for that grade would be compelled to repeat the grade. It is estimated that at least half of all students were held back at least one grade sometime in their school career. It was so common that it was no major disgrace. With the advent of "progressive education" in the thirties the practice of making a student repeat a grade gradually fell into disrepute. It was considered less traumatic to give the failures a social promotion—pass them on to the next grade regardless of what they had learned.

Thus, we began to find youths in junior high who hadn't the foggiest idea of what was going on, who couldn't even read the assignments. For them, the class might as well have been taught in Swahili. They either dropped out or continued on to join the ranks of the hundreds of thousands of illiterate graduates.

While it would seem logical to return to the practice of holding these students back, research has consistently shown that it seldom helps them academically. And it frequently does serious harm to their self-esteem.

The difficulty is not in the old concept that children should be required to learn what is expected of them at each level. Rather, it is in the way these failures have been handled after they are retained. Usually they are compelled to repeat the same classes with the same materials, same techniques, and same teachers that have already proved ineffective for them. Their classmates all know they are the dumb bunnies who flunked last year. In the meantime nothing is done to help solve their learning difficulties. Understandably it turns out to be a destructive practice.

In the structure being proposed here, no student would be held back in elementary school except at two gateway points—the end of the third and sixth grades. At these points proficiency tests with emphasis on reading and math would determine whether the student had successfully mastered the skills necessary for further learning.

But no child would be "failed." At the end of the third grade all would be promoted. Based on these tests, some would be promoted to "4B" for a year's remedial work. Most would be allowed to skip 4B and go directly to 4A (which would be the traditional fourth grade). A few might even be permitted to skip 4A and go to fifth grade.

Instead of being a boring and embarrassing repeat of the third grade, 4B would be a vigorous year-long remedial program, populated solely by children with similar problems. Extensive diagnostic tests would determine in what areas the student was weak and what help was needed. Much of the actual classwork would make use of computer-based lessons and individual tutoring.

At the end of the year the 4B students would again be given the proficiency exam. Those who still failed would be transferred to the Opportunity School, a special-education alternative school described in the next chapter. This very critical decision would be reached only after four years of help from the Child Development Services System starting in kindergarten, extra tutorial help after school, and now an intensive year of remedial classes. It would thus have been conclusively demonstrated that the child could not progress satisfactorily in regular classes.

Depending on the socioeconomic level of the student body, the number who would be promoted only to 4B would be expected to range from 10 to 60 percent. While being held back can be a traumatic experience for a child, it is not nearly as damaging as the accumulated feeling of failure that otherwise will exist all through school. And the program here is carefully designed to avoid many of the psychological pitfalls of the past while really doing something constructive for the child.

The second gate, at the end of the sixth grade, would operate in a similar manner. No student would be allowed to enter the seventh grade functionally illiterate. All would have to have sufficient proficiency in reading and math to survive in today's world. Unprepared students who were still unable to pass the sixth-grade final exam after a remedial year in the junior-high prep class would be transferred to the Basic High Alternative School, also described in the next chapter.

In the total restructuring of the traditional school system that follows, it is expected that a student will have completed most of the present requirements for high school graduation by the end of the tenth grade. This does not mean that everyone would be expected to complete these requirements by age sixteen. Age would no longer be of major significance. Some could finish the tenth grade at fourteen, others at eighteen or even twenty. Each student would be permitted to progress at his or her own pace. No longer after the sixth grade would better students be held back by the slower, nor would slower students be pushed out of the system just because of a need for more time or remedial help.

1. *Primary Levels—Kindergarten Through Grade Three*

Here the student would master the basic skills needed for learning, both social and educational. Teachers would rely heavily on the Child Development Services System proposed in the previous chapter to help solve any problem a youth might exhibit. Because reading ability seems to be the keystone for almost all future academic achievement, beyond the third-grade level there would be no child who could be labeled a "nonreader."

At this level through grade six there would be no tracking, that is, no grouping of children into ability levels—a highly controversial practice that generally leaves slower students shortchanged on attention. Instead, remedial help would be given slower students after regular school hours or on Saturdays. As far as possible, class projects would involve a team approach—one superior student, two average and one slow, all working cooperatively.

We have noted that grades that rank-order students can be destructive to the losers. Consequently, grades as now used would not be continued. Generally, grades would be limited to "satisfactory" or "unsatisfactory" and "completed" or "unfinished." Grades of A, B, C, and so on would be given on papers and tests, but here the measurement would be against the individual's own previous performance. Thus, the most gifted student might receive a D while a struggling youth might be given an A for having made the most progress.

2. *Elementary Levels—Grades Four Through Six*

Generally these grades would continue as in the primary years, with a minimum-competency test at the end of the sixth. Beyond the minimum requirements, each school would determine other content areas for each grade. This would be a community decision determined by the teachers and principal *working with a committee of parents*. Specialized teachers (e.g., for art, music, and exercise) would conduct classes on a rotation basis throughout the three levels.

Creative use of a sort of rank-ordering would continue. In spelling tests, for example, it would be difficult not to notice the number of misspelled words on each paper. By pairing the child having the least errors in a "spelling buddy team" with the child having the most errors, some interesting dynamics could be created. The child with the second-least errors would be paired with the one with the second-most errors, and on down the line. The teams would compete for the month in a weekly spelling contest—sort of a pro-am academic tournament. The winning team would be the one with the fewest misspelled words on the two combined papers.

For the best spellers to win they would need to help their buddies improve their spelling skills—an introduction to peer tutoring. The slower learner would have a chance to be a winner, and most important of all, both partners would receive valuable training in cooperation. The next month a different subject with new teams might be selected.

3. Basic High—Grades Seven Through Ten

This stage begins a more radical restructuring of the system. Eliminated is the concept of a junior high (or middle school) and a senior high. Instead, a student promoted from the sixth grade would enter a four-grade-level "Basic High." This would be followed by a two-grade level "Career High." In an effort to improve the achievement level of the American education system, more demands would be made on the students. It is expected that on completing the four grades of Basic High, a student would have gained competency in most of the academic skills now required by the average high school.

On the first day at Basic High, new students would meet their homeroom teacher, who thereafter would become like a caring parent. They would continue to meet with their mentor daily. He or she would see that none of the twenty to twenty-five protégés fell through the cracks, that they received the remedial and other services needed, and that they were praised for good work, berated for not coming up to expectations. The homeroom teacher would become a friend to whom the student would turn even before going to the school counselors, and in the first year would make at least one home visit to each child's parents, a visit to be repeated as needed.

While it is expected that the "average" student would be graduated from Basic High at age sixteen, having progressed one grade each year, this is only an average. Students would enter Basic High after having taken from five to eight years to pass the elementary school competency exam. And once in Basic High, students would progress at different speeds. Those who failed to pass the final exam in a subject would be given an incomplete and would be required to repeat the class to obtain credit. Some could earn enough credits to finish in three years; others would require five or six. But a diploma would now mean something—not just that the recipient had been enrolled in school for a given number of years.

Forty half-units of academic credit would be required for graduation—normally four in each spring and fall semester, two each summer. There would be six class periods during the school day (excluding lunch), with the average schedule calling for four academic class units, a study or library period, and an enrichment period.

While tracking would be prohibited in the elementary grades, it would be encouraged here, largely through the selection of courses made with the homeroom teacher's advice. In some areas there would be different levels of the same subject—for example, Basic English I and Advanced English I. At this level the fact must be faced that all students are not created intellectually equal. To try to pretend otherwise is to penalize everyone. In Basic High, students would be scheduled into those classes where each could progress as rapidly *and as far* as possible.

The classes offered for enrichment each year would seek to broaden the horizons of all students and to capitalize on the diversity of interests and cultural backgrounds of the student body. The offerings would be wide: athletics, music, gymnastics, art, academic clubs, health and nutrition clubs, foreign language clubs, and on and on—any areas considered important by the community.

Graduation from Basic High would guarantee that no youths leave the tenth grade illiterate and unable to function in modern society. They would be ready to pursue further education geared to their chosen career.

4. Career High—Previously Grades Eleven and Twelve*

The final two years of public education at the local level would be primarily career-oriented, although a continuing core of liberal arts subjects—literature, social studies, and science—would be required in order to make adult life more fulfilling for all students regardless of their career goals. The ratio of students going into college-track pro-

---

* For the basic concept of this section (and other ideas in the chapter) I am indebted to a 1988 study, "Restructuring California Education," prepared by BW Associates for the California Business Roundtable, a group of chief executive officers of prominent corporations.

grams and career-track programs would vary greatly between schools in different communities, even different areas of a city. It could be expected that from one-fourth to three-fourths of the students in any given school would be heading toward college.

Nearly 70 percent of America's teenagers *do not* go to college. Yet the educational establishment has succeeded in pawning off on the public the myth that anyone who isn't college-bound is a second-class citizen. Paramount to the success of these proposals is the elimination of this destructive myth. College per se is not really necessary for many personally rewarding and socially meaningful careers.

Career High would consist of many specialized two-year programs, the number limited only by the size and resources of the local school system. A student would enroll in one of four major sequences: Junior College, Applied Technology, Human Services, and Performing and Fine Arts. Each of these would in turn be divided into a number of specialized programs. Not all programs would be offered at every location. Instead, specialty programs would be scattered throughout the community as magnet schools. All would be tuition-free. Among the core options might be some of the following, plus any others for which there was a demand and interest in the community:

A. Junior College and/or College Prep

As it is the intention to make graduation from Basic High virtually the equivalent of today's high school graduation, many or most students would be ready for college or for college-level courses. Those students planning for advanced academic education would be given a battery of tests similar to the present SAT precollege tests. Depending on the results a youth would enroll directly into college, into a college-prep sequence, or into a combination of the two. In the latter instance additional background courses would be required in deficient areas (e.g., math or English) while the student took college-credit courses in areas in which he or she was adequately prepared.

The structure of this college-level sequence could vary from state to state, even from district to district depending on local preference. In school districts where community colleges (or cooperating universities) are available the state would permit Basic High graduates who qualified to enroll directly in the college. In other districts, particularly smaller ones, the junior college could be operated by the local undergraduate school board, even in the present high school buildings.

While any youth who made a high enough score on the precollege tests would be allowed to enter the college program, careful counseling should be provided to all slower-learning students to make certain they are not interested in college merely as a status symbol or are likely to have academic difficulties. They should be made aware of the vast array of satisfying careers not requiring college degrees that can be achieved through the two-year career training being offered. For college-bound youths the restructuring would speed up the educational process and permit more time for advanced-level professional study.

B. Applied Technology

As the name implies, the courses to be offered in this sequence are a far cry from the traditional concept of "vocational education." They would be the equivalent of a two-year technical school or college. While most classes would be organized around the career being pursued, enrichment classes would also be included. Specific sequences might include the following, although not all would be available in every school:

- electronic and computer technology
- construction (plumbing and heating, electrical, carpentry, mechanical drawing)
- motors (auto and other mechanics)
- horticulture (landscape architecture, nursery skills, yard and garden installation and maintenance, park management)

C. Human Services

This is perhaps the fastest-growing area of employment in the present decade. Among the possible areas:

- paraprofessionals (paramedics, teacher assistants, health care technicians, graduate practical nurses, library assistants)
- office management (accounting and bookkeeping, computer operation, word processing, secretarial)
- community safety (police officers and firemen)

D. Performing and Fine Arts

Among possible courses would be music of many forms, drama, dance, painting and drawing. This would be the smallest of the four major sequences, and selection of courses to be offered would be based on local demand. A school would attempt to specialize in one or more areas and become a magnet school for that specialty. Students in other majors would be allowed to take courses in this sequence for personal enrichment.

This radically restructured school system—from kindergarten through high school—would be true dropout prevention, true delinquency prevention. It has been demonstrated that even marginal students will remain in school when they are able to do the work expected of them. And here they would be. The promise of being able to obtain two-year specialized training in the individual's field of interest—free of tuition—would be a strong incentive to stay in school for many youths who now feel that school is irrelevant. Benefits equally as valuable would accrue to better students because they would be permitted to progress as rapidly as they were capable of doing. They would be competing against themselves, not against slower learners.

TEACHERS: MORE FOR THEM, MORE FROM THEM

Early in the chapter the need for greatly increased teachers' salaries was expounded. To attract teachers to do the jobs that have been outlined, this is essential. *But*—there always seems to be a but—in return for higher pay, certain concessions must be made by the teachers, many of which involve negotiations with their unions. The most obvious is the considerable increase in the total school hours during the year: an hour longer each day for compensatory aid and an additional eight weeks for the summer semester. It is only reasonable, however, that if teachers' salaries are to be brought up to the levels of other professions, so should their hours be brought up to those levels.

Teachers' unions have been effective in protecting teachers' rights, but at times a shortsighted view has been self-defeating for the teachers, destructive for the schools. For example, it is virtually impossible for a school to rid itself of an unqualified teacher, even one who can't spell the name of the course being taught. To do so often requires an expenditure of as much as $75,000 and months and months of work documenting gross inabilities on the job. Consequently, the average school system is loaded with ineffectual teachers.

In a number of cities enlightened school boards and enlightened teachers' unions are getting together for the good of the students. In Rochester, New York, top teachers can now earn up to $70,000 a year. In 1987 the Rochester Teachers Association signed a landmark contract which has been hailed as a blueprint for converting a blue-collar job into a professional one. The teachers received an overall 40 percent pay raise, effective over a three-year period. But instead of being based solely on seniority, much of the raise is now contingent on merit and longer hours. Teachers will be held accountable for their students' performance. Experienced teachers will assist weaker ones, and the union has agreed to the removal, with certain safeguards, of those whose incompetence is found to be beyond peer assistance.

The Rochester agreement drew heavily on the teachers' contract in Toledo, Ohio, negotiated in 1981, when the system was in shambles and reeling from two disastrous teachers' strikes. In return for other concessions, the union agreed to become an active participant in removing incompetent teachers. Many qualified teachers agreed to a three-year assignment as mentors and evaluators of new teachers. Each monitors and critiques the work of eleven neophytes, offers advice and support, and maintains this helping relationship until such time as either the new teacher is considered qualified for a permanent assignment or his or her contract is terminated. In addition, the mentor is assigned to give guidance to one older teacher who has been reported as being unsatisfactory. Should the personalized assistance prove insufficient to turn the teacher's performance around, the union permits his or her contract to be terminated.

DISCIPLINE AND THE BEHAVIORAL REVIEW BOARD

It is impossible for learning to take place where bedlam prevails. The rapid spread of drugs throughout inner-city schools has magnified what has always been a serious problem. But an atmosphere conducive to learning cannot be achieved by having uniformed police patrol the halls (as is being done in many chaotic schools today), or by installing airport-type metal detectors to prevent weapons from being smuggled in (as was tried in one Detroit school and is being considered by others), or by requiring students to wear identification badges (as is done in some Baltimore schools). These and similar tactics produce a repressive, prisonlike atmosphere that is incompatible with creativity and learning, and have failed to produce evidence that school crime was reduced.

The chapter on status offenders made a pitch for limiting the jurisdiction of the juvenile court to those acts which are also a crime when committed by an adult. Under such terms school administrators could no longer turn to the court to punish students who were habitually truant or beyond the school's control. This proposal was made for the very pragmatic reason that generally the court's intervention in these cases exacerbates the problem instead of solving it.

Such a change would force the schools themselves to take responsibility for these unruly, disinterested youngsters. The restructuring proposed here would greatly decrease the problem of disruptiveness because students would no longer be in classes beyond their abilities. Realism, however, suggests that there would still be youths unable to adjust even to this system. And there are thousands of youths already in the educational pipeline who have been socially promoted to levels beyond their abilities. Without some mechanism to replace the court a serious vacuum would be created.

To tackle this problem, a Behavioral Review Board (BRB) within the school system should be mandated by the legislature. Such a board would be, for older children and teenagers, the equivalent of the Child Development Services System for early elementary students—a board that would seek to determine and ameliorate the causes of their recalcitrance.

The causes are, of course, virtually endless. It could be that the disruptive youth is in an academic program where he or she has no remote hope of success, or is suffering from the severe prejudices of a teacher, or is embarrassed about the clothes she has to wear, or has a debilitating health or nutritional problem, or is strung out on drugs, or is being forced to stay home to take care of younger children, or is afraid of physical or sexual attack from another student, or has parents who aren't concerned enough to awaken their child in the morning, or has been forced to run away from parental abuse and is living on the streets. These offer but a hint of the vast array of problems the board might face.

Depending on demand, one Behavioral Review Board might serve an entire district, or a group of schools, or only a single school. Among possible members of the board would be a school psychologist or counselor, a nurse, a social worker (if the system has them), a representative of the pupil personnel department, one or more classroom teachers, and one or more parents.

Parents of the problem student would be invited to attend the hearings. The board could request an in-depth investigation of what appeared to be the problem area—family situation, academic program, health or psychological need.

Some solutions might be found within the school system itself by making academic changes to accommodate the youth's special requirements. This could involve transfer to the alternative schools discussed in the next chapter. For many social and economic needs the board might turn to other community agencies (as was proposed in the Child Development Services System). As a last resort it might turn to the court. This would not be to punish the youth. Rather, it would be to compel the parent or some other person or agency to provide needed services to the youth.

Included in the BRB's authority should be the right (within court-approved guidelines and subject to parental appeal) to permanently expel a youth guilty of continual disruptive behavior, or of drug use and/or peddling while at school. Such power is not to be used lightly or without sufficient warning given the student. But after all avenues of help have been exhausted, there comes the time when a youth's public school days must be terminated. Despite all the tear-jerking rhetoric about totally destroying that youth's future, the fact remains that in the final analysis *it is better that the system finally give up on one youth who refuses to cooperate than it is to destroy the educational opportunity for dozens of others.*

The California legislature has established on a statewide basis the School Attendance Review Board (SARB) upon which the proposal here is largely patterned. It grew out of the reluctance of the legislators to remove status offenders from the jurisdiction of the court without establishing some other means of dealing with their problems. The broad outline in the law provides flexibility to meet local needs, and the system is now operating in all California counties.

Experience in Los Angeles County demonstrated how dramatic the results can be. Prior to the establishment of SARB, schools in Los Angeles County were filing delinquency petitions with the courts on 1,200 to 1,500 pupils a year. In the first year of the new system under 200 were filed. Based on the costs of court processing and supervision, it was calculated that the reduced number of students taken to court saved the juvenile justice system $1.8 million in that year alone.

The tremendous savings in youthful lives cannot be calculated in dollars and cents.

KENTUCKY, A POOR STATE, BLAZES THE WAY

Many educational authorities will shrug their shoulders and dismiss this proposal for restructuring as being too massive, too radical to be practical. No state legislature or school district board, they will claim, would even consider mandating a major portion of such a program except over a period of years—or decades. But the commonwealth of Kentucky has proved such critics to be of little faith.

While an ever-increasing clamor for educational reform is coming from business leaders and the general public, last year Kentucky became the first state to bite the bullet and attempt a major overhaul of its educational system. Overnight the legislature amended the entire philosophy of public education, bringing a radical shift in the traditional view of a school's responsibilities.

Because of the inequality in financing between richer and poorer school districts, in a dozen or more states either the educational system has been declared unconstitutional or the courts have the case under advisement. But in Kentucky the court went much further. Not only was the inequitable financing unconstitutional (a spread of $1,800 to $4,200 per pupil depending on the district's wealth), the entire educational structure was in default because the state ranked near the bottom nationally "in virtually every category that is used to evaluate educational performance."

The legislature accepted the challenge. It hired David Hornbeck, former superintendent of education in Maryland as a consultant, and in eight frenzied months came up with the most extensive, most radical reform measure for public schools ever attempted at a single time in the history of American education.

Control is to be decentralized by transferring much of it to the parents, administrative staff, and teachers in each of 178 local districts. No longer will the state department of education be concerned with the local school's day-to-day operations and policies, including curriculum and textbook selection.

Instead, a much leaner department will now monitor the progress of individual schools in meeting the state's specific learning goals. A school's improvement will be measured against its own past achievement, not that of other schools. As long as a school is improving, it will be left alone to do its own thing. Those schools and staffs exceeding their goals will be given bonuses; those falling behind will be warned and offered assistance. If a school still fails to improve, the state may take over, mandate changes in ineffective policies, transfer or dismiss inadequate administrators and teachers, and, in the extreme, even close the school.

In poorer areas of the state the schools will virtually become a comprehensive social service agency with objectives paralleling those of CDSS proposed in the previous chapter. Dr. Hornbeck, principal architect of the program, defends this new mission as a primary need: "If a child is hungry, or if a child is sick or otherwise unhealthy—if a child can't hear or see or has an abscessed tooth . . . the child can't learn."

Those schools in which at least one-fifth of the students qualify for free lunches (approximately 40 percent of the schools) will be required to establish in or near the school one of two types of centers. Patrick Howington, writing in the *Louisville Courier-Journal*, describes these:

- Elementary schools will have *family resource centers* that will serve parents as well as children, including those who are still years from entering kindergarten—or still in the womb.

  Services will include year-round care for needy children between the ages of two and twelve, and health care and literacy programs for the entire family. Expectant and new parents will get advice on child development, and day-care providers can receive training.
- Middle and high schools will establish *youth service centers* to offer teenage students a wide range of counseling—about drugs, alcohol, family crises, mental health—and job training and placement services. They will also make health care referrals.

David Richart, executive director of Kentucky Youth Advocates, which played an important role in bringing about the changes, says that critics of this nontraditional role for schools are "people who believe that we still live in an 'Ozzie and Harriet' type world—with the typical husband at work and the mother at home. That simply doesn't exist anymore."

The restructuring will be put in place in steps over the next five years, starting in September 1991. Many details remain to be worked out. The legislature backed up its plan with a half-billion dollars of new tax money, and there are requirements and incentives for the districts to increase local funding. The service centers will be largely financed through the state's Department of Human Resources. But it remains to be seen whether a relatively poor state can on its own bring about these far-reaching changes without additional massive financial support from the federal government.

To educational reformers all across the nation, Kentucky's leadership offers new optimism. To the pessimistic who despair that legislatures are far too reactionary to meet the challenges of a new era, Kentucky has demonstrated that it is not necessarily true. If convinced of a need, politicians and legislators can show considerable vision *and guts*. Reformers can take renewed hope that major proposals, such as are being made in *Saving Our Kids*, are not beyond the realm of possibility.

The restructuring outlined in this chapter was introduced as a delinquency prevention program. But in the truest sense it is a process for providing the best possible educational opportunities for *all* students—the fast, the average, the slow. Sadly, however, not all of a community's children will fit into even this expanded, restructured program. There are those who are already so damaged that special allowances must be made for them. And there are those of such limited mental ability that even the extra time, extra tutoring, and extra concern will not meet their needs.

Wealthier families have always had alternatives available in a wide array of private schools—boarding schools for youths with behavioral problems, Ivy League prep schools, military academies, special-education schools, religious schools, and so on. But for those not so economically fortunate the only alternative often has been a delinquency institution for which the taxpayer is forced to pay the high tuition fee. In the next chapter we will examine other more productive alternatives.

Chapter 13

ALTERNATIVE SCHOOLS THAT FIGHT ILLITERACY AND DELINQUENCY

Several groups of problem children were not considered in the previous two chapters. Among them are those who are mentally retarded, those who are too great a behavioral problem to be retained in normal classes, those whom the system has permitted to fall so far behind that catching up is unlikely, those new teenage mothers who lose interest in school—in general, all those who cannot profit from the regular school or whose presence would be seriously disruptive. Alternative programs must be provided for such children if they are to develop into first-class, productive citizens. Failure to meet their needs in the past has added greatly to the delinquency statistics and to the tragic loss of human resources.

Virtually every major school system has one or more alternative schools for troubled youths. All too often these are merely dumping grounds for unwanted misfits. Out of sight, out of mind. These schools and their clients are usually given an extremely low priority. The unofficial policy has been to get by as cheaply as possible while satisfying the state's requirement to give every child an education.

Fortunately, intensive research over the past few decades in education and the social sciences has come up with techniques whereby virtually all these children may be reached. Many of the techniques were first developed during the Vietnam War in the military's successful "Project 100,000," in which youths failing to pass academic entrance requirements were accepted and given special remedial training in basic educational projects. Later the Job Corps developed educational programs for vast numbers of the nation's most economically disadvantaged youths. Educational gains of one to one and a half grade levels have been achieved with only a hundred hours of computer-based instruction. This gain is twice the gain in the average classroom situation and over four times the gain previously achieved by those Job Corps members while in regular schools. Many smaller experimental programs funded by the U.S. Department of Education, various foundations, and coalitions of businesses have produced exciting results with targeted groups.

One of the most promising approaches to large-scale remediation on a practical, cost-effective basis is the Comprehensive Competencies Program (CCP), which has proved that disadvantaged students, even those with multiple problems, can learn basic skills. The CCP was developed in 1983 by Robert Taggart with a multiyear grant from the Ford Foundation. Instead of undertaking new research, he proposed to integrate into a single package the best materials, technologies, and approaches of many already proven remedial efforts. Tested and fine-tuned the following year, the program has since been shown to be effective with minority groups, welfare recipients, unwed mothers, dropouts, and delinquents. Instruction time of only twenty-eight hours has produced an average gain of a full grade in reading; with math the gain has been 1.4 grades.

The package covers a vast array of basic-skill subjects ranging from elementary reading and arithmetic through high school math, humanities, writing, and social studies. Parallel with the academic subjects are lessons in functional competencies related to job getting, consumer economics, citizenship, health, and community resources. Each subject is divided into levels of difficulty which are in turn divided into lessons to be covered in a single learning period.

The program is based on the proven theory that remedial learning is accelerated when it depends on the successful completion of well-defined, short goals that build upon each other. Regardless of the length of time spent on a lesson—brief or long—the student does not move on until that lesson is mastered. Thus, the program provides individualized, self-paced instruction.

A variety of teaching techniques is utilized. Each lesson contains instructions on the computer, an assignment in the workbook, an audiovisual component, and supplementary reading materials. Frequent electronic tests (with results available in thirty seconds) provide the student with instant feedback and positive reinforcement. The detailed packaging permits a small staff in a learning center to provide flexibly scheduled instruction to a diverse group of learners at the same time while also providing a great deal of individualized attention.

The CCP is distributed on a franchise basis by U.S. Basics, a non-profit corporation based in Alexandria, Virginia. It is already being used by some four hundred learning centers in thirty-eight states. It is described here because it, *or a similar technique*, can be effectively used in most remedial situations.

THE OPPORTUNITY SCHOOL

Generally the severely retarded and handicapped are beyond the purview of this book, for the extent of their delinquency is minimal. At times, as the price for acceptance, a severely retarded youth may be led into an antisocial behavior by another delinquent youth. At other times, just for kicks, an adolescent may play a cruel game with a retarded youth by persuading him to do absurd and often illegal acts.

More often delinquency is a problem with those who are borderline or marginal. These would be children roughly in the 70–85 IQ range. They are the troublemakers and perpetual failures in regular school, particularly beginning at the junior-high level where suddenly they no longer have the security of a single teacher, and the academic demands exceed their abilities. A Basic High *Alternative* School would provide opportunities for them.

For younger children, regardless of their physical or mental handicap, it would be best to keep them in regular classes as long as possible. The proposed special tutoring and the extra two-month summer semester during the primary years would permit many marginal youngsters to complete several grade levels before reaching the limit of their capabilities. Only after failing the third-grade competency test following the extra year of remedial work should most of these retarded children be transferred to the Opportunity School.

When possible, the Opportunity School for special education should probably be physically separated from regular school. This segregation of the extremely slow learners is a difficult decision, and admittedly there is no ideal solution. Compassionate instincts rebel at the thought of segregating youths because of a problem not of their own making. But after the age of ten segregation is usually preferable to the steady frustration and humiliation that can otherwise be experienced. All too often children in special-education classes are shunned by the more fortunate, and their classes are called "dummy rooms." It is better to be where acceptance comes more easily and where everyone has a chance to be a winner.

It is not possible to attempt here a consideration of the various techniques and approaches now used with special-education students, but techniques similar to the CCP are often successful. A caring public must insist that Opportunity School not be allowed to become mere baby-sitting. Gifted special-education teachers have been able to accomplish miracles with children who deserve society's finest efforts.

In planning for restructuring, however, it must be realized that the number of children needing to be enrolled in the special-education classes of the Opportunity School would dramatically drop when policies proposed in Chapter 9 on breaking the poverty cycle were instituted and the Child Development Services System was in place. Prenatal and postnatal nutrition and medical care would prevent much of the mental retardation seen today. Early sensory stimulation, constructive experiences in the child care centers, and training in Head Start programs would prevent much of the cultural lag that all too often has been diagnosed as mental retardation.

THE BASIC HIGH ALTERNATIVE SCHOOL

The following essay will not be found in any anthology of philosophical writings, but it deserves recognition for its insight into the soul of a young social misfit:

CRYING

Some people cry because they are lonely. They need love and care. Sometimes they're in trouble for fighting. Maybe they're in trouble for sneaking off. Maybe they've been bad in school. That's why they cry. They cry sometimes because they're scared. They're scared to be home by themselves. It is spooky. Sometimes people cry tears. Sometimes they cry in their hearts.

This composition was written by Butch Jackson, a fourteen-year-old student at a Louisville Alternative Junior High School who knew what it was to "cry in his heart." While it didn't win a Pulitzer Prize for literature, it did win two movie tickets in the school's weekly creative writing contest. It was one of the few times in his entire life that Butch had been a winner. He was as excited as if he had hit a home run in the World Series. It also marked a dramatic shift in the academic career of a habitual truant. In this school for misfits he found a place where classes were geared to his capabilities, a place where he felt wanted, a place where he could be a winner. Seldom now did he miss a day. School was too exciting.

Basic High Alternative Schools should be designed to keep young people like Butch out of delinquency institutions, give them the most useful education possible at this stage in their lives, improve their self-esteem, and reduce their hostility to society.

The "official" grade levels in the proposed program would be seven, eight, nine, and ten. Actually, any behavioral or academic misfit aged thirteen through sixteen who met the criteria would be admitted regardless of the official grade. The target group would be identified under seven categories:

1. Students unable to pass the sixth-grade comprehensive exam after an additional remedial year
2. Retarded fourteen-year-olds "promoted" from the Opportunity School
3. Habitual truants referred by the Behavioral Review Board
4. Students at any level who are beyond control of the school
5. Basic High students who fail to complete a single unit of work in a year, except under extenuating circumstances, e.g., being sick
6. Delinquency institution returnees whose prior school records suggest insurmountable academic difficulties
7. Youths on court probation for whom it is determined that school problems are a contributing cause of their delinquency

Freedom of Choice

Students promoted to the alternative school or referred by the Behavioral Review Board would have no choice about enrollment. For all others "voluntary" enrollment would be preferred. Students facing disciplinary action, suspension, or referral to the juvenile court would be *offered* the opportunity of transferring to the alternative school geared to their needs. But it would also be made clear that enrollment involved a two-way contract with the staff. Misbehavior or noncooperation could cost the youth the privilege of attending.

This freedom of choice is a Hobson's choice. The unappealing alternative is for the student to remain in a school where he or she is experiencing failure, is being continually hassled by the teachers and administrators, and in many states may be facing a court hearing for truancy or being beyond the school's control. While some students might consider the offer to be a choice between cyanide and hemlock, few would refuse to give the new school a trial.

While this "choice" would make little difference in who is enrolled, the psychological difference would be vast. A youth and, more important, his peers would view a compulsory transfer as a jail sentence for being bad. Embarrassment, bitterness, and increased alienation would be the consequence. Freedom of choice removes part of the stigma by making attendance a privilege. It produces at least an illusion of control.

The Program—"Every Kid a Winner"

Academics would concentrate on basic essentials needed in applying for and holding almost any job—the legendary reading, writing, and arithmetic. Instruction would be individually tailored to the level where the student could experience success. Mastery tests as supplied in the Comprehensive Competencies Program would determine at what level a youth should begin. For the youth reading on a first- or second-grade level, instruction would begin at that level. Classes would be small, from one-on-one tutoring up to a maximum of eight. Since the attention span of these students is explosively brief, class periods would be short.

Highly effective individualized instructional methods as incorporated in CCP would be utilized, permitting students at different levels to be in the same classroom. Schoolwide programs would also be included. Writing, for example, would focus on a weekly school newspaper produced on a copying machine. Students would write short articles, interviews, observations and stories, even jokes and riddles. As Butch Jackson demonstrated, seeing one's own words in print is a strong motivator.

The core curriculum would be interspersed with other courses that carry traditional school titles but would be highly nontraditional in content. They would offer skills needed for survival. "Health" would incorporate a heavy emphasis on the dangers of alcohol, drugs, and tobacco. Sex education would be emphasized and reemphasized; the content would be both philosophical and practical. "Business" might include how to open a bank account and write a check, the dangers of borrowing from loan sharks, taxes, Social Security, and unemployment insurance.

Consider this agenda for a continuing course in civics: Study of how the city operates would include field trips to the city hall and aldermanic council meetings. The principal activity, however, would be running student government, patterned after the city system. Students would have a genuine voice not only in planning extracurricular activities but, more important, in setting and enforcing rules. There would be a mayor, board of aldermen, police department, and other necessary municipal officers and services. Elections could be held monthly so that the multitude of offices could be passed around. In one alternative school the students voted a "tax" in order to raise money for an outing. Payment was made by bringing in aluminum cans, newspapers, and glass bottles to be sold to a recycling plant.

Youths who in the past have been left out of school honors and projects would now become "somebodies"—officers in student government.

In Butch Jackson's school much of the disciplinary action was handled by the "judicial" branch of the student government. With prosecuting and defense attorneys and a judge, trials were held for those who broke certain school rules which had been legislated by the students. The decisions rendered by that month's panel of jurors could be appealed by either the prosecutor or the defendant to the supreme court—the staff.

"Economics" might be a sheltered workshop, patterned after the Junior Achievement model. Students would set up a "corporation" to produce items for sale through stores, community fairs, or even door-to-door. Among the unlimited possibilities of items to be sold might be seasonally decorated candles, crocheted or knitted items, woven rugs, cookies and other baked goods. One school ran a successful plant nursery, growing tomato, cabbage, and petunia plants for sale. Piecework contracts might be made with a local industry, and in some communities actual Junior Achievement programs, sponsored by local corporations, might he arranged.

Student absences would have to be investigated immediately by a paraprofessional staff member. Low attendance, however, will not be a problem in a school that is meeting the needs of its students. Learning can be exciting. One year while I was with the Louisville school system, an alternative junior high with seventy-five formerly habitual truants had an attendance record comparable to the other schools in the system. One month it even had the best attendance of all junior highs.

Nonacademic Goals

Equally important as academic improvement would be improvement in the participants' self-concept and in their attitudes toward law-abiding society. Great strides in the latter would come simply from a rebellious youth's realization that somebody genuinely cares that he or she gets a fair shake.

Building self-esteem should be a minute-by-minute priority of the staff. Habitual losers must be "set up" to succeed. As they began to experience more and more success they would begin to believe in themselves as worthwhile individuals. Success is a strong motivator to try even harder. The smallest academic improvement or positive change in behavior should be noted and warmly praised ("You've been on time every morning this week. That's really great."). Scores of awards and small prizes such as Butch Jackson won should be given out regularly. Inexpensive trophies pay big dividends.

Few have understood this need to deal with the negative self-concept of alternative school students better than Fran Chamberlain, who in 1984 was selected by the California Department of Education as the Teacher of the Year. He discovered that for these social failures "the joy of giving is a powerful experience." So he arranges for each student to spend time every week in some constructive volunteer work like visiting patients in a veterans' hospital and tutoring elementary school students. In his alternative school classroom in Napa, California, Chamberlain builds self-esteem by concentrating on positive comments instead of negative. Simple things are important. When grading tests, for example, he checks the correct answers instead of the wrong ones. "Look," he says, "you got this many right. Great! Now let's see what we can do about these others."

Testimony to the fact that positive reinforcement and successful experiences can change "troublemakers" was dramatically provided by the basketball team of a Louisville alternative school. In the city-wide round-robin junior-high tournament they won few games. But they won the sportsmanship trophy! These were kids who for disciplinary reasons had previously been kicked off other school teams by the very same coaches who now praised their behavior.

In a similar vein vandalism virtually disappeared from the Louisville alternative schools which continued to operate until the city system was consolidated with the county system under a desegregation court order. School administrators were stunned to discover that the boys' rest rooms were among the few in the system where the walls were not marred with graffiti. In fact, these junior highs were the only ones in the inner city able to keep toilet paper available in the lavatories. These were the schools for "bad" kids!

Staffing and Location

Attempting to operate an alternative school in the same building with a regular program can be disastrous. It just does not work. Regular students can't understand why they aren't permitted to get by as easily as the alternative students. They are jealous of "bad" kids getting special favors. On the other hand, the alternative students are made to feel they are second-class human beings. Usable vacant buildings, abandoned because of decreasing enrollments or new construction, are available in most school systems. At the very worst, even a vacant garage building could serve.

Experience indicates that a staff of one adult to approximately seven students is needed. Two-thirds may be paraprofessionals (assistant teachers) selected for skills other than purely academic ones. A successful program will likely require as much as three times the per-pupil expenditure of a regular school.

Around 75 to 100 youths is probably the optimum size. However, most physical details would be modified for local conditions and needs—and money available. To New York City school administrators, for example, a suggested optimum size of 100 would be a sick joke. There the demand for the few alternative schools available is so great that they are all oversubscribed. In 1989 the West Side (Alternative) High School had to turn away 50 kids in an effort to keep the enrollment down to the 575 considered to be the maximum before chaotic conditions would close the school. Despite program limitations caused by its size, as well as the difficulty in giving individualized attention, the dropout rate in this assemblage of dropouts and pushouts has been around 33 percent, possibly better than that of the system generally.

Under the proposals here, following four years of participation (indicating that the youth had neither dropped out nor been kicked out for noncooperation) and a demonstrated ability to read and write on a sixth-grade level, the student would receive a Basic High Alternative School diploma. This diploma would not certify that the recipient knew the dates of the Holy Roman Empire or the chemical formula of sulfuric acid—or necessarily any specific batch of knowledge established by the state legislature. It would certify that the holder *was not functionally illiterate*, that he or she and the school had worked together to maximize his or her academic and social skills, and, perhaps most important of all, that the youth had demonstrated reliability and determination by sticking with a project over a number of years.

Such a diploma would meet the requirements of many unskilled jobs for which employers routinely demand a high school diploma. And the student would be far better equipped to face the world than he would have been if he had been chained to a school program beyond his capabilities.

At any time a student could petition to be returned to the regular Basic High. But it is expected that 99 percent would remain at least until they passed the state's age for compulsory attendance.

CAREER HIGH ALTERNATIVE SCHOOL

A continuation program (a watered-down equivalent of the regular Career High) would be for seventeen- and eighteen-year-olds who chose to remain in the school. Here more advanced forms of vocational education geared to their abilities would be offered. The program would include core academic classes but would focus primarily on hands-on training. It would be aimed toward developing good work habits in a population of young people distressingly lacking in this trait. One approach would be with school-generated jobs; the other would be with part-time work in local businesses and industry.

Where possible the latter would be the most valuable. Throughout the nation many corporations as part of their civic responsibility have been willing to provide part-time work and special supervision to marginally qualified youths. Frequently, however, it is difficult to find businesses willing to gamble with the types of youths enrolled in alternative programs, and the problem of paying minimum wages to these trainees is often insurmountable.

In many communities the school itself would have to set up businesses that provide work experiences. A number of schools around the country have successfully let students build a complete house under teaching supervisors. Usually it takes two years. When the house is sold the money provides materials for the next one. In other programs the school has leased a service station which is operated by the students under the supervision of an auto mechanic. Some manufacturing plants have been willing to subcontract labor-intensive components, such as assembling or packaging.

The types of businesses that students could run are limited only by the creative imagination of the staff and the special circumstances of a particular community. In Brattleboro, Vermont, a town of only twelve thousand, students operate all phases of Le Cordon Bleu, a gourmet restaurant serving lunch to the public two days a week.

Throughout the nation a large number of school systems have obtained governmental or corporate grants for experimental alternative programs. Many have succeeded in giving help to troublemaking misfits. Unfortunately, despite their success, most disappeared or were fatally watered down after the grant money was exhausted. Spending extra money on bad kids isn't very popular with the public, or with school administrators.

It is a sad indictment of American priorities that we are willing to pay four or five times as much to destroy a youth by locking him up in a delinquency institution as we are to find an educational program that would save him from that institution. Eventually the costs of crime and prison care make us pay dearly for our shortsightedness.

THE CONTRACT HIGH SCHOOL

A fourth alternative school would focus on a different need. This would be primarily for youths who are not failures but for various reasons are unable to attend normal classes:

1. Youths who found it necessary to help support their family by working during hours that were incompatible with school attendance
2. Working teenage parents who were establishing their own families
3. Former dropouts uncomfortable about returning to regular classes with far younger classmates
4. Students who needed to proceed at a slower pace than regular school

5. Students currently enrolled in Basic High but in danger of not graduating because of their inability to pass one or more required courses

The last group would continue in their regular school program but would also go to the Contract School after regular school hours for special help. Availability of this alternative could prevent many youngsters from failing to graduate.

For all categories of students participation would lead to the regular Basic High diploma—indicating completion of normal academic requirements.

The Contract School would operate in a regular high school building during the late afternoon, evenings, and weekends—similar to adult learning centers that exist in many communities. Here the Comprehensive Competencies Program, or a clone, would be invaluable. The inclusiveness of the courses available and the comprehensiveness of the materials make it adaptable to meet virtually any academic need. There would be no formal classes or required number of hours. Students could proceed as fast or as slowly as suited their abilities. A final exam would be given at the conclusion of the lessons for each course. If the student passed, a credit would be entered in the school's records. Those failing could continue studying and retake the exam.

THE TEENAGE PARENTS ALTERNATIVE SCHOOL

As was discussed in the chapter on delinquency and the poverty cycle, *the alarming increase in teenagers having babies has swelled the ranks of those waving goodbye to education. One out of every eight babies born in the United States today has a teenage mother, and 80 percent of these girls never finish high school.* Later the mothers are far more likely to be on welfare and to suffer from debilitating emotional problems. The offspring of these teenage dropouts can be expected to be less healthy both physically and emotionally than the norm, more likely to be victims of parental child abuse, *and* more likely themselves eventually to become teenage mothers guilty of child abuse. Thus the cycle is completed.

Many districts in desperation are experimenting with programs and schools exclusively for these pregnant girls. The quality runs the gamut from excellent to destructively poor. The latter are those created primarily to quarantine pregnant girls from contact with other impressionable students who might catch the disease.

However, following the lead of some pioneering efforts in cities like St. Paul and Louisville in the seventies, a few well-planned programs are beginning to emerge. For example, 95 percent of the students in Harlem's Lyfe Project now graduate or receive their G.E.D. certificates. A survey of teenage mothers who attended Albuquerque's New Futures School between 1980 and 1985 found that only 18 percent were drawing welfare payments. Not only had three-quarters finished high school, more than half had gone on for some postsecondary education or training.

Such programs have value in reducing future delinquency, value in breaking the cycle of poverty, and value in increasing the quality of future life for the unborn child.

An alternative school for pregnant girls should contain the following components:

a. Participants

Enrollment should be voluntary, and would begin with the second trimester of pregnancy regardless of age or grade in school—or marital status. As in the Lyfe Project, after the baby arrives the new mother could elect to remain in the program until graduation (with her child in the school nursery), provided she continues to make satisfactory academic progress.

b. Academic Classes Available

Participation might range from as low as the fifth or sixth grade on up to the tenth. Yet all the subjects required for graduation from Basic High would also be required here. This behemoth teaching task would be impossible without the equivalent of the Comprehensive Competencies Program, which is the high-tech version of the one-room schoolhouse. Even so, nearly three times the staff of a regular school would be needed for the same number of students. Half could be paraprofessional assistants.

c. Counseling Services

Few individuals need more counseling than these girls. Overcome with feelings of worthlessness, many have deliberately become pregnant in the hope that becoming a mother will give meaning to their lives. Others, having become pregnant by ignorance or accident, are suffering from guilt and shame, a condition often intensified by nonsupportive parents. At the same time, they face many practical decisions: Should the baby be given away for adoption? Can the father be forced to marry them, or pay child support?

Since teenage mothers disproportionately become guilty of child abuse, drop out of school, and have repeat pregnancies, a full-time counselor for individual and group sessions is a must for all but the very smallest programs.

Numerous programs have proved that these problems can be successfully met. Over four hundred teenage mothers in the heart of Los Angeles's Watts area have gone through a program offered by the King/Drew Medical Center in cooperation with the schools. In the six years that they have been followed, only five have had repeat pregnancies and only one case of child abuse has been reported.[1]

d. Infant Care Class

All students would be required to participate in a class dealing with prenatal and postnatal child care, health and nutrition, and contraceptive methods for future sexual activity. (*Nationwide more than a fifth of all teenagers giving birth have already had at least one other child.*) The school's full-time registered nurse would teach the class, for which academic credit would be given.

e. Medical Clinic

A complete doctor-staffed prenatal clinic, open as many hours a week as necessary, *would be housed at the school.* Here girls would receive their initial prenatal health exam and regular follow-ups both before and after delivery. The registered nurse would be the administrator of the clinic and available for emergency consultation during the week. While girls would be permitted to use private medical services, most would probably use the obstetrical care available through the school.

Payment for both prenatal care and delivery would be made in the same manner as it would had the program not existed—private payment, insurance, Medicaid and other Social Security programs, or in some cases county welfare and charity. Regardless of the type of payment, all girls would receive the specialized care demanded for these high-risk pregnancies.

Depending on the community's size, various methods might be used to staff the medical component. In some instances, the local public health department would be able to furnish the necessary personnel. In cities with a medical school, the obstetrics department might be willing (as was the University of Louisville in the pioneering program there) to staff the clinic as part of its research and training efforts. In other communities, contracting with a local obstetrician might be the solution, and in smaller programs, even volunteer doctors might be available.

f. Fathers-to-be Class

Experience has shown that many fathers of unborn babies are willing to participate in a weekly class—sometimes even when they do not plan to marry or live with the mother. Contrary to the myth that brands all as irresponsible, many are eager to be of help and to participate in the responsibilities of child rearing. The class would meet outside regular school hours at a convenient time in the evenings or during the weekend. These teenage fathers-to-be are often emotionally confused, guilt-ridden, and anxious to discuss their feelings. Here they could meet with other youths beset with the same problems, consider their responsibilities, and explore available options. Along with this they could receive practical training in how to be a father—everything from changing diapers to providing emotional support to the mother.

g. Nursery

The availability of day care is vital to the ability of most teenage mothers to continue school. A nursery in conjunction with the school not only furnishes a needed service, it offers an unprecedented opportunity in breaking the cycle of poverty by getting the new baby off to a good start. Furthermore, knowing her baby is nearby where she can check, even nurse, between classes permits the young mother to relax and concentrate on her studies.

Work in the nursery would be a class required of all girls, even before their own babies were born. It would be a training laboratory to gain experience in feeding, diapering, and bathing the newcomer.

As noted, numerous programs have demonstrated that the problem of education for teenage mothers can be successfully solved. But nationwide these programs are so few and the demand so great that at best they are only an unfulfilled vision of hope. In New York City schools, for example, there are seventeen programs providing day care at school, yet there are only 350 slots available for the 5,000 school-age girls giving birth each year.

In Chapter 10 it was proposed that AFDC pay for child care while the mother is in school. This should be integrated into the Teenage

Parents Alternative School. Even by utilizing all outside financial help, however, the total program would be expensive. But as with other alternative programs the ultimate benefits would far outweigh the costs. *It is simply a question of whether we choose to be vindictive and punish those who have "transgressed," or choose to be compassionate and view the long-range quality of our society.*

Chapter 14

SHELTER FOR THROWAWAYS AND PUSHOUTS

Roaming the streets of America is a special category of children. They are a sad, hapless group, both male and female, hustling change for a meal, selling their bodies, engaging in shoplifting and other petty crimes, scrounging day by day for the bare means of survival, frequently numbing their minds with drugs in an effort to escape the misery, the discomforts, and the absence of love in their lives. They sleep in abandoned buildings, in parks, and under freeway bridges. Or they cluster into quasi-family groups for support and crowd into the vermin-infested crash pad that they have been able to rent by pooling their money . . . or that has been conveniently provided by exploitive adults—pimps, pornographers, drug dealers, pedophiles, and homosexuals seeking youthful partners.

They are, on the average, fifteen years old.

No one knows for certain how many there are. They exist largely in the underground, successfully trying to escape detection. Less than one out of four ever comes to the official attention of the police. The Department of Health and Human Services estimates that there may be as many as two million. Two million! If that estimate is anywhere near correct, the number is greater than the combined populations of our four least populous states. Even the more generally accepted estimates of somewhat over a million means an incredible mass of children existing on the fringes of an affluent society. To care for them, society magnanimously provides some six thousand emergency beds nationwide

About half are girls, 80 percent are white.

Technically they are called runaways. We met three of them in the chapter on status offenders—Ralph and Chuck and Marie—selling their bodies on the street. As we have seen, a more accurate name for most would be throwaways or pushouts, children of parents who are unable or unwilling to care for them—children running away from nowhere. In an era of deteriorating family stability, where adults have few qualms about disposing of unwanted mates by divorce, why not toss out an unwanted kid who has become only a nuisance? This was underscored by a California survey that found that only one in six runaways was ever reported by parents or guardians to the police as missing.[1] It suited many parents just fine for their children to leave. Before leaving, however, the vast majority have been sexually, physically, or psychologically abused.

One out of four has attempted or seriously considered suicide.

While many of these youths gravitate to the supposedly glamorous spots, the bright lights of Times Square, Miami, and Hollywood, even there police estimate that up to 80 percent are from nearby areas less than fifty miles away. Most runaways have the financial resources only to get to the nearest city they believe is large enough to offer anonymity. Once there, they quickly discover the hazards of survival.

Interviews with runaway girls in San Francisco found that two out of five had been robbed within forty-eight hours of arriving in town. In a matter of days the runaway is reduced to begging, shoplifting, or prostitution. Without protection, many are raped and assaulted. At this stage most of the few who were merely seeking adventure sheepishly return home. For others, however, terror on the streets is preferable to terror at home. For others it is the start of a career. A survey of two hundred active San Francisco prostitutes revealed that the majority had turned to prostitution after running away from home because of parental abuse.

Many simply are unable to survive on the street. Some two hundred unidentified children are found dead each year.

Today these runaways face a far greater danger than cold and hunger. They flirt with a slow, agonizing death: AIDS. While most teenage prostitutes, like my three friends on San Francisco's Polk Street, claim to know about the danger and practice "safe sex," in reality many are naively ignorant. And even among the informed, many are careless or fatalistic—"It won't happen to me." Often their johns will temptingly offer extra money not to use a condom. The problem is intensified by the crack epidemic. Kids become so desperate for a vial of crack that they sell their bodies. And crack so impairs judgment that many fail to do anything to protect themselves.

It is quite possible that the next large epidemic of AIDS will appear in the runaway underground. The conditions are right: promiscuous sex and heavy use of drugs. Already ominous signs are surfacing. In the *New England Journal of Medicine*, Dr. Donald Burke reported having examined medical tests recently given army applicants. Overall the number testing positive to the HIV virus (the precursor of AIDS) remains low. But in New York, San Franciso, and Washington, D.C., where there is the highest concentration of runaway male prostitutes, the number showing exposure to the HIV virus is now approaching twenty per thousand tested. At New York's Covenant House, the large runaway center off Times Square, by the end of 1989 6.5 percent of the sixteen- to eighteen-year-olds were testing positive and among nineteen-year-olds it was a horrendous 17 percent. These are frightening statistics.

Forced into the Underground

As touched on in Chapter 6, the fact that running away from home is an illegal act for juveniles forces them underground.' Believing they will be thrown in jail or returned home if caught, they carefully avoid official agencies. Thus, most are unknown to those who might give help or food and a safe haven. They are left prey to exploitive adults. If escaping an unsatisfactory and often unsafe home were not a crime, many of these youths would surface where they could be counseled and helped.

The proposal to remove status offenders, including runaways, from jurisdiction of the juvenile court erroneously implies that other help is available. Unfortunately, in most cities little exists—even the very basic necessities of an empty bed and a warm meal. In Houston, school officials became so concerned that in 1989 they opened the gymnasium doors in two schools for students who apparently had no home or family.

In Hollywood, *Los Angeles Times* feature writer Jerry Belcher a few years back found forty-one "official" shelter beds provided by public agencies and twenty provided by private groups—a total of sixty-one beds for an estimated three to four thousand runaways roaming the streets of the movie capital. He discovered them by the hundreds crowded into crash pads, frequently in abandoned and condemned apartment houses.[2]

In San Francisco, there are forty beds available for an estimated one thousand homeless youths. At these emergency shelter facilities the stay is limited to from three to ten nights, except for one house with ten beds where a youth may stay up to sixty days. One crisis center worker explained to me that administrators in San Francisco's Department of Social Services don't want to provide too many services—they don't want to make the city an attractive runaway capital.

These homeless youths have the basic needs of all children, the need for food, shelter, and a positive, loving family environment. Since the vast majority of their families have failed to supply their needs, these runaways become society's responsibility. Just as it is grossly immoral to permit Iraq to gobble up a neighboring nation, so it is grossly immoral that society permits these children to be denied their basic needs. Places are needed that can help change the spots on the lousy cards fate has dealt them. If society can find the financial resources to lock them in costly institutions, certainly we can afford less damaging alternatives.

Throughout the nation there are a number of good pioneering efforts. Shelter House run by the YMCA in Louisville has been a national model. One of the more effective programs, and certainly the largest, is the aforementioned Covenant House in New York City, part of a network that also includes houses in Fort Lauderdale, Houston, New Orleans, and Toronto. Annually Covenant House has raised over three times as much as the paltry $29 million the federal government spends for such programs. Each year some eleven thousand adolescents are in and out of the New York center—as many as four hundred a night—taking advantage of the no-questions-asked offer of help and a bed, the latter often only a mattress on the floor. Many are teenage mothers with their babies. An average of seventy desperate youths each day come to the Covenant House health clinic, many fearful that they've "got AIDS." (The personal life of the founder of Covenant House, Father Bruce Ritter, should not be permitted to tarnish the magnitude of the services that he and Covenant House have provided to so many thousands of bewildered, homeless youths.)

Most cities have some sort of runaway center, invariably pitifully inadequate and swallowed up by the overwhelming need. Yet federal money and the time of law enforcement officers are being used to jail these kids and send them back to abusive homes from which they will run again. Vast expansions are needed in two directions: in the depth of services being offered and in the number of beds available.

A Comprehensive Shelter House Program

Seven components are necessary in a program to meet the needs of runaways, pushouts, and throwaway children. Expensive? Yes. But as suggested by the U.S. Senate Judiciary Committee, far less expensive than building delinquency institutions and prisons to house them *and their future offspring.*

1. Crisis Center

The first need is a well-publicized, twenty-four-hour-a-day crisis center, possibly located at a shelter house. Any youth could go there in an emergency to find answers to overpowering questions: What protection is there from physical or sexual abuse by parents? Where can food and shelter be obtained? Where can someone be found to plead his case with parents who refuse to listen? What can a girl do when her older boyfriend dumps her in a strange city? How can a girl determine if she is really pregnant without her parents finding out, and what can she do about it? How can one obtain a desperately needed job? Is there any decent way to get money for a ticket back home after the "adventure" has turned sour?

The crisis center must have a knowledgeable counselor available around the clock. Equally important, it must have a way to let a troubled youth know the center exists. Shelter House in Louisville tackles this latter need with an active community program. Throughout the city hundreds of prominent locations—from fast-food establishments to convenience stores—have been designated as a "Safe Place" and clearly identified by highly visible black and yellow logo signs. Here a youth in crisis may stay while an employee makes a call to Shelter House. A trained volunteer on twenty-four-hour call is then dispatched to pick up the youth.

The public school system cooperates by showing a twelve-minute videotape at middle and senior high schools. At the conclusion of the tape, which explains how help can be obtained by going to a Safe Place site, students are given a wallet-size card containing information about counseling services available at Shelter House, and its twenty-four-hour phone number. In 1988 the National League of Cities cited Shelter House and the city of Louisville for the Most Innovative Program award. The program is now being replicated in 115 cities under a Safe Place franchise.

2. Temporary Shelter

Most youths require a place to stay while the staff seeks a resolution of their problem. Many runaways simply need a safe haven while both they and their parents cool off after an overheated argument. With a bit of counseling, and perhaps some intervention with their parents, they will go back home. (At Louisville's Shelter House, after counseling and a stay as brief as overnight or as long as several weeks, 80 percent go home or to a staff-approved placement.)

Rules must be rigidly observed. The first would be that any youth permitted to stay overnight must make a phone call, or allow the staff to do so, to let a parent know that he or she is okay and in a safe place. When requested by the youth, the location would be kept confidential, but the parents would be told that they will be advised of any change of plans. This contact paves the way for future parent-child counseling.

A second rule would concern behavior while living in the shelter house. While it is essential that the staff refrain from overt moral sermonizing which would turn many off, the youth would be required to sign a behavioral agreement. This would include a promise not to bring any drugs or alcohol into the house, not to fight with or steal from any other resident, and to participate in housekeeping chores. The youth would be made to understand that infractions were cause for expulsion, and if the misbehavior was serious enough, a delinquency petition might be filed with the court.

Finally, there would be an understanding that after a two- or three-day adjustment and/or cooling-off period, to continue living there would require participation in whatever longer-term plans—school or work—have been agreed upon with the staff. A runaway center must not become a free pad for lazing around, goofing off, and watching TV all day.

3. Emergency Care for the Court

The shelter house should also be available to the court for a temporary placement in lieu of holding certain youths in secure detention. This would include juveniles needing immediate protection of the court in child abuse cases and minor offenders whom for some reason the court cannot release to the custody of parents. An understanding must be reached with the court, however, that such temporary place-ment is *not* secure detention, and that legally the youth is free to leave whenever he or she wishes.

4. Family Counseling

When possible, the staff would work toward reconciliation between runaways and their families. Frequently this will be extremely diffi-cult or even impossible. But all parents would be urged to come for a counseling session where the staff would serve as a neutral arbitra-tor. In cases of divorced parents, both would be urged to attend.

Experiences in successful runaway programs show that such a ses-sion is often the first time that parent and child have ever discussed the source of their problems without yelling and screaming at each other. Often it is only after a series of sessions lasting over several weeks that the youth and parents agree to "try again." A staff coun-selor should follow up on these reconciliations.

5. Youth Advocacy

Implied in the shelter house concept is the notion that the staff be-comes an advocate for all young people in trouble. Since staff mem-bers continually see the problems faced by juveniles in the community, no one is more qualified to speak out. They can do so in newspaper and TV interviews and in talks before service clubs, PTA meetings, and other civic groups.

On a more immediate level, the staff must give their clients what-ever support is appropriate. At times this could involve filing charges against physically and sexually abusive parents, having pimps ar-rested, persuading a school system to place the youth in a more attainable program, pleading with the court to give a minor offender another chance, obtaining medical or psychiatric care when needed, or persuading an employer to give a job to a deserving kid.

6. Long-term Shelter

It has become obvious that many young people on the street need more than temporary shelter. They have no home. When no better arrangement is available, *as a last resort* younger children should be assigned to foster care homes by the court. But most fourteen- to seventeen-year-olds are too mature, too worldly wise to fit comfort-ably into most foster care arrangements. Adjustment is often difficult for both the youngster of this age and the foster parent, many of whom have agreed to house an older youth only with the expectation of letting the state foot the bill for an able-bodied handyman. Many runaways are already running from a similar exploitive situation.

Thus a critical need of older homeless juveniles is for long-term shelter, a safe place to mature. This may be provided by group shelter homes where a small supportive staff, substituting for parents, would help eight to sixteen teenagers move toward adulthood and self-responsibility. In an attempt to reproduce a cooperative family situation as closely as possible, the group would include both girls and boys, all of whom would be expected to accept their share of household chores and home maintenance. Group projects to raise money, such as care of yards in the neighborhood or collecting newspapers, bottles, and aluminum cans for recycling, would provide for recreational activities. When appropriate, the court should order a parent to reimburse the center for the dependent's room and board.

Those who were attending school and doing reasonably well would be encouraged to continue and perhaps work after school or on Saturdays. Those not attending school would be expected to work at a job which the staff would help find. Most of the pay would be put aside for the day when the youth could become independent—the ultimate goal for all residents.

7. Supervised Independent Living

The final level in a comprehensive shelter home program is semi-independent living. This would be an arrangement for those who had graduated from the long-term shelter home and for others who became homeless when they were on the brink of taking off as full-scale adults. Also included would be newly homeless youths who had remained in foster homes until age eighteen, at which time they were required to leave, ready or not.

State and federal governments provide subsidized housing for handicapped persons and the elderly, low-rent shelter for those who are physically and financially unable to meet today's high cost of living. These subsidized units usually offer counseling and many of the special services required by the aged. The parallel with many homeless sixteen- to twenty-year-old youths is worthy of consideration. Many similarities exist. Both have financial and emotional needs that they cannot adequately satisfy alone.

Housing for these youths with rents subsidized on a sliding scale, based on the tenant's income, would be a sound investment in humanity and in the future safety of the city. Many would not find it necessary to turn to drug dealing and other crime. Equally important as the affordable rent would be the services available: recreational and social activities, drug and alcohol rehabilitation programs, job counseling, crisis counseling, perhaps even religious counseling, and advice about health care.

While participation in these special services should be strictly voluntary, the housing would nevertheless be "supervised" independent living. This means that behavioral agreements would be required, similar to those signed by shelter house residents but more appropriate to the older age. Strict enforcement would be necessary to prevent the complex from quickly becoming a vandalized slum project filled with pimps, prostitutes, and drug dealers. Failure to abide by rules that the staff and a council of residents agreed upon would result in expulsion.

In addition to rigid rules, "supervised" would mean that the apartment units would be subject to periodic inspection to see that they were properly maintained, and each resident would be required to have a monthly interview with the project counselor. This would be aimed primarily at determining whether special help was indicated. Residents would, of course, be free to leave any time they desired, and would be required to leave when they reached a prescribed age, probably twenty-one. In many ways this concept is reminiscent of the old YMCAs of a half-century ago which helped many a teenager along the way to independent adulthood.

(One further program to offer shelter—and job training—to runaways will be considered in the next chapter. A revival of the old Civilian Conservation Corps would offer a challenging opportunity to homeless youths wanting to escape the streets.)

Community Support

A comprehensive shelter program as outlined here will require strong community support, both emotional and financial. Much of the financial support should come from the city government and federal subsidies. A substantial amount, however, should be raised in the community. A well-directed financial drive is an effective educational program to increase community awareness.

Again it must be emphasized that success of any runaway program is largely dependent upon early intervention. "Early" means within the first few days a youth is on the streets. Outreach workers must be on the lookout for them at places where runaways tend to congregate—bus stations, truck stops, parks—and on the streets where prostitutes vie for customers.

Time is truly of the essence. As has been noted, when their original resources are exhausted and they discover that no one will hire a fourteen- or fifteen-year-old, runaways must resort to illegal activities for survival. One runaway told me, "You do what you have to. If you have to mug a guy in order to eat, then you mug a guy." Many who have previously been sexually abused have no problem with turning tricks for pay. And with the proper connections, hustling drugs can be highly profitable.

At this stage the runaway becomes a real criminal, subject to arrest and criminal sanctions. Quickly he or she will become absorbed into the camaraderie of the underground counterculture. From there escape is possible, provided jobs are available, but it is difficult. Regretfully, for many—like fourteen-year-old Marie whom I met on Polk Street—escape is not even desired. They have seen the quick profits to be garnered in the criminal world. A minimum-wage job is only for wimps.

Chapter 15

JOBS VERSUS DELINQUENCY

A popular song in the era following World War I concerned the behavior and morals of many of the returning doughboys. The song succinctly asked: "How ya gonna keep 'em down on the farm after they've seen Paree?"

A very similar question could be asked of thirteen- and fourteen- and fifteen-year-old juveniles who, with no allowance from home and unable to find a job, have engaged in mugging and purse snatching, in burglary and con games, in prostitution and drug dealing. How ya gonna interest them in a dull, low-pay job after they've seen the big money to be had on the seamy side of the law?

I recall the dismay of a Louisville high school principal some years back when he was trying to persuade an intelligent, personable young dropout to sign up for a new vocational training project. "How much you make a month?" the dropout challenged. When the principal explained that (even back then) it was better than three thousand dollars a month, the youth replied: "Look, man, I made more than that last week. Why should I go through all the hassle just to become a grease monkey?" Then he really rubbed it in. "But thanks. You're an all-right guy. I like you. If you get pushed for bread, man, let me know. Maybe I can help."

Most delinquents fail to achieve the income of that young drug dealer, but it is estimated that more than 25 percent of teenage income in many inner-city areas comes from crime. In American society a teenager must have spending money, and he's going to get it. Many discover it's really not too difficult to obtain—illegally. Later they may have little interest in eight hours of legitimate work at poverty wages.

They've already seen Paree.

When in the spring of 1989 the unemployment rate dropped below 5 percent and for teenagers below 14 percent, many people concluded that teenage unemployment was no longer a critical issue. They pointed to the "help wanted" signs that prior to the Christmas season had become standard window decorations of small shops and fast-food establishments. But it was a faulty conclusion.

Unemployment is allocated unevenly among the various layers and hues of our society and is highly concentrated among racial minorities and children of welfare recipients. The uneducated, the untrained, the undisciplined, are the last to be hired, the first to be let go. Overall unemployment among black teenagers is still above 30 percent. And the figure runs as high as 60 and 75 percent in some blighted areas—areas where future criminals are being bred and nurtured. Here by age twenty-five unemployment has become a way of life. Many have never held a job. Drugs, alcohol, and crime have become quick fixes for their problems.

The obstacles these teenagers face are many: the small demand for youths who are functionally illiterate, the rapidly evaporating pool of even semiskilled jobs, racial discrimination, union hall efforts to limit the competitive supply of additional laborers, the exodus of industry from the inner cities, the unwillingness of many employers to offer entry-level jobs that include a training feature for disadvantaged applicants. When these are all added together along with the youth's total ignorance of the work ethic, the results spell disaster.

Unfortunately, unemployed youths can't sit around idly for years waiting for a paying job. Survival is a basic drive. They can exist for a while, finding an odd job now and then, occasionally begging a few dollars from some relative. Eventually they give up. The Labor Department estimates that nearly a million are in this category, so discouraged they no longer are looking for jobs and are uncounted in unemployment statistics.

But worthy or unworthy, these young people still have to eat, and they have to have pocket money. They'll get it—one way or another.

It is easy for society to say, "Go to work or starve." But if no one will hire these uneducated, untrained, undisciplined youths, it is society that in the end is the real loser.

There is a cliché among youth advocates: find jobs for teenagers and most of the problems of delinquency and drug trafficking will disappear. But it's not that simple. Many soundly conceived demonstration projects have laid eggs. All too often the delinquent has soon quit or is fired—or stays on the job and keeps right on getting into trouble with the law. Those youngsters for whom jobs have been found seem to pop up in court with about the same frequency as control groups for whom the program did not provide jobs.

The success of the few favorably evaluated programs can usually be explained by one of two factors, one good, one bad. In the latter case, project directors, anxious about their own jobs and intent on making a good showing, carefully skimmed the cream of the applicants, selecting only educated and highly disciplined youths who probably would have succeeded anyhow. They excluded those less likely to find work whose failure would put a black mark on the program's record. Consequently, despite the program's "success," it failed to reach those for whom it was designed.

In the case of the positive factor, the successful program could have been one of the few able to provide jobs in which the participants could see some future, a future worth *working* for. Unlike jobs usually found for delinquents, these were not low-prestige dead-end jobs that generated neither hope nor pride.

So consistent have been the research findings that it should now be considered axiomatic: *To be effective in preventing a youth from turning to crime, the proposed job must offer some hope of advancement, must give the youth some hope of eventually being able to join the mainstream of affluent America.*

A number of these successful programs do exist, proving that runaways, dropouts, and untrained ghetto youths can be trained. IBM, for example, has invested heavily in its Job Training for the Disadvantaged Program. In nine urban-area centers, job training is offered to largely Hispanic youths unable to afford commercial training programs. Many are on public assistance when they start. IBM records show that graduates have a job placement record of 86 percent at an average salary of over twelve thousand dollars. This is training for jobs with a future.

The Vocational Foundation Inc., a nonprofit institution in midtown Manhattan, has been working with troubled youths for fifty-three years. It was created by a visionary industrialist, Walter N. Thayer, who over the years was able to coax money from corporate leaders. Training a teenager for a job has cost around ten thousand dollars including a hundred-dollar-a-week stipend while training—considerably less than the forty thousand a year it costs to keep one in a reform school. Around 70 percent of those enrolled have been placed in building trades, clerical offices, and the food and apparel industries—again, jobs with a future.[1] Unfortunately, the $1.5 million the foundation has been able to raise each year hardly touches the need. And the approach would not be effective with all youths.

For many disadvantaged youths the federal student-loan program permitting them to go to college and trade schools has been a godsend, even though frequently proprietary schools have been scams, ripping off enrollees and giving them false hopes. But again, this program fails to reach the really hard-core unemployables. To provide enough jobs and training to be effective, a coordinated effort of the federal and state governments, local communities, and the public school system will be required.

FEDERAL OFFICE OF YOUTH EMPLOYMENT AND TRAINING

Admittedly, the warm glow of success has not shone forth from many of the federal youth programs stemming from Lyndon Johnson's Great Society. Federally funded efforts over the past three decades—from WIN (Work Incentive Program) to CETA (Comprehensive Employment and Training Act) to JTPA (Job Training Partnership Act)—have often been merely disguised welfare payments. At best they have had only marginal success.

Frequently they have proved to be local boondoggles encountering poor planning, graft, corruption of purpose, and all the ills of bureaucratic administration. And in many instances the young people they would train have been so severely damaged by all the debilitating problems of the underclass that the help being offered is the proverbial too little, too late.

Despite all the hoopla of many congressional hearings, the lawmakers themselves are to blame for many of the difficulties. Politics have often taken priority over sound policy. The reluctance to act forcefully is at times incredible. Year after year, for example, Congress has dillydallied about funding a summer youth work program until vacation time is actually well under way. Community leaders are forced to hastily scrape together a makeshift program, frenziedly recruit both a staff and teenage workers, and make compromise after compromise to keep the program from being a total fiasco.

Pointing the finger at past mistakes should not be an excuse for giving up. The stakes are too high. As part of a comprehensive effort five programs are needed. To be properly coordinated, they should be located in *one* federal office, an Office of Youth Employment and Training, logically within the Department of Labor.

1. School Training Programs

The first tier of a comprehensive job-training effort should be within the public school system. School-based vocational and/or career programs need to be radically upgraded for the two-thirds of America's high school graduates who don't go on to college—who now leave with no salable skill by which they can earn a living. This has been explored in considerable detail in Chapter 12 on restructuring the school system. New areas of public education to prepare youths for work in modern society were proposed for the Career High, and training for less demanding vocations was scheduled for the alternative schools.

2. Community Service Corps

Projects under this program would employ youths aged twelve through sixteen in part-time public service jobs. Participants would be selected from schools in high-delinquency areas on the basis of family need. Some people may claim that this program would be little more than merely paying kids to be good. Well? Basically they would be right. Would it be better to reward them for being bad as delinquency now does? It is designed to help keep underprivileged youths in school instead of sending them to see Paree.

The Community Service Corps would strive to accomplish a number of goals. It would (1) prevent many from becoming delinquent because of having no spending money, (2) teach welfare children that money is something that can be obtained by working, not just something that comes in the mail each month, (3) give early training in good, responsible work habits, and (4) permit many economically disadvantaged teenagers to remain in school. This is a pretty healthy group of goals—goals that have become increasingly important in view of the rapidly growing number of America's children who are living in poverty.

The program would operate year-round, but would be stepped up in the summer months. Features of both FDR's National Youth Administration (NYA) and LBJ's Neighborhood Youth Corps (NYC) would be incorporated. Well-publicized mismanagement in the NYC has tarnished the concept. But instead of abandoning a greatly needed effort, past abuses should be corrected and the program scrupulously divorced from both state and federal politics.

While activities would be limited only by the imagination of community leaders (and approval of the state agency), emphasis would be on improvement of the environment and on services to the elderly and disabled, particularly relieving the loneliness many must endure. In Pittsburgh the housing authority has instituted a "read-aloud partners" program which employs students to read to small children of parents who don't know how to read.

New York City's Department for the Aging has a successful program designed to keep potential dropouts in school. High-risk students are given training and work experience at senior citizen centers and nursing homes and with the homebound elderly. Four half-days of work a week are provided, with the youth going to school the rest of the time. A strict "no school, no work" policy is maintained. Begun two years ago, the project now employs more than two hundred students from fifteen high schools; some sixty senior citizen programs benefit. The project has brought a bridge of understanding across the generation gap, and early indications are that students are being kept in school—and out of trouble with the law.

In my files are dozens of accounts of successful projects which give some indication of the range to be considered for the Community Service Corps. Among them:

- Making life easier for totally or partially incapacitated individuals by doing marketing or laundry, running errands to the post office and bank, walking dogs, or helping clean house
- Reading to blind, elderly, or disabled persons
- Maintenance and other work at senior citizens centers, hospitals, and nursing homes

- Group performances—choral, dance, or drama—at nursing homes and homes for the aged or disabled
- Repair and painting of deteriorating homes belonging to needy, elderly individuals
- Supervision of recreational activities for handicapped children, including taking retarded children on camping trips
- Reading to children at the public library
- Individual tutoring of slow learners in elementary schools
- Restoring neglected cemeteries and other historic spots around the community
- Creating new city parks and improving existing ones
- Development of nearby wilderness areas by constructing hiking trails and paths, clearing away brush and undergrowth, and building picnic tables and bridges
- Painting colorful murals, under supervision of a professional artist, on unsightly city walls and fences and on dismal cafeteria and activity rooms in schools and nursing homes

These jobs are made work—deliberately so. They provide a teenager with a job without taking one away from another individual. They are jobs that perform a meaningful service—a service our affluent society can well afford to provide to its less fortunate citizens. And they are jobs in which a youth can take pride for having reached out and contributed to another human being.

Although these jobs would do little to teach specific work skills, they would underscore principles of the work ethic. Failing to show up, or being late, or doing poor work, or being disrespectful would be causes for dismissal. First infractions would bring a warning and an explanation of the need to abide by work rules. Further infractions would place the youth on probationary leave—without pay—for a week or more, and would eventually bring dismissal. Loss of the job and the pay for unsatisfactory performance would not go unnoticed by other workers.

3. Training Programs by Industry

The two-tiered minimum wage, which President Bush insisted upon to allow for a "training wage," will be a bonanza to those who employ teenagers—primarily fast-food restaurants, supermarkets, and service stations. These do not require extensive training, so the lower wage will let them save on employee costs. But the differential is too small and is available over too brief a time to permit a meaningful training program for most business and industrial jobs offering a promising future.

Private industry could, however, be extremely effective in training disadvantaged youngsters. The current shortage of qualified youths (qualified by educational attainment, social skills, and attitude toward the work ethic) makes this a propitious time to prod industry into establishing training programs for those who are only marginally qualified. The problem is finding the proper carrot to entice industry.

The National Commission on Youth, a think tank created by the Charles F. Kettering Foundation, has urged the use of tax credits as an incentive for employers to set up apprenticeship, internship, and training programs. This would not be entirely new. The 1986 tax overhaul bill revived (over the administration's objections) the Targeted Jobs Tax Credit program which had expired in 1985. This program promotes jobs for various handicapped and economically disadvantaged groups. Unfortunately, the modest funds were reduced. The program allows tax credit for hiring "certified" youths aged sixteen through nineteen who are participating in a qualified cooperative educational project. It fails, however, to encourage industry to set up its own internal training programs designed for its specific needs.

For an effective program, tax credits should be given to the employer for up to 75 percent of the wage of a youth in strictly nonproductive training, then 50 percent for six months of apprenticeship training, and finally, if needed, up to 25 percent of the wages during the next six months. Original approval of a company's training program design would be obtained from the official state youth employment agency, which would then monitor the operations and periodically grant continuation status. Approval would not be given to companies that offered only dead-end jobs, thus preventing industries that required no real training from benefiting from the tax subsidy.

The same state agency would also have the important task of certifying potential trainees as being members of targeted groups. Companies could be encouraged to develop innovative approaches. For example, an older worker could be assigned as an "industry brother" to counsel and encourage the underprivileged neophyte. Such a training program could open up jobs to presently unemployable youths—jobs with a future.

4. Youth Conservation Corps

Perhaps no New Deal program met with such universal favor among liberals and conservatives alike during its heyday as did the Civilian Conservation Corps, the federal agency that put depression-era youths to work. Many business and community leaders of the past few decades look back in gratitude to the financial and emotional boost the program gave them. Living in invigorating camps, eating nutritious food, learning the discipline of honest work, those young Americans blossomed. And even today, a half-century later, we still find pleasure in the parks and recreational areas they created.

As teenage unemployment among certain groups continues to mount in a nation now far more financially able to offer this helping hand than in the 1930s the time has come to reinstate such a program on a major scale. It need not necessarily be residential, as was the old CCC, but could employ teenagers living at home or in subsidized housing (as proposed in the previous chapter). Regardless of whether the Corps was nonresidential or utilized camp-style living, it would be an opportunity to hand out a check for hard work instead of a welfare check, an opportunity for the nation to receive material benefits for the money paid out to the unemployed—and an opportunity to salvage thousands of our problem teenagers.

A dozen or so states and at least fifteen communities have grown weary waiting for Congress to act. As they have watched penniless youths turn to crime they have in desperation begun small programs on their own. The Human Environment Center, a Washington, D.C., clearinghouse, reports that in 1985 these programs were serving 7,000 jobless youths.[2] The largest is California's Conservation Corps, which employees 2,200. Their activities range from renovating parks to weatherproofing homes of the needy. It is claimed that for every $1.00 spent, their work returns $1.77 in benefits to the state.

The figure of 7,000 job slots means that these programs are serving only a tiny fraction of the number who could benefit. The full potential will be achieved only with the infusion of massive federal support. Grants to be matched by the states should be awarded by the proposed Office of Youth Employment and Training. Projects would range over the entire area of conservation and public recreation, anything the state or community felt would contribute to the well-being of the citizenry. In addition to working in parks and recreational areas, many environmental projects would clean up polluted areas. Again, these would be new jobs that would not take employment from another person.

A residential Youth Conservation Corps would be particularly advantageous to the thousands who are homeless—a wholesome alternative to prostitution and living on the streets. A healthy camp environment, away from the crime and drugs of the inner city, could be the life jacket needed by many who have been kicked out of, or are running away from, their homes.

5. Job Corps

It is difficult to name a federal social program of recent years that has received more accolades—and more brickbats—than the Job Corps, the surviving showpiece of Lyndon Johnson's Great Society. The typical youth in the Job Corps is an eighteen-year-old school dropout, frequently black, reading on the sixth-grade level, and from a socially and financially impoverished family of the inner city. He has never held a legitimate job, has no skills or know-how to obtain one. Only crime and/or welfare loom in his future.

Trainees are enrolled in Job Corps centers across the nation, many located hundreds of miles away from the squalor and deprivation of their homes. For four to six months they are paid to learn marketable skills such as welding, auto mechanics, carpentry, electrical repair, nursing, cooking, secretarial and clerical skills, landscaping and yard maintenance. Considering the background of the youths enrolled, it is not surprising that there are many social and disciplinary problems in the centers, and that many enrollees have not succeeded. Unfortunately, it has been the problems and the failures that have made the news.

To obtain a clearer picture of just how good or bad the program is, Mathematica Policy Research, Inc., was engaged for an independent, long-range evaluation. The report, released in 1982, included follow-up interviews with hundreds of 1977 Job Corps members and with a comparative group who did not receive the training. It declared that the program had been a resounding success in putting disadvantaged youths to work and in keeping them out of jail and off welfare rolls. In addition to the humanitarian values, the reported stated, great economic benefits to society had been achieved.

For fiscal year 1984 Job Corps director Peter E. Rell claimed an incredible success of 75.6 percent. Of those who could be contacted, 60.6 percent had found jobs or entered the army, while 15 percent went on for further education. Some centers have at times shown close to 90 percent post-training employment.

With reports such as these, it is difficult to understand the brickbats that were thrown at the program, most audibly by former Office of Management and Budget director David A. Stockman and President Reagan himself while in office.

George Lardner, Jr., a feature writer for the *Washington Post*, points out an ironic aspect of the twentieth-anniversary celebration of the Job Corps. A telegram from President Reagan was read acclaiming it as a "vital program," one that was "in keeping with the American spirit of helping others to reach their full potential, a spirit that has sustained our nation from its very founding." He included best wishes for its continued success. This was six weeks prior to the 1984 election. Five months later, with the election behind him, he submitted his proposed 1986 fiscal budget, which would have totally wiped out the Job Corps.

This flip-flop was likely promoted by the then OMB director's extreme dislike of the program. (One supporter suggested that Stockman must have been mugged by a former Job Corps member.) He refused to believe the Mathematica Policy Research's report and demanded further assessments of the program and even verification of the report itself. Three separate reviews by outside experts, all upholding the report, failed to sway Stockman. He resorted to deceptive statistics, later repeated by Reagan.

Stockman claimed that each of the program's slots cost $15,200 a year, which "nearly equals the annual cost of sending a student to Harvard or Stanford universities"—as if these trainees could have been accepted at the universities, regardless of the cost. Making such a statement was dirty pool, for it implied that this was the cost for each trainee. Actually, a youth spent on the average only five months in the program, so that the slot furnished training for nearly two and a half individuals during that year. The per-trainee cost was nearer $6,000. (And on the other hand, to be comparative, the understated college cost would have to be multiplied by four years.)

Furthermore, Stockman stated that only one-third of the members were employed a year after leaving the Corps. This dubious statement was based solely on incomplete reports of state employment services listing the number of known former Job Corp trainees for whom they had found jobs. It totally ignored the many who found jobs on their own or through other agencies. (It is incredible that back in 1976 a *Wall Street Journal* writer once complained that *only* two-thirds of the graduates found jobs—as if that were not a fantastic achievement considering the social history of the enrollees.)

Despite Reagan's and Stockman's deceptive criticism, Congress refused to go along, and the Job Corps survived. The most vocal support came from senators within Reagan's party, particularly Lowell Weicker, Jr., of Connecticut and Orrin Hatch of Utah. Of the proposal to reduce the budget by eliminating the Job Corps, Senator Hatch said that this would "give us black ink today and red ink tomorrow."

But the victory was also a tragedy. As has happened with so many youth programs, a legislative compromise with the administration forced a reduction. This came at a time when the Job Corps needed to be vastly expanded. The widening gap between the haves and have-nots and the widening cycle of poverty that encompasses many of our youth today are dark clouds on the horizon. As the Department of Labor has observed, for some the Job Corps is the last best hope to join the mainstream of society. Of the five programs proposed here for the Office of Youth Employment and Training, this is the only one capable of reaching many really hard-core, unemployable delinquents.

No time has been more propitious for expanding the Job Corps (and for inaugurating the Youth Conservation Corps) as the present. The military bases that are to be deactivated would provide already owned, instant campuses. Without extensive capital expenditure, there would be all the dormitories, training areas, and service facilities needed. For Congress to ignore this opportunity to expand a program that has demonstrated its ability to reach many of the "unreachables" would be an American tragedy.

It would compound the present tragedy: that the greatest nation in the world fails to see to it that every youth is trained for and has the opportunity to hold a dignified job that can provide for the basic needs of life.

Chapter 16

JUVENILES AND DRUGS—A WAR THAT WAS LOST

When President Reagan campaigned for election in 1980 he promised a gigantic war on drugs. That promise was fulfilled. Under his leadership both money and rhetoric in ever-increasing and unprecedented amounts were thrown into the battle.

But the wrong side won!

Despite an increase in the war chest from $800 million in 1981 to $4.8 billion in 1988, there is general agreement that the situation seriously deteriorated. Drugs have become more plentiful, easier to obtain. Alarming speeches, tougher laws, and more money proved to be an inadequate arsenal for attacking an insidious rodent gnawing away at the social fabric of America.

President Bush likewise promised a gigantic war on drugs: "This scourge will stop." But he turned the word "war" from a metaphor into a bloody reality—the destructive and costly invasion of a sovereign nation to capture a known drug criminal. That such an option remains high in his priorities was indicated early in 1990 when he said, "Narco-gangsters must be dealt with as such by our military—in the air, on the land and on the seas."[1]

Despite the souped-up war, despite additional billions of dollars, despite the hysterical passage of a rash of harsher laws (in Los Angeles a twenty-two-year-old youth is sentenced to life in prison *without* possibility of parole for selling five ounces of cocaine), the result has been the same as with Reagan's war: drugs on the streets remain plentiful and increasingly easier to obtain. There is such a glut of cocaine that the price is now only a quarter of what it was when the "wars" began a decade ago.

To those concerned about juveniles, the most terrifying aspect has been the participation of inner-city teenagers *and even preteens* in the violent gangs that control the distribution of drugs. *Herein lies today's most intractable delinquency problem.*

The convergence of two factors suddenly made juveniles the mainstay of the street drug scene: a do-nothing juvenile court and tougher laws for adults. By the court's repeatedly electing only to slap juveniles on the wrist, the gates were opened for drug lords to circumvent the increasingly harsh and mandatory penalties for adults. Many police don't even bother to arrest suspected juveniles, knowing the slim odds of punishment. It is not uncommon to find eleven- and twelve-year-olds earning a hundred dollars a day as lookouts for crack cocaine houses. Runners can make three hundred. When they graduate to become dealers, the sky's the limit—a thousand or more a night.

These mere children use high-tech equipment and untraceable cellular phones and wear beepers to school. Big profits make it worth the slight risk of arrest, even the greater risk of assassination by rival dealers. Jaguars and high-speed sports cars (at times owned by juveniles too young to drive them legally), heavy gold-chain necklaces worth thousands of dollars, and flashy designer clothes mark the successful dealer. Sadly, the quick money has dulled the appetite for education in the ghetto. Why bother? Drug trafficking is an easier, more certain way out of poverty.

Despite their age, this is not child's play. The violence and the magnitude of shoot-outs among youth gangs armed with automatic assault rifles make the violence of the Al Capone era look like a polite parlor game. In major cities hundreds of innocent victims have been caught in the cross fire of juvenile dealers trying to protect or establish their turfs. School administrators in Long Beach, California, had to erect a $160,000, ten-foot-high concrete wall around a junior high to deflect the bullets from rival youth gangs headquartered in nearby public housing projects.

No, it is not child's play.

Ten or fifteen years ago concern about juveniles and drugs largely revolved around the relatively innocuous use of marijuana and scattered experimentation with LSD and pep pills, even occasionally heroin—a fairly serious concern, but certainly no national disaster. Then suddenly crack appeared on the streets. In just six or seven years it galloped through large areas of the ghettos, leaving a shattered no-man's-land in its wake. Today delinquency cannot be discussed without considering the entire drug picture among both juveniles and adults.

The Drug Problem in Perspective

Few will deny that drug abuse is a serious social problem. But number one? Hardly.

Despite all the political rhetoric and media hype, it pales in comparison to the danger to America posed by poverty in the midst of affluence, by inferior education for many, by the lack of adequate health care for large segments of the population, by the deterioration of the family unit, by discrimination in the halls of justice. The escalation of the drug problem is in large measure only a visible symptom of these larger social problems which have been permitted to fester during the past decade.

A more immediate understanding of the parameters of the drug problem, however, is to be found in a comparison of the social and physical effects of legal versus illegal drugs. Invariably the general public considers the "drug problem" only in terms of illegal drugs, conveniently ignoring the destruction wrought by legal drugs including both prescription and over-the-counter drugs as well as nicotine and alcohol. For the moment consider only the latter.

The majority of all alcohol consumers—a population that includes most community leaders, most state and federal legislators, and most law enforcement personnel—haughtily shrug their shoulders and with righteous disdain declare that it is ridiculous to compare alcohol and *illegal* drugs.

And right they are! When one considers the tremendous death toll from alcohol abuse, the skyrocketing social costs and economic losses, it is indeed ridiculous to equate that with the damage done by *all* illegal drugs combined. According to a 1990 report from the U.S. Department of Health and Human Services, some 10.5 million adults exhibit symptoms of alcoholism, and the annual economic costs of disabilities and lost productivity add up to $136 billion. Like illegal drugs, alcohol leaves in its wake lost jobs, broken marriages, and shattered lives—but in far greater numbers. The recently identified fetal alcohol syndrome caused by drinking during pregnancy is the leading preventable cause of mental retardation. Over fifty thousand babies are born in the United States each year with alcohol-related defects.

Overall, the 100,000 annual deaths in America directly attributable to alcohol are some twenty times those attributable to illegal drugs.

Our concern goes beyond those alcoholics who in effect commit suicide by alcohol-induced failure of the kidneys, liver, or pancreas (and who often leave society stuck with their astronomical medical bills). There is concern for the innocent persons they kill—nearly 25,000 deaths caused each year by drunk drivers, a number that alone dwarfs the entire illegal drug abuse toll.

And this, again, is but a part of the tragedy. The half-million individuals who are seriously injured in these crashes must also be considered. Four out of every ten Americans will be involved in an alcohol-related crash during their lifetime. On weekends 62 percent of fatal accidents involve a driver with a detectable level of blood alcohol.

When newspeople sensationalize the tragedy of drug abuse, they fail to include such stories as the flaming deaths of twenty-seven youths from Radcliff, Kentucky, on a church outing, killed when a drunk driver crashed into their bus . . . or the oil tanker captain who caused a billion dollars' worth of damage to the Alaskan environment. Those who refuse to consider the damage caused by alcohol when discussing drug abuse are today's counterpart of the biblical hypocrites who could see the speck in their brother's eye but were unaware of the log in their own.

Nowhere is this hypocrisy so clearly evident as in the fanatical demands for drug testing. These demands have been made with little evidence of the need or value of such testing. A recent Texas study, however, published in the *Journal of Occupational Medicine*, specifically addresses this question.[2]

In Houston postmortem tests are made on virtually all victims of fatal job-related accidents. Researchers at the University of Texas analyzed these records for the presence of substances that could have affected job performance in nearly two hundred industrial deaths over a two-year period. They found that prior to their deaths 13 percent had been using alcohol. Only half as many, 7 percent, tested positive for all other drugs, and of these, most were legal medications available only by prescription. *Only one worker* (one-half of one percent) *had been using an illegal drug*—marijuana—prior to the accident. The researchers modestly suggested that "reducing or eliminating alcohol consumption among workers may help prevent some work-related fatalities."

Between 1978 and 1988 there were 6,175 accidents among commercial and private aircraft investigated by the National Transportation Safety Board. Of these 33 (or, again, one-half of one percent) were found to be related to drug use, while 299, nine times as many, were found to be alcohol-related. Yet despite these government statistics, in the fall of 1988 when the Department of Transportation launched a random drug-testing program for pilots, it refused to include tests for the far more dangerous drug, alcohol.

More than a year later the Department of Transportation announced the results of its Drug-Free Workplace Program. Less than 1 percent of the 15,352 random drug tests conducted on department employees during the sixteen-month period had turned up indications of drug use. Of the 99 positive tests, two-thirds were for marijuana. Cocaine accounted for virtually all of the rest. With the total cost of the program, including collecting and testing the samples, coming to more than $4 million, this meant that it cost an average of over $120,000 to uncover each hard drug user.

So far this attempt to put the drug problem in perspective has considered only one legal drug, alcohol. I have not mentioned the far more lethal drug nicotine, which accounts for nearly four times as many deaths. Perhaps no one has made the comparison of tobacco with other drugs more succinctly than did former president Carter recently when speaking before a national symposium on health. *"It saddens me,"* he said, *"to know that more Colombians died last year from American cigarettes than Americans died from Colombian cocaine."*[3]

Some would protest, "But cigarettes are legal," as though a person isn't just as dead if he is killed by a legal drug as an illegal one. In the first five months of 1990 U.S. tobacco companies increased cigarette export sales by 37 percent, mostly to undeveloped nations already suffering from the effects of poverty, malnutrition, and ill health. (Agriculture Secretary Clayton Yeutter called a press conference to extol "the marvelous success story.") But at the same time, we threaten to use our military against those countries guilty of exporting death of a lesser degree to the United States.

Yes, drug abuse is a serious problem. But we need to wade through all the media and political hysteria to place the problem in proper perspective.

Like the vast majority of social drinkers, most of the millions using illegal drugs pose no threat to society; most are not even seriously threatening their own health or well-being. Despite an occasional or even fairly regular recreational use in the evenings or on weekends, most of today's drug users—from bankers to football players—continue to function normally in society and at their jobs. *They are so inconspicuous and the observable effects so minimal that frustrated reactionaries want to resort to random urine testing to ferret them out.*

(The most visible example of this is Washington's mayor Marion Barry on whom the FBI spent thousands of man-hours to determine if he was using drugs. The concern—which was possibly politically motivated— was not that his alleged seven years of heavy cocaine use was affecting the quality of his job performance but simply that he was a black high official who might be breaking a felony law.)

Having said all this, I must backtrack a bit. Any discussion of the drug problem must be clearly delineated B.C. or A.C.—before or after crack. Many fear that this epidemic will become, in the words of a *New York Times* editorial, "a disaster of historic dimensions . . . reaching out to destroy the quality of life, and life itself." The diabolical insidiousness of crack lies in the intense euphoria it produces instantaneously but which lasts only for some twenty minutes, leaving the victim desperate for another hit.

The destructive violence has largely been confined to the ghetto areas of major cities where, as already noted, it has turned thousands of juveniles into dangerous, predatory animals. The effect on many inner-city mothers and mothers-to-be has been particularly devastating. Unlike many drugs, crack appeals to women, and consequently there has been a steady increase in the number of "crack babies" being born—in some inner-city hospitals as many as one-half of all newborns. These babies are often premature, malformed, and brain-damaged, requiring long-term intensive hospital care costing as much as ninety thousand dollars a case. Thus, two generations are being destroyed and society is left to pay for the destruction.

But again, as insidious as the problem is, crack has sometimes been overplayed in the media blitz. Because the stories are so dramatic—drive-by shoot-outs spraying innocent bystanders with bullets from automatic rifles, pictures of public housing projects looking like war-ravaged cities—many have the impression that all of America's teenagers are being engulfed in the smoke of crack. This is far from true. While the crack epidemic, both using and dealing, is rampant among juveniles of the underclass, its use remains relatively small in the total population of teenagers.

The usual history of a drug's use offers a ray of hope. When news of any drug—be it heroin or LSD or marijuana—first becomes common knowledge, there is a sudden surge in experimentation with it. At its peak it threatens to engulf the entire population. Then as observations of the ill effects become more obvious and knowledge of the dangers spreads, a reaction sets in and use begins to decline. There are good indications that this reaction to crack has already begun.

The long-range danger of crack is not that it will entrap such a large percentage of the population. Rather, it is that the devastation it causes among certain groups may be so costly that the entire welfare system, the health delivery system, and the justice system will all become paralyzed by the overload. When that happens chaos will truly ensue.

Teenage Drug Use Today

Oddly enough, the concern of the media and the public (and of vote-conscious politicians) began at a time when drug use, particularly among most juvenile groups outside the ghetto, was steadily decreasing. Since 1975 the University of Michigan's Institute for Social Research has conducted for the government an annual nationwide survey of seventeen thousand high school seniors. The survey finds that the use of illicit drugs peaked in 1979, more than a decade ago, and has decreased every year since. At its height 37 percent of the seniors stated they had smoked marijuana in the previous month. By 1989 the percent had dropped to 17. Overall the drop was from a peak of nearly 40 percent of seniors admitting to use of an illicit drug in the previous month to less than 20 percent.

Cocaine use did not peak until 1986 when a sudden drop occurred. Wide publicity about the cocaine-related deaths of two sports idols, University of Maryland basketball star Len Bias and Cleveland Browns defensive back Don Rogers, alerted teenagers to the danger. Use of crack, the cheaper derivative of cocaine, finally began to decline very slightly in 1989, when only 1.4 percent acknowledged having used it in the previous month.

This teenage decline in drug use parallels a similar drop in casual use in the general population. The National Institute on Drug Abuse reported in 1989 that the number of individuals using an illicit drug in the previous month dropped by 37 percent in the three prior years. (Cocaine-related deaths plunged 47 percent in the final three months of 1989.) The report forced drug czar William Bennett to drastically revise the preamble to his antidrug strategy program presented to the President and Congress. He had to tone down the inflaming rhetoric. Nevertheless, despite the dramatic drop, he called for a massive increase in troops and funds for his war.

The government's expensive war to stop the flow and sale of drugs cannot claim credit for the dramatic decrease among middle-class teenagers. Like the national decline in cigarette consumption, this decline has been the result of public education. The government's war has been a failure. Despite all the hoopla about arresting pushers and confiscating supplies, a steadily increasing number of seniors—nearly 60 percent in the 1989 survey—said that illegal drugs, including cocaine, were now either "very easy" or "fairly easy" to obtain. This was the highest percent in the fourteen years of the survey.

Unfortunately, surveys of high school seniors can be misleading. They fail to account for the habits of the 27 percent of all teenagers who drop out of school—over a million a year. Among these are a disproportionately large number of blacks and Hispanics, permanent members of the underclass. The fact that crack thrives in the worst of America's slums and in deteriorating housing projects offers a hint as to both a cause of the problem and possibly even an answer. And it highlights a theme running through these pages—the growth of two different cultures within our national borders. *For the haves, the problem of drug abuse is abating; for the have-nots, the problem is accelerating.*

THE SUPPLY AND DEMAND EQUATION

Two factors determine how widely any product is consumed: supply and demand. Drugs are no exception. Cut off either—the supply or the demand—and the drug problem would vanish.

Federal efforts have been fanatically directed toward only one side of the equation, an effort to eliminate supply. Here over 70 percent of the $9.5 billion budget is focused. The attack has been in three dimensions: (1) interdiction, the government's code name for interception of drugs being smuggled into the country, (2) destruction of drug crops in the countries supplying the drugs, and (3) smashing the distribution network in this country by arresting anyone connected with the trade from the kingpins at the top on down to the runners on the street. Although the war has been intensified on all three fronts during the past eight years, the net result has been a costly fiasco. Consider, for example, our highly illegal and highly immoral invasion of Panama, which brought havoc and bloody terror to that small sovereign nation. The invasion amounted to an undeclared war condemned by virtually all the civilized world. And for what? Instead of putting a stop to the cocaine shipments being smuggled through that country from Colombia, they have increased. The end of Noriega's tight military control of the traffic (for his own benefit) opened up the lucrative pursuit to unlimited new entrepreneurs.

1. Interdiction

Despite almost daily news reports of the "biggest bust ever"—in the fall of 1989 a single cache of cocaine containing twenty tons with a wholesale value of $2 billion and a street value of $20 billion . . . a barge filled with forty-three tons of hashish, enough to furnish a hit for every man, woman, and child in the United States—despite the yearly claims of dramatically increased interception of planes and yachts, despite stories of dogs sniffing out cocaine hidden in attaché cases, despite all the hoopla of beefed-up border patrols and the use of radar and high-tech devices to identify smugglers, despite all this, as high school seniors testify, drugs are far easier to obtain today than ever before. In many areas they are a glut on the market.

While the expenditure for interdiction has quadrupled in the past eight years, the supply of cocaine getting safely into the country has doubled. As would be predicted by the law of supply and demand, the price of cocaine continues to fall. Unless drug seizures reduce supplies sufficiently to cause higher prices, interdiction does absolutely nothing to reduce consumption. But this has proved to be impossible. The profits are so vast—as much as a half-million dollars to a pilot for delivery of a single planeload—that the small danger of being stopped is no deterrent. Obviously, America did not get much in return for its billion-dollar-plus expenditure on interdiction in 1989.

Drug enforcement officials desperately seeking evidence of some good accomplished by the multibillion-dollar effort grasped at a straw in the summer of 1990. A slight bulge in the wholesale price of cocaine (but not the street price) was noted in several cities for the first time in ten years. This, they cautiously announced, could be the result of having sealed off the borders.

But critics, while conceding that this could be the case, suggested that it was more likely the result of one of two other conditions: (1) the cocaine cartels were holding back deliveries in an attempt to drive up prices which had fallen so low that some peasants were finding other crops more profitable, or (2) the slight increase was a temporary phenomenon while production and distribution dislocated by Colombia's war on drugs became reestablished in any of hundreds of other peasant economies throughout the world.

It is amazing that supposedly intelligent people are unable to recognize the total futility of this approach. The skies are too vast, the seas too wide, the borders too long. The entire interdiction effort is merely the little Dutch boy with his finger stuck into a leak in the dike. Unfortunately, the dike is a sieve and in no way are there enough fingers to plug up all the leaks.

Even if we could succeed in building an impregnable barricade across the entire Mexican border, drug traffickers would simply go around it and come in across the Canadian border. Ingenious smugglers stay two steps ahead of the latest high-tech interdiction efforts, even dreaming up such bizarre methods as transporting a pound of cocaine in golf-ball-size condoms concealed in the carrier's intestines. As long as there is a demand and the profits are so enormous, a way will always be found.

2. Attacking Production

The attempt to destroy or eliminate drugs at their source has produced an even greater fiasco. The U.S. State Department officially admitted in 1990 that despite President Bush's highly publicized efforts to persuade other nations to reduce their drug supply, the global production of coca, opium poppies, and marijuana soared. The report stated very bluntly:

> Worldwide narcotics production reached new levels, corruption undermined enforcement efforts, and a number of governments still failed to exhibit a serious commitment to reducing drug production and trafficking.[4]

The effort first became a comic opera scene in July 1986 when six U.S. helicopters and 160 American troops were dispatched to conduct a Gilbert and Sullivan–type raid on cocaine-processing laboratories in Bolivia. Despite elaborate plans, the three-month invasion produced no operators and little equipment. The processors were apparently warned well in advance by the "cooperating" Bolivian antinarcotics police. Adding to the comic scene, the Bolivian ambassador in Washington immediately requested a $100-million loan from the United States to help compensate for the potential loss of some $600 million a year in illegal drugs.

Since then production has continued to increase in Bolivia to the point where overproduction caused a collapse in the market in 1990. While a hundred pounds of coca leaves brought two hundred dollars early in the 1980s, the price plunged to as low as twelve dollars by the end of the decade.

When President Bush in the spring of 1990 met with the presidents of Colombia, Bolivia, and Peru, he was given a lesson in elementary economics. While they were publicly profuse in their sympathy with Bush's problem, they pointed out that over 600,000 of their peasants were dependent on the production and processing of coca leaves. To destroy their means of survival would topple the fragile economies of all three poverty-ridden nations and bring severe deprivation and possibly even mass starvation to the workers. The presidents could become genuinely enthusiastic about eradication only if the United States could find a substitute crop which would grow in their climate and soil, and which we would purchase in sufficient quantity to provide gainful employment to the 600,000 peasants.

An alternative would be for the United States to pay the farmers to stop growing coca. We have been offering to pay Bolivian farmers two thousand dollars for each hectare (2.47 acres) on which they destroyed their coca plants and started growing some other crop. But there were few takers until the 1990 price collapse. To eradicate all of Bolivia's forty thousand hectares in this manner would require $80 million. While this might be commendable humanitarian aid to a handful of the world's hungry peasants, it would do little to stop the global production of cocaine. There will always be thousands upon thousands of other hungry peasants around the world anxious to take their place.

Experience in Thailand underscores the futility of efforts to buy a reduction in world production. For a short time American drug enforcement administrators congratulated themselves on the success of a program that paid farmers to substitute other crops for the profitable opium-producing poppies. Thai production fell from 40 metric tons in 1984 to 15 metric tons in 1987. Success at last! But the enthusiastic back-patting was suddenly stifled by the revelation that the reduction in Thai opium had been a windfall to neighboring Laotian farmers. In this same "victory" period production in Laos increased from 30 tons to 290 tons. The stage is now set for a similar international transfer of cocaine production from Bolivia to peasants of other countries.

America's efforts throughout the world to eradicate drug crops at their source have been merely whistling into the wind. It would take only twenty-five square miles of land producing opium poppies to supply the entire U.S. demand for heroin. Somewhere that acreage will always be found. It is folly to think that we would have the resources to pay every poverty-ridden farmer in the Third World to destroy the crop that keeps him from starving.

The Andean presidents also preached a polite sociological sermon to President Bush at their spring 1990 meeting. If America was genuinely interested in solving *its* problem (drug abuse being no major problem in their countries despite the ready availability), the only effective place to start was right in the United States—stopping the demand of the American people for drugs.

The Mexican government had preached the same sermon to President Reagan, but no one was listening. To cover up for its failure, the Reagan administration attempted to make foreign countries the scapegoat. In the spring of 1986 officers in the State Department and the Drug Enforcement Administration sharply castigated Mexico for its failure to control production of marijuana and heroin. The Mexican Embassy issued a reply:

> It is deeply unfair and even ridiculous for certain officers of a country like the United States, who have been unable to solve their own internal drug-trafficking problem despite almost unlimited resources, to ask a poor country like Mexico to solve not only its own problem but the United States' problem as well.[5]

To honestly expect leaders of poverty-stricken nations to cooperate enthusiastically in wiping out their principal source of Yankee dollars requires a mental flight from sanity.

Even if we could manage the impossible and somehow destroy all the narcotic crops around the world or even more improbably seal off all our borders, the war would still be a failure. Such a victory would be a bonanza for amateur and professional chemists. From basement laboratories all across America would come a flood of synthetic substances—LSD, angel dust, hundreds of man-made narcotics, designer drugs of every description.

Already waiting in the wings as the next star of the drug world is "ice," a smokable form of crystallized methamphetamine, the stimulant commonly known as "speed." Whereas a puff of crack gives the user a twenty-minute high, the euphoria from ice lasts for twelve to twenty-four hours. But most significant, while cocaine and crack must begin with a plant grown abroad, ice can be synthesized in a clandestine lab by anyone able to follow a cake recipe. Already popular in Hawaii, it is now being found in high social circles on the mainland.

Demand will be met. Always! Against all odds!

3. *Attacking the Supply Network*

The third strategy to reduce the supply of drugs—arresting sellers, big and small—is the same old story. Good intentions that have miserably failed.

The city of Washington, D.C., shines out as a symbol of the futility of using legal force to control drug abuse. When drug czar Bennett took office his first major initiative was to muster all his ammunition and forces to make the capital a showplace demonstrating the effectiveness of his drug control policies. But other than driving an alleged drug-using mayor out of office, the only demonstration was one of failure. Drug use and sales continued unabated, and the rate of drug-related murders and crime continued to climb.

Making drug arrests is not difficult because today deals are made brazenly under the eyes of law enforcement personnel. Undercover agents have little trouble in tracking down high-level distributors. In fact, it is so easy to make arrests—44,000 drug dealers and users in the past two years in Bennett's showplace, the District of Columbia; 28,000 *felony-level* arrests in New York City; 2,000 during a single weekend in Florida—that a gridlock has all but paralyzed the criminal justice system in larger cities. The courts are unable to process the offenders, the jails and prisons unable to house those who are brought to trial. Because of the overload, the vast majority are permitted to plead guilty to lesser offenses and receive either a probated sentence or a short time in jail. Within a day of being placed on probation, many are back hustling on the street.

In November 1988 New Yorkers were cheered by the police department announcement of the formation of TNT (Tactical Narcotics Teams), which would apply saturation techniques to clean out pushers in particularly troublesome sites. But TNT blew up in the face of the taxpayers, not the drug dealers. There were not enough prosecutors, judges, or courtrooms to handle the overflow. And the drug hot spots merely moved to new locations.

Just as there have always been dozens of peasants worldwide ready to take up the slack for every producer who is eliminated, so are there dozens of individuals eager to take the place of every pusher who is put in jail or prison. Ghetto youths are a dispensable commodity and in very great oversupply.

William Bennett has given verbal approval—only figuratively, we pray—to beheading drug pushers. But even a punishment too horrible to contemplate would have little effect. The profits are so great that there will always be those willing to take the gamble. *The New Yorker* points out that over the past few years Malaysia has hanged eighty-one offenders. Yet the addiction rate continues to climb. Meanwhile in Holland where the government is quite tolerant of drug use, the addiction rate is declining.[6]

Inviting Corruption

Because of the easy profits available in the drug world, America now suffers the greatest corruption among law enforcement personnel since the Al Capone days of Prohibition. The corruption touches all levels of the criminal justice system, from the rookie cop on the beat on up to the judge on the bench, from drug enforcement agents at the border on up to the FBI, and in an illegal effort to supply money to the contras in Nicaragua possibly to the highest levels of government.

After a crackdown on air shipments into Florida, planes were rerouted to nearby states where small airports were deserted at night. According to the Georgia Bureau of Investigation, by 1988 nearly a dozen county sheriffs had been implicated in drug-smuggling cases. A payoff of $50,000 to $100,000 is an irresistible incentive to a sheriff and his deputies to look the other way during a single night while planes from Central America unload their cargo into waiting cars and trucks.

For all these reasons, the virtually total failure of the multibillion-dollar attempt to reduce the supply of drugs would suggest that the war, as now being structured, is unwinnable. It should be obvious that the war is being fought on the wrong battlefield. Attention needs to be turned to the other side of the equation. Instead of attacking supply, hope rests in attacking demand.

Basically, demand can be reduced in either of two ways—willingly or forcibly. Here again drug fighters have chosen the macho approach: trying to *force* people not to use drugs. In a word, "prohibition."

THE FOLLY OF PROHIBITION

Americans always seem to opt for the quick and easy solution to complex problems. Here the approach even seems reasonable. Just threaten to lock up the 23 million recreational and addicted users for long enough sentences, and out of fear they will stop. Cold turkey! Unfortunately, as we have noted in dealing with delinquent youths, force is seldom an effective way to get people to change their behavior.

The great American experiment in trying to save man from his own weakness legislatively, that is, from the demon rum, was a resounding failure. Only slightly less dramatic has been the failure of legal prohibitions of prostitution and gambling. Saving mankind from its sins has been done more successfully by churches than by governments.

Embedded in the democratic philosophy of America is the belief that an individual should be free from governmental harassment unless his conduct is harmful to other individuals or to society. This is the very heart of the conservative agenda. So it is confusing that the same ultraconservatives who preach "getting government off our backs" are so vocal in getting government onto the backs of drug users for whom there is no public reason to worry about the ill effects of their private activity.

Certainly there are personal risks in drug use. Many socially accepted recreational activities (in addition to the use of alcohol and tobacco) involve considerable personal risk. In the morning's paper side-by-side headlines report: "Two Californians Die in Skydiving Competition" and "Six Climbers Freeze to Death on World's 2nd-Highest Peak." Fatal injuries in hunting accidents are so common they hardly make the news. Yet we don't try to prohibit any of these activities by legal action. Even though society must pay the medical expenses for most of the thousands of motorcyclists who have accidents but no insurance, many states have turned down bills requiring them to wear life-saving helmets. It would be an invasion of their personal rights!

That great American pastime, overeating, has high lethal potentiality. I am still haunted by the fatal heart attack of a grossly overweight friend who refused to abide by his doctor's order to lose forty pounds—necessary before he would have any chance of surviving a desperately needed coronary bypass operation. But my friend's addiction to rich foods was so overpowering that despite the pleas of those concerned about him he kept right on gaining weight.

His death raises a viable question. To protect him against himself, should the government have thrown him into jail? Or committed him to a food abuse rehabilitation center?

Students of American history could have predicted the failure of Reagan's and Bush's wars on drugs. Similar efforts have inevitably been fiascoes. Apparently long forgotten by legislators today are the days of the Volstead Act when small-time criminals selling bootleg whiskey formed a network that grew into the crime syndicates of the Al Capone era. Forgotten is the experience of the California legislature that enacted draconian laws against the use of marijuana only to watch it increase tenfold among teenagers in the next few years. The counterproductive law had to be repealed. Forgotten is the result of Governor Nelson Rockefeller's massive 1973 war on drugs that was hailed as the answer to New York's mounting drug problem.

With the slogan "Life in Prison for the Pusher," Rockefeller had persuaded the legislature to enact the nation's strongest antidrug law, carrying long-term mandatory prison sentences for both sellers and users. The state spent half a million dollars just to advertise the harsh penalties. In the first four years $76 million was used for additional court personnel needed to deal with the new law. But the law failed to reduce drug use, even failed to increase the number of convictions. Juries were reluctant to convict, and prosecutors reluctant to prosecute where mandatory penalties seemed too severe. Nevertheless, the courts became critically overloaded.

A million-dollar evaluation of the law, sponsored in 1977 by the New York City Bar Association and the Drug Abuse Council, called the crusade "a complete failure." For a few months, the researchers conceded, street pushers had been "far less open." Instead of dealing openly on the street, they moved into doorways to make their sales. Even this effect soon evaporated. Two years later most of the law was repealed.

Seldom indeed do we seem to learn from history. Also forgotten has been the advice of that New York evaluation committee: "Drug problems can't be dealt with adequately through the criminal process."

Writing in the *Wall Street Journal*, Hodding Carter III last year insisted:

> Every argument that is made for prohibiting the use of currently illegal drugs can be made even more convincingly about tobacco and alcohol. The effects on the newborn? Staggeringly direct. The effects on adolescents? Alcoholism is the addiction of choice for young Americans on a ratio of about 100 to one. Lethal effects? Tobacco's murderous results are not a matter of debate anywhere outside the Tobacco Institute.[7]

The effect of stringent drug laws was succinctly summarized by Ira Glasser, executive director of the American Civil Liberties Union. He pointed out that only three groups benefit: One is organized crime because the laws permit them to make fortunes. The second group is law enforcement agents whose jobs depend on the law. And finally, there are the politicians who garner votes by passing the tough laws.

Two Problems Confused as One

Drugs and crime are tightly intertwined. But this was not always true. Before the Harrison Narcotic Act of 1914 today's illegal drugs were freely available in America and they bore little relationship to crime. There was no bootlegging or hustling, no gangsters or drug lords, no corruption of officials or police, no widespread robbery and burglary by users getting money to pay artificially high prices.

Heroin, opium, morphine, marijuana (cannabis), and cocaine could be purchased at low prices in the local pharmacy, even by mail order through magazine ads. They were not only regularly prescribed by doctors, they were also the active ingredient of highly touted patent medicines. Cocaine was the "lift" in the original formula for Coca-Cola until it was replaced by caffeine in 1903. Heroin pills were pushed by the Bayer Company. Coca wine, heavily laced with cocaine, was advertised as a brain tonic that "Nourishes—Fortifies—Refreshes," and promoted by temperance leaders as a nonalcoholic beverage. Among its fans were President William McKinley, Thomas Edison, and Sarah Bernhardt.

Some individuals did become addicted. Because of this, narcotic drugs without a prescription were outlawed. But the law did not resolve the problem of addiction. Those who craved drugs still managed to obtain them, although at a higher price. The law succeeded only in creating an additional, more serious problem—the problem of drug-related crime and corruption. It is the laws making drugs illegal, not the drugs themselves, that create the serious problem in America. (Rejected Supreme Court nominee Douglas Ginsburg stands as a symbol of this fact. He was damaged not by the effects of marijuana but rather by the law that made it illegal.)

There are two very distinct problems. One is the problem of drug abuse, the damage it does to the individual; the other is the problem of drug-related crime, the damage it does to society. They are highly different; their solutions are even more different. But the public and politicians confuse the two. Because of this confusion the war has been ineffective against both.

The Unmentionable Word—"Legalization"

More and more social reformers are suggesting something that would have been unthinkable a few years back—the repeal of these unenforceable, counterproductive laws. This is not an endorsement of drug use but rather a recognition that there are two different problems which must be separately attacked. Proponents are not confined to the liberal establishment. They include conservatives tired of seeing American cities being ravaged by drug dealers. Among them are archconservatives like William F. Buckley, Jr., editor of the *National Review*; President Reagan's secretary of state, George Shultz; William Randolph Hearst, III, publisher of the *San Francisco Examiner;* and free-market economist Milton Friedman.

The latter said in a letter to the *Wall Street Journal* that he was "revolted at the prospect of turning the United States into an armed camp, by the vision of jails filled with casual drug users and an army of enforcers empowered to invade the liberty of citizens on slight evidence."[8]

Many advocates of legalization are law enforcement personnel and city officials, particularly those from the major cities who have watched tons of drugs being confiscated and thousands of dealers and users being locked up while the problem continues to escalate.

Among the most vocal has been Mayor Kurt Schmoke of Baltimore whose city is being suffocated by the drug problem.

Legalization would mean that instead of drugs being hustled on the streets, they would be sold to adults in government-regulated, tax-paying stores or pharmacies. While individuals would not be prosecuted for possession or use, they would be severely prosecuted for any drug-induced behavior endangering the lives or safety of others. Likewise bootleggers selling drugs outside regulated channels would be prosecuted. By taking the gigantic profits out of drug trafficking, legalization would eliminate a major portion of the crime and delinquency in America. Consider the many advantages:

- Organized drug syndicates would collapse.
- Violent gang shoot-outs between rival juvenile dealers would cease.
- Purer quality and standardized potency would reduce deaths from overdosing and poisoning.
- Robbery and burglary would drop by as much as 60 percent in many areas as addicts no longer needed to pay artificially inflated prices to support their habits.
- The temptation of big payoffs would no longer corrupt public officials and the police.
- A frustrated law enforcement system would be relieved of an unwinnable assignment and be freed to fight other crimes.
- The costly need to build more and more jails and prisons to house drug prisoners would be eliminated.
- The billions being wasted in a futile attempt to stop the flow of drugs could be more effectively spent on prevention and rehabilitation.
- Instead of giving $50 billion a year to organized crime, taxation of legalized drugs would put money into public treasuries.

Admittedly, there would be social costs to legalization. At first the low prices might possibly bring a rush of experimentation. Even so, legalization would bring a large net gain in social benefits over costs. It is true that while legalization would eliminate most of the drug-related crime, it would not solve the personal health and psychological problems of drug abuse. But neither has prohibition made a dent in these. Here society must rely on preventative measures and rehabilitation.

The reasons for legalization can be very powerfully and statistically argued. But alas! This book presents a pragmatic approach to the problems of delinquency and crime. The American public has been so traumatized by the political and media hysteria that it is not yet prepared to listen to these arguments. Much public education is needed before legalization becomes a realistic goal. In the interim a compromise is necessary. This will be pursued in the next chapter.

Chapter 17

TOWARD A WINNABLE WAR ON DRUGS

Americans are not ready to face up to the fact that with drug abuse we struggle with a health and cultural problem, not a law enforcement problem. In time, with research and public education, a majority may agree to withdraw from an unwinnable war. They may finally realize that the war against drug abuse should be headed by the U.S. Surgeon General, not the U.S. Attorney General. In the meantime America cannot sit by waiting for the age of enlightenment.

So . . . what to do? Now.

A four-pronged attack is proposed:

1. Law enforcement primarily directed at only two classes of offenders: drug users whose behavior is endangering the safety of others, and those selling illegal drugs
2. Legalization of marijuana as a preliminary step in removing all penalties for drug possession and use
3. Recognition that drug abuse is largely a health problem, not a criminal one, by concentrating on treatment programs for all who wish an escape from addiction
4. Massive antidrug educational programs—including the dangers

of alcohol, tobacco, and marijuana—in both the schools and the public media

1. CHANGED FOCUS OF LAW ENFORCEMENT

Under the compromise proposal being made here, while the penalties for personal possession and use of drugs would be sharply reduced, these would continue to be illegal. Arrests and prosecution, however, would in effect be limited to those whose use directly affected others—for example, individuals whose belligerence was physically threatening and those driving under the influence. In this regard enforcement would be similar to that with drunk driving, prosecution of which, it is hoped, would also be stepped up.

Of particular concern to law enforcement personnel would be women whose drug-related behavior was endangering their children including those yet unborn. As proposed in Chapter 9, dealing with the poverty cycle, an infant would be taken away from a seriously addicted mother unable to care for it, unless she agreed to a residential treatment program where the infant would remain with her. After release custody of the child would be contingent upon periodic tests of the mother for drug use.

The extremely expensive, totally futile, and often bloody efforts to stop production of drugs in other countries would be abandoned. In similar vein, although smuggling of drugs would continue to be illegal, no longer should billions of dollars be tossed away in the impossible task of sealing off the wide skies, two seacoasts, and thousands of miles of deserted national borders. Interdiction would be utilized primarily in the effort to identify and prosecute drug kingpins and their organizations.

Law enforcement activities would be concentrated on the pusher and those higher in the distribution hierarchy. But it should be a rational policy. There is no place for such rhetoric as "death [or even life in prison] for the pusher." As has been frequently noted, deterrence of crime comes from the *certainty* of punishment, not its severity. It is counterproductive to overfill the jails and prisons by insisting on long-term sentences for those guilty of selling drugs. Instead, it would be far more effective to see that all pushers—including juveniles—spend a brief time behind bars, the length steadily increasing with each subsequent arrest.

Even more important, heavy emphasis should be placed on taking the *profit* out of drugs. Steep fines should be levied against those arrested. As has been approved by the Supreme Court, all money and other material possessions gained through the illegal sale of drugs should be confiscated and used in drug rehabilitation programs. For the juvenile this could mean the heavy gold chains he wears or the expensive sports car he drives; for the kingpins it could mean large real estate holdings and Swiss bank accounts.

This policy will accomplish two goals: discourage pushers by confiscation of their profits along with repeated short-term imprisonment; and second, allow the enormous profits from drugs to help pay for the damage.

2. LEGALIZATION OF MARIJUANA

Marijuana was not among the drugs outlawed by the Harrison Narcotic Act of 1914. At that time it was viewed as a valuable medicine. After it was discovered in 1839 being used as a painkiller in India, it became the aspirin of the day. Doctors used it in the powdered form of cannabis for a vast array of ailments from menstrual cramps to migraine headaches. In the hundreds of medical reports published in the late nineteenth and early twentieth centuries, there was no mention of users losing their motivation to work or dropping out of society. With the discovery of aspirin, however, marijuana quickly lost its popularity.

It became the "killer weed" only in the 1930s when Harry Anslinger, the U.S. Narcotics Commissioner, sought to beef up his power and influence. He concocted wild stories about the weed that caused smokers to go on rampages, shooting policemen and innocent bystanders. Until he publicized the drug, the principal users were on the fringes of society—poor blacks, itinerant Mexican farm workers, and jazz musicians. There was no one in Congress to challenge Anslinger's horror stories as the unadulterated fiction they really were. He easily lobbied the Marijuana Tax Act of 1937 through Congress.

And when the law declared marijuana to be a problem it quickly became one.

Most medical studies today give marijuana a "relatively" clean bill of health when compared with other drugs. It is not addictive. Unlike alcohol, it does not cause the user to become violent or belligerent. It seldom causes toxic reactions; no one has ever been known to die from an overdose. (Animal studies indicate that it would require a dose a thousand times greater than the amount needed for a high to become lethal.) And when it is used in moderation, the health hazards are minimal, certainly far less than those of either tobacco or alcohol.

Well-documented, major studies in Jamaica, Greece, and Costa Rica of the effects of heavy, long-term use found no evidence of intellectual or neurological damage. Furthermore, there was no indication of personality change or loss of the will to work. By and large, pot smokers were as healthy and functioned in society as well as nonsmokers. *The Harvard Medical School Mental Health Letter* of November 1987 observed:

> Most people who develop a dependency on marijuana would also be likely to develop other dependencies because of anxiety, depression, or feelings of inadequacy. . . . The problem of distinguishing causes from symptoms is particularly acute here. Heavy drug users in our society are often bored, depressed, and listless, or alienated, cynical, and rebellious. . . . Marijuana smokers may be using the drug to demonstrate rebelliousness, cope with anxiety, or medicate themselves for early symptoms of mental illness.[1]

Because symptoms were confused with cause, marijuana was given an unjustifiably bad name when its use first became widespread among teenagers. It would have been better if those adults and authorities concerned about the loss of motivation had looked more carefully into the unmet needs of these turned-off youths rather than screaming about the hazards of pot. (The easy solution!)

Marijuana use is not without some danger, and like alcohol and tobacco it should be strongly discouraged. It causes some temporary impairment of memory, cognitive functioning, and motor skills. Just recently, for example, researchers found that even twenty-four hours after he smoked a single marijuana joint, an airplane pilot's skill in operating a flight simulator was still impaired. But putting this finding in perspective, the effects of a sleeping pill taken before retiring last up to seventeen hours and have been found to impair one's driving ability the next morning. Like many legal drugs (particularly alcohol), marijuana may adversely affect fetal development. And long-term heavy use has the same dangerous effect on the lungs as does tobacco, although few people smoke twenty joints or more day after day.

The Reagan administration's long-standing war on marijuana was based largely on former U.S. attorney general Edwin Meese's erroneous belief that it was the "gateway drug"—the means whereby youths were enticed into the world of serious drug abuse. But no reputable study has ever demonstrated this effect. True, many heroin addicts first used marijuana. But more of them also previously used cigarettes and alcohol. Even Coca-Cola! The fact that one event precedes another does not necessarily indicate a causal relationship.

While it has not influenced Bush's gung ho drug czar, the chief administrative law judge of the Drug Enforcement Administration, Francis L. Young, in discussing the medicinal use of marijuana called it "one of the safest therapeutically active substances known to man."[2]

Marijuana does contribute dramatically to the delinquency picture. It does so because its possession and use, even occasionally or experimentally, is defined by law as being illegal. Young people who otherwise are law-abiding automatically become delinquents. And because alcohol is legal, these young people see the hypocrisy in our justice system.

Effect of Legalization

Many have long argued that the use, growth, and possession of marijuana should be totally decriminalized—subject to governmental controls and taxes. Instead of being a $14-billion illegal industry, it would become a major source of tax revenue and save the billion dollars a year now being used to confiscate it. But conscientious legislators fear they might be opening the floodgates to abuse.

The most relevant indication of the effect of legalization is the experience of the eleven states that between 1973 and 1978 eliminated jail penalties and drastically reduced fines for the possession or cultivation of small amounts of marijuana for personal use. In these states casual users are seldom arrested. In Alaska it became legal to smoke marijuana in one's home. Opponents were loud in their prediction of the wave of drug abuse that would follow. But the catastrophe did not occur. Most states witnessed no increase at all.

Nowhere has the effect of total removal of restraints on marijuana use, possession, growth, and sale been so clearly demonstrated as in the Netherlands. In 1978, after years of unsuccessfully trying to round up users, the Dutch government decided that marijuana was a relatively harmless drug and that trying to enforce prohibition was an ineffective use of law enforcement officers' time. All penalties were removed. Exotic brands from all over the world can now be legally purchased as easily as a bag of peanuts, even at municipal-financed youth recreational centers. Most is sold in six- and twelve-dollar packets at neighborhood coffeehouses.

Now that pot in the Netherlands is no longer a point of contention between teenagers and the establishment, the drug has lost its glamour. No longer is it forbidden fruit. Fewer Dutch youths now use it than their counterparts in most countries that still maintain stiff penalties. In a recent survey 80 percent said they had no interest in the drug.

Decriminalization of marijuana in the Netherlands was part of a carefully thought-out drug policy. It is similar to the one being proposed here. Cocaine and heroin are technically still illegal, but police ignore users except to suggest a rehabilitation program to those appearing to be using a drug to excess. Sellers, however, are vigorously sought by the police, and the penalties are by Dutch standards quite tough. With this policy the use of marijuana and heroin is down, although there has been a slight increase in cocaine use. There are far fewer heroin addicts than in the United States. Overall, Dutch drug authorities are pleased and are cautiously optimistic that they have finally gotten a handle on their country's drug problem.

3. REDUCING DEMAND THROUGH THERAPY

While casual drug use has decreased, the number of addicts has steadily increased. Yet funds for research and development of treatment programs have been hard to find. As a result, today there are thousands of addicts nationwide desperately pleading for the help that is not available.

In New York City there are three times as many addicts seeking admission to rehab programs as there are slots. Those who come are told they must wait for up to six months. While an estimated 1,800 are on Los Angeles's waiting lists, many treatment centers do not even bother to keep lists—the task is too overwhelming. At the Haight-Ashbury Free Clinic in San Francisco nearly 800 addicts are being treated, but each month up to 400 are turned away. The tragedy? Up to 80 percent never return. They die, or are arrested and sent to jail, or become so debilitated by their addiction that they are no longer in sufficient control to know they need help. A study in Washington, D.C., found that 15 percent of those turned away attempted suicide while awaiting admittance.

That America is so hard-pressed for dollars it is unable to provide treatment to those who cry for help should be an embarrassment to a supposedly compassionate society. The legislators, both federal and state, who refuse to appropriate sufficient funds for treatment centers should be required to sit in on sessions where desperate youngsters are told: "Sorry, son. Come back in six months. Then if you are still alive or haven't caught AIDS by turning tricks to pay for your addiction, we'll see if there's room for you." Or where young girls are counseled: "Now don't worry. If you become pregnant before you get into the program, society will pay the ninety thousand dollars or so in medical costs of your drug-addicted, physically afflicted newborn."

Despite the tremendous social costs of babies born of drug-addicted mothers, fewer than one out of ten of these mothers receive treatment.

Drug treatment programs are far from being 100 percent successful, but with experience and research they are improving. A role model for all who feel they are forever caught in the clutches of drugs is Chris Jacobs, a 1988 Olympic gold medal winner in swimming. Already an accomplished swimmer at the age of twelve, Chris began using cocaine in junior high school, the start of a nine-year romance with drugs. Although still in training at college, he became severely depressed as drugs took over his life. He lost forty pounds. He tells of sitting time after time in a closet with the barrel of a .357 magnum in his mouth.

Finally a psychiatrist at the campus counseling service, his swimming coach, and his parents ganged up to persuade him to return home and go into eight months of therapy at the Fair Oaks Hospital in Summit, New Jersey. Since that day his strongest drug has been caffeine. He resumed training with renewed vigor. Two years, four months, and two days after opening the door of the hospital, he was sitting in Seoul waiting for the Olympics to begin.

The therapy currently needed most desperately by juveniles is for crack addiction. Unfortunately, this has been largely ineffective, particularly in nonresidential programs. In these as many as 90 percent drop out in the first month, a majority after the first day. Of those who remain for the entire program, it is estimated that less than 25 percent remain drug-free for as much as six months.

It has been discovered that the craving for crack is situationally induced. (To a lesser degree this is true for all addiction. Those who have attempted to stop smoking cigarettes know how certain events—drinking a cup of coffee or talking on the phone—can trigger an intense craving.) For the crack addict the lure of the anticipated euphoria is so powerful that it is virtually impossible to be rehabilitated while remaining in the community. Meeting a friend with whom crack has been smoked, the sight of a crack hustler on the street, or just the return to the same boring, unfulfilled life can instantaneously destroy any resolve to stay clean. Few have the stamina to resist outside the treatment center. Even most graduates of short-term residential programs of three or four weeks go out the front door of the center and head straight to the nearest crack house.

Because of the easily induced situational craving, long-term residential programs have been considerably more successful. Addicted youths live in a highly controlled therapeutic community for fifteen to eighteen months. At Phoenix Academy, in Yorktown Heights, New York, a short distance from New York City, for example, 250 young male and female drug addicts are immersed in a multiservice treatment program for eighteen months. Enrollees put in a full day at school, do the cooking and housework, and spend the evenings in intensive group therapy. According to the director, Dr. Mitchell Rosenthal, some 70 percent of the addicts who stay the full time will remain clean for at least six months.

Residential treatment is expensive—from thirty-five to forty-five dollars a day. But this is less than half as much as it costs to keep the youth in a delinquency institution. And needless to say, it is far more effective. But hope that addicted underclass teenagers will be turned into productive citizens is largely dependent upon a new life being opened to them after treatment—a job and a realistic hope of escaping the despair in which they have lived.

Methadone substitution has been successful in blocking the effects of heroin and reducing the agony of withdrawal. But methadone has no effect with crack addiction. It must be remembered, however, that crack is new. Few pharmacological studies have been undertaken; experimental programs are untested. (Reagan's last budget increased funds for interdiction and law enforcement but *cut* research funds available to the National Institute on Drug Abuse.) Although impeded by lack of funds, research on the biochemistry of crack addiction is making progress. Already there is hope that newly developed drugs will help suppress the intense craving during the first weeks of withdrawal.

All leads should be explored. The ancient Chinese art of acupuncture, for example, has proved to be surprisingly successful in reducing the craving of many addicts. The scientific explanation is uncertain, but even if it is psychological, the technique should be further tested. With adequate money for research and for the development of therapeutic programs, there is hope that the success rate will improve.

For a compassionate nation to fail to provide the means to make that hope come true is inhumane. But the extreme difficulty of rehabilitation emphasizes the primacy of prevention. The ultimate solution is in removing those conditions that cause people to turn to drugs of abuse.

4. THE PROMISE OF DRUG EDUCATION

Juveniles (and adults) use drugs for two highly different reasons. The two are usually confused. One, *recreational use,* is relatively innocuous; the other, *escapism,* is devastatingly destructive to both the individual and society.

Recreational use—for pleasure and sociability—is by far the most common reason that drugs (including alcohol) are used. In the case of marijuana, this is usually self-limiting, both in frequency and amount, and also in the number of years that it is used. Young people generally begin to phase it out in their early twenties, and most have entirely stopped by the time they are thirty. This recreational use is, at worst, only a very minor social problem.

Likewise, most other drugs are not serious problems as long as they are used to facilitate socialization or relaxation and not as an aid to psychologically drop out of life. This does not imply that efforts to reduce, or stop, the recreational use of drugs should be abandoned. Definitely not! America knows all too well the tragic results of the recreational use of alcohol and tobacco.

But how are we to slow the recreational use of drugs?

Trying to reduce supply has been ineffective. Legal prohibition has been a fiasco. What remains is education . . . education to help young people decide on their own to reject drugs.

While education will not be the overnight miracle that many seek, there is considerable proof that it will work, albeit slowly. The twenty-five-year public health campaign on the dangers of tobacco has brought a dramatic reduction in smoking. It has been accomplished without passing laws, or putting people in jail, or requiring urine tests, or spraying fields of tobacco with dangerous herbicides. Ironically, the campaign has been least successful among the one group for whom cigarettes are illegal—juveniles. The health messages have not been youth-oriented and have been made largely in media not seen by most teenagers.

The "How-not-to" of Drug Education

Drug education got off to a disastrous start back in the 1970s when President Nixon made drug prevention money available to schools. An avalanche of hastily prepared materials was produced by greedy publishers out to make a fast buck. Most were based on two faulty assumptions: that young people lack sufficient information about drugs to make intelligent decisions, and that they can be scared away from experimentation by horror stories. Some of the educational "facts" came straight from the "killer weed" tales concocted by Anslinger. Teachers lost credibility when they repeated these facts to youngsters who personally knew they were false.

The results? The "education" in the early seventies caused a rapid escalation of use among students. Films and pamphlets designed from an adult point of view to show the evils of drugs merely succeeded in introducing the youngsters to an exotic new world to be explored. Students figured they must be missing out on something pretty hot if adults were all that uptight.

Nearly twenty years ago Louie Nunn, while governor of Kentucky, unwittingly became the commonwealth's most successful drug pusher. To show the state's young people the dangers of drugs (at the time principally marijuana, pep pills, and LSD), he organized a state-wide alert. A large exhibition hall in Louisville was filled with booths showing different stages of the evil weed from growth to a rolled joint, bottles of colorful prescription-only pills, exotic paraphernalia used with various drugs, and movies depicting wild hallucinogenic trips in which objects whirled madly about the room in psychedelic colors. Horrifying to adults, electrifying to juveniles.

To this drug carnival thousands of students from every corner of the state were bused in each day. They stared goggle-eyed at all the wonders. One streetwise city youth told me, "Them country dudes keep asking me, 'Hey, where can I get some of that stuff?' "

Teenage drug use in the state skyrocketed.

Prevention Through Drug Education

Fortunately, educators learned from those counterproductive beginnings. A more honest approach to drug education has begun to get the message across. Program planners have learned that efforts must begin at the earliest elementary levels before the start of experimentation, which occurs at an ever younger age, even in the second and third grades. And the education must be continued all through school.

Adolescents are now-oriented, not future-oriented. This is an important key. In successful junior-high antismoking programs, the emphasis has been on immediate effects such as bad breath, discolored teeth, and reduced athletic ability, even sexual prowess. This has been more effective than the warnings about death from lung cancer or heart disease that have reached adults. For ten- and twelve-year-olds such things are too far in the future to be frightening. Many have not even internalized the concept of death.

A few schools are zeroing in on the reason most young people start using drugs: peer pressure. They are attempting to turn the tables and use it to prevent drug use. Discussions center on ways to avoid going along with the crowd without becoming an outcast. Effective lessons concentrate on providing accurate information about alcohol and drug dangers, teaching students decision-making skills, and giving them ideas for alternatives to drug use. Innovative approaches are being used. "Super Teams," for example, is a peer counseling program made possible by the National Football Players Association and other professional athletes. Featuring visits by athletic luminaries, the program promotes self-respect and personal discipline.

D.A.R.E. (Drug Abuse Resistance Education), sponsored nationwide by Kentucky Fried Chicken, now has more than two thousand chapters in forty-nine states. It is expected that in 1991 nearly 5 million children in elementary school exit grades will hear a semester-long program designed to give them facts about drug abuse and to "inoculate" them against peer pressure. While a few critics question the use of uniformed policemen as teachers, preliminary evaluations indicate that the program is reducing the incidence of drug abuse, truancy, and vandalism.

One unsung hero of the drug war is Sheila Tate, who was the former First Lady's press secretary at the time Nancy Reagan's public image was that of a shallow and aloof ex–movie star, obsessed with designer clothes and a lavish life-style. Tate persuaded Mrs. Reagan to embark on her "Just Say No" campaign in an effort to create a new image.

While "Just Say No" by itself is far too simplistic, it does head in the right direction—persuasion instead of force. There are indications that it has had more effect than have the billions Mrs. Reagan's husband used to fight supply. With encouragement from concerned parents and educators, voluntary youth programs sprang up. State networks were established in Mississippi, Texas, Florida, and Ohio. In May 1986, the nearly ten thousand "Just Say No" clubs sponsored a nationwide drug alert day in which it was claimed 5 million young people in six hundred communities participated.

Other groups with similar agendas, such as World Youth Against Drug Abuse and REACH (Responsible Adolescents Can Help), have been formed. Memberships range from fourth- and fifth-graders on up to college students. At the moment these groups exist primarily on the fringes of the in-group youth culture and probably fail to reach those at greatest risk for drug abuse. But their growth is evidence that peer pressure can be used as a positive force.

Along with these student programs other parts of a multidiscipline, multimedia effort have already begun. The Media Advertising Partnership for a Drug-Free America campaign has demonstrated that social attitudes toward drugs can be changed, although not as dramatically as some have hoped, and possibly least effectively with teenagers. TV and radio commercials and printed advertisements worth over $300 million in space and time have been donated in the past two years. In addition, the Advertising Council, the industry's nonprofit public service arm, has aimed much of its annual half-billion dollars' worth of free advertising to the drug abuse problem.

The findings of a two-year study by the Harvard School of Public Health, published in the summer 1990 issue of *Health Affairs,* are critical of these media efforts.[3] Among recommendations to make mass media campaigns more effective:

- Resist the use of scare tactics such as showing an egg in a frying pan which the commentator identifies as "your brain on drugs." As has been discovered in drug education in the classroom, viewers tune out scare tactics by denying that the message is relevant to them. Instead, the ads should be geared toward adopting healthy life-styles and obtaining love and acceptance.

- Persuade the advertising industry to utilize the same marketing techniques used in successful commercial campaigns. Instead of the scattergun approach, for example, ads should be targeted to specific segments of the population based on age and demographic characteristics (as is now done by the cigarette industry).

Ads also should be market-tested for effectiveness before being used on a large scale.

• In a similar manner, persuade managers of TV and radio stations and publishers of printed media fillers to schedule these ads with programs attracting the targeted audiences, particularly teenagers, instead of using them at odd periods as fillers.

• Persuade independent television producers to insert dialogue with an antidrug message into prime-time network shows.

The report points to the 1988 success of the Harvard Center for Health Communications in persuading fifteen producers to include in their shows favorable mention of the designated driver program to prevent drunk driving accidents. When combined with prime-time commercials on all three major networks, a Gallup poll found a 15 percent increase in persons reporting the use of a designated driver.

Too easily ignored in most drug education plans is the number-one drug of abuse—alcohol. Despite the many pompous pronouncements about marijuana, *alcohol* is the gateway drug that introduces virtually all youths to the euphoria and mood-altering excitement to be found by taking chemicals into the body. If recreational drug use is to be slowed, a tremendous educational effort in the schools is required to counter the effects of the annual $1.4 billion spent on media advertising to promote beer, wine, and hard liquor. Much of this, particularly the $800-million advertising budget for beer, only thinly disguises its appeal to the youth of America.

The Workshop on Drunk Driving assembled by former U.S. Surgeon General C. Everett Koop reported that a two-year-old will have seen 100,000 beer commercials by the age of eighteen. Many of these will have been in connection with sports events such as baseball and football games, and others will have included youth-oriented celebrities. Special promotions at Florida's ritualistic spring break, at rock concerts, and on college campuses are brazenly addressed to audiences where the majority is too young to drink legally. Is it any wonder that two-thirds of America's high school seniors report they are currently consumers of alcohol? Virtually all underage! And with this introduction to mind-altering substances, many have gone on to illegal drugs.

Just as efforts to reduce cigarette consumption made it necessary to require tobacco companies to modify their advertising, so it is necessary if drug education is to be successful that the alcohol industry be forced to modify its advertising and promotions so as not to be so blatantly targeted to youth. To head off legislative restrictions, brewers have been offering public service ads promoting "safe" drinking.

The slogan "Know when to say when" is a compelling public relations gimmick, but few youngsters approaching the dangerous level of intoxication are in sufficient control either to know or to say when. However, the slogan succeeds in conveying to teenagers a false sense of confidence that they can always be in control. So it is safe to guzzle beer. If youngsters really were able to say when, beer would not be the number-one cause of drinking-and-driving accidents. One hopes such public relations ploys will not silence demands that advertising be prevented from imprinting on juvenile minds the excitement to be found in this gateway drug.

The Big Three

Antidrug education in the schools should be targeted at three drugs, two legal, one currently illegal—alcohol, tobacco, and marijuana. Efforts should begin in the early elementary levels. If young people could be steered away from these three, problems with drug abuse would be 98 percent eliminated.

The June 1989 issue of the *Journal of the American Medical Association* reports a comprehensive community program involving 22,500 sixth- and seventh-graders in forty-two schools in Kansas City, Missouri, and Kansas City, Kansas. For evaluation the schools were randomly assigned to the experimental program or to a control group being given the regular drug education curriculum. Efforts were aimed primarily at the same big three—alcohol, tobacco, and marijuana. Students were taught the dangers of using drugs and ways to avoid peer pressure. Parents were involved in parent-child discussions, rule setting, and role-playing. Newspaper articles along with TV and radio spots were coordinated with the school activities.

At the end of the year results of this coordinated school, home, and community program were dramatic. In the control schools 13.1 percent of the students reported having smoked cigarettes in the previous month compared to 3.4 percent of those in the program. With alcohol the comparison was 9.4 percent to 4.2 percent, and with marijuana 7.1 percent to 3.4 percent. Even more encouraging, follow-up data three years later indicated that not only had the program effects been maintained, in some cases they had increased.

Report of the project, headed by Mary Ann Pentz of the University of California, is indeed good news in an arena sadly lacking in good news. It indicates that school-based drug education can be successful.

DRUGS AS A MEANS OF ESCAPE

While we are hearing promising news about reduction in the recreational and experimental use of drugs, this offers little hope for that second type of drug user—the one who uses drugs as an avenue of escape. Those who deliberately anesthetize their minds to blot out the pains of everyday life present the most challenging problem.

All youths possess certain basic needs and desires, no matter if they are black or white, rich or poor, smart or dumb. Among these are the need to be loved and wanted, the need for self-esteem, the desire to share in the material delights of life, the desire for pleasure and excitement. A youth faced with the frustration of being unable to satisfy these normal needs and desires may respond in a number of ways.

The most common reaction is to redouble efforts to gain whatever is missing—love, respect, a share of life's goodies. Mild frustration is a strong motivator. But frustration can become overpowering. Then a youth will turn to other efforts. He may simply resort to property crime, stealing what he cannot gain legitimately—or peddle crack on the streets.

Or his frustration may turn to bitterness. He will strike out angrily at the society that denies him what he perceives to be his fair share of the glamour and glitter flashed across the television screen. Senseless acts of vandalism and unprovoked acts of brutal violence, often against people he doesn't even know, become outlets for his frustration. As we have increasingly witnessed in recent years, society is paying dearly for the vengeance he seeks.

Or he may give up and retreat into the euphoric world of drugs. It is quiet and comfortable there. For a little while rage and hostility are rocked to sleep by the narcotic effect. There is peace in the soul no longer tormented by the sense of perpetual failure, by the feelings of inferiority, by the pains of discrimination. The ultimate retreat is, of course, suicide. But heavy drug abuse is a living suicide.

This frustration may come from many different unfulfilled needs. Perhaps the most damaging is the inability to gain a measure of self-esteem. It may come from continually being unable to satisfy parental expectations, whatever those expectations are—grades, social success, athletic achievement. It may come from being trapped in the tragic clutches of child abuse. It may come from sexual frustrations for both the heterosexual and the homosexual. It may come solely from within the individual, his inability to achieve whatever he believes to be vitally important.

Thus, drug abuse cuts across all social and economic levels. But in the ghettos these frustrations zap a youth from all sides. Poverty and drug abuse thrive in a symbiotic relationship, feeding on each other, suffocating their victims.

The cost of crimes committed by these addicted dropouts is horrendous. Drug czar William Bennett points to a crack addict with a $60-a-day habit. To support that habit he has to steal $600 worth of goods each day since he gets only 10 percent when fencing the stolen property. That adds up to $219,000 a year. Just one addict!

Neither drug education nor strict law enforcement will dent this problem. Laws calling for death to pushers and mandatory prison for users might as well be addressed to aliens from another planet. Even therapy of the most effective modality offers little long-term hope. Here the problem is the same as with most delinquency rehabilitation programs. No matter how successful the therapy, when "cured" the youth is returned to the same environment and conditions that fostered the delinquency in the first place. Any resolve to stay clean quickly erodes.

Clearly the only effective long-term hope is in primary prevention. The number of those using drugs to escape the misery and the hopelessness in their lives will be reduced only when America is willing to attack the sources of that misery and hopelessness.

Heading the list must be the attack on the cycle of poverty fervently urged in earlier chapters. Ameliorating the agony of abject poverty will automatically ameliorate much of the tragedy of serious drug abuse. But there are other arenas in which the attack must be pursued—meaningful schools, job opportunities for unskilled and poorly educated youths raised in cultural deprivation, shelter for runaway youths who have been pushed out of uncaring homes.

Political rhetoric and governmental programs err in looking at drug abuse as an isolated phenomenon. It is only an outward manifestation of a much broader malaise. Prevention of delinquency and prevention of serious drug abuse call for the same artillery. Both are spawned by the same unmet needs. It is not enough to tell children of the ghetto,

"Just say no." They must also be shown something to which they can proudly say yes. They must be given a chance to say yes to self-esteem. A chance to be proud of themselves and of their community. A legitimate hope to participate in the bounty of America.

Earlier it was stated that it is highly significant that the crack epidemic has been concentrated in the inner cities, particularly in public housing projects. The flames of this epidemic were fanned by the withdrawal of federal funds from social programs during the Reagan years. Deep cutbacks in antipoverty programs such as job training for disadvantaged youngsters imprisoned many in the ghetto. And these prisoners of the ghettos discovered that hustling crack could be the wings to lift them over those prison walls.

In city after city many housing projects are totally out of control because of the necessity of reducing critically needed security forces and maintenance crews. Many have been virtually abandoned to the crack trade as dealers set up distribution centers in rented apartments. Vacant units have become crack dens. With the eviction of more tenants made penniless by drug purchases, looting and vandalizing of unprotected empty apartments left the projects in shambles. The problem was intensified when responsible tenants literally fled for their lives, an exodus that further diminished inadequate operating budgets.

It is primary prevention aimed at the very heart of the drug problem to restore funds sufficiently to recapture the housing projects. Beefed-up security forces to throw out dealers, addicts, deadbeats, and felons squatting in abandoned apartments; repair crews to refurbish vandalized apartments, making them again occupiable by stable tenants; money for programs and services designed to restore pride among those who live there—these are basic needs for primary drug prevention. Until they are met, boarded-up apartments in desolate housing projects will remain as testimony to a shortsighted drug policy—one that could find billions to squander on futile efforts at interdiction but slashed the few pennies being spent to ameliorate the basic causes of drug abuse.

And where will the money come from to pay for these expensive programs? For a start there needs to be a reallocation of money now being wasted in the war on drugs to more hopeful activities. After that it becomes simply a matter of priorities. If the government can find the billions to develop more deadly weapons to fight an unidentified enemy, surely it can find the billions needed to fight a known enemy—find the means to bail out a large segment of our youth population from a debilitating environment not of their own making.

"Take my word for it. This scourge will stop." President Bush's lips formed this rosy promise about the drug problem during his inaugural address. But there has been little evidence of any serious intention of doing anything other than more and more of those same expensive measures that have failed so miserably. Can it be that his kinder, gentler answer to the desperate cries of the downtrodden will continue to be more prisons . . . and then still more prisons?

Again, is this the response that a compassionate nation really wants to make?

PART III

Society's Last Chance:

PUTTING JUSTICE INTO THE JUVENILE JUSTICE SYSTEM

Chapter 18

THE FAMILY COURT: COMPULSORY PREVENTION

Two Problems—Two Courts

The ultimate hope of reducing juvenile delinquency—and indeed, adult crime—is unquestionably through prevention. This has been the thrust of the many proposals that have been made—meeting the needs of children and youths before those unmet needs trigger delinquent behavior. These included removing many of the root causes of delinquency; early and noncoercive intervention into the lives of children with physical, psychological, or learning problems; alternative educational programs to meet the needs of all youngsters; programs to assure that all youths are trained for and have available a dignified job.

When such programs are implemented, it is to be hoped that the never-ending stream of juveniles passing in and out of the revolving door of the court will slow to a trickle. But alas! Realism must prevail. There will always be those who slip through the cracks. And for many of today's young people the reforms that have been proposed here will come far too late. With these the court must intervene.

After all, court intervention is society's last chance.

But what legal and moral justification does a court have for intervening in the life of a juvenile? Two basic reasons stand out: (1) the juvenile's life or well-being is endangered by the actions of another person or agency, or (2) the juvenile is endangering the safety or rights of others by committing an act that the legislature has declared is unlawful for both adults and juveniles.

The first includes all forms of neglect and abuse of the juvenile by others. As such it is the opposite of the second, which is the youth's own doing. One is done *to* the juvenile, the other is done *by* the juvenile. Yet in most states both are handled, along with status offenses, by the same court. This tends to confuse in the public's mind such terms as "dependent," "neglected," and "delinquent." The youth who appears in juvenile court for a reason beyond his own control is often considered by the public to be as much a delinquent as is a youth who has robbed and beaten an elderly woman.

Because the two justifications for intervening in the life of a juvenile differ so vastly, there are strong reasons to argue that the two should not be handled by the same court. Cases involving criminal acts committed by the juvenile can best be heard in a "Youthful Offender Court." Cases involving abuse and neglect of the juvenile could be heard in a "Family Court."

What follows is not to be considered a precise blueprint for the two courts. To make it so would require a vast volume of codes and regulations. And specifics that might be appropriate in North Dakota or West Virginia might not be so in New York or California. Instead, broad suggestions are made as to how the two courts might be structured.

Unfortunately, the public's concern with juvenile delinquency is narrowly focused on punishing those youths who threaten the peace and safety of the community. It is a costly, shortsighted concern. It ignores the fact that *delinquents are made, not born.* Some person or persons, some agency or institution is responsible. These are the legitimate concern of the Family Court.

As envisioned here, the Family Court would have jurisdiction over all legal difficulties—criminal and civil—arising out of the various phases of family life, including troublesome but *noncriminal* behavior of juveniles. These would include:

- child neglect and/or abuse
- termination of parental rights
- foster home placements

- Truants and dropouts referred by the school's Behavioral Review Board
- Runaways
- Those beyond parental control
- Contributing to delinquency of a minor
- Adoptions
- Paternity suits
- Child custody and child support
- Supervision of court-ordered custody cases
- Emancipation of teenagers
- Divorce, alimony, and annulments
- Intrafamily assault and other criminal acts
- Appointment of legal guardians for incompetents and minors
- Commitment of the mentally ill or mentally deficient

Additionally, the Family Court would have jurisdiction over children under ten years of age who commit criminal acts. For these preadolescents punishment may not be the appropriate response. But their needs should have high priority with the court. Criminal behavior of the extremely young usually reflects serious family dysfunction or serious psychological abnormality in the child. Earlier we noted that such children have the potentiality of becoming the most dangerous of adult criminals. It is critical that the Family Court seek the early determination of the social, psychological, or educational services required by these children—and their parents—and make arrangements for the delivery of those services.

Despite the many important and varied functions of the Family Court, this chapter is primarily concerned with only one phase of those functions, the court's jurisdiction over the persons and agencies responsible for the "making of a delinquent." As contrasted to the Youthful Offender Court, which would "do something to" a teenager as punishment for a criminal act, this court could only "do something for" a child with problems not of his own making, problems that have high likelihood of fomenting delinquent behavior.

Support for the Behavioral Review Board

Consider some hypothetical truants, dropouts, or habitual troublemakers at school who could be referred by the Behavioral Review Board (BRB) or by some school official unable to solve the difficulty (see Chapter 12). Upon hearing evidence presented by the BRB, the court could order whatever services or support the youth needed and when appropriate permit the school to permanently expel the troublemaker.

There is Marie. Despite her impoverished background she had made good grades in school until this year. Suddenly her attendance became erratic and her grades collapsed. A school officer found that when her mother became seriously ill Marie had to stay home to do the housework and take care of younger children. The problem was referred to the court. After hearing the report of the court's investigative social worker, the judge ordered the county welfare department to furnish temporary homemaking services and to arrange for proper medical attention for the mother.

On the other hand, the court ordered Mike's father, under threat of prosecution for contributing to the delinquency of a minor, to stop forcing Mike to work during school hours. The judge found that the job was not necessary for the family's support. The father simply didn't believe school was of any value to a fifteen-year-old boy.

And there is Vince, who for years had been failing in school but had been socially promoted by his teachers, possibly to get him out of their hair. Tired of being the classroom dummy, at age fourteen he had finally rebelled and begun hanging out during school hours. The BRB could make no headway, and he was referred to the court to back up the school's threat of expulsion. The judge, however, ordered the principal to provide Vince with a classroom situation that would be meaningful and in which he would have some chance of success. One can only hope the court order did not come too late. But at the very least the approach is far more hopeful than making the expensive, counterproductive, and tragic mistake of tossing Vince into a reform school because of truancy.

Whatever the basis of a youth's school problem—lack of proper medical attention, lack of family cooperation or support, improper school placement, insufficient money for decent clothes, an unsatisfactory place to live, or any of a hundred factors over which the youth has little control—the court would have the power to demand help for the juvenile.

But there are also students like Rick, another habitual truant. The BRB was unable to determine any educational, physical, or social cause for his behavior. After a hearing the court agreed with the BRB's finding and made Rick's parents responsible: they were ordered to see that he attend school every day. Should this prove ineffective, Rick and his parents will be brought back to court, and if the parents can show they have been reasonably diligent in their efforts, Rick will be declared in contempt of court and remanded to the Youthful Offender Court for punishment. Thus Rick, like other students below the state's cutoff age for compulsory attendance, could be punished for continual truancy, *but only after* it was determined that others, including school personnel and parents, were not at fault.

And finally there is Grover, better known as "Snake-Eyes," who comes to school regularly enough but never makes any pretense of doing schoolwork. Receiving all F's doesn't faze him. He merely laughs. Most days he is obviously high on some drug or other, and twice he has been caught selling drugs to other students. For him school is a great place for socializing and for terrorizing all the "goody-goodies." After the court agrees that the school has exhausted all reasonable efforts to accommodate Grover's needs, it will grant the board's request for permanent expulsion and order him to stay away from the school.

Neglect and Abuse

Listen to Karl Menninger, the venerated psychiatrist of the Menninger Clinic. At the age of eighty-four, after a half-century-long crusade to bring about justice for criminals, he observed: "Nearly every inmate I ever interviewed at length had been brutally beaten as a child by his father or stepfather or other power figure . . . Everything we call crime is a rather stupid, mismanaged, pitiful struggle by angry kids to get revenge in the most evil way they can."[1]

It is possible that no single factor, outside of school failure, correlates so positively with crime and delinquency as does having been a victim of child abuse and neglect. Furthermore, the crimes later committed by these abused juveniles are far more likely to be crimes of violence. A child forced by severe physical punishment to obey parental demands has been taught that the way to get what one wants is through violent force. And a child unable to love an abusive parent learns to hate, learns to get revenge with violence against anyone who stands in his way. This nationwide problem has reached crisis proportions due to the skyrocketing epidemic of drug addiction, severe unemployment among disadvantaged groups, and the many other urban problems of modern times.

After California in 1982 made it mandatory for teachers, counselors, police officers, and neighbors to report suspected cases of physical or sexual abuse, dependency cases in Santa Clara County jumped from 5 percent of the court's caseload to 50 percent. In New York City, because of the overload in the foster care system, endangered children at times must sleep on mats on the floor of the welfare office. "Boarder babies"—infants forced to stay in hospitals for months because of a shortage of foster homes—have steadily increased.

Abuse and neglect take many forms. There is Katie, whose mother draws AFDC money because of her but spends it on her unemployed live-in boyfriend and forces Katie to beg or steal in order to obtain her own clothes and school supplies . . . and sixteen-year-old Jeremiah, whose fanatically religious parents make him wear a plain black suit to school and refuse to let him participate in any school activities . . . and Chuck, on whom his alcoholic father takes out his frustrations with frequent and savage beatings . . . and not too bright Bobbie, who has been denied all normal teenage privileges by his middle-class parents because he doesn't bring his C-average grades up to the level of his brilliant older sister . . .

And in the chapter about runaways and pushouts we met the teen-age prostitutes, both male and female, who had been victims of physical or sexual abuse at home.

A million and a half children are reported each year as suspected victims of abuse. Many more never come to the attention of the authorities. The Family Court should have jurisdiction over the following categories of abuse of these children:

- *Physical abuse*—nonaccidental injury inflicted by the parent or those responsible for the child's welfare
- *Sexual abuse*—of both girls and boys by fathers, stepfathers, other relatives, mothers' boyfriends, and even at times mothers
- *Neglect*—the failure of a parent or custodian to provide basic necessities such as food, shelter, clothing, education, and medical treatment
- *Psychological abuse*—failure to provide the psychological nurturing necessary for a child's growth and development
- *Abandonment*—leaving a child without adequate care, supervision, support, or parental contact for extended or excessive periods of time (particularly common among drug-addicted mothers)
- *Unwilling or unable parents or custodians*—who refuse to care for the child or are unable to do so due to their own mental retardation, mental illness, or physical disability[2]

Under the proposals made in Part II many individuals would have the opportunity to detect evidence of child abuse, including the staffs of the Child Development Services System and runaway centers as well as intake officers of the court. Combined with the observations of neighbors, friends, teachers, doctors, and hospitals, this should ensure that most instances of child abuse are uncovered. Getting them reported, however, is difficult even when mandated by law. Becoming involved is not a favored pastime of modern Americans living in the fast lane. We need a return to a feeling of neighborliness and concern for others. A media educational blitz might encourage getting involved.

Early Delinquency Prevention

It is ironic that so many youngsters charged with delinquency for the first time have already been seen in court—years earlier as babies or toddlers when their parents were charged with child abuse. One research study conducted by the New York State Assembly's Select Committee on Child Abuse found that over half of the families officially suspected of child abuse later had one or more children arrested for delinquency.[3] For these young children, the court obviously failed to offer protection and guidance. The follow-up was inadequate.

In routine child abuse cases a social worker usually makes a few home visits to parents under court order to reform. But most caseloads are far too heavy to permit any in-depth supervision or therapy. Some parents may manage a few superficial changes, but rarely is anything done to ease the emotional trauma of the abused child or to provide educational and social experiences to overcome the cumulative effects of neglect.

Some 300,000 of these endangered children are placed in foster homes each year for either temporary or semipermanent custody. Highly publicized incidents of abuse and neglect by foster parents are testimony that this is not always the ideal solution.

While it is possibly no more inadequate than most systems around the nation, the problems are epitomized by San Francisco's scandal-ridden child welfare department, which each year takes charge of some eight hundred neglected or abused children. In recent years an abnormal number of children have died in city-supervised foster care homes. These included a toddler who died of injuries after being beaten by his department-approved foster parents, a transvestite and his male lover posing as a married couple—both with previous arrest records. An investigative panel placed the blame for the department's problems on an undermanned, overworked, undertrained, and inadequately supervised staff.

In fairness it must be pointed out that for many, many children, foster home placement has turned out to be a successful, nurturing experience. There are foster parents so beautiful in their love and care that they qualify for a heartwarming account in *Reader's Digest*. Unfortunately, there is a vast shortage of these. Many women who in the past would have been willing to care for a foster child are now working outside the home, part of the trend toward two-income families. And foster parents interested primarily in the pay can be as unqualified as the maltreating natural parents. Love cannot be bought.

Disturbing studies indicate that a foster home placement often proves more damaging than keeping the child with its biological parents, or parent, even though they are morally irresponsible and psychologically unstable. Children who have been placed in foster care appear with tragic frequency in delinquency and runaway statistics. Many of the more violent criminals, like Charles Manson, have histories of multiple placements.

No matter how justified, no matter how necessary the separation may have been, the child is forever haunted by one of the most traumatic events in human experience—the feeling of having been rejected by one's mother. The emotional destruction is often magnified by the child's belief that the rejection was caused by something bad he or she had done. In working with runaways I have been bewildered to discover that this imagined guilt causes many of these throwaways to be unjustifiably defensive of their uncaring mothers. They still cry out for the maternal love they were denied.

Even short-term separation may sever the tenuous bond of affection between a marginal parent and a child. The problem of what to do with unloved, abused children has no easy solution. Often it seems you are damned if you do, damned if you don't.

The Need for Permanency

The greatest tragedy in foster home placements lies in the lack of concern given to the overriding need in a child's life for continuity and a secure feeling of permanency. Most maltreated children are taken from their homes on a supposedly temporary basis while a search is made for a suitable placement or while the inadequate parent is being counseled or "treated." Yet, according to government surveys, in some states as many as half are still in this "temporary" status six years after being taken from the home.[4]

A 1989 study of foster care made by the New York City Office of the Comptroller found a majority of these temporarily placed children were still without permanent homes after three years. Little Matilda who had not been seen by her mother in twenty-two months was still listed as "expected to be returned to parent." And Mickie had not yet been freed for adoption after three years even though he had *never* been visited by either parent.

The inaction, the indecisiveness, the insensitivity of many in the child welfare system are truly criminal. These children are emotionally crippled for life because of child welfare workers' vain hope that the parents might eventually straighten out.

This tragedy is exacerbated by the fact that these children are bounced around from one unsatisfactory foster home, group home, or institution to another. The majority have lived in three or more different placements (many in a dozen or more) before they are old enough to successfully run away or are officially released. With each change of caretaker they again go through the trauma of rejection. No one wants them. The feeling of being a no-good, worthless, bad individual is reinforced. All the dynamics for the internalization of antisocial attitudes—rebellion and hate and revenge—come into play.

Incredibly, these frequent changes are often deliberately ordered by the welfare workers. It is done because of a misguided, unofficial policy of preventing the child from becoming too attached to a foster parent, just in case the abusive parent eventually reforms and wants the child back. In the meantime the child grows up in emotional limbo.

This process, termed "foster care drift," thwarts normal development. Security is a primary need of all children—the security of permanent family ties, of uninterrupted love and care, of familiar, unchanging surroundings and friends. Lacking this feeling, they are likely to become emotionally disturbed and antisocially inclined. (Even intact families that move frequently are much more likely to produce delinquent children than those families who remain settled in one place.)

Four years ago a San Francisco youth who had legally been a "child of the city" for fifteen of his sixteen years was arrested for murder. After being taken from a mentally disturbed mother and an alcoholic father, he had over the years been continually shifted from one temporary home to another, from one institution to another—more than twenty placements. This finally ended the day the youth fatally stabbed a stranger in a park. In retrospect it is hard to claim that the "best interests of the child" were served by taking him at age one from his natural parents, unsuitable as they were, and setting him out on a roller-coaster ride through unsatisfactory placements. He epitomizes many of the difficulties with foster care.

Changing the Criteria

One of the more astute students of the problems of child abuse and foster care is Douglas Besharov, a scholar with the American Enterprise Institute for Public Policy Research located in Washington, D.C., who incisively places blame for the misuse of foster care upon the criteria used in the selection process.[5] He proposes that abused and neglected children brought to the attention of authorities should be separated into two categories:

1. Children in Immediately Harmful Situations

This would include those who face momentary life-threatening physical injury, those who are left in extremely dangerous situations (e.g., abandoned), and, less frequently, those who need immediate medical attention or nourishment to prevent starvation. By definition, these children must be quickly provided with protective services. If their safety cannot be ensured by some arrangement such as placement in the care of relatives, they should be taken into custody and placed in emergency foster care. Here they will remain until the home situation is made safe or parental rights are permanently terminated.

2. Children in Cumulatively Harmful Situations

This category would include those to whom the parents' behavior will eventually cause serious harm if permitted to continue. The concern is more for emotional harm than for physical. Included would be use of excessive but not life-threatening physical punishment, minor neglect such as failure to provide medical care or a nutritionally adequate diet, educational neglect and emotional maltreatment, and psychological abuse in general. Together these account for 80 percent of all abuse charges.

While more children die of physical neglect than physical abuse, these children, again by definition, face no immediate physical danger. Although many are now routinely removed "temporarily," only rarely do they actually require emergency foster care. They should be left with the natural parent or parents, who would be given appropriate supervision, counseling, and/or therapy. An in-depth case study should determine what social services would help the parent to become nonabusive. Extensive home visits would be needed at least twice a week in the early months of supervision. Expensive? Yes. *But the cost even for daily supervisory visits pales in comparison to the cost of foster care.*

Recognizing that keeping a child with the natural parents, if at all reasonably possible, is preferable to the perils of institutional or foster care, authorities in Tacoma, Washington, established the Homebuilders, a team of professionals with master's degrees in social work, psychology, or counseling.[6] The services of one or more of the team are made available to any family in imminent danger of having a child removed from the home. No team member works with more than three families at a time. They go into the homes, provide therapy as needed, and help the abusing parents learn more effective ways of coping. Counseling continues as intensively as required. Cooperation is obtained from other community agencies, including the schools.

Of the abused Tacoma children who were headed toward out-of-home placements, 90 percent have been able to remain in their homes with the Homebuilders' counseling and help. The average cost has been $2,600 per family. This has been calculated to be some five or six times less than the projected long-term cost of foster or group care.

Those young abused children who can be kept at home become priority candidates for the day-care and early-education projects proposed in Chapter 10. Even if the therapy for the parents is less than fully successful (as most frequently is the case), the child's well-being may nevertheless be better served by providing compensatory services than by placing him or her in foster care with the accompanying dynamics of rejection.

Besharov also cautions against the common practice of temporarily removing a child while the parent undergoes treatment. This short-sighted practice is damaging to both. In addition to the psychologically jarring effect on the child, it can also complete the destruction of the parent's self-image as a worthwhile human being.

It is the temporarily placed children who are most readily trapped in foster care drift. Because of the myth of rehabilitation (adult as well as juvenile), authorities keep assuming that the parent will in time be cured of an intractable emotional problem. But major improvement seldom occurs. In the meantime the child is shuffled back and forth to unsuccessful home visits on trial tests of the parent's emotional stability and again back to yet a different foster home residence.

Under some circumstances, Besharov suggests, there might be cause to remove a child from the parents even though he or she faces only nonemergency, cumulative danger, such as when (1) the parents refuse to permit the child to receive compensatory services, (2) the child needs diagnostic tests and/or treatment available only through residential care, (3) there is an irreconcilable conflict between the parents and an adolescent youth, or (4) foster care is a planned precursor to the termination of parental rights and subsequent adoption.

With the arrival of crack in the ghettos, there has been an explosion of child abuse including neglect and even total abandonment by drug-addicted mothers. Treatment is difficult and frequently unsuccessful. At present the best hope is in relatively long-term residential treatment for the addict. But it is critical that during treatment the child not be separated from the mother. Doing this would make rehabilitation even more difficult for the mother and would be traumatic for the child. When the mother is released from residential treatment, as noted, her right to keep the child would be contingent on remaining drug-free as determined by periodic urine tests.

If Besharov's suggestions were followed the demands for foster care would be dramatically reduced, making it possible to be more selective in recruiting competent foster parents. And many children would escape the emotional limbo of foster care drift.

Termination of Parental Rights

In life-threatening cases where it becomes obvious that the situation is not likely to improve, the termination of parental rights should quickly free the child for adoption or some permanent intrafamily arrangement. Thus, the irreparable damage of multiple placements can be avoided. In marginal cases a time limit of perhaps six months should be established. At that time an evaluation including, if relevant, a psychiatric study would be conducted. If it is apparent that an insufficient change in the threatening situation has been achieved, permanency plans should be instituted.

Greater consideration should be given to the use of grandmothers, aunts, and cousins, even older siblings, who might be willing to give a child a loving home but are unable to take on the additional financial burden. Blood ties often generate greater interest and concern. It would be far better to make foster care payments to a concerned relative, *screened for being capable and responsible,* than to a stranger who may be interested only in the money. If the arrangement with the relative was made permanent through adoption, the "new" mother might qualify for AFDC payments.

It is a tragedy that millions are spent on years of foster care for children who should have been released earlier for adoption by the thousands of childless couples pleading for the opportunity to give them a permanent home.

It must be reiterated, however, that terminating parental rights is not in the best interest of the child *unless* a better arrangement is at hand. Adoption is a hopeful solution when potentially good parents are available. But many of the children being considered here are not the most sought-after young, blue-eyed, psychologically and physically sound candidates. The many babies of drug-addicted mothers have escalated the problem. We come back to the original question of whether or not to opt for protective custody. Unless the circumstances are immediately dangerous, removing a child from admittedly inadequate parents may merely make a bad situation worse.

We have had to admit that there is no ideal solution to the problem of what to do with unwanted children. Perhaps, as was suggested in Chapter 9, the only real solution lies in prevention—in education to prevent unwanted children from being conceived. But they are. And studies have consistently shown that child abuse often has its genesis in the emotional rejection of an infant born from an unwanted pregnancy. Birth control clinics, even abortions if necessary, could avoid the agony of many who are doomed from birth to lives of unrelieved misery.

Unfortunately, we are brought back to the sad fact that the very vocal, self-righteous right-to-lifers seem to be more interested in producing more and more of these unwanted children than in trying to ease the misery of the thousands whom their misguided morality has already caused to be born.

For the Child's Best Interest—CASA

The admission that there is no ideal solution to the problems of abused children should intensify efforts to guarantee that each child get the most appropriate (or least destructive) of the available alternatives. One successful approach is CASA, a program begun in 1977 by Seattle judge David Soukup. It utilizes volunteers to help make certain that the child's best interests are presented to the court and that no child is allowed to fall through bureaucratic cracks. Following the success of the Seattle program, some 250 similar programs (sometimes under different names) have been established throughout the nation. In Delaware, Florida, North and South Carolina, and Rhode Island the program is now mandated by law.

In Spanish *casa* means home. In court CASA identifies a Court Appointed Special Advocate—a volunteer who has received special training in the causes of child abuse and the availability of resources to rescue a child. The judge assigns a CASA to each battered or neglected child who comes before the court.

The CASA becomes the child's advocate as the legal case makes its way through the court and also in the follow-up. At times this may last for years, regardless of whether the child is placed in foster care or remains at home. The volunteer advocate conducts an independent investigation, consulting with the child, family members, neighbors, teachers, doctors, and others who may be involved. Finally a formal report is submitted to the judge recommending what action will best ensure the child's right to a safe and permanent family and home. At the hearing the presence of the CASA ensures that the abused child's best interests will always be articulated to the court.

As most CASAs are assigned only one or two children, they have far more time to thoroughly research the case than a court social worker, some of whom may have up to a hundred cases. Furthermore, the volunteer will have the time to monitor compliance with the court orders and, as the advocate, to arrange for needed services. In evaluating the CASA approach, the president of the National Council of Juvenile and Family Court Judges, Judge Forest Eastman, summed up the benefits: "An effective CASA program can assure the court that a child is prospering in the ordered placement, and that no child will be lost in the system."[7]

Custody of Runaways

In the case of runaways who have not violated a criminal law, protective custody should be available upon their personal request. As has been discussed at length, most of these youths are running away from physical, psychological, or sexual abuse at home. Protective custody would offer a safe haven while their charges were being investigated. The case would proceed in a manner similar to child abuse cases where the charges have been brought by a third party.

After an investigation and hearing the judge would make a placement decision. In some instances the long-term shelter houses proposed in the chapter on runaways would be the most promising option for older juveniles. In consultation with the youth, creative solutions should be explored. For example, a subsistence allowance might make it possible for the youth to stay with the parents of a friend. At times, with the youngster's approval, arrangements might be made for him or her to receive room and board with an older couple in return for minor household duties. With similar placements the teenager would remain a ward of the court, which would provide a clothing and spending allowance. Ideally a CASA would be assigned.

Engraved in stone must be the legal prohibition against placing any child in a locked delinquency institution, detention center, or jail solely for protective custody. These abused youngsters should be spared the additional trauma of hearing the chilling clank of a door being locked behind them. Instead, the court should maintain contracts for temporary care with shelter houses, group homes, hospitals, and other places housing noncriminal children. Smaller communities may find that contracts for emergency care with one or two private families on a standby basis are a humane and economical solution.

At one time Florida was able to locate some nine hundred homes around the state willing to take a child for a few days *at no charge to the state*. In one year well over a million dollars' worth of goods and services were provided.[8] These crisis homes were utilized on a voluntary basis particularly for runaways. (As with so many other successful experimental programs, this one gradually petered out after the expiration of the federal grant to pay workers for recruiting the voluntary providers.)

Next we turn our concern to those juveniles who commit criminal acts—juveniles whom prevention programs failed to reach.

Chapter 19

PUNISHMENT AS A REHABILITATIVE TOOL

From the day the juvenile court was conceived, punishment has been considered a no-no. Because of the tenderness of their age, because of the unfortunate circumstances of their home life and other conditions for which they were not responsible, these young delinquents were to be pitied and helped—not punished. Despite this compassionate philosophy, juveniles *have* been punished. At times unmercifully. But always under the guise of therapy, not as punishment per se.

Liberals finally came to realize that the court was failing to live up to its promise to rehabilitate wayward youths. Conservatives came to realize that increasingly it was failing to protect society from the rampages of young hoodlums. And herein lies the Catch-22 of the juvenile justice system. *If the court steps in, almost invariably those youths get worse. But because the court is reluctant to do anything, society is being ravaged.*

This impasse is bringing to the forefront a revolutionary concept about juvenile justice—a concept that reverses a castigating philosophy which long ago put the court on a track to nowhere. It even sounds a little old-fashioned. Gradually emerging is the realization that the juvenile court's function is not that of being just another social service agency. Instead, like adult courts, it exists to punish those who break the law, and through this punishment deter them and other youths from future crime.

This change has been dictated for the pragmatic reason that court-ordered rehabilitation simply doesn't work. As was documented in Chapter 3, with rare, rare exceptions the juvenile comes out of delinquency institutions more criminally inclined than when he or she began therapy. And society pays the high tuition required to keep a youth in this crime school.

But this new concept of punishment is a radically changed concept—it is *the use of punishment as a teaching tool*. Indeed, punishment as rehabilitative therapy!

Unfortunately, the word "punishment" conjures up visions of brutal beatings, sadistic treatment, and bread and water in solitary confinement. It need not be so. Punishment can be humane, fair, and done with love. Most parents know this instinctively. From the dawn of history it has been one of the principal devices whereby the child is socialized and learns to accept the rules of the family. In the past many child development specialists have scoffed at anything so primitive. But gradually punishment of children by their parents is regaining respectability among child psychologists who work with problem children and their families.

Punishment as a Learning Experience

In the forefront of this change has been the Oregon Social Learning Center in Eugene.[1] In the past decade the Center has successfully helped hundreds of families deal with problem children—children whose antisocial behaviors range from temper tantrums to lying, stealing, and setting fires. At first the therapists worked with the psychological theory that to mold a child's conduct, proper behavior should be richly rewarded while undesirable behavior was studiously ignored. But this did not work, at least not with these children at Oregon who had already established undesirable patterns. The staff concluded—as most successful parents have always known—that to properly socialize children, not only must they be rewarded for proper behavior, they also must be punished for undesirable misbehavior.

For parents, *or the court,* to ignore an improper act violates the pleasure-pain equation that motivates behavior. We try to do those things which bring pleasure, try to avoid those things which bring pain, be it physical or emotional. To pretend not to notice the child who is stealing a sibling's candy is to leave him or her without any pain but solely with the pleasure derived from eating the candy—perhaps even sweeter because it was stolen. In effect, the act of stealing has been condoned.

Punishment, justifiably, got a bad name in some circles. Because of improper applications it failed as a positive learning experience. Among these improper uses by parents:

- *Inconsistency*—to punish a certain behavior one time and ignore it another is to leave the child confused as to what is expected. The punishment only serves to create tension and rebellion.
- *Inappropriateness*—to make the punishment unduly severe for a mildly disobedient act (making TV off-limits for a month for having failed to take out the garbage) also spawns rebellion and an inclination to violate all rules when not being observed.
- *Insincerity*—the parent who continually threatens punishment but seldom carries it out will become totally ineffectual as an authority figure. In time he or she will be ignored on all counts.
- *Arbitrariness*—to suddenly punish a youth for an act that had not been forbidden by a previously announced rule causes a loss of respect for authority and disrupts the learning experience whereby a youth comes to abide by rules.
- *Selectiveness*—to punish a youth for behavior that is permitted for a brother or sister, without a previously announced reasonable explanation for the discrepancy, tends to destroy the youth's self-concept as a worthwhile, socially acceptable individual and increases his rejection of the parent.

The harm done by these improper uses of punishment is exceeded only by the harm done by parents who are so uncaring or so busy that they don't bother to provide supervision of any sort.

It has been noted frequently that delinquency first arises in the home. So it follows that sociologists making in-depth studies of the families of delinquents regularly uncover improper patterns of discipline. Seldom have these destructive patterns of punishment been deliberate. Frequently they have been developed by parents out of misguided love or a lack of concern. Only years later as they sit with their child in juvenile court do they ask themselves, "What did we do wrong?"

Toughlove is a self-help association of distraught parents of serious delinquents and drug addicts critically damaged by inconsistent and inappropriate discipline—or, more frequently, by the lack of any at all. Drawing strength from the Toughlove group, many parents have finally learned how to set limits on their son's or daughter's behavior as a condition to being a part of the family. In some instances it has been successful. Unfortunately, the limit setting comes far too late for most.

The Court as Surrogate Parent

If the juvenile court is to succeed as a surrogate parent it must do better than these ineffective parents. But alas! The juvenile court has been guilty of the very same omissions and transgressions. It, too, has been *inconsistent, insincere, arbitrary,* and *selective* in ordering punishment which often turns out to be *inappropriate* to the severity of the youth's misdeed.

As previously noted, the frequency with which the juvenile court has dismissed charges time after time has left the delinquent confused as to what is socially permissible. The court becomes a joke. Power to enforce laws is effective only if a would-be violator believes that the power will actually be used. But the delinquent who is repeatedly dismissed or placed on simple probation sees the court as an impotent paper tiger. "It won't punish me. I'm too clever."

Then when the court does do something, often quite arbitrarily, the youth is left embittered because the boy down the street (or more likely, the boy on the other side of the tracks) is getting away with exactly the same thing. The end result is that instead of learning to accept authority, the delinquent rebels even further. And the juvenile court has failed in its role as a surrogate parent.

The Key to Deterrence

Going hand in hand with this resurgence in approval of properly applied punishment has been the rediscovery of a phenomenon that most criminologists have known for decades but politicians and legislators have ignored: *The key to deterring a person (young or old) from crime is the certainty of punishment, not the severity of the punishment.*

The public generally has failed to realize that most individuals planning crimes, be they juvenile or adult, do not anticipate being caught. Cockily, they know they will outwit the authorities. Only half-wits get caught. Consequently, whether the penalty is a month in jail or two years in prison is irrelevant in the minds of most would-be criminals.

Take the extreme example. It has never been shown that capital punishment is even slightly more effective in preventing premeditated murder than is life in prison. Jim Murphy, director of the New York State Coalition for Criminal Justice, points out that in the twelve states that have actually used the death penalty the 1978–88 murder rate was 106 per million population. But in the thirteen states *without* a death penalty the murder rate was only half as high—53 per million. Apparently the fear of capital punishment has not been a deterrent.[2]

If the would-be murderer thought there was a real possibility of being caught, the threat of even ten long years behind bars would be sufficient deterrence. But being caught is not in the plan. Neither does the killer in a crime of passion stop and say, "Now let's see, what is the penalty . . . ?"

This is similarly true for lesser offenses. Increasing the severity of a sanction seldom increases the deterrent effect. And while harsher penalties will produce little increase in deterrence, they can cause increasingly severe damage to those who are punished. As Dr. Karl Menninger in *The Crime of Punishment* succinctly put it, "The more fiercely, the more ruthlessly, the more inhumanely the offender is treated—however legally—the more certain we are to have *more* victims."[3]

Back in 1961 when marijuana first crept into the youth culture, the California legislature panicked. It passed a law calling for a mandatory sentence of from one to ten years for anyone convicted of possession of marijuana, even a single joint. The year the law was passed, there had been 3,500 arrests for marijuana offenses. Six years later, there were 37,000 arrests—a tenfold increase. Obviously, harsh sentences had failed as a deterrent. Finally the legislators stopped daydreaming. (Their own kids were being busted.) They backed off from their tough stance.

On the other hand, stiffer penalties for speeding and drunk driving do reduce auto accidents and deaths. This contradiction exists because these are very visible offenses. The driver is continually aware of the possibility of arrest. He can count the number of patrolmen on the highway. And he may coolly calculate the amount of the potential fine, weighing it against the odds of being caught. But even here the likelihood of being arrested weighs more heavily in the equation than the size of the fine.

Under our juvenile court system the equation is further distorted. A youth can be justifiably optimistic that even if by remote chance he should be caught, the odds are good (about eight to one) he will escape punishment by a do-nothing court.

On the other hand, *the court would be a deterrent if a juvenile believed that it would actually punish those who break the law.* Among the research substantiating this fact is a project that grew out of the observations of an astute juvenile judge in Grand Rapids, Michigan.

Judge Randall Hekman had noticed that in his state there were nearly twice as many arrests of sixteen-year-olds as there were of seventeen-year-olds. He couldn't believe that the difference was merely that the police had it in for sixteen-year-olds and overlooked the crimes of those a year older. He suspected that the explanation lay in what he frequently heard former delinquents say. Now that they were seventeen they were going to stay out of trouble because they didn't want to go to an adult court and get thrown into an adult jail.

So the judge persuaded Martin Gold at the University of Michigan Institute for Social Research and David Ruhland at New York University Medical Center to check out his suspicion. The two researchers agreed to test the hypothesis that juveniles are less likely to engage in crime if they know they would be tried in adult court instead of in the much more lenient, do-nothing juvenile court. Fortunately, a situation exists whereby this theory could be readily tested. In some states the juvenile court has jurisdiction of seventeen-year-olds; in others the jurisdiction stops with sixteen-year-olds. Would there be a difference in the crime rate of seventeen-year-olds who knew they would be tried in adult court and seventeen-year-olds who knew they would go to juvenile court?

In 1983 the results were reported in the *Juvenile and Family Court Journal.*[4] Delinquency was measured by the two researchers in two ways: by official records and by self-reported data. The two measures were in agreement. In states where they are legally adults seventeen-year-olds committed *less than half* as many offenses as did seventeen-year-olds in states where they are treated as juveniles. Here was compelling evidence that the do-nothing policy of the juvenile court was ineffective in stopping youth crime. Instead, the court may actually have been encouraging juveniles to commit crimes.

The Two Forms of Control

Two quite different forms of control wave red flags when a juvenile is about to commit an illegal or undesirable act: social (or external) control and personal (or internal) control. Both influence an individual's behavior. Both work because of the payoff involved. In simple terms, this means that a juvenile believes he will garner more goodies and avoid more thorns by acting in a certain way instead of another.

Social control is effective when those who enforce the rules are in a position to see or know that a rule is broken. But this control loses its punch when a youngster hides in the bushes or is simply out of sight. Most will likely commit the forbidden act if they believe that chances of being caught or of being punished are slim.

Many individuals and groups attempt to exert social control over a juvenile—parents, school authorities, peer groups, and the police. Frequently, competing groups (e.g., parents and peers) may make different demands on the juvenile. Then the youth will weigh the potential pleasure and the potential pain promised by each and act accordingly. It is a simple equation. Peers frequently are the winners.

Personal, or internal, control is by far the most important reason juveniles generally abide by the rules of society. Consider the youth who is invited to share a marijuana joint with friends. He may be tempted because of his need to be a part of the group, or because of the promise of fun, or the need to satisfy a curiosity about the effect of pot, or the need to "prove" himself a man. And yet he may decline. An increasingly large number are deciding to "just say no." Most likely the reason is not the fear of being caught and punished. Rather, it has to do with something deep within the youth's own personal makeup or conscience, something that says, "Stop."

Personal control is effective whether anyone is watching or not. It arises out of two sources. One is the youth's moral value system. This is something that most could not put into words but that in large measure was internalized early in the home. Later it was slowly modified by social and educational experiences.

The other source is the individual's feeling about the person or group making the rules. Those who love and respect their parents, feel a strong emotional attachment to them, will tend to follow their instructions even when unobserved. The same holds true with attachments to school and to peer groups. The juvenile who feels good about the community and society, believes he or she is getting a fair shake, enjoys taking part in the activities being offered, is ambitiously looking forward to participation in that society as an adult—such a juvenile will likely abide by the law most of the time even without considering the threat of being punished.

While personal control is the most compelling, unfortunately it is too weak in some juveniles to be an effective deterrent. The moral code internalized in the home may have been defective at its inception. For these it may be necessary for the court to intervene and add to the pain side of the equation with punishment.

Criteria for Effective Court-ordered Punishment

Many factors inclining young people toward delinquency are beyond their immediate control—poverty, racial discrimination, child abuse, inadequate parents, ineffective schools, to name a few. These delinquents may truly be victims of society. But understanding why these youngsters became delinquent does not mean they can be absolved of responsibility for their actions. No matter how lousy a hand they have been dealt, to live peacefully in society they still must learn to obey the rules. This the court can help them do through the proper use of punishment. But a fine line exists between punishment that is beneficial and punishment that is detrimental. If punishment is to serve as a rehabilitative tool, important criteria must be met:

1. Punishment as a Primary Function

It should be made clear to youthful offenders that laws must be observed. They are on trial to determine their guilt or innocence. Those found guilty will be punished. If they break the law again, they will be punished again, most likely more severely. Youths who are told that they need treatment or therapy instead of punishment are given the impression that society has absolved them of their personal responsibility. The constructive value of punishment has been negated.

2. Certainty of Punishment

Being found guilty of breaking the law should automatically trigger an addition to the pain side of the pleasure-pain equation. Youths who were not punished following many, many trips to the court justifiably believe they have been given a dispensation to continue committing crimes. And so do their friends.

3. Punishment at the Second Offense

The majority of juveniles who appear in court do so only that one time. So despite the need for the certainty of punishment, it is probably counterproductive (and a needless expenditure of taxpayer dollars) to punish first offenders except for major felonies or particularly violent crimes. But it should be made clear at that first appearance that breaking the law will not be tolerated and that punishment will be forthcoming at the next apprehension. And that threat must be carried out.

4. Immediacy of Punishment

Anyone who has struggled to housebreak a puppy knows the necessity of delivering the punishment for a mishap immediately. If it is done later the puppy merely associates the punishment with his mean master, not with the forbidden act. While a juvenile's time span for associating cause and effect may be a trifle longer than a puppy's, the psychological effect of delayed action is the same. A long-delayed trial produces behavior modification of the wrong sort. If delivered too long after apprehension, the punishment will cause the youth to feel aversion to the authorities and the system, not to the illegal act. Alienation will be increased and recidivism made more probable.

5. With Punishment, Less Is Best

There is a sizable body of research showing that the deterrent effect of punishment progressively *decreases* as the severity or length of imprisonment increases. John Conrad and his colleagues at Ohio State University found that among 1,138 juveniles arrested for violent crimes in Columbus, Ohio, the more *severe* the sanction, the sooner the juvenile was likely to be rearrested after release.[5] Instead of encouraging the delinquent to stay out of future trouble, punishment that is too abusive or unfairly long increases the youth's alienation from society.

On the other hand, a low level of punishment can be amazingly effective. In Chapter 7 it was pointed out that in low-crime Scandinavian countries unbelievably mild sanctions—fines as small as a half-dollar and jail sentences as short as one day—have proved to be effective deterrents.

An interesting research project in Des Moines, Iowa, demonstrated this fact with five hundred juveniles held in a detention facility. Inmates who committed seriously disruptive or antisocial acts while in the facility were locked in their rooms—but only for periods as brief as fifteen minutes on up to a *maximum* of forty-five minutes. Sounds like an ineffectual slap on the wrist. Yet in 80 percent of the cases this mild sanction was effective in preventing any subsequent serious misbehavior while the youth was in the center.[6] The mild punishment got the message across: Rules must be obeyed.

Quite by coincidence, on the morning I was writing this the newspapers reported the death of a seventeen-year-old who hanged himself in a San Francisco detention center. He had been locked in solitary confinement for over twenty-four hours as punishment for causing a disturbance. The emotional terror this engendered "proved" to the youth how worthless he really was. Suicide was the solution to his agony. A heartrending contrast to the forty-five-minute maximum in the Iowa experiment!

6. Punishment That Is Fair

To be an effective learning experience, the punishment must be perceived by the youth as being fair. Fairness has several components. First, the severity must be commensurate with the severity of the crime. Second, the punishment must be administered to all lawbreakers indiscriminately, regardless of their socioeconomic or racial status—the mayor's son as well as the janitor's. And finally, it must be for a clearly stated, prescribed length of time. No longer should a sentence be for an indeterminate time until the institutional staff "thinks" the delinquent has been rehabilitated.

7. Punishment as Penance

Over the centuries the Catholic Church has recognized the cleansing value of doing penance. It helps the individual restore faith in himself. First make amends; then you are forgiven. "Go and sin no more." For many delinquents this can be the most valuable component of punishment, affording them the opportunity to rebuild belief in themselves as worthwhile human beings.

R. Foster Winans, who served nine months in a federal prison in 1988 for his participation in insider stock trading, wrote in a letter to the *New York Times* on March 14, 1990, that his incarceration, by itself, had little redemptive value. It merely reinforced the notion that "the system stinks." But his four hundred hours of community service caused more soul-searching. He was required to be a "buddy" to a man dying of AIDS.

"He could not walk or feed himself or read," Winans wrote. "I washed his dishes and emptied his urinal. I was doing real penance for my crimes, returning something of measurable value to my community . . . It provided society with something beyond the smug satisfaction that I had been hurt in return for the hurt I had caused."

Whenever possible a juvenile's punishment should aim toward letting the youth do penance for his or her crime. If the punishment causes the youth to make some contribution to the community, particularly to an unfortunate individual, the effect can be far more cleansing than months of "therapy" in an institution.

Since the successful completion of the sentence legally repays the debt, no further strings, such as a period of probation, should be attached. When punishment is completed the former delinquent should be able to say, as did a young offender in Louisiana: "Yes, I committed a crime, one that I am terribly ashamed of. But, I also paid my debt to society without whimpering and begging . . . Because of this, I can look every other human being in the eye."[7]

No one should fault the child savers who brought about the juvenile court for wanting to show compassion to unsocialized children. But they erred in how to accomplish it. Trying to make the court a social service agency instead of an enforcer of laws was not the way. Frequently the most compassionate act a court can perform is to punish the misguided youth. Thus he or she may learn early in life that for civilization to function, the participants must abide by certain rules. Compassion of this nature may save the youth from years of agony in the future.

Chapter 20

THE YOUTHFUL OFFENDER COURT

BASIC CONCEPTS

Throughout history four reasons have been put forth for "doing something to" criminals: rehabilitation, retribution, incapacitation, and deterrence. Wisely or not, each has historically played a role in our handling of unruly juveniles. But the objective of the proposed Youthful Offender Court is primarily the last—deterrence. The court is designed to protect society from future crimes and acts of violence perpetrated by those juveniles for whom all preventative measures have been inadequate.

This special criminal court would have jurisdiction over all persons not less than ten years or more than seventeen years of age who have committed a criminal offense. (The upper age limit of seventeen corresponds to that of the present juvenile court in forty-one states.) Children under ten years of age can best be served by the Family Court. Juvenile behavior known as status offenses (such as being truant, beyond parental control, and running away) would be excluded. Minor traffic offenses committed by a youth of legal age to drive would fall within the jurisdiction of the traffic court and be subject to the same sanctions as adults. Major traffic offenses, as well as those committed by underage drivers, would be tried in the Youthful Offender Court.

Although punishment is the tool by which the goals of deterrence are to be achieved, society will be the winner if that punishment is administered in the most humane and least destructive manner possible. Those who clamor for tougher treatment of juvenile lawbreakers forget that short of life in prison or a death sentence, these youths will eventually be returned to the community. Self-interest dictates that they not be returned bitterly determined to get even with society in the most vengeful manner possible.

We have seen that for the court to repeatedly do nothing has been ineffective. And we have also seen that long, inhumane punishment only increases recidivism. An effective system is to be found somewhere between these two poles. To achieve this balance, the Youthful Offender Court should be designed within the parameters of guidelines suggested in previous chapters.

1. In all phases of the juvenile justice system, fairness and justice must prevail—a requirement that includes a mandate that:
   a. Race, economic status, or social history must not be factors in the court's decision-making process.
   b. Punishment must be proportionate to the seriousness of the offense.
   c. The terms of the sentence should be fixed by the court, not to be altered later at the whim or bias of program and institutional administrators.
   d. Basic constitutional and human rights must not be denied.
   e. Juveniles must not be punished for their thoughts or beliefs, or even for their actions, no matter how reprehensible they may be, as long as they do not infringe on the rights or welfare of others.
2. Speedy trials and speedy administration of punishment are necessary since long delays destroy the effectiveness and emotional impact upon the youth.
3. All juvenile defendants should be provided with counsel, either personally retained or court-provided, and this should be a nonwaivable right.
4. It must be kept in mind that it is the certainty of punishment, not the severity, that is effective in deterring juveniles from criminal activity.

5. All dispositions in juvenile cases should seek the least restrictive alternative that will still serve as a learning experience and will provide reasonable protection of society.
6. Sentences must be based on three factors and these alone: seriousness of the crime, age of the delinquent, and the number of prior offenses.
7. Other than in rare instances necessary for the protection of society, juveniles should not be held in secure detention while awaiting court action.
8. While mild punishment, consistently and fairly administered, will often be an effective deterrent, the punishment should become progressively more severe for those youths who persist in breaking the law.
9. Whenever possible, sentences should be designed so that when they are completed the delinquent will have a feeling of having paid his debt to society by making a constructive contribution to the community.
10. Long-term institutionalization should be reserved for the small percentage of violent and/or habitual delinquents who pose an immediate and serious threat to society.
11. Since the majority of juveniles appear in court only once, except for those who have committed serious violent crimes first offenders should be warned, counseled, and then released without further official involvement in the justice system.
12. In order to ensure that the civil rights of juveniles are protected and that they are not prey to the biases or capriciousness of the judge, all delinquency hearings should be open to the public and the press.

GETTING INTO THE SYSTEM—THE POLICE

Virtually all juveniles would receive their invitation to visit the Youthful Offender Court via the police—being picked up on suspicion of having committed a crime or on a complaint lodged by another person. The policeman represents the first tier in the selection process whereby some youths become involved and others escape. Traditionally he is given or assumes wide discretion in deciding what to do with the juveniles he apprehends. Police are caught in a dilemma. They face an aroused citizenry demanding a crackdown on what appears to be a rising tide of youthful violence and crime. At the same time they hear youth advocates claiming that "getting tough" only exacerbates the problem.

Being taken into custody can be one of the most crucial events in the making—*or unmaking*—of a delinquent. This is the event that initiates the process whereby in the public's eye a youth is branded as a "delinquent"—a label that often becomes a self-fulfilling prophecy.

Consistent with the guideline calling for the least restrictive alternative commensurate with the protection of society, an officer should at times merely warn and release young lawbreakers. This would include instances of trivial infractions: mildly disturbing the peace, peer fights that do not result in serious injury, petty shoplifting when the store management does not wish to prosecute, public intoxication, casual use of marijuana, nondamaging trespass, loitering, insignificant vandalism. Such behavior is indeed undesirable and certainly not to be condoned. Even so, in the vast majority of instances, legal action will create more problems than it solves.

An effective officer will talk it over with minor offenders, explaining the necessity of enforcing the laws of the community. He may demonstrate a genuine concern for the youth's problem (which may vary from simple boredom to the need of a job) and offer suggestions as to where help might be found. If the youth is convinced of the officer's sincerity he may come away from the encounter with a new respect for the law and those who enforce it. Under certain circumstances the officer might take unofficial action, such as carrying an intoxicated juvenile home to his parents or taking a runaway to a shelter house.

There is a grave danger here, however. While the man on the beat may at times be the best judge of whether or not a youth should be officially charged, the door is left wide open for blatant discrimination. Because of this danger, those in authority as well as citizen watchdog groups should be alert to all forms of bias in arrest records. A loud alarm should be sounded if such a situation is suspected.

INTAKE AND THE FIRST OFFENDER CONFERENCE

A youth whom the officer has decided to take into custody should be taken directly to the intake department of the Youthful Offender Court, bypassing the police department's youth bureau. This will necessitate the intake department's being open twenty-four hours a day, seven days a week. In small jurisdictions a person in authority should be on immediate call at all times, just as a doctor is always on call at the emergency room of even a small hospital. If intake units are open only from 9:00 A.M. to 5:00 P.M., Monday through Friday, a youth arrested on Friday evening, no matter how minor the cause or even how unjustified, could be held in secure detention for nearly three days. This is child abuse.

Under extenuating circumstances the intake department of the court could waive jurisdiction and transfer certain offenders to the Family Court. Such action would be appropriate, for example, for those who were mentally retarded, those whose theft was prompted by genuine hunger or need for shelter, and those who were defending themselves against abuse by an adult.

Secure Detention

The practice of locking up a youth while awaiting court action is possibly the most abused, misused, and overused segment of the juvenile justice system. At times the incarceration may be only overnight or for a few days while court workers get around to deciding upon the juvenile's suitability for release. At other times it may stretch on for months while the youth awaits his or her day in court (actually, most often their fifteen minutes in court).

The uncertainty of what is going to happen and how long the stay will be . . . the fear of physical and sexual abuse by tougher and older inmates (or staff) . . . the feeling of having been stripped of all dignity and self-respect by indifferent staff members who won't even bother to listen—all these can convey to sophisticated adults only a hint of the terror that fills the heart of a child on the first night behind iron bars or barbed-wire fences. Rejected at home, rejected at school, the youth bitterly feels the ultimate rejection by society. A wavering self-esteem is now totally demolished.

The devastation is magnified when the incarceration is in an adult jail (as is the case with some 1,600 juveniles nationwide on any given day, 100,000 a year). If juveniles are not separated from adults, they become prey to physical assault and homosexual rape and are also given the opportunity to get a criminal education from real pros. If they are separated, juveniles are frequently placed in isolated cells where continuous surveillance is impossible. This setting invites pathological depression and, all too frequently, suicide.

Those who lock up kids in pretrial detention justify it on two grounds. One is that it is necessary for "the protection of the child and protection of society." Yet after the court hearing nine out of ten of those who have been locked up will be released back into the community without being committed to a secure institution. It is only fair to ask: What suddenly happened to all that pressing need for community protection?

The other official explanation is that it is necessary so that the delinquent will show up in court. But studies have shown repeatedly that only an infinitesimally small number will run away before their impending court hearing when warned that they will be subject to further arrest and punishment if they fail to appear. The few who don't show up can usually be rounded up easily by the police. While the Children's Bureau was a part of HEW a survey was made of all juvenile courts in jurisdictions of over 100,000 population. Half of the courts reported that less than 1 percent of those juveniles *not* being held in detention failed to show up at the appointed time.

Few research projects have so clearly demonstrated the destructiveness of detention as that done by Robert Coates at the Harvard Law School Center for Criminal Justice.[1] He was searching for factors that could predict whether or not a juvenile who had been arrested would later turn out to be a serious criminal. His research came up with an alarming surprise. The most significant single predictor was neither the seriousness of the offense nor the number of offenses committed. It was whether or not the youth had *on his first arrest* been held in a locked detention center or jail.

Some quickly interpreted this finding merely to reflect that those locked up naturally had been the more serious and dangerous delinquents. But a careful review of the data revealed virtually no relationship between the seriousness of the offense and being locked up. Rarely was this first lockup due to a violent crime. More often it was a reflection of the offender's socioeconomic status—and whether or not there were beds available in the center. Being locked up greatly increased the odds that this first offender's future behavior would become more serious and more violent.

It has often been claimed that delinquency is a contagious disease. If this is so, then juvenile jail is a good place to catch it.

Measures to reduce the abuses of detention were included in the Juvenile Justice and Delinquency Prevention Act of 1974. However, a study by the General Accounting Office, sent to President Reagan in 1983, indicated that while practices had improved, massive problems still existed: Four out of ten of those juveniles being held in detention centers and jails were not charged with a serious offense.

Despite standards calling for expeditious handling of juvenile cases and only very brief stays in detention, more than one out of five youths were held for over thirty days without having been found guilty by the court. Frequent instances of abusive conditions of confinement, including isolation cells in adult jails, continued to be found.

Given the previously mentioned Reagan responses to studies of juvenile problems, it is almost redundant to add that instead of trying to alleviate these problems, the administration stepped up its effort to zero out of the budget the Office of Juvenile Justice and Delinquency Prevention.

By following provisions of the JJDP Act a number of jurisdictions have proved that widespread use of detention is unnecessary. Take, for example, the Gateway Juvenile Diversion project in a seven-county rural area of Kentucky. In 1980, prior to the program, 276 of 479 arrested juveniles were jailed. Then the counties began using national guidelines for detention, and by 1984 a 94 percent reduction had been achieved—only 17 of the 461 juveniles arrested that year were held in detention. And there was no problem about the juveniles showing up for their court hearings.

But that is not the really exciting, the truly significant news. *By not subjecting these youths to the destructive effects of being locked up, recidivism was cut in half.* That's a pretty fair social payoff for a program that also saved the counties the heavy expense of locking up kids.

Under the proposals being made here, a youth would be held in detention pending court hearings *only* if the juvenile was

1. accused of a serious crime of violence or a property crime for which an adult could be sentenced to as much as ten years in prison, or
2. currently under court order for having committed another crime, or at liberty while awaiting court action on another charge, or
3. known to be a fugitive from the juvenile justice system and legally wanted by authorities either at home or in some other jurisdiction, or
4. known to have previously failed to appear for a court hearing, or
5. known to have previously been convicted of three or more offenses, regardless of their severity, or
6. believed to be a threat to his or her own physical safety (e.g.,

dangerously intoxicated with drugs or alcohol, or making sui-
cidal threats), or

7. so deranged or emotionally upset, even temporarily, that he or
she was a physical threat to some person or persons in the
community (this so-called preventive detention should be used
cautiously, for no method of accurately assessing potential dan-
gerousness has been devised), or if

8. it was impossible to verify the juvenile's identity or name and
address so as to notify the parents or guardian.

At times the youth might request, in writing, to be held because of
outside threat of possible injury. Otherwise he would be released to
the custody of his parents, or on his own recognizance to appear in
court.

The Intake Hearing

Along with the citation for the juvenile to appear at the intake hearing
would be a citation calling for one or both parents also to attend. By
way of the hearing, a number of important functions would be per-
formed:

First, it would screen out for dismissal all frivolous and nonserious
charges, including complaints about annoying behavior that is not
illegal.

Second, it would screen charges for legal sufficiency—that is, determine that reasonable grounds exist to support the charge. It
is important that a youth be protected from the damaging effects of
court appearances resulting from unjustified or vindictive charges
made by a disgruntled neighbor or a prejudiced police officer.
In screening for legal sufficiency the staff should guard against efforts of the police or court officials to punish status offenders by
improperly labeling their actions as criminal. (An example of such
an effort: changing a charge of "beyond parental control" to "theft"
on the basis of the juvenile's having lifted fifty cents from the cookie
jar.)

Third, most of those arrested *for the first time* would be referred to
a "first offender conference" in lieu of further official processing
through the court. This policy is dictated by the fact that most juveniles who are arrested for the first time are never arrested again. It
would be an expensive mistake to subject them to the potentially

harmful effects of deeper involvement in the justice system. To qualify for the first offender conference four requirements must be met:

1. The youth has never before been convicted of an offense.
2. The offense was not a violent crime which if committed by an adult would be subject to a possible sentence of as much as ten years.
3. The youth admits his guilt after being told that although he will not be punished at this time, he will be given a record of a "conviction" which automatically increases the degree of punishment at the next conviction. For those who feel they have been unjustly accused, it would be to their advantage to clear their record by having the court find them not guilty.
4. The youth agrees to return (with the threat of arrest for failure) at a later date and participate in the first offender conference which may take as much as half a day.

The First Offender Conference

The goal of the conference would be to increase greatly the percentage of first offenders who are never arrested the second time. To do this will require far more than a perfunctory recitation of moralistic phrases. An attempt should be made to impress on a youth the gravity of breaking the law, the reasons why laws must be enforced, and—perhaps most important of all—the fact that next time he is arrested and found guilty, he will not get by so easily: he will surely be punished.

Even higher on the agenda would be the effort to engage these first offenders in an honest dialogue about their problems. An effort would be made to determine if their delinquency was triggered by unmet needs. Help would be arranged when appropriate.

And finally, if there are indications that the underlying problem results from the failure of some adult or agency, a request for investigation would be forwarded to the Family Court. Because of the strong correlation between delinquency and abuse by an adult, the conference leader should be trained to ask a series of medical and nonmedical questions to uncover indications of maltreatment. If necessary the Family Court would be asked to provide protective services.

At the conclusion of the conference the first-time offender would be released *unconditionally*—no meaningless probation or other strings attached.

THE YOUTHFUL OFFENDER COURT HEARING

After the intake staff screened out those charged with minor or trivial offenses, those for whom there was insufficient evidence to justify a court hearing, and those who qualified for a first offender conference, all others would be scheduled for a court hearing. Here there would be a number of radical changes from the present court:

Social Histories

No longer would these have any legitimacy in the proceedings, either during the hearing to determine guilt or in the selection of the punishment to be levied. Used in the past supposedly for determining a child's need for therapy, social histories have been responsible for many of the injustices in the system. As noted in Chapter 2, their use has led to the punishment of juveniles because of the color of their skin, the moral character of their parents, the depth of poverty in which they live, and countless other factors over which the youths have no control. Juveniles should be punished for what they have done, not for the sins of others.

(In the Family Court, however, social histories will be highly useful in determining what help is needed by the youth.)

Speedy Trial

Instead of the court being operated at a snail's pace for the convenience of the court workers, as is now so common, it should be operated in the best interests of the juvenile. Because of the emotional and psychological needs of juveniles, the trial should be scheduled at the earliest possible date—preferably within a week of intake but no longer than two weeks in the future.

The Sixth Amendment guarantees to the accused the right to a speedy and public trial. Although this right is possibly more critical for juveniles than for adults, the Supreme Court has not considered it to apply to juveniles. Consequently, a speedy trial should be structured by the state into any reform of the juvenile court. The stepped-up timetable is possible because of the elimination of the time-consuming need to develop the extensive social and family history.

Public Trial

Traditionally in many states the public and the press have been excluded from most juvenile hearings, supposedly in order to protect the identity and reputation of the juvenile. It is this policy of secrecy, however, that has masked the injustices that often permeate the court—a policy that has left it unaccountable to the public for its actions. Opening the court to the scrutiny of the public and press would afford a measure of protection from incompetent, arbitrary, and capricious judges, from overzealous prosecutors, from inadequate representation by court-appointed attorneys, and from convictions based on social histories and rumors rather than solid evidence.

Furthermore, a major goal of the court is to deter other juveniles from criminal behavior by demonstrating that lawbreakers will be punished. Hence it is essential that the public, including other juveniles, know that punishment is actually being delivered.

It should be noted that this proposal for open hearings runs counter to the position taken by many responsible groups seeking to improve the juvenile justice system, including the National Council on Crime and Delinquency. And it may be in conflict with some aspects of the labeling theory which says that a youth is locked into a delinquent role because of the public's knowledge of his criminal behavior.

Critics who view open hearings as a backward step should realize that most child advocates, including myself, who decry the debilitating effect of the delinquency label are concerned in the main with this stigma being applied to status offenders. It is tragic that a child who may have done nothing worse than being truant from school or running away from abuse in the home would be branded with the same label as a tough young hoodlum. Since under these proposals status offenders are to be eliminated from the jurisdiction of the Youthful Offender Court, the danger of labeling these youths as delinquent would no longer exist.

The potential harm from labeling would be further reduced by barring the press and the public from intake proceedings and the first offender conference. Thus, only those who continue to break the law would come under public scrutiny. When explained to first offenders, this threat of future publicity would in itself become a deterrent to crime.

Extenuating Circumstances

A plea of "not guilty by reason of undue adult influence to do wrong" would be applicable in a number of instances. A child who commits a crime could make this plea if the act was done on orders from a parent or other controlling adult. Charges of violence against another person, including a parent, could be dismissed if it was provoked by excessive abuse from that person. A judge could consider this plea by a defendant whose normal resistance to breaking the law had been weakened by an adult plying the youth with drugs or alcohol or promises of exciting rewards. A juvenile who ran away from a delinquency institution might be found not guilty because of the undue severity of the treatment administered by a staff member.

As these examples illustrate, undue adult influence could take widely different forms. This would not, however, automatically relieve the juvenile of responsibility. Many would be mature enough to be expected to resist the influence. Deciding how "undue" the influence had been would be a judicial determination. In the event a youth was found not guilty on this basis, the case would then be turned over to the Family Court or even the adult criminal court for prosecution of the offending adult.

With this as the basic structure of the Youthful Offender Court, we now turn to a consideration of the type and severity of punishment the judge could order.

Chapter 21

PUNISHING THE JUVENILE OFFENDER

PUNISHMENT ALTERNATIVES

The fact that the focus of the Youthful Offender Court is to be on punishment does not mean that an erring youth need be brutalized. The certainty of even mild punishment will usually be effective. A wide range of sanctions is needed to make it possible to start with mild punishment and progressively step up the severity for those who continue to break the law. In order of least stringent to most stringent these are:

Category A: First Offender Conference and Release

This alternative has been discussed as a disposition for the intake department and would apply to all first offenders except those charged with serious and/or violent crimes.

Category B: Nonresidential Community Alternatives

1. Restitution

This relatively new dispositional alternative now gaining favor is one of the few bright spots in the juvenile justice system. Restitution made to the victim by a guilty youth is possibly the most desirable and effective of all forms of punishment whenever age and circumstances make it feasible. Research studies show that youths ordered to pay financial restitution or to perform community service generally have had lower recidivism rates than those given traditional sanctions. The sentence appeals to the public in that it compensates the victim, and it helps to teach personal accountability to the youth. It is particularly appropriate in the case of property crimes, vandalism, damage to property during the commission of a crime, and theft or burglary.

Restitution might be made in the form of money, services, or the repair of damages. Any money paid as restitution must have been earned through efforts of the juveniles themselves, not by the parents. This is necessary not only to prevent discrimination against juveniles from poorer families but also to make juveniles personally responsible for their actions. Thus, a youth may make cash payments only from the proceeds of a current, nonfamily job, not from a family allowance. If he or she does not have a job or is unable to find a job, the court staff should help to find one—or create one for the youth.

In other instances, as symbolic restitution, the offender may perform a specified number of hours of service for the victim.

Restitution was one of the most publicized and effective of the many programs funded by LEAA (Law Enforcement Assistance Administration) back in the mid-seventies and, fortunately, was one of the few enthusiastically continued by the Reagan administration. (It has been promoted as RESTTA, the Restitution, Education, Specialized Training and Technical Assistance program.) A typical example is Prince Georges County, Maryland, where in three years over $750,000 was collected for victims of juvenile offenders at a cost of about five cents on the dollar.

A pioneer program, "Earn-It," started by the Quincy (Massachusetts) District Court in 1975 has caused victims to be paid nearly $2 million in restitution, and over 300,000 hours of community service have been performed by delinquents without pay. This program got off to a fast start due to the cooperation of the local chamber of commerce, which recruited over seventy-five businesses, ranging from large department stores to service stations; each agreed to make 100 hours of part-time work available. It remains a prime example of the effect of strong community support in creating meaningful juvenile programs.

At times it might be necessary for the court to create jobs for a restitution program to be effective. In 1981 the court in Pinehurst,

North Carolina, sent seventeen youthful offenders to state delinquency institutions. All but one were committed for failing to pay the
restitution ordered by the court. They had been unable to find jobs.
The next year the court set up its own work program. Offenders spent
Saturdays and school holidays cutting wood in the fall and winter,
raising vegetables in the spring and summer. Youths were paid the
minimum wage with all but fifty cents an hour being set aside for the
victim. The balance was given to the juveniles only *after* they paid
the entire debt, which averaged around two hundred dollars. In contrast to the previous year, all but one of the offenders met their
obligations. Sale of the firewood and vegetables came close to covering the costs of the program.[1]

2. Community Work Fines

Increasingly, adult courts in America are sentencing offenders to
specified hours of community service in lieu of monetary fines or time
in jail, a sanction long popular in Europe. Such a practice could be
particularly valuable as a sanction for youthful offenders when there
is no victim needing restitution. It is punishment yet avoids the
trauma and stigma of incarceration. Furthermore, it permits the delinquent, by constructively contributing to society, to make moral
restitution for his antisocial act.

The hours would be served during the afternoon, evening, or weekends and would be tailored to the juvenile's school and/or work schedule. A community service supervising staff would oversee the work to
be done in public and charitable institutions—hospitals, parks, municipal buildings, schools, and so on. Depending on the skills and
abilities of the youth, the work could be as menial as washing police
cars and picking up trash in the park or as responsible as tutoring
younger children and serving as an aide in a hospital or day-care
center.

3. Day Detention

Under terms of this sanction, the convicted delinquent would serve
the hours of his or her sentence in a nonsecure, daytime detention
center. The court would order the youth to be present at the center
for all or part of certain days, most likely after school and on Saturdays. Entertainment and recreational activities would not be
permitted—no TV, radio, smoking rooms, cards, or other games!
Experience in similar programs has shown that out of boredom many
youths will participate voluntarily in self-improvement activities when

available. These could include the opportunity for catching up on schoolwork, supervised group discussions, vocational or personal counseling, and from time to time programs presented by professionals on such subjects as drug abuse, sex education, job skills, and physical development.

Penalty for Noncompliance

These three nonresidential community sanctions require voluntary compliance. Facts of life suggest that most youths would refuse to comply if they could get away with it. Sanctions such as these are effective only when backed up by some coercive threat. A youth would be warned that those refusing to do the required work or failing to show up would be picked up by the police and returned to court. The judge would find the youth in contempt of court and impose a more severe disposition, one calculated to bring about compliance. One option would be to order a weekend stay in secure detention, after which the remainder of the original sentence would be served. Continued refusal to participate would bring increasingly longer hours of secure detention.

Category C: Nonsecure Group Homes

While group homes have not been particularly successful as a rehabilitative measure, they are generally less destructive than institutions. And less expensive! Care in a group home frequently costs only half as much as institutional care. As punishment, group homes can be an intermediary step between noncustodial punishment and secure incarceration.

A group home should house six to eight adjudicated delinquents supervised by a live-in married couple, at least one of whom devotes full time to the home. It should be run as much like a family unit as possible, with rewards and punishments given out freely.

A major difficulty with most group home operations has been the philosophical confusion between punishment and therapy. Under current practices, as we have seen, the usual sentence is for an indeterminate period of time—until the delinquent is "cured." Thus, the youth is encouraged to play a con game to gain release. Much destructive potential could be avoided by eliminating overt attempts at rehabilitation and by making it clear to the delinquents that they are there for punishment. The stay would be limited to the time specified by the court. If a youth ran away or refused to be reasonably cooperative, the court (not the staff) could extend the sentence or commit him or her to a secure facility.

In the meantime, the youth would continue going to school or a job, and would have to abide by clearly posted rules. Houseparents would be permitted to reward good behavior by a slight reduction in the time to be served—perhaps one day off for each week in which the youth had no serious infractions of the rules. This reward system, a slight tip of the hat to behavior modification therapy, would help houseparents to maintain control.

Category D: Community-based Secure Detention

A locked facility (other than the jail) should be available in the community for short periods of incarceration—from one to fourteen days. It would be used primarily in combination with the less punitive dispositions listed above. Its value would be in its shock effect and as a very vivid warning to delinquents of what they can expect in big doses if they continue to break the law. In the short-term facility the youth would be treated humanely but with Spartan rigidity.

Category E: State-operated Custodial Facilities

1. Small Group Camps

Repeated convictions of a youth become prima facie evidence that mild sanctions are insufficient to deter him or her from continued criminal behavior. At this stage the court is able to identify potential habitual criminals, those for whom normal maturational reform is not likely to occur. To protect society, progressively more severe sanctions including time in a secure facility become a necessity. In most instances a juvenile camp holding some forty youths may be the preferred choice. Such a camp would be used for sentences of up to six months. Although it is classified as secure, security would be minimal—no walls or barbed-wire fences. "Secure" would mean that a juvenile who went AWOL would be arrested and given a longer, more severe sentence, possibly in a closed secure facility.

Many operational principles established in other dispositional alternatives would apply: no mandatory participation in therapeutic programs, but availability of educational and counseling programs including information on relevant subjects such as drug abuse, sex education, finding a job, and health maintenance; required partici-

pation in housekeeping chores; a day off for each week of good behavior.

Whenever possible, outside work would be available: forestry and
conservation activities, work in state parks, maintenance of public
grounds in nearby communities. A youth would receive a small hourly
wage, most of which would be held in an account until time of release. This work would be optional. But again, experience indicates
that out of boredom and the desire for spending money most youths
will opt for work assignments.

2. Closed Secure Institutions

A facility providing maximum control and from which escape would
be difficult is needed as the most secure punishment alternative. It
would serve two functions: protecting society by isolating for extended periods those youths who have repeatedly committed serious
and violent crimes, and providing a place to send youths who run
away from the small group camps. It is the threat of being sent to a
juvenile "prison" that would make it possible to handle many nonco-
operative delinquents in a less secure setting.

It is hoped that in the comprehensive dual system of prevention
and punishment being proposed here—a system of intervention that
begins even before a youth is born—few delinquents will progress to
the stage requiring a juvenile prison. For those who do, the prognosis
is indeed poor. But there is always hope—hope that the experience of
being securely isolated from normal society, combined with the
knowledge that further criminal activity will bring increasingly longer
sentences, may persuade the delinquent that crime really is not worth
the risk.

Every effort must be made to prevent the prison experience from
increasing the youth's alienation. Otherwise society is the ultimate
loser. For this reason the capacity of secure facilities should be in the
neighborhood of a hundred, certainly no more than two hundred.
Larger institutions, particularly those monstrosities housing a thousand juveniles, tend to be dehumanizing. A culture of brutality de-
velops among both staff and inmates. Members of former gangs have
been known to form the nuclei for powerful in-house gangs that rule
large institutions with the same violence they spread on the outside.

Operational guidelines should be patterned after the successful
federal Job Corps camps. Small group living units within the institution would vary considerably as to the quality of furnishings and the
privileges allowed. A newcomer would be assigned to the lowest

ranking unit and by good behavior could progressively earn the privilege of more desirable quarters. Noncooperation would bring about a lowering of rank.

SENTENCING BY THE COURT

As noted in Chapter 20, three factors, *and these alone,* are to be taken into consideration in deciding upon a juvenile's sentence. These are:

1. severity of the crime
2. age of the juvenile
3. record of past convictions

To incorporate these three factors into a fixed sentence, a matrix must be developed. (Only one state, Washington, has attempted a matrix with these factors. It was adopted, however, in response to a public outcry to crack down on juvenile terrorism rather than as an effort to reform the court. Consequently, it tends to be unduly harsh and loses much of the potential in the use of mild but certain punishment. But it is a comprehensive attempt to answer the charge of a do-nothing court and at the same time establish fairness in the juvenile justice system.)

The matrix proposed here first establishes a fixed sentence based on two factors, severity of the crime and the number of prior convictions. Once this is determined, the age of the delinquent then determines the percentage of the fixed sentence to be applied. Before diagraming this matrix, the punishment alternatives that have been discussed should be summarized:

- Category A—First offender conference and unconditional release
- Category B—Nonresidential community correctional alternatives: (1) restitution, (2) work-hour fines, (3) daytime detention
- Category C—Nonsecure group home in the community
- Category D—Community-based, short-term secure detention
- Category E—State-operated facilities: (1) minimum-security small group camps, (2) closed secure institutions

All offenses are assigned to one of six classes of punishment. These are directly proportional to the severity of the punishment mandated by the state legislature for specific crimes when committed by an adult. Thus, sentencing of a juvenile would reflect how serious the state considered a particular offense to be. Classification of crimes is as follows:

- Class I—crimes for which the maximum adult sentence is a fine or less than six months in jail
- Class II—for which the maximum adult sentence is six to twelve months in jail or prison
- Class III—maximum adult sentence of over a year and up to five years in prison
- Class IV—maximum adult sentence of over five years and up to nineteen years in prison
- Class V—maximum adult sentence of twenty years to less than life in prison
- Class VI—maximum adult sentence of life in prison (or death, if applicable)

In instances of multiple charges the classification of the most serious charge would be used. Based on these classifications and the number of prior criminal convictions, a punishment would be mandated for the offense.

The age of the delinquent at the time of the offense would then determine what percentage of this punishment he or she was to serve:

Ages 16 and 17—100%
Ages 14 and 15— 70%
Ages 12 and 13— 40%
Ages 10 and 11— 20%

It will be noted in the following matrix that for most crimes the judge is given a discretion of roughly a 100 percent spread (for example, a range of between ten and twenty hours of community work). A spread of this size will permit the judge some leeway for extenuating circumstances and for the varying severity of crimes listed in the same category.

Citizens Advisory Committee

Each facility should have an official citizens watchdog committee. This group, appointed by the governor (or a judge in case of community programs), would have an advocacy role in protecting the

MATRIX OF PENALTIES FOR JUVENILES AGES 16 AND 17*
(70% for ages 14–15—40% for ages 12–13—20% for ages 10–11)

	CLASS I OFFENSES	CLASS II OFFENSES	CLASS III OFFENSES	CLASS IV OFFENSES
FIRST CONVICTION	Category A	Category A	Category A or B—30/60 hours	Category D—2/5 days plus B—40/80 hours
SECOND CONVICTION	B—10/20 hours or Restitution	B—20/40 hours or Restitution	D—2/5 days plus B—40/80 hours	C—4/8 weeks
THIRD CONVICTION	B—20/40 hours or Restitution	D—2/4 days plus B—40/80 hours or Restitution	C—4/8 weeks	C—8/16 weeks or E—2/4 months
FOURTH CONVICTION	D—2/4 days** plus B—40/80 hours or Restitution	D—4/8 days plus B—80/160 hours or C—3/6 weeks	C—8/16 weeks or E—2/4 months	E—6/12 months
FIFTH CONVICTION	D—4/8 days** plus B—80/160 hours or C—3/6 weeks	C—6/12 weeks or E—2/4 months	E—4/8 months	E—12/24 months
SIXTH CONVICTION	Classes I through IV—penalty will double for each succeeding conviction			

CLASS V OFFENSES—First conviction: Category D—10/20 days plus C—4/8 months.
Second conviction for Class V or VI offense: Categories C or E—6/12 months.
Each succeeding conviction, penalty doubles previous penalty.

CLASS VI OFFENSES—First conviction: Category E—6 months to 3 years.
Second conviction for Class V or VI offense: Category E—4 years to maximum age of 21.
Or, at arrest for Class V or VI offense after previous Class V or VI conviction a youth 16 or 17 may be transferred to adult court after waiver hearing.

Notes: * If the offense for which the youth is being sentenced is in Classes I through IV, the sentence will be based on the total number of convictions, regardless of the class of previous offenses. The judge should take severity of previous offenses into consideration in setting sentence within the range allowed.
 ** This portion of the sentence may be waived if the penalty for an adult is punishable only by fine and no jail sentence.

rights of the youths. It should have legislative authority to inspect the facility, activities, files, disciplinary actions, and budget ledgers as well as to conduct confidential interviews with the juveniles. Reports and recommendations would be made to the proper authorities, and when appropriate, press releases would be prepared.

Grievance Procedures

As a safeguard against staff abuse and dehumanization, any youth in a court-ordered program should have the right to protest the treatment he or she was receiving by petitioning the court for a hearing. The citizens advisory committee would be the official conduit for transmitting these petitions. The complaint would be investigated by a representative and then considered by the whole committee. If the complaint appeared to have merit the petition would be referred to the court for a hearing.

Health Services

A complete physical examination, including eyes and teeth, should be given to every youth committed to a custodial facility. Whenever possible, health problems should be addressed while the youth is in custody. Since physical defects and poor health are known to be contributing causes of delinquency, such a policy should be considered as long-range protection of society.

POST-RELEASE CARE OF INSTITUTIONALIZED DELINQUENTS

Having served his time, whether in a custodial or noncustodial setting, a youth should be released *unconditionally*. He should have a clear feeling that having paid his debt to society, he is no longer a second-rate citizen. Now he is ready to become a part of the law-abiding community. This does not mean, however, that an indifferent justice system would merely toss him back into the jungle from which he came.

It has been noted that among the reasons for the failure of therapeutic programs is the fact that after "treatment" delinquents are returned to the same inadequate family situation, the same meaningless schools, the same delinquent friends, and in general the same conditions that nurtured their delinquency in the first place. Any resolve to go straight is soon smothered by old influences. Few habitual offenders will be able to obtain a legitimate role in the community unless drastic changes occur.

To bring about these changes, plans to resolve the causes of the youth's delinquency should be made *while* he or she is serving the sentence. The National Council on Crime and Delinquency has urged that *"fully as much time, attention and money should be spent in the return of the offender to the community as is given to the program within the institution."*

Under the proposed system, a full social casework study would be unnecessary at the time of the trial because the disposition would be made strictly on the findings of guilt or innocence. And in the interest of speeding the trial, there would be little pretrial study into the youth's background. But in preparation for a prerelease conference this should be done by the staff of the court while the juvenile is institutionalized. Academic, vocational, family, personal, and psychological needs would be evaluated.

A number of states, alarmed at the high rate of recidivism, have already begun to place more emphasis on postcustodial care—care that is considerably more meaningful than mere perfunctory probation. Georgia's Division of Youth Services, for example, now utilizes community-based programs to provide remedial education, individual and family counseling, and cultural enrichment activities to former institutionalized delinquents.

Needs uncovered by the court's investigative staff should be discussed during the prerelease conference. Suggestions as to where help is available *on a voluntary basis* should be made. This might be an alternative school program, a community service job for which the youth would be paid, subsidized vocational training, the Job Corps— or even the army. Or the need might be assistance in overcoming any of hundreds of emotional and physical problems that face a delinquent youth. If legal action against some negligent party was indicated by the court study, the findings would be forwarded to the child advocacy division of the Family Court.

In many instances this prerelease conference and the staff study preceding it could be the turning point in a delinquent's career. After all, it is society's last chance.

THE VIRGIN ADULT CRIMINAL

One further change from the present juvenile justice system should be considered. It deals with the fact that in most states juvenile records are sealed when a youth becomes an adult. Thereafter officially no crimes have been committed. Thus, delinquents are offered a fresh start in life, without the records of their juvenile crimes hanging around their necks.

This is a commendable concept. It has great value for the juvenile who has straightened up and gotten his act together. Without this official forgiveness a juvenile indiscretion could haunt him the rest of his life, his record making it impossible to obtain many jobs and even in some instances to join the armed forces. It is a humane approach.

But conversely, it is a big bonus to the many delinquents who choose to continue their criminal activities into adulthood. Since their past criminal records are not available to judges deciding on the sentence for adult offenders of eighteen or nineteen or twenty, habitual, violent offenders are often permitted to remain out on the street, preying on the public. Many of these dangerous criminals who were habitual juvenile offenders escape severe court sanctions until after they have accumulated an extensive criminal history as adults. Coming to the court as criminal "virgins," they go through a number of probated sentences and brief jail stays before they are finally taken out of circulation.

From age seventeen through the early twenties is the period of the most serious and concentrated criminal activity. Despite this fact, the median age of adults entering prison is considerably older—twenty-five. Ironically, this is the age when these young men have already passed through the years of most serious criminal activity, and normally their criminal careers are winding down. While chronic criminals represent only an exceedingly small portion of all offenders, they account for a staggeringly large portion of the total crime picture. Incarcerating these few during their most active period would have a major impact on crime in America.

Most of these habitual criminals can be identified by their juvenile record. In a recent study of 2,200 inmates of jails and prisons in California, Texas, and Michigan, Jan and Marcia Chaiken identified the most serious habitual offenders. They were designated "violent predators." Most had begun committing especially violent crimes before the age of sixteen, and by the time they were legally adults they had accumulated long records of parole violation and commitment to juvenile institutions. Yet, because of sealed records, it had been difficult to make early identification of them as adults. The Chaikens commented:

> . . . varying degrees of confidentiality, depending on the jurisdiction, envelop these records, the idea that juveniles should not be stigmatized for life by youthful misbehavior. For this and other reasons (including bureaucratic sloth), juvenile records are often unavailable to judges and prosecutors. That fact was driven home to much of the public by the widely reported 1976 Timmons case. Ronald Timmons, 19, arrested in New York for beating and robbing an 82-year-old woman, was released on $500 bail by a judge who was unaware that Timmons had appeared in juvenile court 67 times and was suspected of murdering a 92-year-old man.[2]

Thus we face a dilemma: the conflict between the need to permit a juvenile to reform and escape the lifelong consequences of a youthful mistake and the equally important need to protect society from being terrorized by chronic young adult criminals.

There is a reasonable solution. Legislation is needed to prohibit a potential employer or others (including the armed forces, schools, labor unions, and the government) from discriminating against a young adult because of a juvenile record. This would be very similar to laws prohibiting discrimination because of race or sex. Youths would not be legally required to list juvenile records on applications or official papers. In this regard the slate would be wiped clean. They would be given the chance to start over.

But the record would be available to the judge and prosecuting attorney in all adult criminal proceedings against former delinquents who were later arrested and found guilty as adults. Juveniles who do indeed go straight would have nothing to fear from such a law. Their past record would come to light and become an albatross *only* if they reverted to crime. And such a policy would provide greater protection to society from those chronic criminals who ravish America.

Chapter 22

STATE OFFICES OF CHILDREN AND YOUTH

It will be necessary for the federal government to take the lead in initiating many of the changes proposed. But in the end, regardless of where the money comes from, programs must be implemented on the state and local level. And even if the proposed state and federal legislation is enacted, it will be of no avail unless state officials and courts comply with the legislation. A good law that goes unenforced may be worse than no law at all. It engenders a false belief that the problem has been adequately addressed.

Many commendable laws are already on the books—and ignored. Most states, for example, have laws prohibiting holding juveniles in adult jails. Yet on any given day in America between 1,500 and 2,000 youths can be found locked up with adult criminals, where many are subject to various brutalities including homosexual rape. Because of AIDS this can amount to a sentence of death.

Guilt for the failure to enforce laws protecting juveniles zooms right to top levels of the federal government. The well-planned and comprehensive Juvenile Justice and Delinquency Prevention Act was sabotaged during eight years of the Reagan administration because the President didn't believe in spending money on delinquent kids.

He arrogantly believed he knew better about the needs of children than the overwhelming majority of professionals in the field, better than the virtually unanimous and bipartisan consensus of Congress.

President Bush has done little to correct the damage.

Over the past two decades a series of rulings by the Supreme Court has guaranteed to juveniles most of the constitutional rights granted to adults. Only trial by jury, the right to a speedy trial, and the use of bail have been excluded. Yet at times many states act as though the Court opinions were never written. As H. Ted Rubin of the Institute for Court Management has noted: "Juvenile court judges and other agents repeatedly fail to apply the statutory and constitutional protections that have been mandated."[1]

Because of these problems the governmental structure in each state should include an Office of Children and Youth—an advocacy office to monitor all phases of the state's juvenile justice system. It needs teeth to enforce those laws which have been enacted. Such an office would demand accountability from the numerous youth-serving agencies and would seek to protect the rights of all children including low-income and minority youths.

During the presidency of Gerald Ford the Office of Juvenile Justice and Delinquency Prevention established a National Advisory Committee to design and recommend standards for improvements in the juvenile justice system. After more than five years of study by the Committee and its staff, a report was made to President Reagan shortly after he took office. It included this recommendation:

> The state government should establish an executive office of youth advocates with the responsibility for investigating and reporting misfeasance and malfeasance within the juvenile justice system, inquiring into areas of concern, and conducting periodic audits of the juvenile service system to ascertain its effectiveness and compliance with established responsibilities.
>
> The authority of the agency should extend over all juvenile services receiving state and/or federal funding.[2]

But the Reagan administration wasn't interested in investigating malfeasance anywhere in government, much less in the juvenile justice system.

Most states, however, made a timid start in this direction, largely because the 1974 Juvenile Justice Act had required states to have a juvenile justice advisory committee appointed by the governor in order to receive federal funds authorized by the Act. Most of these became primarily an official conduit for money. But over half of the states now have a governmental bureau, council, commission, or agency designed to promote in one way or another the interests of young people. Typically these are appendages to some other state department, Departments of Education, Human Resources, Social Services, or Program Planning.

The official duties assigned to these advocacy groups sound great on paper. They cover the whole gamut of desirable efforts—planning, program development, coordination of services, monitoring of service programs, providing a forum for youth representatives, youth employment services, consultation with local communities on delinquency problems . . . and on and on. All very commendable. Unfortunately, performance has never matched the legislative rhetoric. Most organizations serve only in an advisory capacity; most are vastly underfunded and understaffed (if staffed at all); most have virtually no political clout.

My personal frustration at serving with such a group came some years ago when the governor of Kentucky, under pressure from child advocates, created the Institute for Children. It was officially charged with overseeing all youth-related programs in the commonwealth. The potential seemed so promising that I cashed in some political chips and managed to get myself appointed to the Institute.

I resigned less than two years later, fully disillusioned by the wasted effort. The studies, reports, and recommendations of the Institute went to the secretary of the Department of Human Resources where apparently they were buried deep in Kentucky's Mammoth Cave. Without any legislative mandate for the Institute the secretary apparently viewed it only as an apparatus for taking the heat off him and his department. He could conveniently refer any criticism or charges of malfeasance to the Institute "for study" and on to oblivion.

The proposed Office of Children and Youth should not just happen, as similar offices have in most states, but should be officially created by the legislature and given absolute independent status from other departments. It would be under the supervision of a Youth Advocacy Commission, the members of which would be appointed by the governor with approval of the legislature. Membership should reflect the diversity of the various political, racial, and social groups in the state, with a balance maintained between professionals and knowledgeable lay citizens.

The enacting legislation should carefully detail the duties and responsibilities of the Office. And the Commission should be allowed an adequate staff to carry out this mandate. Among the duties should be:

1. Monitoring

This would convey watchdog status over all aspects of the juvenile justice system as well as all agencies affecting the well-being of minors. Included would be the delivery of social services, youth employment programs, education, the Family Court, and the Youthful Offender Court, along with programs ordered by the court for punishment. The Office would be empowered to conduct on-site investigations, hold hearings, subpoena records and witnesses, and demand compliance with existing state and federal laws.

2. Legal Advocacy

If it failed to bring any agency or department into compliance by official warnings, the Office would be empowered to bring suit against that agency. While the Office would seldom seek a legal remedy for an individual juvenile, it would, when appropriate, bring test-case litigation to ensure the rights of a given group or class of minors.

3. Research

The Office would conduct studies, research, and public hearings on problems of youth and make recommendations to the governor and the legislature. This would include programs or services needed, particularly those for early correction of conditions that eventually lead to delinquent behavior.

4. Public Education

The Office should periodically release reports to all appropriate media as to the status of youth programs in the state. Increased visibility of the workings of youth-serving agencies will result in greater accountability. Publication of research studies, lectures by the Office staff and Commission members, and educational use of other media techniques would be designed to increase public understanding needed to meet the needs of the state's young people.

5. Local Network

Under the aegis of the state office would be a network of local juvenile advocacy groups designed to carry the job of monitoring and public education to the grass-roots level. Members of local committees would be appointed by the top public official such as the mayor or the county administrative executive. In general, the network would function on a local basis similar to that of the state office to which the committees would report. Additionally, it would recruit and encourage citizens to become involved in youth-serving programs in the community.

6. Advisory Council of Youths

The Office would sponsor a council to officially represent youth in governmental affairs. Such a council could follow the structure designed in North Carolina, where youth members of the local council give input to city planning agencies and encourage peer contribution to community projects. Local councils elect representatives to regional councils, which in turn send representatives to the State Youth Advisory Council. In Massachusetts a somewhat similar organization has been set up by the State Education Department. There forty-four youth representatives sit on a council that advises the Department on the needs and concerns of youth throughout the commonwealth.

This proposed Office of Children and Youth within the official structure of state government would be an insurance policy to prevent good intentions from going astray. It could go far in determining the needs of youth in the state . . . go far in sounding an alarm when programs failed to live up to expectations . . . go far in eliminating those conditions which push our kids into delinquency, drugs, and despair.

A Final Thought

Delinquency, illiteracy, and welfare dependency—these make up the crime bomb that is ticking away, threatening to destroy America. As we have seen, there are no quick, easy answers. Delinquency is a multifaceted, multicausal phenomenon. It cannot be solved solely by the courts. It must involve our entire social structure.

A dual-accountability model has been outlined—making a juvenile accountable for his or her actions, and making society accountable for those conditions which propel a youth into delinquency. This calls for meeting the needs of children before they turn to delinquency— meeting the needs of all children, the underprivileged as well as the privileged.

These proposals have appealed to enlightened self-interest—the protection of society from the ravages of crime and the saving of billions being spent on law enforcement and on jails and prisons. But an affluent society which gave a mandate for a kinder, gentler nation can well afford to leave behind the "me only" decade and enter a new decade eager to show compassion for the less fortunate children of our society.

Many among those who stand to profit by strict maintenance of the economic and social status quo, many among those who are still enamored of the "me only" philosophy will patronizingly dismiss these proposals as being naive. They will protest that the proposals are too extensive, too expensive to be realistic.

But no one who has witnessed the unbelievable world political events of the past year should dismiss the possibility of major social changes if and when the public demands them . . . even when the impossible is demanded. The measures suggested here are well within the realm of practicability if a concerned citizenry places high on the list of priorities the important job of saving our kids.

ACKNOWLEDGMENTS

The seed that some twenty years later matured into this book would never have been sown had it not been for the exceptional opportunities given me by two individuals: Charles L. Owen, while director of the Kentucky Commission on Law Enforcement and Crime Prevention, offered me an unfettered staff position to research the problems and causes of delinquency. Later, Newman Walker, while superintendent of the Louisville public schools, gave me an assignment whereby for several years I could test in the schools many of the concepts and theories that had grown out of my research. Both friends have my sincere thanks.

At the other end of the twenty years during which that seed grew and matured is an extremely dedicated editor, Cornelia Bessie, who saw in *Saving Our Kids* a story that needed to be presented to the American public. For her courage and faith in me I am again most grateful.

In between these two events are the many people who have knowingly and unknowingly contributed to the final version. There are the hundreds of teenagers, both delinquent and nondelinquent, who confided in me their dreams and their agonies . . . and their difficulty in trying to find meaningful roles in a very complex and troubled society. And there are the dozens of sociologists, personally unknown to me, whose research forms the backbone of many of the far-reaching proposals I have made.

Then, special acknowledgments are due several persons who read earlier versions and gave me valuable criticism: John Filiatreau, a Louisville free-lance writer; C. Edwin Baker, my son and a law professor at the University of Pennsylvania; and Michael Kirst, a Stanford University professor of education and director of PACE (Policy Analysis of California Education). And to an incredibly accomplished copyeditor, Jean Touroff, my thanks for trying to save me from the embarrassment of too many ungrammatical sentences, misspelled words, and lapses into inconsistencies.

Many individuals deserve personal mention, such as Danny Diaz, an exceptionally effective social worker, who persuaded a group of delinquents that I was an adult whom they could confide in and trust. And there is Ernest Scott, wise in the ways of publishing, whose unflagging enthusiasm kept me at the task of writing. But alas! There are so many to whom I am indebted that I fear the attempt to name them all would result in embarrassing omissions.

Finally, I must give grateful thanks for the love and unwavering support of my wife, Ernestine Magagna Baker, and for the encouragement of my daughter, Nancy Lynn Baker, a clinical psychologist in Los Angeles.

To all these, named and unnamed, thanks.

—Falcon Baker

NOTES

Chapter 1.

1. *Campus Report,* Stanford University, March 13, 1985, p. 7.
2. *LEAA Newsletter,* U.S. Department of Justice, September 1977.
3. *Report to the Nation on Crime and Justice,* 2d ed., Bureau of Justice Statistics, U.S. Department of Justice, March 1988, p. 44.
4. *Profile of State Prison Inmates,* Bureau of Justice Statistics, U.S. Department of Justice, 1988.
5. Paul A. Kahn, *The Juvenile Offender and the Law,* W. H. Anderson, 1971, p. 18.

Chapter 2.

1. Anthony M. Platt, *The Child Savers: The Invention of Delinquency,* University of Chicago Press, 1969.
2. "The Right to Be Left Alone," *American Criminal Law Review,* vol. 11, no. 1, 1972.
3. *Task Force Report: Juvenile Delinquency and Youth Crime,* The President's Commission on Law Enforcement and Administration of Justice, Washington, D.C., 1967, p. 7.
4. *Juvenile Justice Bulletin,* U.S. Department of Justice, January 1989.
5. *New York Times,* March 1, 1982, p. 1.

6. Simon L. Singer and David McDowall, *The Law and Society Review*, 1988, pp. 521–38.

7. Edward Wakin, *Children Without Justice*, National Council of Jewish Women, New York, 1975.

8. Patrick T. Murphy, *Our Kindly Parent—the State*, Viking Press, 1974.

9. Irving Piliavin and Scott Briar, "Police Encounters with Juveniles," *American Journal of Sociology*, September 1964, pp. 206–14.

10. Sanford J. Fox, "The Reform of Justice: The Child's Right to Punishment," *Juvenile Justice*, August 1974, pp. 2–9.

11. David Gilman, "How to Retain Jurisdiction over Status Offenders," *Crime and Delinquency*, January 1976, p. 48.

12. William Haney and Martin Gold, "The Delinquent Nobody Knows," *Psychology Today*, September 1973, p. 52.

Chapter 3.

1. Karl Menninger, *The Crime of Punishment*, Viking Press, 1968.

2. *Bulletin of the Menninger Clinic*, September 1970.

3. *Juvenile Justice Standards Project: Final Report*, Institute of Judicial Administration, February 1973, p. 551.

4. Dennis A. Romig, *Justice for Our Children* (part 2, "System Intervention as Treatment"), Lexington Books, 1978.

5. Jill Leslie Rosenbaum, "Family Dysfunction and Female Delinquency," *Crime and Delinquency*, January 1989, pp. 31–44.

6. James Q. Wilson, " 'What Works?' Revisited," *Public Interest*, Fall 1980, pp. 3–17.

7. Steven Lab and John Whitehead, *Crime and Delinquency*, January 1988, p. 60.

8. Richard J. Lundman, *Prevention and Control of Juvenile Delinquency*, Oxford University Press, 1948, pp. 80–86.

9. Donald R. Cressey and Robert A. McDermott, *Diversion from the Juvenile Justice System*, National Institute of Law Enforcement and Criminal Justice, 1974, pp. 3–4.

10. Quote from the abstract of the report on the Memphis-Metro Youth Diversion Project in *Criminal Justice Abstracts*, June 1983, p. 154.

11. *National Evaluation of Diversion Projects*, Executive Summary, Behavioral Research Institute, 1981.

Chapter 4.

1. Robert C. Maynard, in *Louisville Courier-Journal*, April 5, 1980, p. A10.

2. William C. Berleman, James R. Seaberg, and Thomas W. Steinburn, "The Delinquency Prevention Experiment of the Seattle Atlantic Street Center," *Social Service Review*, September 1972.

Chapter 5.

1. Sheldon and Eleanor Glueck were sociologists who pioneered in the field of juvenile delinquency. In the study referred to they followed through their thirty-first birthdays five hundred nondelinquent boys and five hundred who appeared before the Boston court. The first of many reports was *Unravelling Juvenile Delinquency,* The Commonwealth Fund, 1950.
2. Kenneth Polk and Daniel Halferty, *Schools and Delinquency,* 1967.
3. *Report to the Nation on Crime and Justice,* 2d ed., Bureau of Justice Statistics, U.S. Department of Justice, March 1988, p. 48.
4. Gordon Berlin and Andrew Sum, *Toward a More Perfect Union,* Ford Foundation, 1988, pp. 24–25.
5. Marvin E. Wolfgang, Robert M. Figlio, and Thorsten Sellin, *Delinquency in a Birth Cohort,* University of Chicago Press, 1972; Delbert S. Elliott and Harwin L. Voss, *Delinquency and Dropout,* Lexington Books, 1974; Delbert S. Elliott, "Delinquency, School Attendance and Dropout," *Social Problems,* Winter 1966, pp. 307–14; Bachman, Green, and Wirthanen, *Dropping Out: Youth in Transition,* vol. 3, Institute for Social Research, 1971.
6. Frank Tannenbaum, "Point of View," in *Crime and the Community,* Ginn and Company, 1938, pp. 8–22.
7. Ray C. Rist, "Student Social Class and Teacher Expectations," *Harvard Educational Review,* August 1970, pp. 411–51.
8. "This World," *San Francisco Chronicle,* February 17, 1985, p. 16.
9. *Juvenile Justice Bulletin,* U.S. Department of Justice, October 1989.

Chapter 6.

1. Lee N. Robins, *Deviant Children Grown Up,* Williams and Wilkins, 1966.
2. Quoted by Jane Gross in "San Francisco Journal," *New York Times,* December 12, 1988.
3. *The Young Criminal Years of the Violent Few,* Office of Juvenile Justice and Delinquency Prevention, U.S. Department of Justice, 1985.
4. U.S. Senate Judiciary Committee, *Homeless Youths: The Saga of "Pushouts" and "Throwaways" in America,* 1980.
5. "Runaway Children and the Juvenile Justice Delinquency Act: What is the Impact?" *Juvenile Justice Bulletin,* OJJDP, U.S. Department of Justice, 1986, p. 2.

Chapter 7.

1. *Special Report: International Crime Rates,* Bureau of Justice Statistics, U.S. Department of Justice, May 1988.
2. Police Chief Joseph McNamara, speech at the Commonwealth Club, San Francisco, April 21, 1989.
3. Richard A. Sundeem. "Swedish Juvenile Justice and Welfare," *Journal of Criminal Justice,* 1976, pp. 109–21.

4. Gerry Fitzgerald, *Common Cause Magazine*, January/February 1990.
5. "Sunday Punch," *San Francisco Chronicle*, September 7, 1986, p. 5.
6. Kevin P. Phillips, *The Politics of Rich and Poor*, Random House, 1990.
7. *Wall Street Journal*, July 24, 1986, p. 21.

Chapter 9.

1. *Special Report: Survey of Youth in Custody*, Bureau of Justice Statistics, U.S. Department of Justice, September 1988.
2. From *Journal of the Alan Guttmacher Institute*, June 1986, as quoted in *San Francisco Chronicle*, July 9, 1986.
3. *The Common Good*, Ford Foundation, New York, 1989, p. 11.

Chapter 10.

1. Diane Camper, "Editorial Notebook," *New York Times*, January 25, 1988.
2. *Business Week*, Special Advertising Section, May 2, 1988.
3. This report is taken from an article by Gina Kolata in *New York Times*, June 13, 1990.

Chapter 11.

1. *From Children to Citizens*, vol. 3, James Q. Wilson and Glenn C. Loury, eds., Springer-Verlag, 1987, p. 30.
2. Description of Dr. Prinz's program is extracted from an article by Daniel Goleman in *New York Times*, February 1, 1990.
3. Robert P. Weissbert, et al., "The Primary Mental Health Project," *Journal of Consulting and Clinical Psychology*, 1983, pp. 100–107.
4. Christine L. Chandler, et al., "Long-Term Effects of a School-Based Secondary Prevention Program," *Journal of Consulting and Clinical Psychology*, April 1984, pp. 165–70.
5. L. A. Rescorla, S. Provence, and A. Naylor, "The Yale Child Welfare Research Program: Descriptions and Results," in *Day Care: Scientific and Social Policy Issues*, E. F. Zigler and E. W. Gordon, eds., Auburn House, 1982, pp. 183–99.
6. *Wellness Letter*, University of California, Berkeley, November 1985, p. 7.

Chapter 13.

1. Lisbeth B. Shorr, *Within Our Reach*, Anchor Press, 1988, pp. 108–9.

Chapter 14.

1. Dorothy Miller, et al., *Runaways—Illegal Aliens in Their Own Land*, J. F. Bergin Publishers, 1980, as quoted in *Juvenile Justice Bulletin*, U.S. Department of Justice, n.d.

2. Jerry Belcher, reprinted from *Los Angeles Times* in "Sunday Punch," *San Francisco Chronicle*, February 12, 1984, p. 3.

Chapter 15.

1. *New York Times*, March 19, 1989, p. 37.
2. *Wall Street Journal*, February 4, 1986, p. 1.

Chapter 16.

1. Speech at Commonwealth Club, San Francisco, February 7, 1990.
2. *Journal of Occupational Medicine*, January 1989.
3. "The 1990 Report of the Carter Center," Emory University, p. 8.
4. *New York Times*, March 2, 1990, p. 1.
5. New York Times News Service, as published in *Louisville Courier-Journal*, June 3, 1986, p. 1.
6. "Talk of the Town," *The New Yorker*, January 1, 1990, p. 22.
7. *Wall Street Journal*, July 13, 1989, p. A11.
8. Letter to *Wall Street Journal*, as quoted in *Common Cause Magazine*, January/February 1990.

Chapter 17.

1. *The Harvard Medical School Mental Health Letter*, November 1987.
2. As quoted by Jim Hankins in the *New York Times*, January 31, 1990, p. A19.
3. This discussion is adapted from an article by Randall Rothenberg in the Business Section of the *New York Times*, February 16, 1990.

Chapter 18.

1. As quoted in *Psychology Today*, June 1978, pp. 84–86.
2. This list has been adapted from "CASA: Court-Appointed Special Advocate for Children," *Juvenile Justice Bulletin*, U.S. Department of Justice, 1988.
3. Douglas J. Besharov, "Giving the Juvenile Court a Preschool Education," in *From Children to Citizens*, vol. 3, James Q. Wilson and Glenn C. Loury, eds., Springer-Verlag, 1987, pp. 214–16.
4. Ibid., p. 238.
5. Ibid., pp. 207–38.
6. This description of the Homebuilders is drawn primarily from Lisbeth B. Shorr, *Within our Reach*, Anchor Press, 1988, pp. 156–61.
7. "CASA: Court-Appointed Special Advocate for Children."
8. *Symposium on Status Offenders: Proceedings*, National Council of Jewish Women, 1976, p. 33.

Chapter 19.

1. G. R. Patterson, *Coercive Family Process,* Eugene, Oregon, Castalia Publishing Co., 1982.
2. Letters to the Editor, *New York Times,* June 10, 1988.
3. As quoted in *Psychology Today,* June 1978, p. 84.
4. *Juvenile and Family Court Journal,* August 1983, pp. 3–6.
5. *Criminal Justice Abstracts,* March 1984, p. 31.
6. *Criminal Justice Abstracts,* June 1983, p. 155.
7. *Crime and Delinquency,* October 1982, p. 527.

Chapter 20.

1. Jerome G. Miller, "The Issue of Violent Juvenile Crime," in *Violent Juvenile Offenders,* Robert A. Mathias, ed., National Council on Crime and Delinquency, 1984, p. 381.

Chapter 21.

1. *New York Times,* December 19, 1982, p. 70.
2. Jan M. Chaiken and Marcia R. Chaiken, "Trends and Targets," *The Wilson Quarterly,* Spring 1983, p. 115.

Chapter 22.

1. H. Ted Rubin, "Retain the Juvenile Court," *Crime and Delinquency,* July 1979, p. 282.
2. *Report of the National Advisory Committee for Juvenile Justice and Delinquency Prevention* (published by the committee itself), July 1980, p. 93.

INDEX

Abbott, Raymond, 75
Abbott v. Burke, 75
abortion, 129, 285
Achievement Place, 43, 44
acupuncture, 260–261
adoption, 86, 285
Advance parenting program, 139
Advertising Council, 264
affirmative action programs, 101–102
AIDS (acquired immune deficiency syndrome), 88, 122, 127, 130, 212–213, 324
Aid to Families with Dependent Children (AFDC), *see* welfare
Alaska, 257
Albuquerque, N. Mex., 136, 207
alcohol, 157, 235–237, 247, 254, 256, 257, 261
  as gateway drug, 265
  illegal drug abuse compared with, 235–237
  juvenile use of, 152, 265, 266–267
  social cost of, 235–237
Alcoholics Anonymous, 47
Allen, Harry, 29

alternative schools, 136, 195–210
  Basic High, 182, 197, 198–204
  Career High, 204–205
  Contract High, 205–206
  Opportunity, 197–198
  for teenage parents, 206–210
American Friends Service Committee, 143
Annandale, 41
Anslinger, Harry, 255, 262
Appalachia, 106
Arkansas, 16–17, 142
Armed Forces Qualification Test, 63
Armstrong, Louis, 38
arson, 6
assault, aggravated, 5, 6, 18
Associated Communications, 103
Australia, 95, 99, 176

Barry, Marion, 238
Bayer Company, 249
Bayh, Birch, 37
Bazelon, David, 9
beer, 265, 266
behavior modification, 43–45

Belcher, Jerry, 213–214
Bennett, William, 240, 245, 246, 268
Besharov, Douglas, 282, 283, 284
Bettelheim, Bruno, 86
Bias, Len, 239
birth control, 126, 127, 128, 129, 131
blacks, black community:
    breakdown in family structure of, 125–126
    Bush campaign and, 102
    delinquency rate of, 62
    double prejudice against, 103, 121
    homicide rate in, 5
    police and juvenile court bias against, 24–31
    post–Civil Rights Act anger of, 108
    scholastic achievement of, 62–63, 69–71, 175
    slavery's legacy and, 97–98, 101–102
    unemployment and, 222
Bolivia, 243
Bosket, Willie, Jr., 19–20, 28–29, 33
Boys Industrial School, 37
Brattleboro, Vt., 205
Breed, Allan, 39
Briar, Scott, 26
Brookwood Center for Boys, 19
Buckley, William F., 250
burglary, 6
Burke, Donald, 213
Bush, George, 105, 325
    blacks and, 102
    drug war and, 233, 242, 243, 244, 248, 270
    Head Start and, 151–152
    minimum wage policy of, 227–228
    Panama invasion and, 98–99
    rhetoric of, 144, 149, 177
BW Associates, 185n

caffeine, 249
California Business Roundtable, 185n
California Community Treatment Project, 45
California Youth Authority, 36
Calvinism, 97, 102, 104
Canada, 99, 125
Carroll, Lewis, 81
Carter, Hodding, III, 110, 174, 249
Carter, Jimmy, 98–99, 105, 237
Carter administration, 92, 175
Catholic Church, 129, 131, 297
Census Bureau, U.S., 111, 135, 140
Chaiken, Jan, 322–323
Chaiken, Marcia, 322–323
Chamberlain, Fran, 202

Charles F. Kettering Foundation, 228
Charles Stewart Mott Foundation, 59
child abuse, 93, 166–167, 277–279, 284
    CDSS and, 166–167, 279
    delinquency and, 8, 11, 129
    detection of, 167
    proposed Family Court and, 277–279, 282–284
    psychological, 85–86, 278
    runaways and, 85–86, 89, 286
    sexual, 8, 11, 85, 89, 220, 277–279, 286
    unwed teenage mothers and, 125, 129
Childcare Enrichment Program, 153
Child Development Services System (CDSS), 156–172, 182, 190, 191, 198
    behavioral problems and, 162–164
    conceptual basis of, 157–160
    diagnostic process of, 160–161
    health problems and, 161
    learning problems and, 167–172
    social problems and, 164–167
Children's House program, 166
Children Without Justice, 22
Civil Rights Act (1964), 108
Clark, Joe, 77
Coates, Robert, 304
Coca-Cola, 249, 257
cocaine, 258, 259
    declining use of, 239, 240
    failed war on, 234, 240–243
    former legal status of, 249
    testing programs for, 237
    see also crack cocaine
college, alternative schools and, 186–187
Colombia, 237, 241, 242, 243
Commission on Law Enforcement and Administration of Justice, 118
Commission on the Skills of the American Workforce, 110
community service, 297–298, 313
Community Service Corps, 180, 225–227
community treatment programs, 42–43, 44–45, 46
Comprehensive Competencies Program (CCP), 196–197, 198, 200, 206
Congress, U.S., 33, 48, 93, 110, 140, 142, 146, 147, 152, 225, 232, 255
Conrad, John, 296
Conservation Corps, 229
constitutional rights, 29–31
Cook County, Ill., 15
Cooper, Andrew, 33
Costa Rica, 256
Court Appointed Special Advocate (CASA), 285–287

courts:
  proposed Family, 273–287, 299, 307,
    308, 310
  proposed Youthful Offender, 274, 275,
    277, 299–310, 311
  see also juvenile courts; Supreme
    Court, U.S.
Covenant House, 213, 214–215
crack cocaine, 127
  babies and, 138, 149, 150, 238
  destructive force of, 235, 238–240,
    259–260, 284
  juveniles and, 213, 234, 235, 238–239,
    259–260, 268
Cressey, Donald R., 49
crime:
  FBI Index classifications of, 6, 8, 18,
    26, 82
  fear of, 3, 4–6
  genetic inheritance and, 12
  increasing violence in, 6–7
  juvenile role in, 6–13
  material promise found in, 47
  organized, 249
  social causes of, 47, 53
  social class and, 102–104
  softness of statistics on, 3
  in U.S. vs. other countries, 95
  white-collar, 102–103
  see also delinquency
Crime and Delinquency (Lab and White-
    head), 46
Crime of Punishment, The (Menninger),
    37, 292

day-care programs, 134–136, 147–150,
    152–155, 209
day detention, 313–314
death penalty, 12, 98, 292
deinstitutionalization, 42–43
Delaware, 286
delinquency:
  child abuse and, 8, 11, 129
  childhood poverty and, 109–110, 111
  court-ordered therapy and, 83
  cultural roots of, 95–112
  economic imbalance and, 106–108
  federal programs for, 58–59
  jobs and, 221–232
  juvenile court system and, 31–34, 116
  legal definitions of, 16–17
  official vs. hidden, 25, 26
  organized recreation and, 56–57
  peak age for, 57
  poverty cycle and, 120–133
  predictions of, 52–54, 117

delinquency (*cont.*)
  prevention of, 52–60, 115–270, 273
  psychiatric vs. sociological approaches
    to, 10–13, 52, 60
  punishment and, 165, 288–297, 300–
    301, 311–324
  race and, 62, 101, 103–104
  scholastic achievement and, 61–63, 65–
    68
  school dropouts and, 62–65
  self-concept and, 57, 60, 64, 72–73,
    96–97, 168–169
  self-fulfilling prophecies and, 54–55
  social services and, 55–56
  status offenses and, 16, 45, 81–94
  top dog syndrome and, 96–97
  unmarried teenage mothers and, 124–
    125
  in U.S. vs. other countries, 95
  by younger juveniles, 6, 7–9, 117
  see also crime
delinquency institutions:
  as criminal breeding grounds, 35, 39, 41
  cruel and unusual punishment in, 22–
    24
  deaths in, 42, 48, 297
  euphemisms for, 35
  GGI used in, 39–42, 43, 44, 46, 66
  inmate survey of, 121
  inmate uprisings in, 48
Dependent Care Tax Credit Program,
    154
Depression, Great, 143
Diaz, Danny, 21
diversion projects, 48–50, 305
Dodd, Christopher, 148
Drug Abuse Resistance Education
    (DARE), 263
drugs, 87, 121, 125, 152, 157, 169, 233–
    270
  alcohol and nicotine vs. illegal, 235–
    237
  cost of war against, 233, 240
  education programs for, 253–254, 261–
    267
  failed war against, 233–252
  "just say no" campaign against, 263–
    264
  juveniles and, 234, 239–240, 259, 261–
    263, 265–267
  legalization of, 250–252, 253, 255–258
  prohibition of, 247–250, 261
  proposed approach to, 253–270
  race and, 101, 240, 268–269
  refocused law enforcement for, 253,
    254–255

drugs (*cont.*)
    rehabilitation programs for users of,
        138–139
    supply-demand equation of, 240–247
    testing programs for, 237, 238, 284
    therapy programs for, 253, 258–261
    use cycles of, 239
    warfare among dealers of, 5, 234
    (*see also* specific drug listings)
dyslexia, 74–75, 169–170, 171

Earn-It, 312
Eastman, Forest, 286
economic imbalance, 106–108
Edison, Thomas, 75, 171, 249
Education, Department of, U.S., 79, 196
Educational Testing Service, 175
Education for All Handicapped Children
    Act (1975), 169
Education Improvement Act (1984), 178
Einstein, Albert, 75, 148, 171
Eisenhower, Milton, 5, 53
Elmira, N.Y., 146
embezzlement, 102–103
Employment and Training program (ET),
    Massachusetts', 142–143

Fairfax High School, 6–7
Family and Nation (Moynihan), 126
Family Life Education Program, 59
Family Support Act (1988), 135
Federal Bureau of Investigation (FBI), 3,
    238, 246
    Index crime classifications of, 6, 8, 18,
        26, 82
Federal Office of Youth Employment and
    Training, 224–232
fetal alcohol syndrome, 236
Fineberg, Harvey, 130
Flint, Mich., 58–60
Florida, 286, 287
Follow Through, 175
Forbes, 104
Ford, Gerald, 93, 325
Ford administration, 92, 175
Ford Foundation, 132–133, 152, 196
foster care, 86, 279–287
Foundation for Children with Learning
    Disabilities, 168
Fox, Sanford J., 27
France, 95, 125
Friedman, Milton, 250

gangs, 5, 56, 234, 316
Garber, Howard, 148
Gateway Juvenile Diversion project, 305

Gault, Gerald Francis, 30
Gault decision, 30
Georgia, 29
Georgia Bureau of Investigation, 246
Germany, Federal Republic of (West), 95
Gilman, David, 31
Ginsburg, Douglas, 250
Glasser, Ira, 249
Glueck, Sheldon and Eleanor, Boston
    delinquency study of, 61
Glueck Social Prediction Tables, 54
Gold, Martin, 32–33, 293
Gonion, Gordon, 82
Great Britain, 5, 95, 99, 125, 161
Greece, 95, 256
Green, Richard R., 153
group homes, 314–315
Guided Group Interaction (GGI), 39–42,
    43, 44, 46, 66
Guinness Book of World Records, The, 96
guns, 99

Habitat for Humanity, 105
Haight-Ashbury Free Clinic, 258
Hamady House Stepping Stones, 59
Harris, Louis, 73
Harrison Narcotic Act (1914), 249, 255
Harvard Educational Review, 69
*Harvard Medical School Mental Health
    Letter,* 256
hashish, 241
Hatch, Orrin, 232
Head Start, 150, 151–152, 165, 175, 198
Health, Education and Welfare, Depart-
    ment of, U.S., 53, 59
Health Affairs, 264
Health and Human Services, Department
    of, U.S., 211, 235
Heber, Rick, 148
Hekman, Randall, 293
Hern, Ruby, 146
heroin, 47, 235, 244, 249, 257, 258, 260
Highfields Training Program, 39, 41, 43,
    44
Hispanics, 139, 223
    illiteracy among, 129
    juvenile arrest rates of, 101
    scholastic achievement of, 63, 71, 240
Homebuilders, 283
homelessness, 111
*Homeless Youths: The Saga of "Pushouts"
    and "Throwaways" in America,* 92
homosexuality, 87, 88
Hong Kong, 174
Hornbeck, David, 192, 193
House of Representatives, U.S., 93

House Select Committee on Crime, 39
Howard, James R., 44
Howard, Judy, 149
Howington, Patrick, 193
Human Environment Center, 229
human worth, 104–106
Hutschnecker, Arnold, 53, 54

IBM, training programs and, 223
ice (crystallized methamphetamine), 245
Illinois, 15
Illinois Juvenile Court Act (1899), 16
illiteracy, 123, 124, 173
    cycle of, 73, 121, 129
indeterminate sentences, 28–29
Indiana, 154
infant mortality, 145, 146
Institute for Children, 326
Institute for Developmental Studies, 151
Institute for Juvenile Justice and Delin-
    quency Prevention, 44
Interior, Department of the, U.S., 58
International Association for the Evalua-
    tion of Educational Achievement,
    174
Ireland, Republic of, 176

Jackson, Butch, 199, 200, 201, 202
Jackson, Michael, 105
Jacobs, Chris, 259
Jamaica, 256
Japan, 177, 179
    crime statistics for, 5, 95, 99, 108
    economic equality in, 107–108
    education in, 177, 179
    out-of-wedlock babies in, 107, 125
Job Corps, 196, 230–232, 316, 321
Johnson, Lyndon B., 17, 58, 110, 224,
    226, 230
Jones, Richard R., 44
Journal of Occupational Medicine, 236
*Journal of the American Medical Associa-
    tion*, 145, 170, 266
Junior Achievement, 201
Justice, Department of, U.S., 18, 121
    affirmative action programs nullified
        by, 101–102
Justice Statistics, Bureau of, 3, 9, 62
Juvenile and Family Court Journal, 293
juvenile courts, 14–34, 122, 159, 216–217
    adult courts compared with, 17
    class and race bias of, 24–31
    constitutional rights denied in, 29–31
    criticisms of, 14, 17–34
    diversion from, 48–50, 305
    establishment of, 15

juvenile courts (*cont.*)
    false assumptions about, 115–118
    false compassion of, 17, 21–24
    harm done by, 14, 17, 31–34, 291–
        294
    indeterminate sentences of, 28–29
    rehabilitation as goal of, 15–16, 24–25,
        28–29, 34, 115–116, 117, 288–289
    "revolving door policy" of, 18, 33
    sealed records of, 21, 118, 322–323
    social history reports used in, 27, 308
    society not protected by, 17–21, 31
    status offenses and, 81–94
    as surrogate parent, 291
    unjustness of, 17, 24–31
Juvenile Court Statistics, 59
Juvenile Justice and Delinquency Preven-
    tion Act (1974), 33–34, 93, 304, 305,
    324, 325–326
Juvenile Justice and Delinquency Preven-
    tion Office, U.S., 50
Juvenile Justice Bulletin, 93
juveniles:
    adult trials for, 20, 292–294
    arrest rates of, 108
    constitutional rights of, 29–31
    crime by, 6–13
    criminal responsibility and, 116–117
    death penalty for, 12
    declining age of first criminal involve-
        ment by, 6, 7–9, 117
    federal job program for, 224–232
    foster care and, 86, 279–287
    increasing violence in crimes by, 6–7
    as later habitual criminals, 9–10, 116
    murder by, 6–7, 8, 12–13, 18–20, 99,
        281–282
    parental pressure on, 96–97
    post-release care of, 320–321
    social vs. personal control over, 294–
        295
    suicide by, 85, 92, 96–97, 212, 297
    see also runaways; unmarried teenage
        mothers

Kansas, 147
Kentucky, 178, 192–194, 262
Kentucky Village, 67
Kent v. United States, 24
Kerner Commission, 110
kindergarten, 69–70, 78, 160, 182, 183
King, Martin Luther, Jr., 109
Koch, Edward I., 127, 128, 152
Koop, C. Everett, 265
Kozol, Jonathan, 70, 129
Ku Klux Klan, 101

Lab, Steven, 46
larceny-theft, 6
Lardner, George, Jr., 231
Larkin Street Youth Center, 86, 88
Law Enforcement Assistance Administration (LEAA), 90, 312
learning disabilities, 74–75, 167–172
Learning in America, 79
Leonardo da Vinci, 171
Levine, Melvin D., 169
life expectancy, 107
Lindbergh, Charles, 39
Los Angeles, Calif., 125, 258
Los Angeles Times, 213
Louisville, Ky., 153, 215–216
Louisville Courier-Journal, 193
LSD, 235, 262
Lueger, Milton, 32, 39
Lyfe Project, 207

McClure, Jessica, 147
McDermott, Robert A., 49
McNamara, Joseph, 99
Maine, 142
Malaysia, 246
Mann, Horace, 69, 72
Manpower Demonstration Research Corporation, 142
marijuana, 235, 237, 239, 254, 265
  failed war against, 242, 244, 248, 292
  former legal status of, 249, 255
  health effects of, 255–257
  juveniles and, 152, 239, 261, 262, 266–267, 292
  proposed legalization of, 253, 255–258
Marijuana Tax Act (1937), 255
Martinson, Robert, 45–46
Maryland, 142, 147
Massachusetts, 36–37, 48, 142–143, 147, 328
maturation reform, 38–39
Matza, David, 38
May, Robert, 31
Medicaid, 111, 125, 129, 145, 146, 161, 209
Medicare Catastrophic Illness Act (1988), 129, 146
Meese, Edwin, 257
Memphis-Metro Youth Diversion Project, 49
Mencken, H. L., 10
Menninger, Karl, 37, 277, 292
mental retardation, 144–145, 148–149, 151, 169, 236
metal detectors, 7, 189
methadone, 260

Mexico, 244
Milken, Michael, 104
Miller, David L., 103
Miller, Jerome, 36–37, 48
minimum wage, 227–228
Minnesota Multiphasic Personality Inventory (MMPI), 53–54
Mississippi, 111
Montessori schools, 76
Montrose training school, 24
Moral Majority, 129
morphine, 249
Motorola, 79
motor vehicle theft, 6
Moynihan, Daniel Patrick, 126, 129
Mudd, Roger, 79
murder:
  death penalty for, 12
  with handguns, 99
  by juveniles, 6–7, 8, 12–13, 18–20, 99, 281–282
  statistics on, 5, 6, 8, 95, 99
Murphy, Jim, 292
Murphy, Patrick T., 22–23

National Advisory Commission on Criminal Justice Standards and Goals, 49
National Alliance of Business, 144, 152, 174
National Commission on Children, 111
National Commission on the Causes and Prevention of Violence, 5, 53
National Commission on Youth, 228
National Council of Jewish Women, 22, 29
National Council on Crime and Delinquency, 90, 309, 321
National Educational Testing Service, 63
"National Evaluation of Diversion Projects," 50
National Institute of Mental Health, 44, 57
National Institute on Drug Abuse, 240, 260
National Juvenile Justice Assessment Center, 90
National Research Council (NRC), 45–46
National School Boards Association, 6
National Teaching-Family Association, 44
National Transportation Safety Board, 237
National Youth Survey, 25–26
Nazario, Sonia, 145
Netherlands, 95, 100, 125, 246, 257–258
New England Journal of Medicine, 99, 213
New Futures School, 136, 207

New Jersey, 146
New Jersey Supreme Court, 75
New York, N.Y., 129, 151, 278
  crime statistics for, 108, 245–246
  dropout program in, 226
  drug rehabilitation in, 258
  Project Giant Step and, 152
  school overcrowding in, 203
  unmarried teenage mothers in, 124
New York City Board of Education, 7
New York City Youth Board Prediction
    Study, 54
New Yorker, The 246
New York State, 20, 51
New York Telephone, 79, 174
New York Times, 18, 174, 238, 297
Nicaragua, 246
Nixon, Richard M., 53, 147, 150, 262
Nixon administration, 92
Noriega, Manuel, 241
North Carolina, 286, 328
Nunn, Louie, 91, 262

Office of Juvenile Justice and Delin-
    quency Prevention (OJJDP), 92–93,
    305, 325
opium, 242, 243–244, 249
Oregon Social Learning Center, 165, 289
organized recreation, 56–57
Our Kindly Parent—the State (Murphy),
    23
Owen, Sasha, 86

Palme, Olof, 107
Palmer, Ted, 45–46
Panama, 98, 241
parens patriae, 15
parents, 54
  CDSS school for, 165–166
  children pressured by, 96–97
  school participation by, 79
  terminating rights of, 284–285
  truancy and, 84
  see also child abuse; unmarried teenage
    mothers
parochial schools, 79
Paterson, N.J., 77
Patton, George, 171
PBS, 79
Perry Preschool Project, 150–151
Peru, 243
Philadelphia High School Academies,
    178
Phoenix Academy, 260
Picasso, Pablo, 75, 104
Piliavin, Irving, 26

Platt, Anthony, 14
police, discretion of, 301–302
Police-School Liaison Program, 59
Policy Analysis for California Education
    (PACE), 125
Positive Peer Culture, 39, 40, 41–42
Positive Peer Group Pressure, 39
Postal Department, U.S., 59
poverty:
  delinquency related to cycle of, 120–
    133
  prejudice against, 102–104, 121
  teenage pregnancy and cycle of, 128–
    130, 206
  widening gap of, 110–112, 147
Prejean, Dalton, 12–13
President's Commission on Law Enforce-
    ment and Administration of Justice,
    90
Prevention Research Center, 157
Primary Mental Health Project (PMHP),
    163, 164
Prinz, Ronald, 162–163
prisons, 121
  alternatives to, 315–317
  minimum-security, 103
  overcrowding of, 4
  total population of, 3–4
private schools, 76
probation, 18, 19, 43, 46, 83, 117
Project Early Start, 144–155
  developmental day care in, 147–150
  long-term savings through, 146
  pre- and neonatal health care in, 144–
    146
  preschool programs in, 150–152
  school-based day care in, 152–155
Project Giant Step, 152
prostitution, 85, 86–89, 212, 278
Protestant ethic, 102
punishment, 165, 288–297, 300–301,
    311–324
  alternatives to, 311–317
  certainty of, 291–294, 295–296
  criteria for, 295–298
  as learning experience, 289
  low levels of, 296–297
  as rehabilitative tool, 288–297
  see also sentences
pushouts, *see* runaways

rape, 5, 6, 18, 22, 95, 324
reactance, 46–47, 83
Reagan, Nancy, 263
Reagan, Ronald, 93, 98, 107, 111, 122,
    177, 231

Reagan, Ronald (*cont.*)
  drug war and, 233, 244, 248, 256–257,
    260, 263, 269
  greed condoned under, 105
  juvenile justice funding cut by, 92,
    106, 304–305, 324–325
Reagan administration, 312
  minimum-wage jobs created under, 111
  poverty programs cut by, 110, 175, 269
  race relations under, 101–102
  school lunch program funding cut by,
    71, 175
recidivism:
  faulty predictions of, 29
  institutional effect on, 36–37, 40, 42,
    45, 46, 48
Reckless, Walter, 57–58
recreation, organized, 56–57
Rector, Milton, 25
Red Wing (Minnesota) School for Boys,
    39–40, 42
reform schools, *see* delinquency institu-
    tions
Regnery, Alfred S., 92, 93
rehabilitation, 35–51
  behavior modification approach to, 43–
    45
  community treatment programs as, 42–
    43, 44–45, 46
  cost of, 51
  deinstitutionalization approach to, 42–43
  diversion projects and, 48–50, 305
  for drug and alcohol abuse, 47
  GGI method of, 39–42, 43, 44, 46, 66
  hopeless cases for, 47–48
  as juvenile courts' goal, 15–16, 24–25,
    28–29, 34, 115–116, 117, 288–289
  maturation reform as, 38–39
  as myth, 35–37
  NRC report on, 45–46
  psychiatric approach to, 37–38
  punishment as, 288–297
  reactance as barrier to, 46–47, 83
Rell, Peter E., 231
Responsible Adolescents Can Help
    (REACH), 264
restitution, 311–313
Restitution, Education, Specialized Train-
    ing and Technical Assistance program
    (RESTTA), 312
"Restructuring California Education,"
    185*n*
Rhode Island, 286
Richart, David, 193
"Rich Get Richer and the Poor Get
    Prison, The" (Reiman), 102

Ritalin, 170
Ritter, Bruce, 214
robbery, 5, 6, 18, 31, 95
Robins, Lee N., 83
Rochester, N.Y., 163, 189
Rockefeller, Nelson, 171, 248
Rodin, Auguste, 171
Rogers, Don, 239
Rosenbaum, Jill Leslie, 45
Rosenthal, Mitchell, 260
Rubin, H. Ted, 325
Ruhland, David, 293
runaways, 85–89, 92, 211–220
  childhood abuse and, 85–89, 212, 278,
    280
  number of, 211–212
  prostitution by, 85–89, 93, 211, 212–
    213, 278
  shelter programs for, 213–219, 286–287
  as status offenders, 45, 82, 85–89, 92,
    93, 213

salaries, 104, 105, 106–107, 176–177,
    188–189
San Antonio, Tex., 139
San Francisco, Calif., 126, 258, 279
Schmoke, Kurt, 251
School Attendance Review Board (SARB),
    191
schools, 61–80, 122, 124, 173–194, 225
  academic grades and, 72–73, 183
  alternative, *see* alternative schools
  charges against, 69–80
  cheating in, 73
  conditions conducive to failure in, 68
  cycle of illiteracy perpetuated by, 73
  day-care programs in, 135–136, 152–
    155, 209
  declining academic standards in, 78–80,
    174
  delinquency and achievement in, 61–
    63, 65–68
  discipline in, 76–78, 79, 189–191
  dropout programs for, 64–65
  dropouts from, 62–65, 69, 71, 121, 125,
    157, 178
  economics of reform of, 176–179
  expulsion from, 77–78
  grade restructuring proposals for, 181–
    188
  homework and, 71
  Kentucky reforms of, 192–194
  lack of alternate programs in, 75–76
  learning disabilities undiagnosed in,
    73–75
  length of day for, 179

schools *(cont.)*
length of year for, 80, 179–180
life skills untaught in, 76
lunch program funding cut in, 71
male teachers as role models in, 80
minority language disadvantage in, 71
parent participation and, 79
parochial, 79
private, 76
race and, 62–63, 69–72
restructuring proposals for, 173–194
self-concept and, 70, 72–73, 109, 159,
168, 181
self-fulfilling prophecies in, 54–55, 69–
71, 72–73
sex education programs in, 130
social class and, 62, 69–72
spending per student in, 72
success stories in, 79–80
suspension from, 78
truancy and, 82, 83–85, 91–92
as two-tiered system, 71–72, 173, 178–
179
violence in, 6–7, 76–77
vocational education in, 76, 187
see also Child Development Services
System
Schools That Work (Department of Education), 79
Schorr, Lisbeth, 79
Schroeder, Pat, 148
Seattle, Wash., 154
Seattle Atlantic Street Center, 55–56
self-concept (self-esteem):
delinquency and, 57, 60, 64, 72–73,
96–97, 168–169
scholastic achievement and, 70, 72–73,
109, 159, 168, 181
Senate, U.S., 11, 32, 37, 93
Senate Committee to Investigate Juvenile
Delinquency, 93
Senate Judiciary Committee, 92, 215
sentences:
indeterminate, 28–29
matrix for, 317–320
see also punishment
Shelter House, 214, 215–216
shoplifting, 25
Shultz, George, 250
Sixth Amendment, 308
skinheads, 101
slavery, legacy of, 97–98, 101–102
Social Security, 140–141
social services, 55–56
Soukup, David, 285
South Africa, Republic of, 4, 111

South Carolina, 178, 286
Soviet Union, 4
Spock, Benjamin, 73
State Department, U.S., 242, 244
State Offices of Children and Youth, 324–
328
status offenses, 16, 45, 81–94, 100, 116,
299, 309
decriminalization of, 89–93
definition of, 16
euphemistic labels for, 82–83
later criminal careers and, 90–91
running away as, 45, 82, 92, 93, 213
truancy as, 82, 83–85, 91–92
Steinberg, Lisa, 167
Stockman, David, 231
suicide, 85, 92, 96–97, 212, 297
Super Teams, 263
Supreme Court, U.S., 250, 255
civil rights weakened by, 102
on constitutional rights of juvenile offenders, 29–31, 308, 325
on death penalty for juvenile offenders,
12
economic equality in schools not addressed by, 71–72
on juvenile court abuses, 24
Sweden, 95, 99, 100, 106–107, 108, 125

Tactical Narcotics Teams (TNT), 246
Taggart, Robert, 196
Tannenbaum, Frank, 68
Targeted Jobs Tax Credit Program, 228
Task Force on Juvenile Delinquency, 17
Tate, Sheila, 263
taxes:
capital gains, 105
for child care programs, 154
credit programs for, 154, 228
income, 105, 110, 154
for school reform, 178
in Sweden, 107
teachers:
proposed school reforms and, 183, 184,
188–189
salaries of, 176–177, 188–189
Texas, 178
Thailand, 243–244
Thayer, Walter N., 224
throwaways, *see* runaways
Time, 77
tobacco, 235, 237, 247, 254, 256, 257,
261, 265–266
Tokyo, 108
top dog syndrome, 96–97
Toughlove, 291

Transportation, Department of, U.S., 237
Trump, Donald, 104, 105
Twain, Mark, 86
twins, studies of, 12
Tyson, Mike, 38

underclass, 72, 138, 240
    definition of, 120–121
    unemployability of, 123
United Federation of Teachers, 7
unmarried teenage mothers, 124–130
    alternative schools for, 206–210
    day-care programs for, 134–136, 137,
        147–150, 152–155
    delinquency and, 124–125
    drug rehabilitation program proposal
        for, 138–139
    ending welfare dependency of, 134–144
    guaranteed family-income maintenance
        for, 136
    learnfare for, 136–137
    male responsibility and, 127–128, 139–
        141
    parenting training for, 139
    poverty cycle and, 128–130
    reasons for, 126–128
    rise in numbers of, 122, 206
    sex education programs for, 130–132,
        140
    in U.S. vs. other countries, 107, 125
    welfare dependency of, 120, 126
U.S. Basics, 197

vandalism, 7
venereal diseases, 127
Vietnam War, 47, 196
violence:
    in schools, 6–7, 76–77
    in U.S. culture, 98–100
    in U.S. vs. other countries, 99
Virginia, 142
vocational education, 76, 187
Vocational Foundation, 224

Volstead Act (1919), 248
Voss, Harwin, 54

Wall Street Journal, 103, 110, 145, 232,
    249, 250
Washington, D.C., 245, 258
Washington Post, 231
Washington State, 146, 317
Watkins, Calvin, 127–128
wealth, reverence of, 104–106
Weicker, Lowell, Jr., 232
Weinrott, Mark R., 44
welfare, 111–112, 120–124, 134–155, 209
    breaking cycle of, 134–155
    cost of, 125
    growth of, 122
    minimum-wage jobs and, 123–124
    poverty cycle and, 123
    temporary recipients of, 120
    unmarried teenage mothers dependent
        on, 120, 126
    workfare and, 137–138, 142
Welfare Reform Act (1988), 140, 141–142
white-collar crime, 102–103
Whitehead, John, 46
Wilson, Pete, 164
Wilson, Woodrow, 171
Winans, R. Foster, 297–298
Winship case, 31
Wisconsin, 140
Wisconsin Juvenile Offender Study
    Project, 92
Within Our Reach (Schorr), 79
Wolfgang, Marvin E., 9, 63
Worcester facility, 48
World Youth Against Drug Abuse, 264

Yeutter, Clayton, 237
YMCA, 56, 153, 219
Young, Francis L., 257
Youth Conservation Corps, 229–230

Zigler, Edward, 147, 148, 150, 153

ABOUT THE AUTHOR

As director of Delinquency Prevention Programs in the Louisville, Kentucky, schools, Falcon Baker developed many experimental and successful methods that have been used as models for programs throughout the country. His book *Delinquency in Kentucky* drew national acclaim in the field, and his articles have appeared in numerous magazines.